The Princeton Review®

Cracking the

AP® STATISTICS EXAM

2016 Edition

Madhuri S. Mulekar

PrincetonReview.com

Penguin
Random
House

The Princeton Review, Inc.
24 Prime Parkway, Suite 201
Natick, MA 01760
E-mail: editorialsupport@review.com

Published in the United States by Penguin Random House LLC, New York, and in Canada by Random House of Canada, a division of Penguin Random House Ltd., Toronto.

ISBN: 978-0-8041-2625-0
ISSN: 1546-9085

Editor: Sarah Litt
Production Editor: Harmony Quiroz
Production Artist: Deborah A. Silvestrini

Printed in the United States of America on partially recycled paper.

10 9 8 7 6 5 4 3 2 1

2016 Edition

Editorial

Rob Franek, Senior VP, Publisher
Casey Cornelius, VP, Content Development
Mary Beth Garrick, Director of Production
Selena Coppock, Managing Editor
Meave Shelton, Senior Editor
Colleen Day, Editor
Sarah Litt, Editor
Aaron Riccio, Editor
Orion McBean, Editorial Assistant

Random House Publishing Team

Tom Russell, Publisher
Alison Stoltzfus, Publishing Manager
Melinda Ackell, Associate Managing Editor
Ellen Reed, Production Manager
Kristin Lindner, Production Supervisor
Andrea Lau, Designer

Acknowledgments

I would like to thank my spouse, Satish Mulekar, for his understanding, patience, and willingness to help during this project. I would not have been able to complete this project without his assistance in making time available for it.

The Princeton Review would like to give special thanks to Eugenia Prezhdo for her hard work and her changes to the 2016 edition.

Contents

Register Your Book Online! viii

Part I: Using This Book to Improve Your AP Score 1

Preview: Your Knowledge, Your Expectations 2

Your Guide to Using This Book 2

How to Begin 3

Part II: Practice Test 1 7

Practice Test 1 9

Practice Test 1: Answers and Explanations 47

Part III: About the AP Statistics Exam 63

How the AP Statistics Exam Is Structured 64

Overview of Content Topics 65

How AP Exams Are Used 69

Other Resources 70

Designing Your Study Plan 70

On The Day of The Test 71

Part IV: Test-Taking Strategies for the AP Statistics Exam 73

1   How to Approach Multiple-Choice Questions 75

2   How to Approach Free-Response Questions 79

3   How to Use Your Calculator 85

Part V: Content Review for the AP Statistics Exam 95

4   Exploring Data 97

Observing Patterns and Departures from Patterns 98

Collecting Data 98

Tabular Methods 100

Graphical Methods for Qualitative Data 103

Graphical Methods for Quantitative Data 106

Numerical Methods for Continuous Variables 121

Boxplots 131

The Effect of Changing Units on Summary Measures 134

Comparing Distributions of Two or More Groups 136

Exploring Bivariate Data 141

Exploring Categorical Data: Frequency Tables 163

Chapter 4 Review Questions 167

Chapter 4 Answers and Explanations 170

5   Sampling and Experimentation 173

Planning a Study 174

Overview of Methods of Data Collection 174

Planning and Conducting Surveys 176

Bias in Surveys 180

Planning and Conducting Experiments............................. 181

Chapter 5 Review Questions 190

Chapter 5 Answers and Explanations.............................. 193

6   Anticipating Patterns 197

Probability... 198

Random Variables and Their Probability Distributions 214

The Probability Distributions of Discrete Random Variables 215

The Probability Distributions of Continuous Random Variables 234

The Normal Distribution 236

Combining Independent Random Variables 246

Sampling Distributions 248

Chapter 6 Review Questions 252

Chapter 6 Answers and Explanations.............................. 255

7   Statistical Inference 259

Confirming Models.. 260

Parameters and Statistics... 260

Estimation.. 261

Point Estimation... 262

Interval Estimation and the Confidence Interval 267

Inference: Tests of Significance..................................... 267

Estimation and Inference Problems................................ 280

Estimation for and Inference About a Population Proportion p 283

Estimation for and Inference About a Population Mean μ................ 293

Estimation of and Inference About the Difference in
    Population Proportions $(p_1 - p_2)$ 314

Estimation of and Inference About the Difference in
    Population Means $(\mu_1 - \mu_2)$ 318

Making an Inference Using Categorical Data 347

Review of Formulas on the Exam.................................... 374

Chapter 7 Review Questions 377

Chapter 7 Answers and Explanations.............................. 380

Part VI: Practice Test 2 385

Practice Test 2.. 387

Practice Test 2: Answers and Explanations..................... 423

Appendix: Formulas and Tables 441

About the Author 449

Register Your

1 Go to `PrincetonReview.com/cracking`

2 You'll see a welcome page where you can register your book using the following ISBN: 9780804126250.

3 After placing this free order, you'll either be asked to log in or to answer a few simple questions in order to set up a new Princeton Review account.

4 Finally, click on the "Student Tools" tab located at the top of the screen. It may take an hour or two for your registration to go through, but after that, you're good to go.

If you are experiencing book problems (potential content errors), please contact EditorialSupport@review.com with the full title of the book, its ISBN number (located above), and the page number of the error. Experiencing technical issues? Please e-mail TPRStudentTech@review.com with the following information:

- your full name
- e-mail address used to register the book
- full book title and ISBN
- your computer OS (Mac or PC) and Internet browser (Firefox, Safari, Chrome, etc.)
- description of technical issue

Book Online!

Once you've registered, you can...

- Find any late-breaking information released about the AP Statistics Exam

- Take a full-length practice PSAT, SAT, and ACT

- Get valuable advice about the college application process, including tips for writing a great essay and where to apply for financial aid

- Sort colleges by whatever you're looking for (such as Best Theater or Dorm), learn more about your top choices, and see how they all rank according to *The Best 380 Colleges*

- Access comprehensive study guides and a variety of printable resources, including formulas, tables, calculator tips, and bubble sheets

- Check to see if there have been any corrections or updates to this edition

The Princeton Review®
Your Goals. Our Expertise.™

Part I
Using This Book
to Improve Your
AP Score

- Preview: Your Knowledge, Your Expectations
- Your Guide to Using This Book
- How to Begin

PREVIEW: YOUR KNOWLEDGE, YOUR EXPECTATIONS

Your route to a high score on the AP Statistics Exam depends a lot on how you plan to use this book. Respond to the following questions.

1. Rate your level of confidence about your knowledge of the content tested by the AP Statistics Exam.

    A. Very confident—I know it all
    B. I'm pretty confident, but there are topics in which I could use help
    C. Not confident—I need quite a bit of support
    D. I'm not sure

2. Circle your goal score for the AP Statistics Exam.

    5   4   3   2   1   I'm not sure yet

3. What do you expect to learn from this book? Circle all that apply to you.

    A. A general overview of the test and what to expect
    B. Strategies for how to approach the test
    C. The content tested by this exam
    D. I'm not sure yet

YOUR GUIDE TO USING THIS BOOK

This book is organized to provide as much—or as little—support as you need, so you can use this book in whatever way will be most helpful to improving your score on the AP Statistics Exam.

- The remainder of **Part I** will provide guidance on how to use this book and help you determine your strengths and weaknesses

- **Part II** of this book contains your first practice test, answers and explanations, and a scoring guide. (Bubble sheets can be found in the very back of the book for easy tear-out.) This is where you should begin your test preparation in order to realistically determine:
  o your starting point right now
  o which question types you're ready for and which you might need to practice
  o which content topics you are familiar with and which you will want to carefully review

Once you have nailed down your strengths and weaknesses with regard to this exam, you can focus your preparation and be efficient with your time.

- **Part III** of this book will take care of the following:
  - o provide information about the structure, scoring, and content of the AP Statistics Exam
  - o help you to make a study plan
  - o point you towards additional resources

- **Part IV** of this book will explore various strategies including:
  - o how to attack multiple-choice questions
  - o how to write high scoring free-response answers
  - o how to manage your time to maximize the number of points available to you

- **Part V** of this book covers the content you need for your exam

- **Part VI** of this book contains Practice Test 2, its answers and explanations, and a scoring guide. (Again, bubble sheets can be found in the very back of the book for easy tear-out.) If you skipped Practice Test 1, we recommend that you do both (with at least a day or two between them) so that you can compare your progress between the two. Additionally, this will help to identify any external issues: if you get a certain type of question wrong both times, you probably need to review it. If you only got it wrong once, you may have run out of time or been distracted by something. In either case, this will allow you to focus on the factors that caused the discrepancy in scores and to be as prepared as possible on the day of the test.

You may choose to use some parts of this book over others, or you may work through the entire book. This will depend on your needs and how much time you have. Let's now look at how to make this determination.

HOW TO BEGIN

1. **Take Practice Test 1**

   Before you can decide how to use this book, you need to take a practice test. Doing so will give you insight into your strengths and weaknesses, and the test will also help you make an effective study plan. If you're feeling test-phobic, remind yourself that a practice test is a tool for diagnosing yourself—it's not how well you do that matters but how you use information gleaned from your performance to guide your preparation.

So, before you read further, take AP Statistics Practice Test 1 starting at page 11 of this book. Be sure to do so in one sitting, following the instructions that appear before the test.

2. **Check Your Answers**

Using the answer key on page 48, count how many multiple-choice questions you got right and how many you missed. Don't worry about the explanations for now, and don't worry about why you missed questions. We'll get to that soon.

3. **Reflect on the Test**

After you take your first test, respond to the following questions:

- How much time did you spend on the multiple-choice questions?

- How much time did you spend on each essay?

- How many multiple-choice questions did you miss?

- Do you feel you had the knowledge to address the subject matter of the essays?

- Do you feel you wrote well-organized, thoughtful essays?

- Circle the content areas that were most challenging for you and draw a line through each one in which you felt confident/did well.
  o Exploring Data
  o Sampling and Experimentation
  o Anticipating Patterns
  o Statistical Inference

4. **Read Part III of this Book and Complete the Self-Evaluation**

Part III will provide information on how the test is structured and scored. It will also set out areas of content that are tested.

As you read Part III, re-evaluate your answers to the questions above. At the end of Part III, you will revisit the questions on the previous page and refine your answers to them. You will then be able to make a study plan, based on your needs and time available, that will allow you to use this book most effectively.

5. **Engage with Parts IV and V as Needed**

   Notice the word *engage*. You'll get more out of this book if you use it intentionally than if you read it passively, hoping for an improved score through osmosis.

   Strategy chapters will help you think about your approach to the question types on this exam. Part IV will open with a reminder to think about how you approach questions now and then close with a reflection section asking you to think about how/whether you will change your approach in the future.

   Content chapters are designed to provide a review of the content tested on the AP Statistics Exam, including the level of detail you need to know and how the content is tested. You will have the opportunity to assess your mastery of the content of each chapter through test-appropriate questions and a reflection section.

6. **Take Practice Test 2 and Assess Your Performance**

   Once you feel you have developed the strategies you need and gained the knowledge you lacked, you should take Practice Test 2. You should do so in one sitting, following the instructions at the beginning of the test.

   When you are done, check your answers to the multiple-choice sections. See if a teacher will read your essays and provide feedback.

   Once you have taken the test, reflect on what areas you still need to work on, and revisit the chapters in this book that address those deficiencies. Through this type of reflection and engagement, you will continue to improve.

   Keep in mind that there are other resources available to you, including a wealth of information on AP Connect. You can continue to explore areas that can stand to be improved and engage in those areas right up to the day of the test.

Part II
Practice Test 1

- Practice Test 1
- Practice Test 1: Answers and Explanations

Practice Test 1

AP® Statistics Exam

SECTION I: Multiple-Choice Questions

DO NOT OPEN THIS BOOKLET UNTIL YOU ARE TOLD TO DO SO.

At a Glance
Total Time
1 hour and 30 minutes
Number of Questions
40
Percent of Total Grade
50%
Writing Instrument
Pen required

Instructions

Section I of this exam contains **40 multiple-choice questions. Fill in only the ovals for numbers 1 through 40 on your answer sheet.**

Indicate all of your answers to the multiple-choice questions on the answer sheet. No credit will be given for anything written in this exam booklet, but you may use the booklet for notes or scratch work. After you have decided which of the suggested answers is best, completely fill in the corresponding oval on the answer sheet. Give only one answer to each question. If you change an answer, be sure that the previous mark is erased completely. Here is a sample question and answer.

Sample Question   Sample Answer

Omaha is a

(A) state
(B) city
(C) country
(D) continent
(E) village

Use your time effectively, working as quickly as you can without losing accuracy. Do not spend too much time on any one question. Go on to other questions and come back to the ones you have not answered if you have time. It is not expected that everyone will know the answers to all of the multiple-choice questions.

About Guessing

Many candidates wonder whether or not to guess the answers to questions about which they are not certain. Multiple–choice scores are based on the number of questions answered correctly. Points are not deducted for incorrect answers, and no points are awarded for unanswered questions. Because points are not deducted for incorrect answers, you are encouraged to answer all multiple-choice questions. On any questions you do not know the answer to, you should eliminate as many choices as you can, and then select the best answer among the remaining choices.

Once you have checked your answers, remember to return to page 4 and respond to the Reflect questions.

STATISTICS
SECTION I
Time—1 hour and 30 minutes

Number of questions—40

Percent of total grade—50

Directions: Solve each of the following problems, using the available space for scratchwork. Decide which is the best of the choices given and fill in the corresponding oval on the answer sheet. No credit will be given for anything written in the test book. Do not spend too much time on any one problem.

1. An outlier is an observation that
   - (A) is seen more frequently than the other observations in the data set
   - (B) is seen less frequently than the other observations in the data set
   - (C) is always smaller than the other observations in the data set
   - (D) is always larger than the other observations in the data set
   - (E) is significantly different from the other observations in the data set

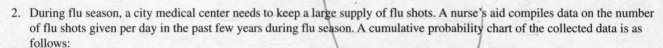

2. During flu season, a city medical center needs to keep a large supply of flu shots. A nurse's aid compiles data on the number of flu shots given per day in the past few years during flu season. A cumulative probability chart of the collected data is as follows:

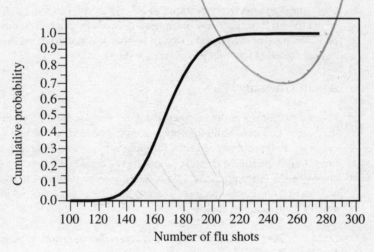

   How many flu shots should the center store every day to meet the demand on 95 percent of the days?
   - (A) At most 190
   - (B) At most 140
   - (C) Exactly 170
   - (D) At least 150
   - (E) At least 200

GO ON TO THE NEXT PAGE.

3. A large company has offices in two locations, one in New Jersey and one in Utah. The mean salary of office assistants in the New Jersey office is $28,500. The mean salary of office assistants in the Utah office is $22,500. The New Jersey office has 128 office assistants and the Utah office has 32 office assistants. What is the mean salary paid to the office assistants in this company?

   (A) $22,500

   (B) $23,700

   (C) $25,500

   (D) $27,300

   (E) $28,500

4. In the northern United States, schools are sometimes closed during winter due to severe snowstorms. At the end of the school year, schools have to make up for the days missed. The following graph shows the frequency distribution of the number of days missed due to snowstorms per year using data collected from the past 75 years.

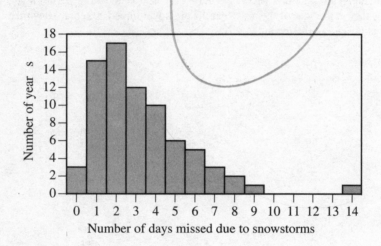

   Which of the following should be used to describe the center of this distribution?

   (A) Mean, because it is an unbiased estimator

   (B) Median, because the distribution is skewed

   (C) *IQR*, because it excludes outliers and includes only the middle 50 percent of data

   (D) First quartile, because the distribution is left skewed

   (E) Standard deviation, because it is unaffected by the outliers

GO ON TO THE NEXT PAGE.

5. The probability that there will be an accident on Highway 48 each day depends on the weather. If the weather is dry that day, there is a 0.2% chance of an accident on Highway 48; if the weather is wet that day, there is a 1.0% chance of an accident. Today, the weather station announced that there is a 20% chance of the weather being wet. What is the probability that there will be an accident on Highway 48 today?

   (A)   0.0004
   (B)   0.0016
   (C)   0.0020
   (D)   0.0036
   (E)   0.0060

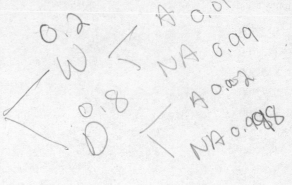

6. An employment placement agency specializes in placing workers in jobs suited for them. From past experience, the agency knows that 20% of all the workers it places will no longer be at the position in which they were placed after one year; however, only 5% of those remaining after the first year leave during the next year. At the start of a year an employer hires 100 workers using this agency, then at the start of the next year the employer hires 100 more. How many of these 200 workers are expected to be on the job at the end of the second year?

   (A)   140
   (B)   144
   (C)   152
   (D)   156
   (E)   171

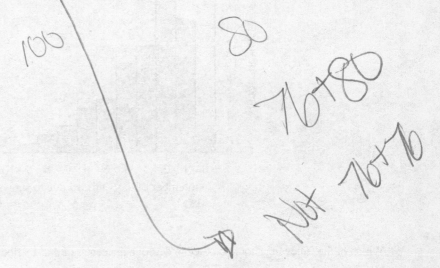

GO ON TO THE NEXT PAGE.

7. The average number of calories in Yum-Yum Good candy bars is 210, with a standard deviation of 10. If the number of calories per candy bar is normally distributed, what percent of candy bars contain more than 225 calories?

    (A)   66.80%

    (B)   47.70%

    (C)   43.30%

    (D)   6.68%

    (E)   3.34%

8. A publisher used standard boxes for shipping books. The mean weight of books packed per box is 25 pounds, with a standard deviation of two pounds. The mean weight of the boxes is one pound, with a standard deviation of 0.15 pounds. The mean weight of the packing material used per box is two pounds, with a standard deviation of 0.25 pounds. What is the standard deviation of the weights of the packed boxes?

    (A)   28.000 pounds

    (B)   5.290 pounds

    (C)   4.085 pounds

    (D)   2.400 pounds

    (E)   2.021 pounds

$$\sqrt{2^2 + 0.15^2 + 0.25^2}$$

GO ON TO THE NEXT PAGE.

9. The principal of a school is interested in estimating the average income per family of her students. She selects a random sample of students and collects information about their family income. A 95 percent confidence interval computed from this data for the mean income per family is ($35,095, $45,005). Which of the following provides the best interpretation of this confidence interval?

   (A) 95 percent of the students in her school are from families whose income is between $35,095 and $45,005.

   (B) There is a 95% probability that the families of all the students in this school have an income of between $35,095 and $45,005.

   (C) If we were to take another sample of the same size and compute a 95 percent confidence interval, we would have a 95% chance of getting the interval ($35,095, $45,005).

   (D) There is a 95% probability that the mean of another sample with the same size will fall between $35,095 and $45,005.

   (E) There is a 95% probability that the mean income per family in the school is between $35,095 and $45,005.

10. The Department of Health plans to test the lead level in a specific park. Because a high lead level is harmful to children, the park will be closed if the lead level exceeds the allowed limit. The department randomly selects several locations in the park, gets soil samples from those locations, and tests the samples for their lead levels. Which of the following decisions would result from the Type I error?

    (A) Closing the park when the lead levels are within the allowed limit

    (B) Keeping the park open when the lead levels are in excess of the allowed limit

    (C) Closing the park when the lead levels are in excess of the allowed limit

    (D) Keeping the park open when the lead levels are within the allowed limit

    (E) Closing the park because of the increased noise level in the neighborhood

GO ON TO THE NEXT PAGE.

11. Extra study sessions were offered to students after the midterm to help improve their understanding of statistics. Student scores on the midterm and the final exam were recorded. The following scatterplot shows final test scores against the midterm test scores.

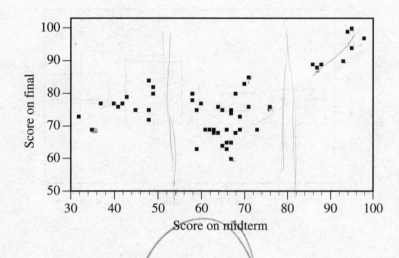

Which of the following statements correctly interprets the scatterplot?

(A) All students have shown significant improvement in the final exam scores as a result of the extra study sessions.

(B) The extra study sessions were of no help. Each student's final exam score was about the same as his or her score on the midterm.

(C) The extra study sessions further confused students. All student scores decreased from midterm to final exam.

(D) Students who scored below 55 on the midterm showed considerable improvement on the final exam; those who scored between 55 and 80 on the midterm showed minimal improvement on the final exam; and those who scored above 80 on the midterm showed almost no improvement on the final exam.

(E) Students who scored below 55 on the midterm showed minimal improvement on the final exam; those who scored between 55 and 80 on the midterm showed moderate improvement on the final exam; and those who scored above 80 on the midterm showed considerable improvement on the final exam.

GO ON TO THE NEXT PAGE.

12. A resident of Auto Town was interested in finding the cheapest gas prices at nearby gas stations. On randomly selected days over a period of one month, he recorded the gas prices (in dollars) at four gas stations near his house. The boxplots of gas prices are as follows:

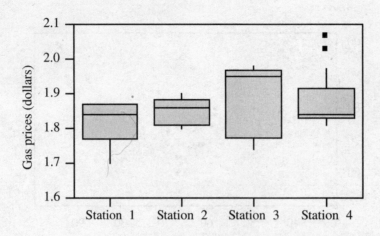

Based on this display, which of the stations had the closest mean and median during the month?

(A) Station 1
(B) Station 2
(C) Station 3
(D) Station 4
(E) We cannot tell without knowing the standard deviation of the gas prices from each station.

GO ON TO THE NEXT PAGE.

13. A botanist is interested in testing $H_0: \mu = 3.5$ cm versus $H_a: \mu > 3.5$, where μ = the mean petal length of one variety of flowers. A random sample of 50 petals gives significant results at a 5 percent level of significance. Which of the following statements about the confidence interval to estimate the mean petal length is true?

   (A) The specified mean length of 3.5 cm is within a 90 percent confidence interval.

   (B) The specified mean length of 3.5 cm is not within a 90 percent confidence interval.

   (C) The specified mean length of 3.5 cm is below the lower limit of a 90 percent confidence interval.

   (D) The specified mean length of 3.5 cm is below the lower limit of a 95 percent confidence interval.

   (E) Not enough information is available to answer the question.

14. A filling machine puts an average of four ounces of coffee in jars, with a standard deviation of 0.25 ounces. Forty jars filled by this machine are selected at random. What is the probability that the mean amount per jar filled in the sampled jars is less than 3.9 ounces?

   (A) 0.0057
   (B) 0.0225
   (C) 0.0250
   (D) 0.0500
   (E) 0.3446

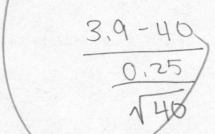

GO ON TO THE NEXT PAGE.

15. The number of customers served per day by a large department store is normally distributed, with a mean of 3,250 customers and a standard deviation of 320. Find the range of customers served on the <u>middle 50 percent</u> of days.

(A) (3,035, 3,464)

(B) (2,930, 3,570) ✓   150

(C) (2,610, 3,890)   250

(D) (2,450, 4,050)

(E) (2,290, 4,210)   350

1 sd = 68% Between 1st & 3rd quartile

---

16. Assume that the masses of chicken eggs are normally distributed with a mean of 45 g and a standard deviation of 4 g. What mass of egg would be the 25th percentile of the masses of all the eggs?

(A) 42.2 g

(B) 42.3 g

(C) 42.4 g

(D) 42.5 g

(E) 42.6 g

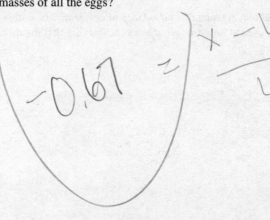

$$-0.67 = \frac{x - 45}{4}$$

GO ON TO THE NEXT PAGE.

17. The observed times (in minutes) it takes a runner to complete a marathon are normally distributed. The z-score for his running time this week is –2. Which one of the following statements is a correct interpretation of his z-score?

    (A) This week his time was two minutes lower than his time last week.

    (B) This week his time was two minutes lower than his best time ever.

    (C) This week his time was two minutes lower than his average time.

    (D) This week his time was two standard deviations lower than his average time.

    (E) This week his time was two standard deviations lower than his time last week.

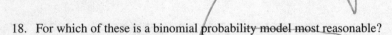

18. For which of these is a binomial probability model most reasonable?

    (A) The number of times, out of 10 attempts, that a particular child can throw a ball into a basket from six feet away

    (B) The colors of the cars in the parking lot of a particular grocery store on a randomly selected Sunday

    (C) The number of times that a randomly selected resident of California has visited a museum in the last 12 months

    (D) The number of cards drawn from a well-shuffled deck until all four aces are found

    (E) The number of people surveyed until someone who owns a parrot is found

GO ON TO THE NEXT PAGE.

19. A dentist has noticed that about two children in every seven whom he sees professionally develop cavities before they turn 10 years old. Last week he examined the teeth of five unrelated children younger than 10. Let *X* be the number of children who develop cavities before turning 10. Which of the following gives the probability that at least one will develop a cavity before turning 10?

    (A) $P(X = 2, 3, 4, 5, 6, 7)$
    (B) $P(X = 2 \text{ out of } 7)$
    (C) $P(X = 1)$
    (D) $1 - P(X = 0)$
    (E) $P(X = 0, 1)$

20. The probability that Ted enrolls in an English class is $\frac{1}{3}$. If he does enroll in an English class, the probability that he enrolls in a mathematics class is $\frac{1}{5}$. If he does not enroll in an English class, the probability that he enrolls in a mathematics class is $\frac{3}{5}$.

    If we learn that Ted enrolled in a mathematics class, what is the probability that he enrolled in an English class?

    (A) 0.067
    (B) 0.143
    (C) 0.250
    (D) 0.333
    (E) 0.500

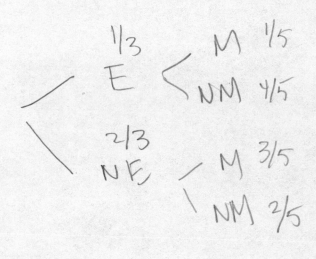

GO ON TO THE NEXT PAGE.

21. Two dice are rolled simultaneously. If both dice show 6, then the player wins $20; otherwise the player loses the game. It costs $2.00 to play the game. What is the expected gain or loss per game?

    (A)   The player will gain about $0.55.
    (B)   The player will gain about $1.44.
    (C)   The player will lose about $0.55.
    (D)   The player will lose about $1.44.
    (E)   The player will lose about $2.00.

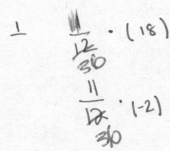

---

22. According to the Central Limit Theorem, the sample mean X is approximately normally distributed

    (A)   for a large sample, regardless of the distribution of random variable X
    (B)   for a large sample, provided the random variable X is normally distributed
    (C)   regardless of the sample size
    (D)   for a small sample, regardless of the distribution of random variable X
    (E)   for a small sample, provided the random variable X is normally distributed

GO ON TO THE NEXT PAGE.

23. A department store at a large mall claims that over 60 percent of the mall's visitors shop at that store. Let p = the proportion of the mall's visitors who shop at the store. Which of the following pairs of hypotheses should be used to support this claim?

   (A) $H_0: p \leq 0.60$ and $H_a: p > 0.60$

   (B) $H_0: p = 0.60$ and $H_a: p \neq 0.60$

   (C) $H_0: p = 0.60$ and $H_a: p < 0.60$

   (D) $H_0: p > 0.60$ and $H_a: p \leq 0.60$

   (E) $H_0: p < 0.60$ and $H_a: p \geq 0.60$

24. A random sample of 16 light bulbs of one brand was selected to estimate the mean lifetime of that brand of bulbs. The sample mean was 1,025 hours, with a standard deviation of 130 hours. Assuming that the lifetimes are approximately normally distributed, which of the following will give a 95 percent confidence interval to estimate the mean lifetime?

   (A) $1,025 \pm 1.96 \dfrac{130}{\sqrt{16}}$

   (B) $1,025 \pm 1.96 \sqrt{130}$

   (C) $1,025 \pm 2.12 \dfrac{130}{\sqrt{16}}$

   (D) $1,025 \pm 2.13 \dfrac{130}{\sqrt{16}}$

   (E) $1,025 \pm 2.13 \dfrac{130}{\sqrt{15}}$

GO ON TO THE NEXT PAGE.

25. A school committee member is lobbying for an increase in the gasoline tax to support the county school system. The local newspaper conducted a survey of county residents to assess their support for such an increase. What is the population of interest here?

    (A) All school-aged children
    (B) All county residents
    (C) All county residents with school-aged children
    (D) All county residents with children in the county school system
    (E) All county school system teachers

26. A manufacturer of ready-bake cake mixes is interested in designing an experiment to test the effects of four different temperature levels (300, 325, 350, and 375°F), two different types of pans (glass and metal), and three different types of ovens (gas, electric, and microwave) on the texture of its cakes, in all combinations. Which of the following below is the best description of the design of the necessary experiment?

    (A) A completely randomized design with nine treatment groups
    (B) A completely randomized design with 24 treatment groups
    (C) A randomized block design, blocked on temperature, with six treatment groups
    (D) A randomized block design, blocked on type of pan, with 12 treatment groups
    (E) A randomized block design, blocked on type of oven, with eight treatment groups

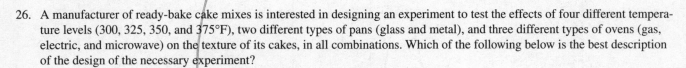

$4 \times 2 \times 3$

GO ON TO THE NEXT PAGE.

27. Which one of the following distributions could have a mean of approximately 12 and a standard deviation of approximately 2?

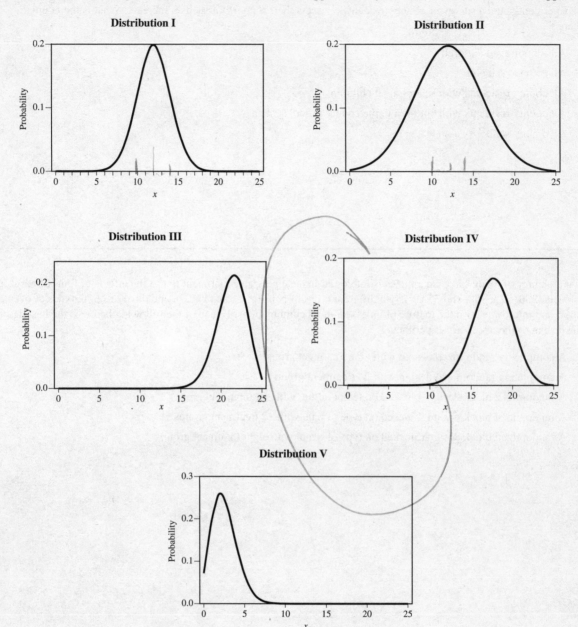

(A) Distribution I
(B) Distribution II
(C) Distribution III
(D) Distribution IV
(E) Distribution V

GO ON TO THE NEXT PAGE.

28. The relation between the selling price of a car (in $1,000) and its age (in years) is estimated from a random sample of cars of a specific model. The relation is given by the following formula:

    Selling price = 15.9 − 0.983(age)

    Which of the following can we conclude from this equation?

    (A) For every year the car gets older, the selling price goes down by approximately 9.83 percent.

    (B) A new car costs on the average $9,830.

    (C) For every year the car gets older, the selling price drops by approximately $1,590.

    (D) A new car costs $16,883.

    (E) For every year the car gets older, the selling price drops by approximately $983.

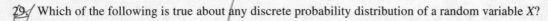

29. Which of the following is true about any discrete probability distribution of a random variable *X*?

    (A) The expected value of $X = np$.

    (B) The sum of all possible values of *X* is equal to one.

    (C) The probabilities of all possible values of *X* must add up to one.

    (D) The probability distribution is bell-shaped and symmetric.

    (E) Approximately 95 percent of the values of *X* fall within two standard deviations of the mean.

GO ON TO THE NEXT PAGE.

X	
x	*P(X = x)*
0	0.4
1	0.3
2	0.2
3	0.1

Y	
y	*P(X = x)*
1	0.1
2	0.2
3	0.3
4	0.4

30. *X* and *Y* are independent random variables; the probability distributions for each are given in the table above. Let $Z = X + Y$. What is $P(Z \leq 2)$?

    (A)   0.07
    (B)   0.15
    (C)   0.24
    (D)   0.40
    (E)   0.80

GO ON TO THE NEXT PAGE.

31. After a frost warning was issued, the owner of a large orange grove asked his workers to spray all his trees with water. The water was supposed to freeze and form a protective covering of ice around the orange blossom. Nevertheless, the owner suspected that some trees suffered considerable damage due to the frost. To estimate the proportion of trees that suffered more than 50 percent damage due to the frost, he took a random sample of 100 trees from his grove. What is the response variable in this experiment?

    (A) The proportion of trees that suffered more than 50 percent damage due to frost

    (B) The number of trees affected by the frost

    (C) The number of trees sampled from the grove

    (D) For each sampled tree, whether it was sprayed with water or not sprayed with water

    (E) For each sampled tree, whether it suffered more than 50 percent damage or at most 50 percent damage

32. For which of the following purposes would it be most unreasonable to use a census?

    (A) To determine the proportion of students with a learning disability in a small rural area high school

    (B) To determine the proportion of red snappers with a high mercury level in the Gulf of Mexico

    (C) To determine the difference between the proportion of engineering professors and the proportion of business professors in favor of the new teaching initiative at a large university

    (D) To determine the mean wage earned by construction workers in a small town

    (E) To determine the mean selling price of houses in your neighborhood

GO ON TO THE NEXT PAGE.

33. A student organization at a university is interested in estimating the proportion of students in favor of showing movies bi-weekly instead of monthly. How many students should be sampled to get a 90 percent confidence interval with a width of at most 0.08?

    (A)   27
    (B)   64
    (C)   106
    (D)   256
    (E)   423

34. A small kiosk at the Atlanta airport carries souvenirs in the price range of $3.99 to $29.99, with a mean price of $14.75. The airport authorities decide to increase the rent charged for a kiosk by 5 percent. To make up for the increased rent, the kiosk owner decides to increase the prices of all items by 50 cents. As a result, which of the following will happen?

    (A)   The mean price and the range of prices will increase by 50 cents.
    (B)   The mean price will remain the same, but the range of prices will increase by 50 cents.
    (C)   The mean price and the standard deviation of prices will increase by 50 cents.
    (D)   The mean price will increase by 50 cents, but the standard deviation of prices will remain the same.
    (E)   The mean price and the standard deviation will remain the same.

GO ON TO THE NEXT PAGE.

35. Two hundred students were classified by sex and hostility level (low, medium, high), as measured by an HLT-test. The results were the following:

	Hostility Level		
	Low	**Medium**	**High**
Male	35	40	5
Female	62	50	8

(handwritten: 120)
(handwritten: 90)

If the hostility level among students were independent of their sex, then how many female students would we expect to show the medium HLT score?

(A) 25
(B) 45
(C) 54
(D) 60
(E) 75

36. After receiving several complaints from his customers about the store being closed on Sundays, a storekeeper decided to conduct a survey. He randomly selected 100 female customers and 120 male customers, and asked them, "Are you interested in shopping at this store on Sundays?" He counted the number of customers answering "yes" and constructed a 95 percent confidence interval for the difference by subtracting the proportions of female from the proportion of male customers in favor of shopping on Sundays. The resulting interval was (–0.23, –0.18). Which of the following is a correct interpretation of the interval?

(A) We are 95 percent confident that the proportion of women interested in shopping on Sundays exceeds the proportion of men interested in shopping on Sundays.

(B) We are 95 percent confident that the proportion of men interested in shopping on Sundays exceeds the proportion of women interested in shopping on Sundays.

(C) We are 95 percent confident that the proportion of women interested in shopping on Sundays is equal to the proportion of men interested in shopping on Sundays.

(D) Because the interval contains negative values, it is invalid and should not be interpreted.

(E) Because the interval does not contain zero, the interval is invalid, and should not be interpreted.

GO ON TO THE NEXT PAGE.

37. A company is interested in comparing the mean sales revenue per salesperson at two different locations. The manager takes a random sample of 10 salespeople from each location independently and records the sales revenue generated by each person during the last four weeks. He decides to use a *t*-test to compare the mean sales revenue at the two locations. Which of the following assumptions is necessary for the validity of the *t*-test?

   (A) The population standard deviations at both locations are equal.

   (B) The population standard deviations at both locations are not equal.

   (C) The population standard deviations at both locations are known.

   (D) The population of the sales records at each location is normally distributed.

   (E) The population of the difference in sales records computed by pairing one salesperson from each location is normally distributed.

---

38. A skeptic decides to conduct an experiment in ESP in which a blindfolded subject calls out the color of a card dealt from a regular deck of cards (half the cards are red; the other half, black). One hundred cards are dealt from a well-shuffled pack, with each card being replaced after a deal. Using a 5 percent level of significance, what is the lowest number of cards that the subject needs to call out correctly in order to show that he is doing better than he would if he were simply guessing?

   (A) 51

   (B) 59

   (C) 75

   (D) 95

   (E) 98

GO ON TO THE NEXT PAGE.

39. A manufacturer of motor oil is interested in testing the effects of a newly developed additive on the lifespan of an engine. Twenty-five different engine types are selected at random and each one is tested using oil with the additive and oil without the additive. What type of analysis will yield the most useful information?

    (A) Matched pairs comparison of population proportions
    (B) Matched pairs comparison of population means
    (C) Independent samples comparison of population proportions
    (D) Independent samples comparison of population means
    (E) Chi-square test of homogeneity

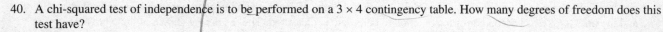

40. A chi-squared test of independence is to be performed on a 3×4 contingency table. How many degrees of freedom does this test have?

    (A) 6
    (B) 8
    (C) 10
    (D) 11
    (E) 12

END OF SECTION I

STATISTICS
SECTION II
Time—1 hour and 30 minutes
Number of questions—6
Percent of total grade—50

Part A
Questions 1–5
Spend about 60 minutes on this part of the exam.
Percent of Section II grade—75

Show all your work. Indicate clearly the methods you use, because you will be graded on the correctness of your method as well as on the accuracy of your results and explanation.

1. A chemical engineering company has developed two different catalysts to accelerate a chemical reaction necessary for one of its products. To test the speed of the reaction of the two catalysts, the company uses catalyst A 12 times in the reaction, then catalyst B 12 times in the reaction. Each of the 12 trials for both catalysts is conducted under identical controlled conditions, and the time it takes (in seconds) for the reaction to complete is measured. The results are shown in the table below:

Trial	Time Using Catalyst A (seconds)	Time Using Catalyst B (seconds)
1	24	8
2	27	7
3	18	26
4	32	30
5	26	11
6	32	19
7	19	22
8	26	30
9	22	23
10	19	16
11	20	13
12	25	26

A → 18, 19, 19, 20

GO ON TO THE NEXT PAGE.

(a) Display the data using two box-and-whisker plots in the space below.

Times of Reactions

A

B

A: 18, 19.5, 24.5 26.5, 32

B: 7, 12, 20.5, 26, 30

(b) If the chemical company is most interested in making the reaction time as short as possible, which catalyst should it use? Please explain.

The company should use catalyst B. The center of the distribution has the smaller time (20.5 vs. 24.5 for the median), and its range encompasses smaller times.

(c) If the chemical company is most interested in making the reaction time as consistent as possible, which catalyst should it use? Please explain.

The company should use catalyst A. A has a smaller range and IQR thus proving to be less variability and less spread.

GO ON TO THE NEXT PAGE.

2. A vegetable oil blend packaged by a food manufacturer consists of canola oil and corn oil. The amount of canola oil in each bottle of the blend can be modeled using a normal distribution with mean 440 ml and standard deviation 10 ml; the amount of corn oil in each bottle of the blend can likewise be modeled using a normal distribution with mean 410 ml and standard deviation 15 ml. The amount of canola oil in each bottle is independent of the amount of corn oil.

(a) Determine the probability that the amount of oil in a randomly selected bottle of this blend will exceed 900 ml.

Mean: $440 + 410 = 850$ mL

SD: $\sqrt{10^2 + 15^2} = 18.0278$ mL

$z = \dfrac{900 - 850}{18.0278} = 2.773$

$P(z \geq 2.773) = 0.0028$

There is a 0.28% that the oil will exceed 900 mL.

(b) Determine the probability that the amount of corn oil in a randomly selected bottle of this blend is greater than the amount of canola oil in the bottle.

$440 - 410 = 30$

$\mu = 0$

$\mu \neq 0$

$\dfrac{0 - 30}{18.0278} = 1.644$

(c) Based on your answer to part (b), what is the probability that, out of five randomly selected bottles of this blend, at least one of the bottles contains more corn oil than canola oil?

Binomial Distribution

GO ON TO THE NEXT PAGE.

Section II

3. Salmon farmers have a choice of three different types of food (type A, type B, or type C) and two different breeds (Sockeye and Chinook). The salmon farmers want you to design an experiment in which you feed the different types of food to the two breeds of salmon to see which type of food leads to the largest salmon by weight. They provide you with 60 salmon divided equally between the two breeds and can provide you with up to 10 different tanks in which to raise the salmon. The farmers would like the results in 10 weeks.

(a) Design an appropriate experiment.

You have 30 Sockeye and 30 Chinook. Hence, for the Sockeye, 10 will be fed A, 10 fed B, 10 fed C. Also, for chinook, 10 fed A, 10 fed B, and 10 fed C. Hence, there are 6 groups, and 6 tanks. Feed all of them normally, and in 9 weeks, weigh each group of fish.

(b) Is your design single-blind, double-blind, or neither? Explain.

Neither. Fish have no conscious of what type of food they will receive. The researchers need to know which fish received which food type.

GO ON TO THE NEXT PAGE.

38 | Cracking the AP Statistics Exam

4. A nutritionist wants to confirm her suspicion that, among Americans, women tend to prefer chocolate for dessert more often than men. She decides that it will be convenient to collect data on customers of a large and popular restaurant owned by her family. The restaurant has a practice of showing the daily selection of desserts on a tray to the customers. For 500 customers selected randomly over a one-week period, the nutritionist notes the sex of the customer and the choice of dessert. The data is summarized in the table below.

	Sex	
	Male	Female
Dessert with Chocolate	140	150
Dessert without Chocolate	160	50

290

210

300   200

(a) Identify the target and sampled populations in this experiment. Are they the same or different? Discuss how their sameness or difference will affect the conclusions drawn from this experiment.

The targetted population
are all men and women.
The sample population is
a random sample, but we
can only generalize it to the
customers of the restaurant.

GO ON TO THE NEXT PAGE.

(b) The nutritionist is considering using a chi-square test of independence to analyze this data. Why is this test inappropriate to justify her suspicions?

she wants to determine
if women prefer more chocolate
than men. The test of
Independence only determines
if there is a relationship between
the two.

(c) Which test would be more appropriate to gather evidence to support her suspicions? Can the test you named be done using this data? Justify your answer.

A two sample z-test. Firstly,
because the sample is randomly
sampled, we may use this
test. Next, we must check if the
size is adequate. So for males,
$\hat{p}_1 = \frac{140}{300} = 0.467$ and $n_1 = 300$. For
females, $\hat{p}_2 = \frac{150}{200} = 0.75$ and
$n_2 = 200$. since all $(\hat{p})n$ and
$(\hat{p})n \geq 10$, we may use this
test.

5. A large security-system management company with clients in Los Angeles and San Francisco installs and monitors security systems in houses and on business premises. The system's alarm sounds at the central monitoring location if the system detects a security break-in, smoke, or fire at any of the clients' premises. Tests have indicated that a false alarm occurs approximately 3 percent of the instances in which the alarm sounds and that in approximately 0.5 percent of actual incidences, the system fails to sound an alarm. The records indicate that about 0.1 percent of its clients have break-in/fire/smoke incidents.

(a) Suppose a client is selected at random. What is the probability that the alarm will sound at this client's premises?

$$0.999$$
$$NI \quad \begin{array}{l} S \ 0.03 \\ NS \ 0.97 \end{array}$$
$$0.001$$
$$I \quad \begin{array}{l} S \ 0.995 \\ NS \ 0.005 \end{array}$$

$$P(NI \ and \ S) + P(I \ and \ Sound)$$
$$(0.97)(0.03) + (0.001)(0.995)$$
$$0.03 \quad or \quad 3.81\%$$

(b) Suppose the alarm is sounded at a client's premises. What is the probability that there was no break-in, smoke, or fire incident?

$$\frac{P(NI \cap S)}{} = \frac{(0.03)(0.999)}{(0.03)}$$

$$0.996 \quad or \quad 99.6\%$$

END OF PART A

STATISTICS
SECTION II
Part B
Question 6
Spend about 30 minutes on this part of the exam.
Percent of Section II grade—25

6. A physician who has delivered babies for over 20 years claims that birthweights of babies tend to be higher than the birthweight of their next older siblings. In other words, a parent's second child tends to have a higher birthweight than the first child, the third child tends to have higher birthweight than the second child, and so on. To verify the doctor's statement, her office assistant gets a random sample of mothers with at least two children from the hospital records and records the birthweights of the first two children. The birthweights for the children of 19 mothers are given in the table below.

Mother	Birthweight of First Child (in Pounds)	Birthweight of Second Child (in Pounds)
1	5.13	5.37
2	5.25	5.65
3	6.71	6.89
4	4.71	5.61
5	3.77	3.37
6	5.81	6.65
7	8.29	8.77
8	6.36	6.13
9	6.08	6.97
10	4.91	5.58
11	3.19	3.43
12	5.64	5.89
13	6.37	6.88
14	5.90	6.21
15	4.73	4.93
16	5.60	6.25
17	4.68	5.30
18	7.79	7.38
19	4.18	4.77

GO ON TO THE NEXT PAGE.

(a) Does this data provide any evidence to support the physician's theory? Justify your answer using statistical evidence.

use t test single. ✓

Can do on calculator

(b) The scatterplot of birthweights of first-born children and second-born children is given below.

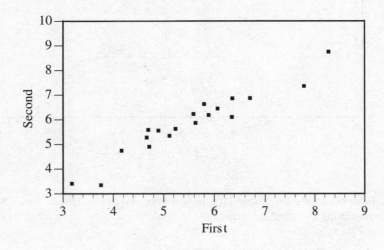

Describe the relation between the birthweights of first-born children and the birthweights of second-born children.

There seems to be a positive correlation or first chidren with large birth weights tend to have second chidren with large birthweight as well.

GO ON TO THE NEXT PAGE.

(c) The regression analysis of the data resulted in the following outcome.

Predictor	Coef	StDev	T	P
Constant	0.5626	0.3966	1.42	0.174
first	0.95939	0.06996	13.71	0.000

S = 0.3772   R-Sq = 91.7%   R-Sq(adj) = 91.2%

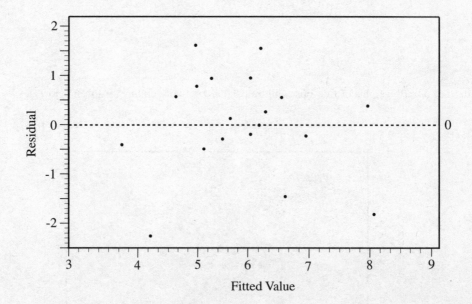

Is there a significant relation between the birthweights of first-born children and the birthweights of second-born children? Justify your answer using statistical evidence.

Residual plot aint pattern so linear.

Slope of regression line

GO ON TO THE NEXT PAGE.

(d) Suppose the doctor is getting ready to deliver the second child of a mother whose first child weighed 7.2 pounds. Predict the birthweight of this second child.

$$6.5626 + 0.95939 (first) = second$$

(e) What is an approximate range of birthweights of second-born children whose first-born siblings weighed 7.2 pounds?

1 : 4
2 : 1.5
3 : 3
4 : 4
5 : 4
6 : 2

STOP

END OF EXAM

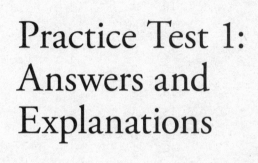

Practice Test 1:
Answers and
Explanations

PRACTICE TEST 1 ANSWER KEY

1.	E	21.	D
2.	E	22.	A
3.	D	23.	A
4.	B	24.	D
5.	D	25.	B
6.	D	26.	B
7.	D	27.	A
8.	E	28.	E
9.	E	29.	C
10.	A	30.	B
11.	D	31.	E
12.	B	32.	B
13.	B	33.	E
14.	A	34.	D
15.	A	35.	C
16.	B	36.	A
17.	D	37.	D
18.	A	38.	B
19.	D	39.	B
20.	B	40.	A

PRACTICE TEST 1 EXPLANATIONS

Section I—Multiple-Choice

1. **E** An outlier is an observation that is significantly different from the other observations in the data set. It is not necessarily just the largest or the smallest observation; it could be either.

2. **E** Look closely at the chart. For example, the point (160, 0.4) indicates that on 40 percent of the days, up to 160 shots were given. To find the number of shots needed to meet the demand on 95 percent of the days, we need to find the 95th percentile. Draw a horizontal line from the cumulative probability of 0.95 to the curve. From the point at which the line meets the curve, draw a vertical line down to the x-axis, and then read the number of flu shots given there. It should be approximately 200.

3. **D** The total amount paid in salaries to the office assistants is 128($28,500) + 32($22,500) = $4,368,000.

    This total amount is paid to 128 + 32 = 160 office assistants. The mean salary paid to office assistants

    $$= \frac{\text{total}}{\text{number of assistants}} = \frac{\$4,368,000}{160} = \$27,300.$$

    An easier method of solving this problem is to use process of elimination. The average must be between $22,500 and $28,500, eliminating choice (A) and choice (E). Next, note that there are far more people in the New Jersey office than in the Utah office, so the average has to be closer to the New Jersey number ($28,500) than the Utah number ($22,500). Only choice (D) meets this requirement.

4. **B** *IQR*, first quartile, and standard deviation are not measures of central tendency. Median and mean are measures of central tendency. The mean is affected by extreme observations—large observations tend to make the mean higher. Because this distribution is skewed, the median should be used to describe the center of the distribution. Note that the median is not affected by the extreme measurements.

5. **D** A tree diagram makes this problem easiest to visualize.

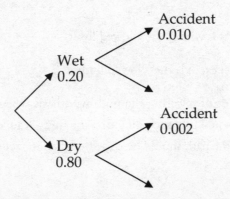

The chance of an accident depends on whether or not the weather is wet, so the weather condition is our first branching on the tree. The probabilities at the next branch are conditional. There are two final branches on the tree that conclude with an accident: $P(\text{wet} \cap \text{accident}) = 0.2 \times 0.010 = 0.0020$ and $P(\text{dry} \cap \text{accident}) = 0.80 \times 0.002 = 0.0016$. Therefore the total probability of an accident is $0.0020 + 0.0016 = 0.0036$.

6. **D** Of the 100 workers hired the first year, we expect 80 percent, or 80, to still be working at the company after the first year. Then we expect 95 percent of those 80, or 76, to be still employed at the end of the second year. Of those hired at the start of the second year, we expect 80 to still be hired at the end of the second year. We therefore expect $80 + 76 = 156$ to still be hired at the end of the second year.

7. **D** It is given that the random variable X = number of calories per bar. Now we need to find $P(\text{Number of calories} > 225)$.

$$P(X > 225) = P\left(Z > \frac{225 - 210}{10}\right) = P(Z > 1.5) = 1 - 0.9332 = 0.0668$$

(Hint: On the TI-83 or TI-84, use the normalcdf function from the DISTR menu, or use Table A with $Z = 1.50$.)

8. **E** Note that the weight of a packed box = weight of books + weight of box + weight of packing material used.

It is given that $\sigma_{\text{books}} = 2$ pounds, $\sigma_{\text{box}} = 0.15$ pounds, and $\sigma_{\text{packing material}} = 0.25$ pounds. So, the standard deviation of the weights of the packed boxes is

$$\sigma_{\text{packed boxes}} = \sqrt{\sigma^2_{\text{books}} + \sigma^2_{\text{books}} + \sigma^2_{\text{packing materials}}} = \sqrt{2^2 + 0.15^2 + 0.25^2} = 2.021 \text{ pounds}$$

Note that variances of independent variables are additive. Standard deviations are not.

9. **E** A confidence interval is a statement about the mean of the population the sample is drawn from; there is a 95 percent probability that a 95 percent confidence interval contains the mean of the population.

10. **A** The hypotheses tested here are:

H_0: The true mean lead level is within the allowed limit

H_a: The true mean lead level exceeds the allowed limit

The Type I error is the error of rejecting the null hypothesis when the null hypothesis is true. In this case, the Type I error would be concluding that the mean lead levels are in excess of the allowed limit—and therefore, that the park should be closed—when in fact the levels are within the allowed limit.

11. **D** The scatterplot shows three different groups. The group of students on the far left of the scatterplot scored lowest on the midterm, in a range of 30–50, but then scored in a range of 65–85 on the final, showing considerable improvement. The middle group scored between 55–80 on the midterm and then between 60–85 on the final, showing very little improvement. The third group, the one on the far right of the scatterplot, scored above 85 on the midterm and then above 85 on the final, showing almost no improvement. To assist you in seeing this, you can add a straight line to the graph, going from a point on the x-axis at 50 (midterm = 50) and the bottom of the y-axis (final = 50) to a point at midterm = 100 and final = 100. Then, people on the upper left of that line did better on the final, whereas those on the lower right did better on the midterm.

12. **B** The mean is strongly affected by skew and outliers, while the median is not. Therefore the mean will be closest to the median when the box-and-whisker plot is most symmetric; the most symmetric of the box-and-whisker plots is from station 2.

13. **B** The right-tailed test is used. So there is a 5 percent area in the rejection region in the right tail of the sampling distribution. If we construct a 90 percent confidence interval, then the upper confidence limit will match the critical value. If the test of hypothesis is rejected at a 5 percent level of significance, then the test statistic fell in the rejection region. In other words, the hypothesized value of mean did not belong to the 90 percent confidence interval.

14. **A** The sample of 40 jars is large enough for us to apply the central limit theorem and get an approximately normal distribution of the sample mean, with $\mu_{\bar{x}} = 4$ ounces and $\sigma_{\bar{x}} = \dfrac{\sigma}{\sqrt{n}} = \dfrac{0.25}{\sqrt{40}} = 0.039$.

    So, $P(\overline{X} < 3.9) = P\left(Z < \dfrac{3.9 - 4.0}{0.0395}\right) = P(Z < -2.53) = 0.0057$

    (Hint: On the TI-83 or TI-84, use the normalcdf function from the DISTR menu, or use Table A with $Z = -2.53$.)

15. **A** Find the first and third quartiles of the distribution because the middle 50 percent of the data falls between the first and the third quartile.

    $P(X < Q_1) = 0.25 \Rightarrow Q_1 = \mu - Z_{0.25}\sigma = 3{,}250 - 0.675(320) = 3{,}035$

    $P(X < Q_3) = 0.75 \Rightarrow Q_3 = \mu + Z_{0.25}\sigma = 3{,}250 + 0.675(320) = 3{,}464$

16. **B** In a normal distribution, the z-score at the 25th percentile is $z = -0.675$. That is, $P(z < -0.675) \approx 0.25$; this can be found using invnorm(.25) on the TI-83, or the table for the normal distribution. This implies the mass of egg that would be at the 25th percentile for all eggs is 0.675 standard deviations below the mean. Therefore, that mass is $45\text{ g} - 0.675 \times 4\text{ g} \approx 42.3\text{ g}$.

17. **D** The z-score $= \dfrac{x - \mu}{\sigma}$. A negative z-score indicates that the x-value is below the average. The value of the score represents the difference between the x-value and the mean in terms of the number of standard deviations.

18. **A** A binomial model counts the number of successes out of a fixed number of attempts at a task when each attempt has a constant probability of success. Only choice (A) meets these criteria. Choice (B) is not even quantitative; choice (C) cannot be reasonably modeled by counting successes over a fixed number of attempts; choice (D) is close, but the probability that we will draw an ace changes from draw to draw; choice (E) can be modeled using the geometric probability model: we are counting the number of attempts until we achieve a success.

19. **D** The probability that at least one child will develop a cavity is equal to the probability that one, two, three, four, or five children will develop cavities. Because X, the number of children developing cavities in a sample of five children, takes values 0, 1, 2, 3, 4, 5, and the sum of their probabilities is equal to 1, then the probability that one, two, three, four, or five children will develop cavities is equal to 1 minus the probability that no child develops cavities.

20. **B** The correct answer is (B). We are asked for a conditional probability: the probability that Ted enrolled in English given he enrolled in mathematics, or P(English|math). The formula for conditional probability tells us that $P(\text{English}|\text{math}) = \dfrac{P(\text{English} \cap \text{math})}{P(\text{math})}$. The tree diagram below shows that $P(\text{English} \cap \text{math}) = \dfrac{1}{15}$ and $P(\text{math}) = \dfrac{1}{15} + \dfrac{6}{15} = \dfrac{7}{15}$. Therefore $P(\text{English}|\text{math}) = \dfrac{\frac{1}{15}}{\frac{7}{15}} = \dfrac{1}{7}$

$= 0.1428 \approx 0.143$.

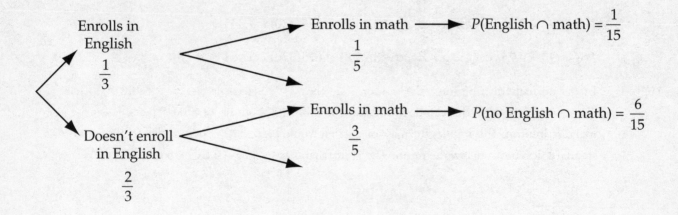

21. **D** P(Both dice roll 6) = $\dfrac{1}{36}$. So there is a one out of 36 chance that the player will win $20, and a $\dfrac{35}{36}$ chance that the player will win nothing. So, the expected amount won by the player is $20\left(\dfrac{1}{36}\right)$ = $0.56. But note that it costs the player $2.00 to play the game. Therefore, the expected gain or loss for the game is 0.56 − 2.00 = −1.44. In other words, on average the player will lose $1.44.

22. **A** The central limit theorem states that for a large sample, the sampling distribution of the sample mean will be approximately normally distributed regardless of the distribution of random variable X.

23. **A** If we're trying to support the claim that more than 60 percent of mall-goers visit the store, we need to make this statement the alternative hypothesis. The null hypothesis should be that the proportion of visitors to the store is less than or equal to to 0.60.

24. **D** The population standard deviation is unknown, and the lifetimes are normally distributed. Therefore, we should use a t-interval to estimate the mean lifetime. With a sample of 16 bulbs, we get 15 degrees of freedom. To construct a 95 percent confidence interval, use α = 0.05. Therefore, using a t-table, find $t_{\alpha/2}\left(df\right) = t_{0.025}\left(15\right) = 2.13$. The confidence interval for the mean lifetime is

$$\bar{x} \pm t_{\alpha/2}\left(df\right)\frac{s}{\sqrt{n}} = 1{,}025 \pm 2.13\frac{130}{\sqrt{16}}$$

25. **B** All county residents will be affected by the gasoline tax increase, regardless of whether they have school-aged children or where their children go to school.

26. **B** We can randomly assign temperature level, type of pan, and type of oven to a particular cake mix, so there is no reason to block by any of the variables. Since we want to try every combination, we must have 4 × 2 × 3 = 24 treatment groups.

27. **A** The distribution with a mean of 12 will be centered around 12. So rule out Distributions III and IV, which have higher means. Also rule out Distribution V, which has a lower mean. Distributions I and II are centered around 12. A fairly symmetric and mound-shaped distribution with mean 12 and standard deviation 2 should have an approximate range of 12: (3 standard deviations around mean, 12 − 3(2) = 6 and 12 + 3(2) = 18). Distribution II has a larger range, so rule it out. Distribution I is centered around 12 and has an approximate range of 12.

28. **E** In the given equation, Y-intercept = 15.9 and slope = −0.983. Note that the car prices are recorded in $1,000. The slope is negative, which means the price decreases as the age increases. The amount of change in price for every unit change in age is equal to 0.983 (in $1,000), which equals $983. So for every year the car gets older, the selling price goes down by approximately $983.

29. **C** For any discrete probability distribution to be valid, one of the two conditions that need to be satisfied is $\displaystyle\sum_{\text{all possible values of } x} P(X) = 1$

30. **B** There are three mutually exclusive ways to get a sum less than or equal to two: $x = 0$ and $y = 1$; $x = 0$ and $y = 2$; $x = 1$ and $y = 1$. Since the random variables are independent, we can multiply each pair's probabilities to get the probability of the pair. That is:

$P(x = 0 \text{ and } y = 1) = P(x = 0) \times P(y = 1) = 0.4 \times 0.1 = 0.04$

$P(x = 0 \text{ and } y = 2) = P(x = 0) \times P(y = 2) = 0.4 \times 0.2 = 0.08$

$P(x = 1 \text{ and } y = 1) = P(x = 1) \times P(y = 1) = 0.3 \times 0.1 = 0.03$

Since each of these different possibilities is mutually exclusive, we can sum these probabilities to get the probability of any of them occurring. Thus, $P(Z \leq 2) = 0.04 + 0.08 + 0.03 = 0.15$.

31. **E** For each sampled tree, one of two possible outcomes will be noted: (1) the tree suffered more than 50 percent damage, or (2) the tree suffered at most 50 percent damage.

32. **B** It would be impossible to catch all the red snappers in the Gulf of Mexico and measure their mercury levels.

33. **E** The margin of error $= \dfrac{\text{width}}{2} = \dfrac{0.08}{2} = 0.04$.

For a 90 percent confidence interval, we need to use $\alpha = 0.10$ and find

$Z_{\alpha/2} = Z_{0.10/2} = Z_{0.05} = 1.645$

Because no prior estimate for p is available, we should use $p = \dfrac{1}{2}$. Then,

$n \geq \left(\dfrac{1.645}{0.04}\right)^2 \left(\dfrac{1}{2}\right)\left(1 - \dfrac{1}{2}\right) = 422.82$

At least 423 students should be sampled.

(Hint: On the TI-83 or TI-84, use the invNorm function from the DISTR menu to find $Z_{\alpha/2}$.)

34. **D** The range and the standard deviation remain unaffected by the constant increment in all the measurements, but the mean will increase by 50 cents.

35. **C** The total number of females in the sample = 120.

The total number of students with medium HLT score = 90.

The total number of students in the sample = 200.

The expected number of females with medium HLT score

$$= \frac{(\text{Number of female students})(\text{Number of students with medium HLT score})}{\text{The total number of students}}$$

$$= \frac{(120)(90)}{200}$$

$$= 54$$

36. **A** The entire interval for $(p_M - p_F)$ falls below 0. This indicates that $(p_M - p_F) < 0$, which means that it is likely that $p_M < p_F$.

37. **D** Equality of standard deviations is not necessary for a t-test to be valid. One of the conditions of a t-test is that the underlying populations must be normally distributed.

38. **B** The hypotheses used in this experiment are

H_0: The subject is guessing, i.e., $p = 0.50$

H_a: The subject is not guessing, i.e., $p > 0.50$

where p = the proportion of correct answers. Using $\alpha = 0.05$, the null hypothesis will be rejected if

$$z = \frac{\hat{p} - p_0}{\sqrt{\dfrac{p_0(1 - p_0)}{n}}} > Z_\alpha$$

i.e., if $z = \dfrac{\hat{p} - 0.50}{\sqrt{\dfrac{0.50(1 - 0.50)}{100}}} > 1.6$

i.e., if $\hat{p} > 0.50 + 1.645\sqrt{\dfrac{0.50(1 - 0.50)}{100}} = 0.5823$

The subject needs to identify at least 58.23 percent correctly. Because 100 cards are dealt, the subject needs to identify at least 59 cards correctly.

(Hint: On the TI-83 or TI-84, use the invNorm function from the DISTR menu to find Z_α, or look in Table A for 0.05. It is midway between 1.64 and 1.65, so 1.645 is the value we want.)

39. **B** Because the question is asking about the lifespan as a whole—and not the number of engines that lasted greater than 5000 miles, for instance—a mean is more appropriate than a proportion. Both engine oils, with the additive and without the additive, are tested on each car. Therefore, each car is acting as a block, or in other words, each car is matched with itself.

40. **A**   For a chi-squared test of independence, the number of degrees of freedom is equal to (# of rows – 1) × (# of columns – 1) = (3 – 1) × (4 – 1) = 6.

Section II—Free-Response

Our answers in this section are just guides to how you could or should answer similar questions. Your answers do not need to match ours.

1.   (a)

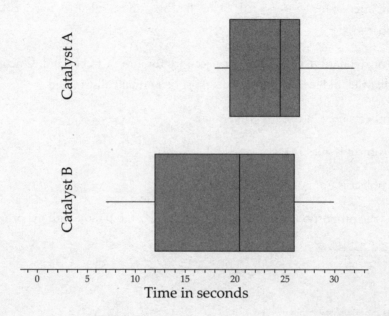

(b)   If the company is interested in making the reaction times as short as possible, then it should use catalyst B. Based on the box-and-whisker plot above, the minimum, Q1, median, Q3, and maximum reaction times are all shorter using catalyst B than catalyst A.

(c)   If the company is interested in making the reaction times as consistent as possible, then it should use catalyst A. Based on the box-and-whisker plot, the *IQR* and the range of the times using catalyst A are lower than the *IQR* and range using catalyst B.

2. (a) The probability that the amount of oil will exceed 900 ml can be determined by adding the independent random variables that give the amount of canola oil and the amount of corn oil in each bottle. When we add independent random variables, their means and variances combine. Therefore the mean amount of oil in a bottle is 440 ml + 410 ml = 850 ml; the standard deviation is the square root of the sum of the variances, or $\sqrt{10^2 + 15^2} \approx 18.028$ ml. Finally, when we sum normally distributed random variables, the sum is still normally distributed. So the z-score for 900 ml is $\dfrac{900 - 850}{18.028} \approx 2.774$; using a calculator or a table, $P(z > 2.774) \approx 0.00277$.

    (b) This is similar to the previous question, except now we are interested in the difference between the amounts of oil. When we subtract independent random variables, the means subtract, but the variances still combine. Therefore the mean of the difference *canola – corn* is 440 ml – 410 ml = 30 ml; the standard deviation is the same as above: 18.028 ml. And, as above, the difference of the variables is normally distributed. We want to determine P(*canola – corn* < 0). The z-score for 0 ml is $\dfrac{0 - 30}{18.028} \approx -1.664$ using a calculator or a table, and $P(z < -1.664) \approx 0.048$.

    (c) This is modeled using a binomial distribution. From part (b), the probability that a randomly selected bottle contains more corn oil than canola oil is 0.048. To get the probability that at least one out of five randomly selected bottles contains more corn oil than canola oil, we consider the complement of the event, which would be that zero out of five contain more corn oil than canola oil. The probability of this occurring is $(1 - 0.048)^5 = 0.952^5 \approx 0.782$. Since this is the complement of our desired event, the probability that at least one out of five bottles contains more corn oil than canola oil is $1 - 0.782 = 0.218$.

3. (a) Since we are trying to yield the largest salmon, and we do not know the weight of the salmon that were used in the experiment before the experiment began, it would be good to weigh the salmon pre-experiment to ensure that the change in weight is due to the food not a tendency in the random samples. Using a randomized block design, randomly divide each breed of salmon into three groups of 10 salmon each. Place each group into a different tank, and feed one tank of each breed one of the three food types, so you have 10 Sockeye eating food A, 10 Sockeye eating food B, and 10 Sockeye eating food C. Likewise, there are 10 Chinook eating each type of food. After 10 weeks, have evaluators weigh each salmon in each of the six tanks and report the results.

    (b) This design could easily be made single-blind: Make sure that those evaluators who weigh the salmon do not know which type of food each salmon ate. Whether or not it could be double-blind depends on whether or not those tending the salmon could be made unaware of the type of food each salmon was eating. If that is possible, this design could be double-blind.

4. (a) The target populations are the population of American men and the population of American women, i.e. about 120 million in each population. The sampled populations are the population of male customers at this restaurant who order desserts and the population of female customers at this restaurant who order desserts. Obviously, the sampled populations are not random samples from the target populations. Because the nutritionist has taken a sample of dessert-ordering customers at this restaurant only, the conclusion will be applicable only to the customers of this restaurant who order desserts, not to all men and women in general.

   (b) The nutritionist is interested in testing a one-sided alternative—specifically, that the proportion of women preferring chocolate is higher than the proportion of men preferring chocolate. But the chi-square test of independence will only tell the nutritionist whether the preference for chocolate is sex-dependent. This test is incapable of making the required determination, because it is not a one-sided test.

   (c) To find evidence to support her theory, the nutritionist needs to do a large sample z-test for difference of proportions with a one-sided alternative. She cannot do a z-test on this data, because the samples of men and women were not drawn independently of each other.

5. Let's define "fire" as an incident of fire, security break-in, or smoke. There are several ways to write this up. Two good ones are:

   I. $P(\text{Alarm}) = P(\text{Alarm} \mid \text{fire})P(\text{Fire}) + P(\text{Alarm} \mid \text{no fire})P(\text{No fire})$

   $= 0.995\,(0.001) + 0.03\,(0.999)$

   $= 0.030965 \approx 0.031$

   II. $P(\text{No fire} \mid \text{alarm}) = \dfrac{P\big(\text{Alarm} \mid \text{no fire}\big)P\big(\text{No fire}\big)}{P\big(\text{Alarm}\big)} = \dfrac{0.03(0.999)}{0.031} = 0.967$

   Or

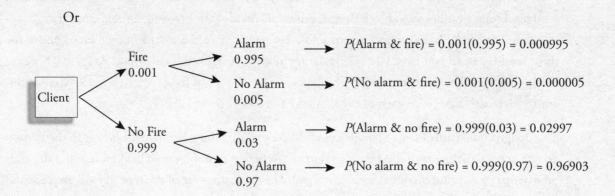

Using this tree diagram, we get

(a) $P(\text{Alarm}) = 0.000995 + 0.02997 = 0.030965 \approx 0.031.$

(b) $P(\text{No fire} \mid \text{alarm}) = \dfrac{0.02997}{0.031} = 0.967$

6. (a) Let $\mu_1 =$ The mean birthweight of the first child

$\mu_2 =$ The mean birthweight of the second child

We are interested in

$\mu_d = (\mu_1 - \mu_2)$

The mean difference in birthweights of first and second children.

We want to test

$H_0: \mu_d = 0$

(there is no difference in the mean birthweights of first and second children)

$H_a: \mu_d < 0$

(the mean birthweight of the second child is higher than the mean birthweight of the first child)

The data is collected on siblings, so it is paired data. Let $d_i =$ (weight of first child − weight of second child) in the ith pair. Then plot all the differences. Use any one of the following four graphs or charts to argue for the normality of the population of differences in birthweights of first and second children.

I.

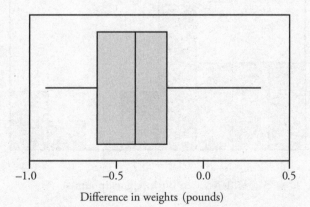

Difference in weights (pounds)

II.

Character Stem-and-Leaf Display

Stem-and-leaf of diff-wt

N = 19

Leaf Unit = 0.10

Stem	Leaf
−0.9	0
−0.8	4 9
−0.6	2 5 7
−0.5	1 9
−0.4	0 8
−0.3	1
−0.2	0 4 4 5
−0.1	8
0.2	3
0.4	0 1

Data points:

−0.9	−0.59	−0.24
−0.89	−0.51	−0.24
−0.84	−0.48	−0.20
−0.67	−0.40	−0.18
−0.65	−0.31	0.23
−0.62	−0.25	0.40
		0.41

III.

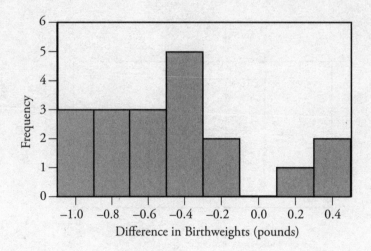

Difference in Birthweights (pounds)

IV.

Difference in Birthweights (pounds)

The pairs of siblings were selected at random, and from the above plots, it is reasonable to assume the normality of the population of differences in weights. The standard deviation of the population of differences is unknown, so we should use the paired *t*-test.

With $n = 19$ observations, we get 18 degrees of freedom. Let's use a 5 percent level of significance. The rejection rule will be "reject null hypothesis if p-value $< \alpha = 0.05$."

(If you chose to use the rejection-region approach, then the rule would be "reject null hypothesis if the $TS < -t_\alpha(df) = -t_{0.05}(18) = -1.734$.")

$\bar{d} = -0.3647$, and $s_d = 0.4079$

$$t = \frac{\bar{d} - 0}{s_d / \sqrt{n}} = \frac{-0.3647}{0.4079 / \sqrt{19}} = -3.898$$

p-value $= P(t(18) < -3.898) = 0.001$

With p-value $< 0.001 < 0.05$ (or because $t = -3.898$ falls in the rejection region), we can reject the null hypothesis and accept the alternative hypothesis. At a 5 percent level of significance, we should conclude that this data provides significant evidence that, on average, the second child tends to weigh more than the first one at birth. However, the physician made a somewhat different claim: that babies are heavier at birth than their next older siblings. There is no evidence here about the second and third children pairs, or about any later pairs

(Hint: On the TI-83 or TI-84, use the t-test function from the STAT $\rightarrow$ TESTS menu on the differences in birthweights. You could also use the calculator's graphing capability to make your graphs. Don't forget to copy the graphs from the calculator screen to your exam paper.)

(b) There is a strong positive linear relationship between the birthweights of first and second children. There are no outliers or influential points.

(c) Let $\beta_1 =$ the slope of the regression line for the weight of the second child as a function of the weight of the first child.

To test H_0: $\beta_1 = 0$ versus H_a: $\beta_1 \neq 0$, let's use a 5 percent level of significance.

The residual plot shows no patterns, indicating that a line is an appropriate model for this data. Also, the assumption of constant variance is reasonable, and the scatterplot in part (b) showed no outliers or influential points. Use a t-test for slope, with $(19 - 2) = 17$ degrees of freedom. The rejection rule is "reject null hypothesis if p-value < 0.05" [or if using p-value approach, "reject null hypothesis if $t > t_{\alpha/2}(df)$ $t_{0.025}(17) = 2.110$ or $TS < t_{\alpha/2}(df) = -t_{0.025}(17) = -2.110$."]

The regression output provided shows that $TS = 13.71$ and p-value < 0.001.

Because p-value $< 0.001 < 0.05$ (or the TS falls in the rejection region, or $TS > 2.110$), we should reject the null hypothesis and accept the alternative hypothesis. At a 5 percent level of significance, we can conclude that there is sufficient evidence indicating that the slope of the regression between the birthweights of first and second children is not zero. In other words, there is sufficient evidence to indicate that there is a significant relation between the weights of first and second children.

(Hint: On the TI-83 or TI-84, use the LinRegTTest function from the STAT → TESTS menu, or use Table B, row $df = 17$, column $d = 0.025$.)

(d)   From the regression output, we can write the equation of the line of best fit as follows:

Weight of a second child = 0.5626 + 0.95939(weight of a first child)
Use this equation to predict the weight of a second child.
Weight of a second child = 0.5626 + 0.95939(7.2) = 7.47 pounds.

The second child is expected to weigh about 7.47 pounds.

(e)   From the regression output, we get an estimated standard deviation of $s = 0.3772$. If the first child weighed 7.2 pounds, then most of the second children should weigh in the range $7.47 \pm 2\,(0.3772)$, i.e., in the range (6.72, 8.22) pounds, and nearly all in the range $7.47 \pm 3(0.3772) = (6.34, 8.60)$ pounds.

Part III
About the
AP Statistics
Exam

- How the AP Statistics Exam Is Structured
- Overview of Content Topics
- How AP Exams Are Used
- Other Resources
- Designing Your Study Plan
- On The Day of The Test

HOW THE AP STATISTICS EXAM IS STRUCTURED

The AP Statistics Exam is made up of two parts: a multiple-choice section and a free-response section. The entire test lasts three hours. Here's how the time is allotted:

- **Part I: Multiple Choice.** This part consists of 40 multiple-choice questions, each with five possible answers. Exactly one hour and 30 minutes is allotted for this part of the exam.

- **Part II: Free Response.** This part consists of six free-response questions, requiring not only that you perform the *right* computations but also that you communicate your reasoning and *justify* your answers clearly. Exactly one hour and 30 minutes is allotted for this part of the exam. This free-response section is further divided into two parts, Part A and Part B:
  - **Part A:** Five free-response questions, on which you are instructed to spend about 60 minutes, or about 12 minutes each.
  - **Part B:** The investigative task question, on which you are told to spend about 30 minutes. This question typically consists of several parts linking different areas of the curriculum. As the name suggests, the investigative task question invites you to investigate a situation and arrive at a solution. It might also require you to expand your knowledge of statistics a bit beyond the course curriculum.

Using a Calculator

Regarding calculators on the AP Statistics Exam, the College Board states: "Each student will be expected to bring a graphing calculator with statistical capabilities to the exam."

Note the word *expected*. Although the Test Development Committee makes some effort to develop tests that can be passed without using a graphing calculator, the truth is that you will be at a disadvantage if you don't have one. Good graphing calculators, such as the TI-83, TI-84, and TI-89 (currently the most commonly used), will not only save you time and prevent you from making minor arithmetic mistakes but will also help compute descriptive statistics such as standard deviation, correlation coefficient, and the equation of a least-squares regression line. These calculators are also capable of making useful graphs, such as histograms, scatterplot graphs, and least-squares regression lines. It goes without saying that these capabilities are extremely useful on the AP Statistics Exam.

Make sure you are thoroughly familiar with the functioning capabilities of your calculator. Don't bring an unfamiliar calculator to the AP Statistics exam. During the months before your exam, practice using your calculator until you feel confident with it.

However, you should always remember that a graphing calculator is only a computational aid. It cannot answer problems for you. Use it carefully. Interpreting numerical answers given by the calculator is still your responsibility. The calculator cannot do it for you. Nonetheless, the calculator will definitely make your computation easier, so use it.

Certain types of calculators may be prohibited from use on exams, such as calculators with QWERTY keyboards. This policy is updated as new and modified calculators enter the market. Refer to the College Board's policy on the use of calculators on exams (it's on the website) before purchasing one.

Using Computer Outputs

Due to time constraints during the exam, students are not expected to do extensive computations. For some questions, computer outputs are provided. Students are expected to make use of these outputs and interpret them correctly. Generally, only very standard, non-program specific outputs are provided. During the weeks before the exam, become familiar with the outputs of statistical programs. Learn to read them, interpret them, and use them, so you won't be caught by surprise on the exam. When you encounter a question on the exam that comes with a computer output, be sure to read the entire question carefully before answering it, and be sure to use the given output. Do not start computing everything again. This will only waste precious time.

OVERVIEW OF CONTENT TOPICS

The curriculum for AP Statistics consists of four basic themes.

- **Exploring data:** describing patterns and departures from patterns

- **Sampling and experimentation:** planning and conducting a study

- **Anticipating patterns:** exploring random phenomena using probability and simulation

- **Statistical inference:** estimating population parameters and testing hypotheses

The following is an outline of the major topics covered by the AP Statistics Exam. The topics may be taught in a different order. Keep in mind that less emphasis is placed on actual *arithmetic computation*, and more emphasis is placed on *conceptual understanding and interpretation*.

I. Exploring data: observing patterns and departures from patterns (20–30%)

    A. Constructing and interpreting graphical displays of distributions of univariate data (dotplot, stemplot, histogram, cumulative frequency plot)

        1. Center and spread
        2. Clusters and gaps
        3. Outliers and other unusual features
        4. Shape

    B. Summarizing distributions of univariate data

        1. Measuring center: median, mean
        2. Measuring spread: range, interquartile range, standard deviation
        3. Measuring position: quartiles, percentiles, standardized scores (z-scores)
        4. Using boxplots
        5. The effect of changing units on summary statistics

    C. Comparing distributions of univariate data (dotplots, back-to-back stemplots, parallel boxplots)

        1. Comparing center and spread: within group, between group variation
        2. Comparing clusters and gaps
        3. Comparing outliers and other unusual features
        4. Comparing shapes

    D. Exploring bivariate data

        1. Analyzing patterns in scatterplots
        2. Correlation and linearity
        3. Least-squares regression line
        4. Residual plots, outliers, and influential points
        5. Transformations to achieve linearity: logarithmic and power transformations

    E. Exploring categorical data

        1. Frequency tables and bar charts
        2. Marginal and joint frequencies for two-way tables
        3. Conditional relative frequencies and association

II. Sampling and experimentation: planning and conducting a study (10–15%)

  A. Overview of methods of data collection

      1. Census
      2. Sample survey
      3. Experiment
      4. Observational study

  B. Planning and conducting surveys

      1. Characteristics of a well-designed and well-conducted survey
      2. Populations, samples, and random selection
      3. Sources of bias in sampling and surveys
      4. Simple random sampling, stratified random sampling, and cluster sampling

  C. Planning and conducting experiments

      1. Characteristics of a well-designed and well-conducted experiment
      2. Treatments, control groups, experimental units, random assignments, and replication
      3. Sources of bias and confounding, including placebo effect and blinding
      4. Completely randomized design
      5. Randomized block design, including matched pairs design

  D. Generalizability of results and types of conclusions that can be drawn from observational studies, experiments, and surveys

III. Anticipating patterns: producing models using probability theory and simulation (20–30%)

  A. Probability as relative frequency

      1. Interpreting probability, including long-run relative frequency interpretation
      2. "Law of Large Numbers" concept
      3. Addition rule, multiplication rule, conditional probability, and independence
      4. Discrete random variables and their probability distributions including binomial and geometric
      5. Simulation of random behavior and probability distributions
      6. Mean (expected value) and standard deviation of a random variable and linear transformation of a random variable

B. Combining independent random variables

1. Notion of independence versus dependence
2. Mean and standard deviation for sums and differences of independent random variables

C. The normal distribution

1. Properties of the normal distribution
2. Using tables of the normal distribution
3. The normal distribution as a model for measurements

D. Sampling distributions

1. Sampling distribution of a sample proportion
2. Sampling distribution of a sample mean
3. Central Limit Theorem
4. Sampling distribution of a difference between two independent sample proportions
5. Sampling distribution of a difference between two independent sample means
6. Simulation of sampling distributions
7. *t*-distribution
8. Chi-square distribution

IV. Statistical inference: estimating population parameters and testing hypotheses (30–40%)

A. Estimation: point estimators and confidence intervals

1. Estimating population parameters and margins of error
2. Properties of point estimators including unbiasedness and variability
3. Logic of confidence intervals, meaning of confidence level and confidence intervals, and properties of confidence intervals
4. Large sample confidence interval for a proportion
5. Confidence interval for a mean
6. Large sample confidence interval for a difference between two proportions
7. Confidence interval for a difference between two means (unpaired and paired)
8. Confidence interval for the slope of a least-squares regression line

B.   Tests of significance

1.   Logic of significance testing, null and alternative hypotheses; *p*-values; one- and two-sided tests; concepts of Type I and Type II errors; concept of power
2.   Large sample test for a proportion
3.   Test for a mean
4.   Large sample test for a difference between two proportions
5.   Test for a difference between two means (unpaired and paired)
6.   Chi-square test for goodness of fit, homogeneity of proportions, and independence (one- and two-way tables)
7.   Test for the slope of a least-squares regression line

HOW AP EXAMS ARE USED

Different colleges use AP Exam scores in different ways, so it is important that you go to a particular college's web site to determine how it uses AP Exam scores. The three items below represent the main ways in which AP Exam scores can be used:

• **College Credit.** Some colleges will give you college credit if you score well on an AP Exam. These credits count towards your graduation requirements, meaning that you can take fewer courses while in college. Given the cost of college, this could be quite a benefit, indeed.

• **Satisfy Requirements.** Some colleges will allow you to "place out" of certain requirements if you do well on an AP Exam, even if they do not give you actual college credits. For example, you might not need to take an introductory-level course, or perhaps you might not need to take a class in a certain discipline at all.

• **Admissions Plus.** Even if your AP Exam will not result in college credit or even allow you to place out of certain courses, most colleges will respect your decision to push yourself by taking an AP Course or even an AP Exam outside of a course. A high score on an AP Exam shows mastery of more difficult content than is taught in many high school courses, and colleges may take that into account during the admissions process.

OTHER RESOURCES

There are many resources available to help you improve your score on the AP Statistics Exam, not the least of which are your **teachers**. If you are taking an AP class, you may be able to get extra attention from your teacher, such as obtaining feedback on your essays. If you are not in an AP course, reach out to a teacher who teaches AP Statistics, and ask if the teacher will review your essays or otherwise help you with content.

Another wonderful resource is **AP Central**, the official site of the AP Exams. The scope of the information at this site is quite broad and includes:

- Course Description, which includes details on what content is covered and sample questions

- Sample questions from past exams

- Free-response question prompts and multiple-choice questions from previous years

The AP Central home page address is **http://apcentral.collegeboard.com/apc/Controller.jpf**.

For up-to-date information about the ongoing changes to the AP Statistics Exam Course, please visit: **http://apcentral.collegeboard.com/apc/public/courses/teachers_corner/2151.html**.

Finally, The Princeton Review offers tutoring and small group instruction. Our expert instructors can help you refine your strategic approach and add to your content knowledge. For more information, call 1-800-2REVIEW.

DESIGNING YOUR STUDY PLAN

As part of the Introduction, you identified some areas of potential improvement. Let's now delve further into your performance on Test 1, with the goal of developing a study plan appropriate to your needs and time commitment.

Read the answers and explanations associated with the multiple-choice questions (starting at page 47). After you have done so, respond to the following questions:

- Review the bulleted outline of content topics on pages 65-69. Next to each topic, indicate your rank of the topic as follows: "1" means "I need a lot of work on this," "2" means "I need to beef up my knowledge," and "3" means "I know this topic well."

- How many days/weeks/months away is your exam?

- What time of day is your best, most focused study time?

- How much time per day/week/month will you devote to preparing for your exam?

- When will you do this preparation? (Be as specific as possible: Mondays & Wednesdays from 3 to 4 P.M., for example)

- Based on the answers above, will you focus on strategy (Part IV) or content (Part V) or both?

- What are your overall goals in using this book?

ON THE DAY OF THE TEST

- Eat a reasonable breakfast. Do not overeat, which may make you drowsy, but definitely do not skip breakfast either. Hunger pangs can prevent you from thinking straight.

- Use the bathroom before you enter the testing room. Avoid drinking beverages that will send you to the bathroom during the exam, such as coffee, tea, or other caffeinated beverages.

- Wear comfortable clothing. Dress in layers, so that you can remove them should the room be too warm.

What to Bring
Pack your bag the night before the exam. Don't forget the following:

- Several sharpened **number two pencils** and a separate eraser.

- A **snack.** Eating a piece of fruit or an energy bar during the break will give you a much-needed boost.

- If you're taking the exam at a different school from your own, or if you're homeschooled, bring a **photo I.D.** and your secondary **school code number** (homeschoolers will be given a code on the testing day).

- Your **Social Security number.** Although it's not mandatory for you to provide your Social Security number, it is used for identification and appears on your AP Grade Report.

- A **watch without a calculator.** If your watch has an alarm, turn it off.

- A **calculator.** Each student is expected to bring a graphing calculator with statistical capabilities. Portable computers, tablets and iPads, pocket organizers, and devices with typewriter-style (QWERTY) keyboards, electronic writing pads, or pen-input devices are *not* allowed. Most graphing calculators currently on the market are acceptable.

- **Extra batteries** for your calculator.

Finally...

Relax. Even if all you've done is read this book carefully, you're probably better prepared than a lot of the other students. Stay positive, and remember: Everyone else is at least as nervous as you are.

Part IV
Test-Taking Strategies for the AP Statistics Exam

1   How to Approach Multiple-Choice Questions
2   How to Approach Free-Response Questions
3   How to Use Your Calculator

PREVIEW ACTIVITY

Review your responses to the first three questions of the Introduction and then respond to the following questions:

- How many multiple-choice questions did you miss even though you knew the answer?

- On how many multiple-choice questions did you guess blindly?

- How many multiple-choice questions did you miss after eliminating some answers and guessing based on the remaining answers?

- Did you find any of the free-response questions easier or harder than the others—and, if so, why?

TIPS FOR BOTH SECTIONS OF THE AP STATISTICS EXAM

Here are two things to keep in mind for both parts of the exam.

- **Statistical tables:** Statistical tables and formulas are provided for you in the exam booklets in both sections. A copy of those tables and formulas is available at the back of this book. In the months before the exam, familiarize yourself with them and practice using them.

- **Calculators:** You may use a graphical calculator with statistical capabilities on both sections of the exam. From the beginning of your statistics course, use only one calculator, and practice with it as much as you can. Being familiar with the capabilities of your calculator will save you time on the exam. And remember that many calculators have distribution functions, which can save you from spending time looking through the tables provided. You should bring spare batteries and know how to change them.

Chapter 1
How to Approach
Multiple-Choice
Questions

CRACKING THE MULTIPLE-CHOICE SECTION

Section I of the AP Statistics Exam consists of 40 multiple-choice questions, which you're given 90 minutes to complete. That works out to 2.25 minutes per question. This section is worth 50% of your grade.

All the multiple-choice questions will have a similar format: Each will be followed by five answer choices. At times, it may seem that there could be more than one possible correct answer. There is only one! Remember that the committee members who write these questions are statistics teachers. So, when it comes to statistics, they know how students think and what kinds of mistakes they make. Answers resulting from common mistakes are often included in the five answer choices to trap you.

Use the Answer Sheet

For the multiple-choice section, you write the answers *not* in the test booklet but on a separate answer sheet (very similar to the ones we've supplied at the very end of this book). Five oval-shaped bubbles follow the question number, one for each possible answer. Don't forget to fill in all your answers on the answer sheet. *Don't* just mark them in the test booklet. Marks in the test booklet will not be graded. Also, make sure that your filled-in answers correspond to the correct question numbers! Check your answer sheet after every five answers to make sure you haven't skipped any bubbles by mistake.

Should You Guess?

Use Process of Elimination (POE) to rule out answer choices you know are wrong and increase your chances of guessing the right answer. Read all the answer choices carefully. Eliminate the ones that you know are wrong. If you only have one answer choice left, *choose it*, even if you're not completely sure why it's correct. Remember: Questions in the multiple-choice section are graded by a computer, so it doesn't care *how* you arrived at the correct answer.

Even if you can't eliminate answer choices, go ahead and guess. As of May 2011, AP exams no longer include a guessing penalty of a quarter of a point for each incorrect answer. You will be assessed only on the total number of correct answers, so be sure to fill in all the bubbles even if you have no idea what the correct answers are. When you get to a question that is too time consuming, or you don't know the answer (and can't eliminate any options), don't just fill in any answer. Use what we call your "Letter of the Day" (LOTD). Selecting the same answer choice each time you guess will increase your odds of getting a few of those skipped questions right.

Use the Two-Pass System

Remember that you have about two and a quarter minutes per question on this section of the exam. Do not waste time by lingering too long over any single question. If you're having trouble, move on to the next question. After you finish all the questions, you can come back to the ones you skipped.

The best strategy is to go through the multiple-choice section twice. The first time, do all the questions that you can answer fairly quickly—the ones where you feel confident about the correct answer. On this first pass, skip the questions that seem to require more thinking or the ones you need to read two or three times before you understand them. Circle the questions that you've skipped in the question booklet so that you can find them easily in the second pass. You must be *very careful* with the answer sheet by making sure the filled-in answers correspond correctly to the questions.

Once you have gone through all the questions, go back to the ones that you skipped in the first pass. But don't linger too long on any one question even in the second pass. Spending too much time wrestling over a hard question can cause two things to happen: 1) You may run out of time and miss out on answering easier questions in the later part of the exam. 2) Your anxiety might start building up, and this could prevent you from thinking clearly and make answering other questions even more difficult. If you simply don't know the answer, or can't eliminate any choices, just use your LOTD and move on.

REFLECT

- How long will you spend on multiple-choice questions?

- How will you change your approach to multiple-choice questions?

- What is your multiple-choice guessing strategy?

Chapter 2
How to Approach
Free-Response
Questions

CRACKING THE FREE-RESPONSE SECTION

Section II is worth 50% of your grade on the AP Statistics Exam. This section is composed of two parts. Part I contains five free-response questions; Part II contains one longer free-response question known as the "investigative task." You're given a total of 90 minutes for this section. It's recommended that you spend the first 60 minutes on the first five questions, and the next 30 minutes on the investigative task. The investigative task question is worth twice as much as each of the other free-response questions. Some students begin with the investigative task for this reason. Remember, it's not harder than the other questions—just longer.

Clearly Explain and Justify Your Answers

Remember that your answers to the free-response questions are graded by *readers* and not by computers. Communication is a very important part of AP Statistics. Compose your answers in precise sentences. Just getting the correct numerical answer is not enough. You should be able to *explain* your reasoning behind the technique that you selected and *communicate* your answer in the context of the problem. Even if the question does not explicitly say so, always explain and *justify* every step of your answer, including the final answer. Do not expect the graders to read between the lines. Explain everything as though somebody with no knowledge of statistics is going to read it. Be sure to present your solution in a systematic manner using solid logic and appropriate language.

Remember: Although you won't earn points for neatness, the graders can't give you a grade if they can't read and understand your solution!

Use Only the Space You Need

Do not try to fill up the space provided for each question. The space given is usually more than enough. The people who design the tests realize that some students write in big letters and some students make mistakes and need extra space for corrections. So if you have a complete solution, don't worry about the extra space. Writing more will not earn you extra credit. In fact, many students tend to go overboard and shoot themselves in the foot by making a mistake after they've already written the right answer.

Read the Whole Question!

Some questions might have several subparts. Try to answer them all, and don't give up on the question if one part is giving you trouble. For example, if the answer to part (b) depends on the answer to part (a), but you think you got the answer to part (a) wrong, you should still go ahead and do part (b) using your answer to part (a) as required. Chances are that the grader will not mark you wrong twice, unless it is obvious from your answer that you should have discovered your mistake.

Use Common Sense

Always use your common sense in answering questions. For example, on one free-response question that asked students to compute the mean weight of newborn babies from given data, some students answered 70 pounds. It should have been immediately obvious that the answer was probably off by a decimal point. A 70-pound baby would be a giant! This is an important mistake that should be easy to fix. Some mistakes may not be so obvious from the answer. However, the grader will consider simple, *easily recognizable errors* (e.g., giving negative probabilities) to be *very important*.

Concepts Versus Computations

The AP Statistics Exam, and particularly the free-response section, emphasizes the understanding and communication of *concepts*, rather than routine *computation*. If you show a clear understanding of why you have selected a particular technique and how you plan to use it, but you make some minor arithmetic mistake, then most likely the grader will not subtract points.

Suppose, for example, in doing a *t*-interval problem, you defined the parameter of interest, justified why using the *t*-interval was appropriate in this case, and checked all the assumptions correctly. Then you showed the correct formula for the margin of error and made the correct substitutions, but in doing the computation, you reversed the digits of the answer and got 1.61 instead of 1.16 as follows:

$$95\% \ ME = t_{0.025}(14)\frac{s}{\sqrt{n}} = 2.145\left(\frac{2.1}{\sqrt{15}}\right) = 1.61$$

This mistake is not so obvious from the answer. So, you then went ahead and computed your interval correctly using the above margin of error to get 14.75 ± 1.61, which gives (13.14, 16.36). And finally, you explained and interpreted the answer correctly. In this case, because everything else was done perfectly, most likely your arithmetic error would be ignored and you would still get full credit for the question.

On the other hand, imagine the following scenario. While computing the probability under the normal curve, you make a mistake and get the wrong answer. Say you compute

$$P(X > 20) = P\left(Z > \frac{20 - 15}{2}\right) = P(Z > 2.5)$$

You look up the number in the normal table and find that the probability corresponding to 2.5 is 0.9938. Instead of subtracting this figure from 1, you subtract it from 0.5 and get the answer −0.4938. This mistake will *not* be ignored, because students are expected to know that a probability value is *always* between 0 and 1. If you get a negative value or a value larger than 1 for probability, you are expected to realize your mistake immediately. No matter how perfect the rest of the solution is, such an easily identifiable error will not be ignored.

Think Like a Grader

When answering questions, try to think about what kind of answer the grader is expecting. Look at past free-response questions and grading rubrics on the College Board website (**http://apcentral.collegeboard.com/apc/public/courses/teachers_corner/2151.html**). These examples will give you some idea of how the answers should be phrased. The graders are told to keep in mind that there are two aspects to the scoring of free-response answers: showing statistical knowledge and communicating that knowledge. You don't need to show all the steps of a calculation, but you must explain how you got your answer and why you chose the technique you used. The table on the following page contains scoring guidelines that the College Board gives to free-response graders on the AP Statistics Exam (remember that each question is scored from 0 to 4).

Once again, responses should be written as clearly as possible in complete sentences.

Think Before You Write

Abraham Lincoln once said that if he had eight hours to chop down a tree, he would spend six of them sharpening his axe. In the free-response problems, Part A asks five questions and you have about 60 minutes to work—that's 12 minutes per question. In Part B, one question should take about 30 minutes. In both parts, it makes sense to spend some time thinking about what the question is, what answers are being asked for, what answers might make sense, and what your intuition is before starting to write. These questions aren't meant to trick you, so all the information you need is given. If you think you don't have the right information, you may have misunderstood the question. In some calculations, it is easy to get confused, so think about whether your answers make sense in terms of what the question is asking. If you have some idea of what the answer should look like before starting to write, then you will avoid getting sidetracked and wasting time on dead-ends.

Scoring Guidelines for the Free-Response Questions

	Statistical Knowledge	Communication
	• Identify the important components of the problem • Demonstrate the statistical concepts and techniques that result in the correct solution of the problem	• Explain clearly what you did to get the solution to the problem and why you chose a particular method • Give a clear statement of your conclusions
Expect this score on a question	**If you do this...**	**and do this...**
4	• Through your answer, show that you understand the problem's different statistical components • Correctly analyze the relation among the different components of the problem • Correctly use the appropriate statistical techniques • Make sure all your answers are reasonable	• Explicitly explain your entire solution, not just the final answer • Describe your reasoning in getting that solution, using the correct terminology • Use the required numerical or graphical aids to explain your solution • State and check all appropriate assumptions for the statistical techniques used in your solution • Give a reasonable and complete conclusion
3	• With some minor exceptions, show an almost complete understanding of the problem's different components • Analyze the relations among the different components of the problem, with a few gaps • Use the appropriate statistical techniques • Give fairly reasonable answers, but with some computational errors	• Provide a clear but incomplete explanation of your choice of statistical techniques • Give a less-than-perfectly-organized explanation of the steps leading to your solution • Neglect a few conditions necessary for the techniques you use • Use graphical and numerical techniques to help justify your solution • Give a reasonable but somewhat incomplete conclusion
2	• Show some understanding of the problem's statistical components • Have trouble relating the different components • Use some statistical techniques correctly but omit or misuse others • Make some computational mistakes that result in unreasonable answers	• Give a vague explanation of your solution • Use inappropriate terminology • Give an explanation that is difficult to interpret • Use incomplete or ineffective graphical methods to support your solution • Totally neglect to use graphical methods to support your solution
1	• Show a limited understanding of the problem's components • Fail to identify some important components • Have difficulty organizing your solution • Use irrelevant information in your solution • Use statistical techniques incorrectly • Fail to use statistical techniques • Make arithmetic mistakes that result in unreasonable answers	• Give little explanation of your solution • Give an unclear explanation of your solution or methods • Give an explanation that does not match your solution • Fail to use diagrams or graphical methods • Use graphical methods incorrectly • Forget to write a conclusion • Give an incorrect conclusion
0	• Show little or no understanding of the problem's statistical components	• Provide no explanation of any legitimate solution

A FEW MORE TIPS

- Include units of measurements in all your computations and answers. You will probably not lose points for missing units, but you might *gain* an advantage by showing them. AP Statistics Exams are graded holistically. The grader will look at the whole question before assigning a grade, and every little bit helps.

- **Beware of presenting conflicting arguments.** Read your entire answer after finishing the question. If your explanation has any conflicting arguments, it will reveal a lack of understanding of the material, and you will most likely lose points.

- **Do not give parallel solutions.** For example, students often realize that a *t*-test is an appropriate procedure in a given situation, but they do not know which *t*-test to use. So they try to play it safe by giving *both* solutions (the matched and the independent sample cases, for example). This is not a good strategy. In the exam, both the solutions will be graded, and the one with the lower score will be counted.

- **Know your Greek letters.** Statistics often makes use of the following Greek letters: α (alpha), β (beta), μ (mu), χ (chi), π (pi), θ (theta), and σ (sigma).

REFLECT

- How much time will you spend on the short free-response questions? What about the investigative task?

- What will you do before you begin writing your free-response answers?

- Will you seek further help, outside of this book (such as a teacher, tutor, or AP Central), on how to approach the questions that you will see on the AP Statistics exam?

Chapter 3
How to Use Your Calculator

USING THE CALCULATOR

Below is a brief outline of how to use the TI-83 or TI-84 calculator. You may need to refer to this section as you work through the examples later in the book. This is not a complete list of the useful functions of your calculator, but it does cover the functions used most often in an AP Statistics course. You may want to refer to your calculator's manual for more options.

The most commonly used statistical features of the TI-83 and TI-84 are the following:

STAT

When you press the STAT button, you are given three different options: EDIT, CALC, and TESTS.

1. **EDIT:** You can access these procedures using STAT → EDIT.

    • **Edit:** Use this option to access lists (similar to a spreadsheet), create a new list of data, or edit an existing list of data. There are six default columns labeled L_1, L_2, L_3, L_4, L_5, and L_6.

    To enter data in a list: Suppose the data to be entered is 3, 5, –2, 6. Enter the data in a list using the following steps. The data will be saved automatically.

    - To **ENTER** data in a list, say, L_1
    - Choose **STAT → EDIT**
    - Press **ENTER**
    - In the list titled L_1, type 3
    - Press **ENTER**
    - Type 5
    - Press **ENTER**
    - Type (–)2
    - Press **ENTER**
    - Type 6
    - Press **ENTER**

    To create a new list: Suppose you want to create a new list, named NEW, in addition to the six default lists. Use the following steps.

- Suppose you want to create a list between, say, L_1 and L_2
- Choose **STAT** → **EDIT**
- Press **ENTER**
- Put the cursor at the title of list L_2
- Press **2nd** → **INS** *A new column will be added to the left of L_2.*
- Use the ALPHA (green) key and alphabet keys to label the new column
- Press **ENTER**

- **ClrList:** Use this option to clear all data in a given list. This option is *not* for deleting a partial list. To delete a partial list, use the DEL key. This action will delete all numbers in a given column, and *this deletion is not reversible.*

- Suppose data is in a list, say, L_1
- Choose **STAT** → **EDIT** → **ClrList**
- Press **ENTER**
- Enter the list name to read ClrList (L_1)
- Press **ENTER**

---

2.   **CALC:** You can access these procedures using STAT → CALC. Use this option to get one or two variable summary statistics, the correlation coefficient, linear regression coefficients (slope and *y*-intercept), and regression using transformed variables. The steps for using these procedures are provided in Chapter 4.

1:1-Var Stats: Use this option to compute summary statistics for one-variable (*univariate*) data. It gives the number of observations (n), mean $\left(\overline{X}\right)$, sum ($\Sigma X$), sum of squares ($\Sigma X^2$), sample standard deviation (S), population standard deviation (σ), median, quartiles (Q_1 and Q_3), minimum, and maximum.

2:2-Var Stats: Use this option to compute summary statistics for *bivariate* data. It gives the number of pairs of observations (n), mean ($\overline{X}$ and $\overline{Y}$), sum (ΣX and ΣY), sum of squares (ΣX^2 and ΣY^2), sample standard deviation (S_x and S_y), population standard deviation (σ_x and σ_y), min and max for each variable, and sum of products (ΣXY).

8:LinReg(*a+bx*): Use this option to get the correlation coefficient and least-squares estimates for slope and *y*-intercept for linear regression.

9:LnReg: Use this option for logarithmic transformation to linearize a regression model.

O:ExpReg: Use this option for exponential transformation to linearize a regression model.

A:PwrReg: Use this option for fitting a power model using logarithmic transformation to linearize a regression model.

3. **TESTS:** Access these procedures using STAT → TESTS.

Procedures for creating confidence intervals and testing hypotheses are located under this option. The steps for using these procedures are provided in Chapter 7.

1:Z-Test: Use this for a one-sample z-test for population mean (known population variance).

2:T-Test: Use this for a one-sample t-test for a population mean (unknown population variance).

3:2-SampZTest: Use this for a z-test for the difference between two population means (independent samples).

4:2-SampTTest: Use this for a t-test for the difference between two population means (independent samples, unknown population variances—equal and unequal).

5:1-PropZTest: Use this for a large-sample z-test for a population proportion.

6:2-PropZTest: Use this for a large-sample z-test for the difference between two population proportions (independent samples).

7:Zinterval: Use this for a one-sample z-confidence interval for a population mean (known population variance).

8:Tinterval: Use this for a one-sample t-confidence interval for a population mean (unknown population variance).

9:2-SampZInt: Use this for a z-confidence interval for the difference between two population means (independent samples).

0:2-SampTInt: Use this for a t-confidence interval for the difference between two population means (independent samples, unknown population variances—equal and unequal).

A:1-PropZInt: Use this for a large-sample z-confidence interval for a population proportion.

B:2-PropZInt: Use this for a large-sample *z*-confidence interval for the difference between two population proportions (independent samples).

C: χ^2 – Test: Use this for a chi-square test for independence of two categorical variables.

E:LinRegTTest: Use this for a *t*-test for the slope of a least-squares regression line.

MATH

Under MATH, there are four options, but the PRB option is the only one you'll need for AP Statistics. The steps for using these procedures are listed in Chapter 6.

PRB: Access these procedures using MATH → PRB.

3:nCr: Use this option to get combinations.

5:randInt(: Use this option to generate a set of random integers from a specified range.

randInt (*lower limit, upper limit, numbers to generate*)

6:randNorm(: Use this option to generate a set of random numbers from a specified normally distributed population.

randNorm (*mean, standard deviation, numbers to generate*)

7:randBin(: Use this option to generate a set of random numbers from a binomial population.

randBin (*n, p, numbers to generate*)

MATRX

Under MATRX, there are three options, but the NAMES and EDIT options are the ones you'll need to use. Access these procedures using 2nd → x^1 key.

1. **NAMES:** Access this option as MATRX → NAMES.
    Use this option to utilize an already-created matrix—for example, a matrix of expected counts created by a chi-square test of independence.

- Choose **MATRX** → **NAMES**
  A list of matrix names with their respective dimensions will be displayed.
- Use the up and down arrows to move up and down the list. Highlight the name of the matrix to be used.
- Press **ENTER** *The name of the selected matrix will be pasted in the window.*
- Press **ENTER** *The matrix will be listed in the window.*

2. **EDIT:** Use this option to create a new matrix or edit an existing one.

Suppose you want to create the following 2×3 matrix:

$$A = \begin{bmatrix} 20 & 5 & 30 \\ 10 & 15 & 25 \end{bmatrix}$$

- Choose **MATRX** → **EDIT**
  A list of matrix names with their respective dimensions will be displayed.
- Use the up and down arrows to move up and down the list. Highlight the name of the matrix to be created, say, 1: [A]
- Press **ENTER**
- Create the appropriate dimensions for the matrix: 2×3
- Press **ENTER**
- Enter 20
- Press **ENTER**
- Enter 5
- Press **ENTER**
- Enter 30
- Press **ENTER**
- Enter 10
- Press **ENTER**
- Enter 15
- Press **ENTER**
- Enter 25
- Press **ENTER**

DISTR

Procedures for computing probabilities and cumulative probabilities for different distributions are listed under this option. The steps for using these procedures are provided in Chapter 6. Access these procedures using $2^{nd} \rightarrow$ DISTR.

2:normalcdf(: Use this option to find the area under any normal curve in a given range specified by a lower limit and an upper limit. The lower and upper limits must be x values.

normalcdf (*lower limit, upper limit, mean, standard deviation*)

If you know the lower and upper scores, you may use normalcdf (*lower z-score, upper z-score*) to find the area.

3:invNorm(: Use this option to find a z-score corresponding to the specified area (p) less than that of the z-score.

invNorm (*p, mean, standard deviation*)

5:tcdf(: Use this option to find the area under the t-distribution in a given range specified by the lower limit and the upper limit—for example, if you need to find a p-value for a t-test.

tcdf (*lower limit, upper limit, degrees of freedom*)

7: χ^2 cdf(: Use this option to find the area under the chi-square distribution—for example, when you need to find a p-value for a chi-square test.

χ^2 cdf (*lower limit, upper limit, degrees of freedom*)

0:binompdf(: Use this option to find the binomial probability of a specific outcome. $P(x) = \binom{n}{x} p^x (1-p)^{n-x}$

binompdf (*n, p, x*)

A:binomcdf(: Use this option to find the cumulative binomial probability of a specified outcome. $P(x \le x_0) = \sum_{x=0}^{x_0} \binom{n}{x} p^x (1-p)^{n-x}$

binomcdf (*n, p, x_0*)

D:geometpdf(: Use this option to find the geometric probability of a specific outcome. $P(x) = p(1-p)^{x-1}$

geometpdf (*p, x*)

E:geometcdf(: Use this option to find the cumulative binomial probability of specified outcomes. $P(x \le x_0) = \sum_{x=1}^{x_0} \binom{n}{x} p (1-p)^{x-1}$

$$\text{geometcdf } (p, x_0)$$

DIAGNOSTICS

Use this option to get the calculator to display values for the correlation coefficient and coefficient of determination when executing regression models. You need to turn diagnostics on only once; it will stay on until you turn the diagnostics off.

- Choose $2^{nd} \rightarrow$ Catalog $\rightarrow$ DiagnosticOn

STAT PLOT

Use this option to make a scatterplot, boxplot, histogram, regression line plot, and residual plot. The steps for making these graphs are given in Chapter 4.

Tips on Using the Calculator Well

The calculator is a valuable tool, but many students lose points by using it improperly or relying on it too heavily. Note that although the TI-83 and TI-84 are currently the most popular calculators, there are many others on the market. You do not know if the readers grading your exam will be familiar with your particular calculator.

Also, remember that readers come from both high schools and colleges. Although most high school statistics classes use calculators, many colleges do not require specific calculators in their courses. It's quite possible that your answers will be graded by people unfamiliar with statistical calculators. So, *do not use calculator talk.* Explain your answer in plain English, using the appropriate statistical terminology. For example, suppose you're faced with this question:

1. Suppose the time 8-to-12-year-olds spend playing video games per week is normally distributed with a mean of 15 hours and a standard deviation of two hours. What percent of children spend more than 20 hours per week playing video games?
    - If your answer to this question is just the number "0.0062," you will probably not get credit. First, you did not describe your reasoning for getting this number. Second, you failed to communicate your answer appropriately. Third, the question asks for a *percentage*.
    - If your answer to this question is just "0.62%," with no further explanation or description of the steps you used to get this number, you might or might not get any credit for the answer. It depends on whether the passage above constitutes the entire question or just a sub-question of the question and how the answer to this sub-question is related to other sub-questions.

- If your answer to this question is "normalcdf (20, 2000, 15, 2) = 0.0062", again, you should not expect to get credit. Those who are familiar with the functions of a TI-83 calculator will understand your answer, but non-users will not. Other calculators, such as Casio or HP, have different formats. This is what statistics teachers refer to as "calculator talk." Statistics teachers and, more importantly, statistics readers do not like calculator talk.
- Instead, you should explain your answer as follows:

Let X = the time spent by 8-to-12-year-olds per week on playing video games.

Then, $P(X > 20) = P\left(Z > \dfrac{20 - 15}{2} \right) = P(Z > 2.5) = 0.0062$

Therefore, about 0.62% of 8-to-12-year-olds spend more than 20 hours per week playing video games.

This will constitute a complete and well-communicated answer, without calculator talk.

Your Work Versus the Calculator's Work

Do not reproduce calculator output just as is. Do not describe how you entered numbers in the calculator or your sequence of keystrokes. This will not give you any advantage. When using confidence intervals or hypotheses-testing procedures, do not copy input or output from the calculator screen. For example, take the following problem:

1. A random sample of fifteen 8-to-12-year-olds was selected. All selected children were monitored for six months and the number of hours they spent playing video games was recorded. The mean number of hours they spent playing video games was 14.75 hours per week, with a standard deviation of 2.1 hours per week. Estimate the true mean time that 8-to-12-year-olds spend playing video games per week using a 95% confidence level.

   - You might be tempted to copy the following from your calculator:

Tinterval	Tinterval
Inpt: Stats	(13.587, 15.913)
$\overline{X}$: 14.75	$\overline{X}$: 14.75
Sx: 2.1	Sx: 2.1
n: 15	n: 15
C-Level: 95	
Calculate	

Do not give in to temptation. This is calculator talk. It is not a complete answer to the question. It will not receive any credit beyond the credit allowed for arithmetic computations.

- Suppose you give the following answer:

$$95\% \ ME = \ t_{0.025}(14)\frac{s}{\sqrt{n}} = 2.145\left(\frac{2.1}{\sqrt{15}}\right) = 1.16$$

$$14.75 \pm 1.16 \text{ gives } (13.59, \ 15.91)$$

This is better than calculator talk, but it is still an incomplete answer. It provides the correct mechanics, but it fails to provide the proper communication. What is the parameter of interest here? Why was the t-interval used? Why is the t-interval appropriate in this situation? Are the conditions required for using the t-interval satisfied? What does the answer tell us in the context of the situation described? All those questions need to be answered. The above answer might get you credit for correct mechanics but nothing else. It might be worth one point out of four.

Showing Graphs

If you make plots on your calculator for, say, checking the conditions for a certain procedure used to answer a question, be sure to do more than just say that the graph shows that the required conditions were met. The grader has no way of knowing what graph you made, what your graph looked like, why you think the conditions were met, or whether you even looked at a graph. Instead, copy the graph from your calculator screen onto your answer sheet so that the grader can see what it is that you looked at when arriving at your answer. Discuss how you used the graph to make a decision. Even if your answer is wrong, you might get partial credit for using the correct reasoning. For example, you would probably lose points for using the wrong graph, but you might get some credit for drawing the correct conclusion from the wrong graph.

Part V
Content Review
for the AP
Statistics Exam

4 Exploring Data
5 Sampling and Experimentation
6 Anticipating Patterns
7 Statistical Inference

HOW TO USE THE CHAPTERS IN THIS PART

For the following content chapters, you may need to come back to them more than once. Your goal is to obtain mastery of the content you are missing, and a single read of a chapter may not be sufficient. At the end of each chapter, you will have an opportunity to reflect on whether you truly have mastered the content of that chapter.

Chapter 4
Exploring Data

OBSERVING PATTERNS AND DEPARTURES FROM PATTERNS

Statistics is a science of data. We all use data to estimate unknown quantities, to make decisions, and to develop and implement policies. To draw any sensible conclusions from collected data, we need to summarize the data or examine the patterns that it forms. This chapter will discuss graphical and numerical techniques used to study data. In the multiple-choice section, this topic appears in eight to 12 out of 40 questions. In the free-response section, this topic appears in one to two out of six questions.

COLLECTING DATA

Who collects data and what do they do with collected data?

- Businesses collect data on their products and on consumer behavior. For example, they might use the collected data to determine the marketability of new products.
- Real estate agents collect data on market trends and on the availability of certain types of properties. They might use the collected data to identify popular locations for first-time home buyers.
- Doctors collect diagnostic data on their patients. They might use collected data to identify the appropriate treatment for a patient.
- Police collect data on criminal behavior and the frequency of certain crimes. They might use the collected data to determine where to increase police patrols.

Data is rarely collected in a form that is immediately useful for decision-making. For example, imagine that a polling group was conducting a telephone survey to estimate the percent of state residents in favor of the governor's new proposal. Five interviewers called a total of 1,800 residents over a period of five days and recorded the result for each resident as "supports" or "does not support." So at the completion of the survey, the polling group had a list of 1,800 responses listed as "supports" or "does not support." What can we say based on the data? Unfortunately, nothing—until somebody takes the time to organize it.

To use collected data, it needs to be organized and summarized. The different methods for doing this are known as **descriptive methods**. Different descriptive methods might result in different outcomes, leading to different conclusions. Descriptive methods are useful for data presentation, data reduction, and summarization. The best method depends on the type of data being collected.

Types of Variables

There are two types of variables: **categorical** and **continuous**. A variable is categorical if it can only take on a fixed number of values. Some examples of categorical data are sex (male or female) and eye color.

A variable is continuous if it can take on any value. Some examples of continuous variables are age, height, and weight. In practice, variables that can take on a great many values are often treated as continuous: For example, IQ can take on any value between about 40 and 200. Technically, that is a fixed number of values, but it is so large that methods for continuous variables can be used. Different methods of analysis must be used for the categorical and continuous variables.

If we take only one measurement on each object, we get **univariate data**. With two measurements on each object, we get **bivariate data**. For example, measuring the heights of a group of children will result in a *univariate* data set of the heights of the children. On the other hand, if we measure the height and the weight of each child, then we will get a *bivariate* data set consisting of the heights and weights of the children.

Both types are discussed in detail later in this chapter.

Types of Descriptive Methods

We use different descriptive methods depending on the type of data collected. Descriptive methods are divided into three basic categories:

- Tabular methods
- Graphical methods
- Numerical methods

Different descriptive methods answer different questions about data. Naturally, different questions have different answers. In general, we cannot look at data from all possible angles using only one method. So it's best to use more than one method when we're summarizing a data set, even if the different methods produce some overlap of information. Let's look at each of these three categories in more detail.

TABULAR METHODS

Collected data generally need to be rearranged before analysis. One tabular method is the frequency distribution table. This table facilitates the analysis of patterns of variation among observed data.

- The letter n is used to denote the number of observations in a data set.

- The **frequency** of a value is the number of times that observation occurs. Frequency is usually denoted using the letter f.

- The **relative frequency** of a value is the ratio of the frequency (f) to the total number of observations (n). It is usually denoted by rf, and $rf = \frac{f}{n}$.

- The **cumulative frequency** gives the number of observations less than or equal to a specified value. It is usually denoted by cf.

- A **frequency distribution table** is a table giving all possible values of a variable and their frequencies.

Example 1: The Student Government Association (SGA) at a university was interested in how much students spend per month on housing. Because students who live in dorms pay a fixed housing fee per semester, it was decided not to include those students in the study. The SGA selected a sample of students living off campus and collected data on their housing type and on the amount they spent per month on housing. The collected information is listed in the table below. The columns titled "Exp" (for "Expenditure") give the amount each student spent per month on housing (in dollars). The columns titled "Type" give the type of housing for each student, classified as:

A = Apartment   C = Condominium   H = House   T = Townhouse

Exp	Type	Exp	Type	Exp	Type	Exp	Type	Exp	Type	Exp	Type	Exp	Type	Exp	Type
304	C	323	H	529	T	482	A	406	H	628	T	259	C	330	A
342	A	350	A	358	A	423	A	440	H	333	A	424	H	595	C
437	A	349	A	278	A	530	A	384	H	327	A	529	H	383	C
446	A	384	H	482	H	404	H	391	T	581	A	466	H	437	C
362	C	394	A	270	A	393	A	501	T	398	T	834	T	416	C
552	H	296	C	462	H	450	C	550	T	516	T	558	A	351	T
411	C	435	A	503	A	364	T	306	T	478	T	332	C	385	T
330	C	334	A	367	H	264	A	450	H	358	H	317	H	376	T
673	H	525	T	353	H	276	A	309	C	439	H	430	A	408	C
309	H	391	A	760	A	297	T	255	T	377	A	282	T	385	A

Table 1: Housing expenditure (in $) and type of housing data

These numbers are useless unless we rearrange and summarize them in a meaningful fashion. Note that data were collected for two variables: type of housing and housing expenditure per month. Type of housing is a *qualitative*, or *categorical*, variable and housing expenditure is a *quantitative*, or *continuous*, variable.

One possible grouped frequency distribution table for housing expenditure is as follows:

not related, independent.

Housing Expenditure ($)	Frequency f	Relative Frequency $rf = f/n$	Percentage 100 rf	Cumulative Frequency cf
250–299	9	0.11	11	9
300–349	14	0.18	18	23
350–399	20	0.25	25	43
400–449	14	0.18	18	57
450–499	7	0.09	9	64
500–549	7	0.09	9	71
550–599	5	0.06	6	76
600–649	1	0.01	1	77
650–699	1	0.01	1	78
700–749	0	0.00	0	78
750–799	1	0.01	1	79
800–849	1	0.01	1	80

Table 2: Frequency distribution for housing expenditure

Note the following:

- The numbers in the frequency column add up to the total number of observations, $n = 80$.
- Housing expenditures are grouped into different classes. For the class 400–449, the number 400 defines the lower limit and the number 449 defines the upper limit.
- All classes are of length equal to 50.
- The class mark is the halfway point for each class. For class 400–449, the class mark is 424.5.

- The numbers in the relative frequency column add up to 1. In some charts, due to rounding-off errors, the total may not add to exactly 1, though it should be close.
- The numbers in the percentage column add up to 100. As with the proportions, the total should be very close to 100.
- The last entry in the cumulative frequency column is equal to the total number of observations, $n = 80$.

What do the numbers in this table mean? Below are some examples.

- The frequency for group 300–349 is 14. This means that 14 students of those interviewed spend $300 to $349 per month on housing.
- The relative frequency for group 300–349 is 0.18 and the percentage is 18. This means that 18 percent of students interviewed spend $300 to $349 per month on housing.
- The cumulative frequency for group 300–349 is 23. This means that 23 of the students interviewed spend less than or equal to $349 per month.

The frequency distribution table for housing type is as follows:

Type of Housing	Frequency f	Relative Frequency $rf = f/n$	Percentage $100\ rf$
Apartment	29	0.36	36
Condominium	14	0.18	18
House	19	0.24	24
Townhouse	18	0.23	23

Table 3: Frequency distribution for housing type

Again, note the following:

- The figures in the frequency column add up to the total number of observations, $n = 80$.
- The figures in the relative frequency column add up to 1.01. This is another example of rounding-off error. Although the total is not exactly 1, it is very close.
- The figures in the percentage column add up to 101.
- For this categorical variable, there is no sensible ordering of values. So, cumulative frequency is meaningless.

We can interpret the numbers in this table as follows:

- The frequency for apartments is 29. This means that 29 of the students interviewed live in apartments.
- The relative frequency for apartments is 0.36 and the percentage is 36. This means that 36 percent of students interviewed live in apartments.

GRAPHICAL METHODS FOR QUALITATIVE DATA

Presenting data in tables is not always useful and will rarely give a full picture of the data. Almost every statistical problem will benefit from good charts and graphs. With today's technology, it has become much easier to generate useful charts and graphs. To summarize and describe qualitative data, bar charts are particularly useful. Pie charts are frequently used but are not recommended.

Graphical Methods for Categorical Data: Bar Charts and Pie Charts

Bar Charts

Bar charts are very common. Economists use them to display financial data. The business section of any newspaper usually has at least one bar chart. A bar chart can have either horizontal or vertical bars. Bar charts look very similar to histograms (you will see an example of a histogram later on this chapter), but they are used only for categorical data.

This is how to make a bar chart:

- Draw horizontal (x) and vertical (y) axes.
- On the horizontal axis, mark the categories of the variable at equal intervals.
- Scale the vertical axis in order to plot frequencies, relative frequencies, or percentages.
- Note that the above three steps would result in a vertical bar chart. For a horizontal bar chart, transpose the x-axis and y-axis.
- For each category, draw a bar whose height (or whose length, for horizontal bars) is equal to the data plotted, frequency, relative frequency, percentage, etc.

Example 2: Create a bar chart summarizing the data on housing type in Table 3.

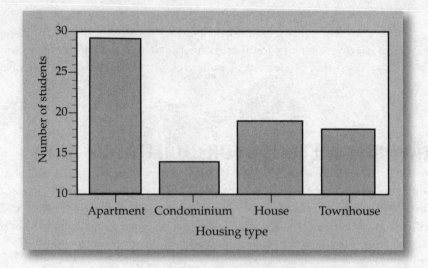

Figure 1: Bar chart for type of housing data

The bar chart above clearly shows that an apartment is the most popular type of accommodation among these students. There's not much difference in popularity between houses and townhouses, with houses leading townhouses by a narrow margin. The fewest students live in condominiums.

How do we read a bar chart?

- Each bar indicates a different category.
- The height of a frequency bar chart indicates how often that category occurred in the data set. For example, the first bar in the bar chart shown above corresponds to "Apartment." The height of this graph can be read off the vertical axis as 29. This means that 29 students out of all those interviewed live in apartments.

Pie Charts

A pie chart displays the groups formed by a data set. It is commonly used to describe the different spending categories of a budget, for example. Businesses use pie charts to display the various components of their entire production output. For example, a paper company producing copying paper, notebook paper, trifolds, etc., could use a pie chart to describe what proportion of its entire production is made up by each of these products. While popular, they are rarely, if ever, the best method of displaying data and have been shown to be misleading and hard to read accurately.

This is how to make a pie chart:

- Prepare a frequency distribution table.
- Compute the percentages for each category.
- Equate one percentage point to an angle of 3.6 degrees. For each category, compute angle = 3.6 × percentage.
- Draw a circle of the desired size and then draw one radius within the circle to be used as a starting point.
- Form "slices" of the pie with sizes equal to the corresponding angles computed earlier.
- Go all the way around the circle.

Example 3: Create a pie chart summarizing the housing type data in Table 3.

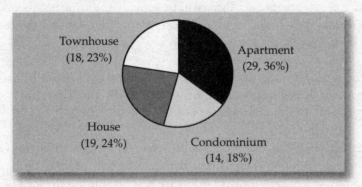

Figure 2: Pie chart for housing type (frequency, percentage)

This pie chart shows clearly that the highest percent of students lives in apartments.

How do we read a pie chart?

- Each piece of the pie corresponds to one category.
- The category corresponding to the largest piece is the one that occurs most often.

GRAPHICAL METHODS FOR QUANTITATIVE DATA

To summarize and describe quantitative data, dotplots and stemplots are used for small sets of data. For larger sets, histograms, cumulative frequency charts, and boxplots are often employed.

Examining Graphs

We can describe the overall pattern of the distribution of a quantitative variable set using the following three terms:

Plan on taking the SATs soon? Check out *Cracking the SAT* for proven tips and techniques to help you get your highest score.

- The **center** of a distribution describes the point around which the data points are spread. There will be roughly the same number of data points to the left and right of the center. For most graphs, the center will be roughly the same as the median and the mean.

- The **spread** of a distribution describes how the data points deviate from the average. Spread can be quantified through the range, standard deviation, or variance of a distribution.

- The **shape** of a distribution can be described in a few different ways. Some distributions have simple shapes; others are more irregular. Some basic shapes of distribution are described using the idea of symmetry. Here are the classifications:
  - **Symmetric distribution:** If the left half of the distribution is approximately a mirror image of the right half, then the distribution is described as symmetric. In other words, a symmetric distribution has the same number of observations on its left half as it does on its right half.
  - **Left-skewed distribution:** If the left half of the distribution extends further from the center than its right half, then the distribution is described as left-skewed. In other words, a left-skewed distribution has a longer left tail than right tail. There are more observations with higher values than there are with lower values. The distribution of scores on an easy exam is generally left-skewed, because there will be more students with higher scores and fewer with lower scores.
  - **Right-skewed distribution:** If the right half of a distribution extends further from the center than its left half, then the distribution is described as right-skewed. In other words, a right-skewed distribution has a longer right tail than left tail. The distribution of scores on a difficult exam is generally right-skewed, because there will be more students with lower scores and fewer with higher scores.

The following three graphs show three basic shapes of distributions.

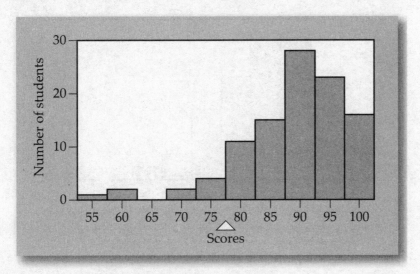

Figure 3: **Left-skewed distribution**

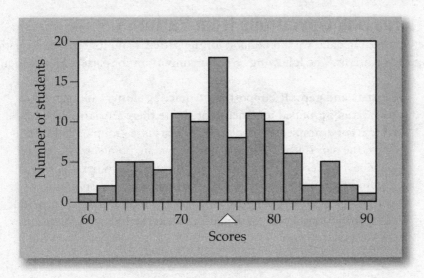

Figure 4: **Symmetric distribution**

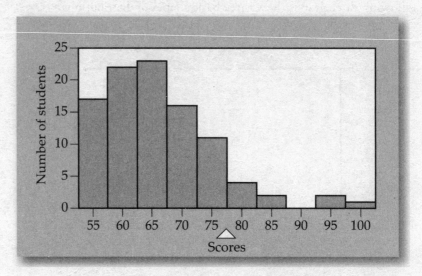

Figure 5: Right-skewed distribution

Patterns and Deviations from Patterns

When examining data, we should look for the patterns and for striking deviations from those patterns. The following terms are important for pattern recognition:

- **Clusters and gaps:** It's important to describe clusters and gaps. Are observations grouped together tightly? Are there any large gaps in the values? For example, if you plot the heights of a group of college students, the plot is likely to peak at two separate points, with a trough (or valley) in between. The reason for this is that women in general tend to be a bit shorter than men. The first peak corresponds to the women's most common height, whereas the second peak corresponds to the men's most common height. Look at the following figure:

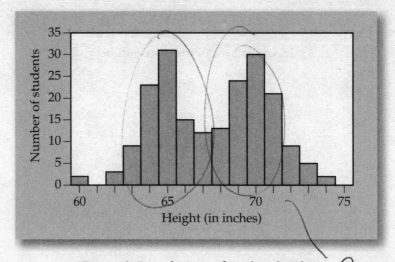

Figure 6: Distribution of student heights

2 clusters

- **Outliers:** An outlier is an observation that is surprisingly different from the rest of the data. For example, imagine a class in which most of the students scored between 60 and 98 on a test. But one student scored 18. This score is an outlier because it's so much different from most of the others. In a distribution of the salary of employees of any company, the salary of the highest official is typically an outlier. Consider the following distribution, which shows the salaries of employees at one company:

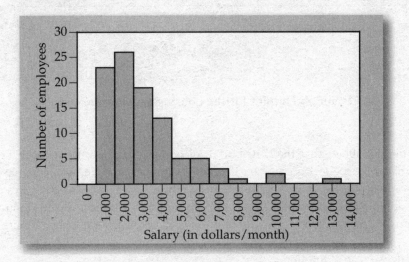

Figure 7: Distribution of salaries

Note that the distribution is highly right-skewed. A few employees on the higher end earn much more than the rest of the employees. Those higher observations are outliers, because they deviate so much from the rest.

Graphical Methods for Continuous Variables: Dotplots, Stemplots, Histograms, and Cumulative Frequency Charts

Dotplots

This is one of the easiest plots to make. It's most effective for smaller data sets. If the data set is too large, then the dotplot will be very cluttered. For large data sets, it's best to create a boxplot (described later in this chapter).

This is how to make a dotplot:

- Draw a horizontal line (the *x*-axis) to indicate the data range.
- Scale the line to accommodate the entire range of data.

- Mark a dot for each observation in the appropriate place above the scaled line.
- If more than one observation has the same value, then add dots one above the other.

Example 4: Create a dotplot for the housing expenditure data in Table 1.

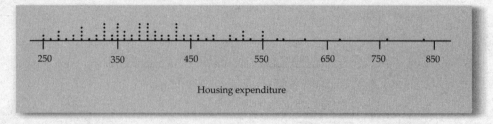

Figure 8: Dotplot for the housing expenditure data

This dotplot shows that the distribution of housing expenditure is right-skewed, and that there are at least two outliers on the higher end (i.e., students paying a lot more for housing than what most of the others spend). The expenditures range from about $250 a month to almost $850 a month, with most of the amounts in the range of $250 to $550. The distribution is centered around $414 a month.

How do we read a dot plot?

- Each dot on the plot indicates the location of the value of the data point.
- For any data point, we can look directly down at the scale to determine the value of the point.

We can use the dotplot to determine:

- How the data points are spread.
- What kind of shape the points make collectively.
- Where the approximate center of the distribution is—in other words, where this picture of dots is likely to balance if it were held on an outstretched finger.

Stemplots

Stemplots, also known as stem-and-leaf plots, are also commonly used. When turned on its side, a stemplot resembles a histogram. One advantage of using a stemplot is that it shows every value, but stemplots are inconvenient for very large data sets.

This is how to make a stemplot:

- Separate each observation into two parts. The left-most part of each observation is called the **stem** and the remaining part is called the **leaf**. There is no definite rule for determining where to make the division. Use a scheme that gives a reasonable number of stems. Too few stems can distort the picture by hiding patterns, whereas too many stems can distort the picture by diluting patterns. For example, if you have a sample of 80 numbers between 1 and 99, you may want to divide the data into groups of 10. So for stems, you might choose the first digit of each number in the sample (0, 1, 2, 3, 4, 5, 6, 7, 8, 9). If the sample was of 80 numbers between 1 and 49, you might want to make 10 stems by writing in the first digit of every number twice (0, 0, 1, 1, 2, 2, 3, 3, 4, 4). The first occurrence of each 1 would be the stem for all numbers from 10 to 14; the second occurrence of each 1 would be the stem for all numbers between 15 and 19. The first occurrence of each 2 would be the stem for all numbers from 20 to 24; the second occurrence of each 2 would be the stem for all numbers between 25 and 29; and so on.
- Draw a vertical line on the left side of the page to separate the stems from the leaves.
- Write all possible stems in increasing order on the left of the line, making sure that the entire range of the data is covered.
- For each observation, write in the leaf to the right of the corresponding stem on the right side of the vertical line.
- After leaves are created for all observations, write all leaves for the same stem in increasing order of value.

Example 5: Create a stemplot for the housing expenditure data in Table 1.

Stemplot of housing expenditure data
N = 80   Leaf Unit = 10

Stem	Leaves
2	556777899
3	00001223333344
3	55555666778888899999
4	00011223333344
4	5566788
5	0012223
5	55589
6	2
6	7
7	
7	6
8	3

Figure 9: Stemplot for the housing expenditure data

This stemplot shows that the distribution of housing expenditure is right-skewed, with at least two outliers at the high end. Expenditures ranged from about $250 a month to almost $850 a month, with most of the amounts (all but seven) in the range of $250 to $550 per month. The distribution is centered around approximately $414 a month.

How do we read a stemplot?

<table>
<tr><td>Note: There is only one 2 because no value was under $250, and also one 8 because no value was above $850.</td><td>
• The numbers on the left of the vertical line are stems. In this stemplot, notice that there are two 3s, two 4s, and so on. The first of each pair of stems corresponds to the lower half of a group of each hundred dollars spent per month and the second stem of the pair corresponds to the higher half of each hundred. For example, in the pair of 5s, the first 5 corresponds to the expenditure between $500 and $549 per month, and the second 5 corresponds to the expenditure between $550 and $599 per month.
</td></tr>
</table>

- The numbers on the right of the vertical line are leaves. Each stem has a different number of leaves, indicating the frequency of that class. For example, stem 2 has nine leaves, which means nine observations belong to this stem. In other words, nine students pay $250–$299 per month for housing.
- Each leaf indicates a single observation. Four leaves with the value 0 on stem 3 indicate that four students spend $300–$309 per month on housing.
- The lower stem 7 has no leaves. It means that no interviewed student pays between $700 and $749 per month for housing.

We can use the stemplot to determine:

- How the variable is spread. To do this, we might turn the graph on its side with the stems at the bottom.
- The shape of the distribution of the variable.
- Where the center of this variable is—in other words, where this picture of stems and leaves would balance if it were turned on its side with the stems at the bottom and held on an outstretched finger.

Histograms

This is probably the most popular form of displaying data. It looks like a stemplot on its side. Unlike the stemplot and dotplot, the histogram is useful for displaying large data sets. For very small data sets, however, a histogram might fail to show a pattern, so a dotplot or stemplot would be more appropriate.

Another disadvantage of the histogram is that, due to grouping, the pattern of data within each group is lost. For example, suppose 18 students get A's (score 90 and above). From a histogram, it would not be possible to tell how the grades of those 18 students are spread within the range of 90 to 100. All of them could be at 90 or all could be at 100 or they could be evenly spread from 90 to 100.

A histogram can be drawn for ungrouped as well as grouped data. It can be drawn using frequencies, relative frequencies, or percentages.

This is how to make a histogram:

- Create groups of equal length.
- Draw the x-axis and the y-axis.
- Scale the x-axis to accommodate all the data groups.
- Scale the y-axis to accommodate the range of frequencies used (or relative frequencies or percentages).
- Draw bars of heights equal to the corresponding frequencies (or relative frequencies or percentages) and add a label for each group. Draw the bars next to each other without any gaps.

Example 6: Create a histogram to describe the housing expenditure data in Table 2.

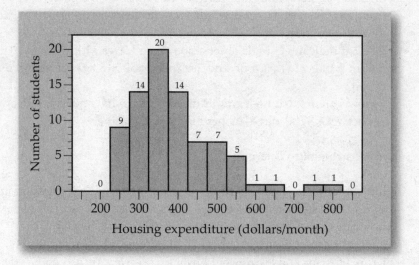

Figure 10: Frequency histogram of housing expenditure data

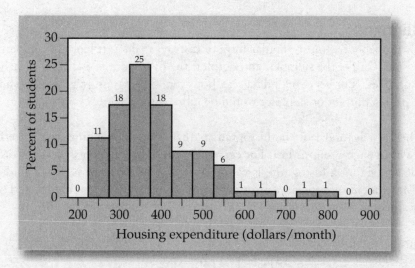

Figure 11: Percent histogram of housing expenditure data

Both these graphs show that the distribution of housing expenditure is right-skewed. In other words, more students spend lower amounts for housing, and fewer students pay higher amounts for housing. The expenditures ranged from about $250 per month to $850 per month. The expenditures seem to be centered around approximately $414 per month.

How do we read a histogram?

- Each bar represents a single group or class. There is only one bar for each class.
- The classes are placed on the x-axis in numerically increasing order, just like on a number line.
- The height of a bar in a frequency histogram corresponds to the frequency of that class. For example, the height of the first bar of Figure 10 is equal to 9. This indicates that nine students spend at least $250 but less than $300 per month on housing.
- Note that on both of the graphs on the previous page, there's one gap with no bar. This means that no student interviewed spends at least $700 but less than $750 on housing.
- The total of heights of the bars beyond 700 in Figure 10 is $0 + 1 + 1 = 2$. This means that two students spend at least $700 per month on housing.
- The total of the heights of the second and third bars in Figure 10 is $14 + 20 = 34$. This means that 34 students spend at least $300 but less than $400 per month on housing.
- **Percentage frequency** or **relative frequency** histograms can be read similarly. In a relative frequency histogram, the height of the bar reflects the relative frequency corresponding to the class. In the percent frequency histogram, the height of the bar reflects the percent frequency that corresponds to the class.

You can also use your calculator to draw a histogram. Here's how to do it on the TI-83 or TI-84:

TI-83 or TI-84:

Making a histogram using the entire data set:
- Choose **STAT** → **EDIT**
- Enter the housing expenditure data in L_1
- Choose **2nd** → **STAT PLOT** → **1: PLOT1**
- Turn the plot1 ON by highlighting **ON** (selecting it) and pressing **ENTER**
- Out of six available choices, select "histogram" by highlighting the figure that looks like a histogram and then pressing **ENTER**
- Enter Xlist: **2nd L_1**
- Enter Freq: 1

  (a) To let calculator determine classes:
- Choose **ZOOM** → 9: **ZOOMSTAT** → **TRACE**

  (b) To use classes of your choice:
- Choose **WINDOW**
- Enter the required numbers in the window

  WINDOW
  Xmin = 250
  Xmax = 850
  Xscl = 50 (group width)
  Ymin = −1
  Ymax = 20 (highest frequency)
  Yscl = 1 (depends on frequency)
  Xres = 1
- Choose **GRAPH** → **TRACE**

Making a histogram from a frequency distribution table:
- Enter class midpoints into L1
- Enter frequencies into L2
- Choose **2nd** → **STAT PLOT** → **1: PLOT1**
- Turn the plot1 ON by highlighting **ON** and pressing **ENTER**
- Out of six available choices, select "histogram" by highlighting it and pressing **ENTER**
- Enter Xlist: **2nd L_1**
- Enter Freq: **2nd L_2**
- Choose **WINDOW**
- Enter the required numbers in the window

  WINDOW
  Xmin = *enter minimum value*
  Xmax = *enter maximum value*
  Xscl = *enter group width*
  Ymin = −1
  Ymax = *enter highest frequency*
  Yscl = 0 (for no occurrences)
  Xres = 1
- Choose **GRAPH** → **TRACE**

Cumulative Frequency Charts

The cumulative frequency for any group is the frequency for that group plus the frequencies of all groups of smaller observations. Many cumulative frequency charts are S-shaped.

The cumulative frequency chart is also known as the ogive chart.

Here's how to draw cumulative frequency charts:

- Draw the *x*-axis and the *y*-axis.
- Scale the *x*-axis to accommodate the range of all groups. Mark the upper boundary of each group.
- Scale the *y*-axis from 0 to *n* for a cumulative frequency chart (from 0 to 1 for a relative cumulative frequency chart or from 0 to 100 for a percentage cumulative frequency chart).
- Place a dot at the height equal to the cumulative frequency for that group above the upper boundary for each group. Connect all the dots with straight lines.

Example 7: Create a cumulative frequency chart to describe the housing expenditure data in Table 2.

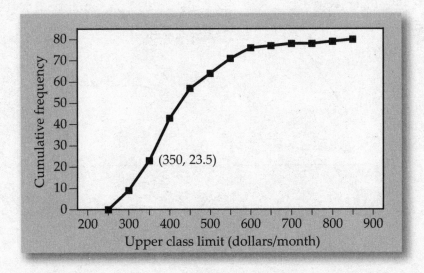

Figure 12: Cumulative frequency chart for the housing data

The line's steep climb in the beginning combined with its tapering off at the higher end of the graph indicates that the distribution is right-skewed (see Figure 13).

How do we read a cumulative frequency chart?

- From any point on the graph, we can draw a vertical line to read the
  x-value from the *x*-axis and a horizontal line to read the *y*-value from
  the *y*-axis. For example, take the third point from the bottom. Draw
  a vertical line to read *x*. It's about 350. Then draw a horizontal line to
  read *y*. It's about 23 or 24. This tells us that about 23 (or 24) students
  spend less than $350 per month on housing.

- Because a total of 80 students were interviewed, we can also say that
  about 80 − 23 = 57 (or 80 − 24 = 56) students spend at least $350 per
  month on housing.

- The steepness of the line is an indicator of the shape of the distribution.
  Refer to the following graph, which shows cumulative frequency lines
  for left-skewed, symmetric, and right-skewed distributions.

Note that for right-skewed distributions, the curve increases quickly in the beginning but then steadies in the later part. For left-skewed distributions, the curve increases slowly in the beginning, but then steeply later on.

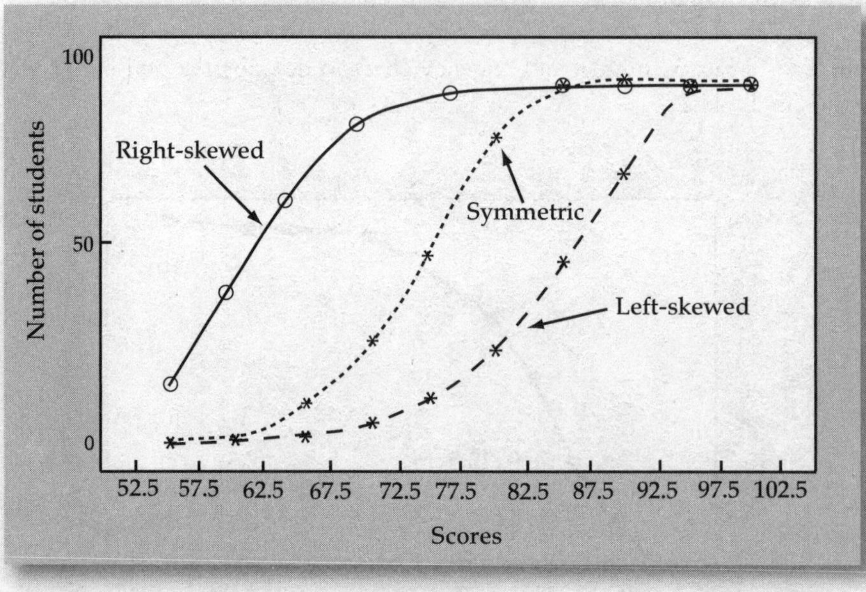

Figure 13: Comparison of cumulative frequency charts

The table on the following page shows different graphs summarizing the scores of
students on an easy exam, a fair exam, and a difficult exam. Examine the graphs
carefully to see how the symmetry or the skewedness affects the shape of the different types of graphs. If you know how symmetric or skewed distributions look,
then you can determine the nature of the distribution by examining the graphs.

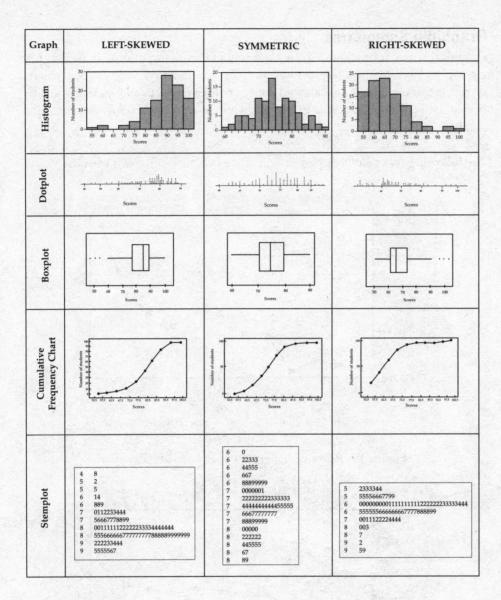

Table 4: Comparison of shapes of different graphs

Note that boxplots, which are included in the table, are discussed later in this chapter, following the discussion of Measures of Position.

Summarizing Distributions

First, two important terms: The **population** is the entire group of individuals or things that we are interested in. The **sample** is the part of the population that is actually studied.

For example, when a shopper buys a bag of a dozen oranges, he might squeeze one or two to determine how fresh they are. In this case, the entire bag of oranges constitutes the *population*, and the one or two oranges inspected constitute the *sample*.

Graphical Summaries

Graphical summary measures are a good way of conveying information, but they are also subject to misinterpretation and can be distorted very easily. Two researchers can take the same data and convey completely different messages just by manipulating the layout of a graph. So, you have to be careful when reading graphs.

The following two graphs display revenue for a business in the last calendar year.

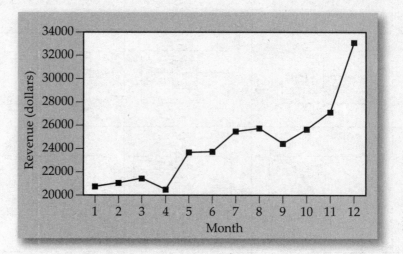

Figure 14: Revenue generated over one calendar year

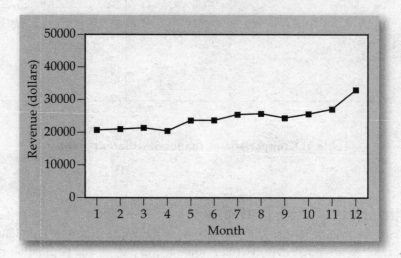

Figure 15: Revenue generated over one calendar year

- The first graph gives the impression that the revenue increased dramatically over the last calendar year.
- The second graph gives the impression that the revenue increased steadily but only slightly.

A closer inspection of the scale on the *y*-axis tells a different story. Both the graphs are displaying *exactly the same revenue data*. The only difference is that one has a more extended scale than the other. But the impressions they leave with the viewer are totally distinct.

Describing a Distribution

When examining a graphical summary of a distribution of univariate data, use the following three measures to describe the data:

- Center
- Spread
- Shape

In addition, you should always note any clustering of data, any gaps in the data, and any outliers. If possible, try to provide explanations for such features.

NUMERICAL METHODS FOR CONTINUOUS VARIABLES

Numerical, tabular, and graphical methods complement one other. Numerical methods are precise and can be used in a wide variety of ways for statistical inference; however, they are dull and can be overwhelming. Graphical methods allow us to view a large amount of data and a large number of relationships at once, but they are not precise and are often abused. Tabular methods allow us to find precise values but are not as good for grasping relationships among variables.

There are three types of numerical measures:

- Measures of central tendency
- Measures of variation (spread)
- Measures of position

Each type is discussed in detail in the following sections, but first, let's review the notation we'll be using.

Review of Summation Notation

A Greek capital letter Σ (read as "Sigma") is used to indicate the sum of a set of measurements. For example, if we denote the first through the fifth measurements of something by X_1, X_2, X_3, X_4, X_5, then

$$\sum_{i=1}^{5} X_i = X_1 + X_2 + X_3 + X_4 + X_5 = \text{the sum of first five measurements}$$

Example 8: The following list shows one student's scores on 10 quizzes:

$$8, 9, 0, 10, 10, 8, 7, 9, 10, 5$$

What is this student's total score on the quizzes?

Solution: Let X_i = the score on the ith quiz. So $X_1 = 8$, $X_2 = 9$, … $X_{10} = 5$. Then, the total score is

$$\sum_{i=1}^{10} X_i = X_1 + X_2 + \cdots + X_{10} = 8 + 9 + 0 + 10 + 10 + 8 + 7 + 9 + 10 + 5 = 76$$

Measures of Central Tendency

Measures of central tendency determine the central point of a variable or the point around which all the measurements are scattered. The two main measures of central tendency are the mean and the median.

Mean: The arithmetic mean (often called the **average**) is the most commonly used measure of the center of a set of data. The mean can be described as a data set's center of gravity, the point at which the whole group of data balances. Unlike the median, the mean is affected by extreme or outlier measurements. One very large or very small measurement can pull the mean up or down. We say that the mean is not resistant; it is not resistant to changes caused by outliers.

- The *population mean* is denoted by Greek letter μ (read as "mu"). It is computed as $\mu = \dfrac{\sum_{i=1}^{N} X_i}{N}$. That is, simply add up all of the values in the entire population and divide by the number of values.

- The *sample mean* is generally denoted by an English letter with a bar on top, such as $\overline{X}$ (read as "X bar") or $\overline{Y}$ (read as "Y bar"). It is computed as $\overline{X} = \dfrac{\sum\limits_{i=1}^{n} X_i}{n}$, where n = the number of measurements in the sample.

Median: The median is another commonly used measure of central tendency. The median is the point that divides the measurements in half. That is, half of the values are at or below the median, and half are at or above the median. The median is *not* affected by outliers. Therefore, for skewed data sets or data sets containing outliers, it's better to use the median rather than the mean to measure the center of the data. The median is resistant; it resists changes caused by outliers.

Let's denote the median by M. Use the following steps to determine the median:

- Suppose there are n measurements in a data set.

- Arrange the measurements in increasing order (i.e., from smallest to largest).

- Compute $l = \dfrac{n+1}{2}$

- Then the median M = the value of the lth measurement.

Note that if the data set contains an odd number of measurements, then the median belongs to the data set. But if the data set contains an even number of measurements, then the median may not belong to the data set. It is instead the mean of the middle two measurements. For example, if a data set contains five measurements, then the median is the third smallest (or third largest) measurement. But if the data set contains six measurements, then the median is the mean of the third smallest and the fourth smallest measurements (see Example 12 on page 132).

Measures of Variation

Measures of variation (or "measures of spread") summarize the spread of a data set. They describe how measurements differ from each other and/or from their mean. The three most commonly used measures of variation are range, interquartile range, and standard deviation.

Range: The range is the difference between the largest and the smallest measurement in a data set.

$$R = \text{range} = \text{largest measurement} - \text{smallest measurement}$$

Range is the simplest of the measures of spread. It is very easy to compute and understand, but it is not a reliable measure because it depends only on the two extreme measurements and does not take into account the values of the remaining measurements.

Interquartile range: The interquartile range (*IQR*) is the range of the middle 50 percent of the data, the difference between the third quartile (Q_3) and the first quartile (Q_1).

Quartiles are defined in the next section under Measures of Position.

$$IQR = Q_3 - Q_1$$

Interquartile range is not affected by outliers. If you choose to measure the center using the median, you should use the IQR to measure the spread.

Standard deviation: Standard deviation is often a more useful measure of variation than range is. Unlike range, standard deviation takes every measurement into account. However, like the range, the standard deviation is affected by outliers. When there are outliers, the IQR may be a more useful measurement. The square of the standard deviation is known as **variance**.

- A lowercase Greek letter σ (read as "sigma") is used to denote a population standard deviation. So σ^2 denotes a population variance. The population standard deviation is defined as

$$\sigma = \sqrt{\frac{\sum_{i=1}^{N}(X_i - \mu)^2}{N}}$$

  That is, we square the difference between each point and the mean, add those squares, divide by the number of points, and take the square root.

- The letter *s* is used to denote a sample standard deviation. So s^2 denotes a sample variance. The sample standard deviation is defined as

$$s = \sqrt{\frac{\sum_{i=1}^{n}(X_i - \overline{X})^2}{n-1}}$$

- Note that standard deviation is measured in the same units as are data values, whereas variance is measured in squared units of the data values. For example, suppose the standard deviation of a set of housing expenditure data is 110 and the variance is 12,100. The associated units of measurement would be the following: standard deviation $s = 110$ dollars, and variance $s^2 = 110^2 = 12{,}100$ squared dollars (or dollars^2).

- Standard deviation can be used as a unit for measuring the distance between any measurement and the mean of the data set. For example, a measurement can be described as being so many standard deviations above or below the mean. (See the discussion of *z*-scores, below.)

- A standard deviation (or variance) of 0 indicates that all of the measurements are identical. For example, if a student scores 8, 8, 8, and 8 on four quizzes, then the standard deviation of the scores is 0.

- Standard deviation is the positive square root of variance. Because variance is a squared quantity, it is *always* a positive number. So if your computation gives you a negative value for variance, go back and check your work.

- A larger standard deviation (and consequently, variance) indicates a larger spread among the measurements. The larger the standard deviation, the wider the graph. For example, two students score the following on their quizzes:

    Student A: 8, 9, 4, 8, 6, 8, 7, 9, 10, 5 $s_A = 1.897$

    Student B: 7, 8, 6, 6, 6, 6, 7, 5, 5, 7 $s_B = 0.949$

The dotplots and boxplots (we'll discuss boxplots in more detail later in this chapter) of scores for the two students are shown in Figures 16 and 17. Compare the spread of the scores from the plots. Both graphs show that the scores for student A are more spread out (they vary more) than the scores for student B. So it makes sense that the scores for student A have a larger standard deviation than those for student B.

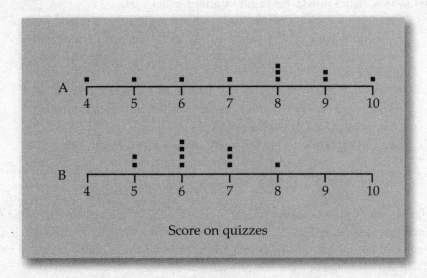

Figure 16: Dotplot of students' scores on quizzes

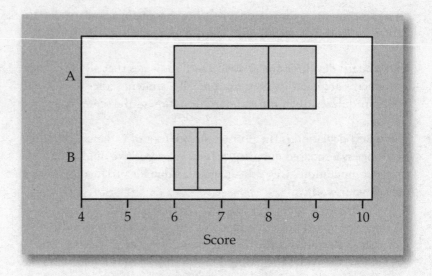

Figure 17: Boxplot of students' scores on quizzes

Measures of Position

These measures are used to describe the position of a value with respect to the rest of the values of the variable. Quartiles, percentiles, and standardized scores (z-scores) are the most commonly used measures of position. To compute quartiles and percentiles, but not to compute z-scores, the data must be sorted by value.

Quartiles: Quartiles divide a data set into four equal parts:

- Q_1: First quartile. The number such that, at most, 25 percent of the values are at or below it, and, at most, 75 percent of the values are at or above it.
- Q_2: Second quartile, same as the median. A number such that, at most, 50 percent of the values are at or below it, and, at most, 50 percent of values are at or above it.
- Q_3: Third quartile. A number such that, at most, 75 percent of the values are at or below it, and, at most, 25 percent of values are at or above it.

In other words, 25 percent of the values are below Q_1, 25 percent are between Q_1 and Q_2, 25 percent are between Q_2 and Q_3, and 25 percent are above Q_3. Refer to the discussion of percentiles for instructions on how to compute quartiles. Quartiles can be calculated using STAT/CALC/1-Var Stats on your calculator.

Percentiles: Percentiles divide a set of values into 100 equal parts. For each variable, there are 99 percentiles, denoted by P_1, P_2, ... P_{99}.

P_k = The kth percentile, which is the number such that, at most, k percent of the values are at or below it, and at most $(100 - k)$ percent of the values are at or above it.

For example, P_{95} is the 95th percentile, which means that, at most, 95 percent of the values are at or below P_{95}, and, at most, 5 percent of the values are at or above P_{95}. Note that $P_{25} = Q_1$, $P_{50} = Q_2 = M$, and $P_{75} = Q_3$.

- Suppose there are n measurements of a particular variable in a data set.

- Suppose we are interested in determining the kth percentile.

- Arrange all measurements of that variable in increasing order, i.e., from the smallest to the largest.

- Compute $l = \dfrac{(n+1)k}{100}$

- The percentile P_k = the value of the measurement in the lth position when counted from the lowest measurement.

Standardized scores or **z-scores**: Standardized scores, commonly known as z-scores, are independent of the units in which the data values are measured. Therefore, they are useful when comparing observations measured on different scales. They are computed as:

$$z\text{-score} = \frac{\text{measurement} - \text{mean}}{\text{standard deviation}}$$

A z-score gives the distance between the measurement and the mean in terms of the number of standard deviations. A negative z-score indicates that the measurement is *smaller* than the mean. A positive z-score indicates that the measurement is *larger* than the mean.

Example 9: Suppose a teacher gave her students a test. The class average was 74 and the standard deviation was 6. Suppose student A got an 88 and student B got a 70. Let's calculate the z-scores:

Student A: $z\text{-score} = \dfrac{\text{measurement} - \text{mean}}{\text{standard deviation}} = \dfrac{88 - 74}{6} = 2.33$

Student A scored 2.33 standard deviations above the class average.

Student B: $z\text{-score} = \dfrac{\text{measurement} - \text{mean}}{\text{standard deviation}} = \dfrac{70 - 74}{6} = -0.67$

Student B scored 0.67 standard deviations below the class average.

Note that student B scored closer to the class average than student A.

Example 10: The mean and the standard deviation of the daily high temperatures in degrees Fahrenheit for two cities are given below:

City	Mean	Standard deviation
North Bend	80	12
South Bend	84	4

Yesterday, both cities reported a high temperature of 95 degrees. Which city had the more unusually high temperature?

Solution: Because the mean daily high temperature at North Bend is 80 degrees—which is lower than the mean daily high temperature at South Bend (84 degrees)—we are tempted to say that 95 degrees is more unusually high at North Bend. But that would be incorrect, because it does not take into account the spread of the temperatures at these two cities.

Compute z-scores for both cities:

$$\text{North Bend: } z\text{-score} = \frac{\text{measurement} - \text{mean}}{\text{standard deviation}} = \frac{95 - 80}{12} = 1.25$$

$$\text{South Bend: } z\text{-score} = \frac{\text{measurement} - \text{mean}}{\text{standard deviation}} = \frac{95 - 84}{4} = 2.75$$

Ninety-five degrees Fahrenheit is 1.25 standard deviations above the average in North Bend, whereas it is 2.75 standard deviations above the average in South Bend. This means that 95 degrees Fahrenheit was more unusually high in South Bend.

Example 11: A small used car dealer wanted to get an idea of how many cars her dealership sells per day. Listed below is the number of cars sold per day over a two-week period:

14	9	23	7	11	23	17
11	3	24	21	2	20	20

Compute:

    (a) the mean number of cars sold per day

17.857

    (b) the range of cars sold per day

22

    (c) the standard deviation of the number of cars sold per day

    (d) the median number of cars sold per day

    (e) the first and third quartiles of the number of cars sold per day

    (f) the interquartile range of the number of cars sold per day

    (g) the 90th percentile of the number of cars sold per day

Solution:

    (a) Let X_i = the number of cars sold on the ith day.

$$\sum_{i=1}^{14} X_i = 14 + 9 + \cdots + 20 = 205, \text{ and the number}$$

of observations = n = 14

The sample mean is $\overline{X} = \dfrac{\Sigma X}{n} = \dfrac{205}{14} = 14.64 \; cars$

On the average, she sells 14.64 cars per day. See the calculator instructions on page 130.

    (b) The smallest number is 2 and the largest number is 24. On the best day, her dealership sold 24 cars, and on the worst day it sold only two cars. *Range* = largest measurement – smallest measurement = 24 – 2 = 22

Therefore, the range of the number of cars sold is 22.

    (c) To compute the standard deviation, use your calculator. The sample's standard deviation is s_x = 7.5611 cars. Note: the TI-83 and TI-84 denote standard deviation.

    (d) To find the median, first arrange the data in increasing order:

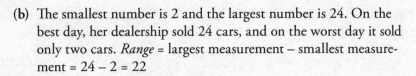

2, 3, 7, 9, 11, 11, 14, 17, 20, 20, 21, 23, 23, 24

Compute:

50

$$l = \frac{n+1}{2} = \frac{14+1}{2} = 7.5$$

So the median is the value of the 7.5th observation, i.e., the average of the seventh and the eighth observations. When counted from the smallest observation, the seventh observation = 14 and the eighth observation = 17, and M = median = $(14 + 17)/2 = 15.5$. In other words, there is an even number of values in the list, so we need to take the average of the middle two values.

On half of the days, fewer than 15.5 cars were sold, and on the other half of the days, more than 15.5 cars were sold. Because you can't sell a fraction of a car, another way to say this is that, on half of the days, 15 or fewer cars were sold, and, on the other half, 16 or more were sold.

(e) The first quartile (Q_1) is the median of the lower half of the observations. The median number of cars sold on the seven days that 15 or fewer cars were sold is nine, so $Q_1 = 9$.

The third quartile (Q_3) is the median of the upper half of the observations. The median number of cars sold on the seven days that 16 or more cars were sold is 21, so $Q_3 = 21$.

(f) Interquartile range = $IQR = Q_3 - Q_1 = 21 - 9 = 12$
(g) To find the 90th percentile (P_{90}), compute:

$$l = \frac{(n+1)k}{100} = \frac{(14+1)90}{100} = 13.5$$

So the 90th percentile is the value of the 13.5th observation, and when counted from the smallest observation, the 13th observation = 23 and the 14th observation = 24.

Interpolating between the 13th and 14th observation for the 13.5th observation, we get:

$$P_{90} = 90\text{th percentile} = 23.5$$

Therefore, on 90 percent of the days, 23.5 (equivalently, 23) or fewer cars were sold per day, and on the remaining 10 percent of the days, 24 or more cars were sold per day.

TI-83 or TI-84:
- Enter data in L1
- Choose **STAT → CALC → 1: 1-Var Stats**
- Press **ENTER**
- Choose 2nd → 1 (to get L1) This will result in 1-Var Stats L1
- Press **ENTER**

Note: This option gives output that contains the following:
$\overline{X}$, ΣX, ΣX^2, sx, σx, n, $Minx$, Q_1, Med, Q_3, $Maxx$
Scroll down using the down arrow to read the entire output.

BOXPLOTS

A boxplot, also known as a box-and-whiskers plot, is a graphical data summary based on measures of position. It is useful for identifying outliers and the general shape of the distribution.

Here's how to make one:

- Draw a horizontal number line.
- Scale the number line to cover the range of observations.
- Draw a rectangular box above the line from the first quartile to the third quartile (Q_1 to Q_3).
- Draw a vertical line at the median, dividing the box into two compartments.
- Compute "whisker" length = $1.5IQR$
- Compute $L = Q_1 - 1.5IQR$
- Compute $U = Q_3 + 1.5IQR$
- Make a lower whisker by drawing a line from the lower (left) wall of the box at Q_1 to the farthest observation greater than or equal to L.
- Make an upper whisker by drawing a line from the upper (right) wall of the box at Q_3 to the farthest observation less than or equal to U.
- Plot any points with values smaller than L or larger than U in their respective places above the number line beyond the whiskers.

How do we read a boxplot?

- Any points below the lower (left) whisker are identified as outliers on the lower end.
- Any points above the higher (right) whisker are identified as outliers on the higher end.
- The length of the box indicates the IQR, i.e., the range of the middle 50 percent of data, when the data is arranged in increasing order of value.
- The length of the lower whisker (with any outliers) shows the spread of the smallest 25 percent of data, when the data is arranged in increasing order of value.
- The length of the first compartment of the box shows the spread of the next smallest 25 percent of data.
- The length of the second compartment of the box shows the spread of the third smallest 25 percent of data.
- The length of the upper whisker (with any outliers) shows the spread of the largest 25 percent of data.
- Compare the lengths of the four parts to compare the respective spread of the data. Use the information about spread to determine the shape of the distribution.

Example 12: Make a boxplot for the car sales data given in the previous example.

Solution: As shown earlier, for the car sales data,

$Q_1 = 9$, $M = 15.5$, and $Q_3 = 21$

$IQR = Q_3 - Q_1 = 21 - 9 = 12$

Compute $L = Q_1 - 1.5IQR = 9 - 1.5(12) = -9$

Compute $U = Q_3 + 1.5IQR = 21 + 1.5(12) = 39$

- Draw a box from 9 to 21.
- Draw a divider in the box at 15.5.
- Draw a whisker from 9 to 2 (lowest observation within the range of L).
- Draw a whisker from 21 to 24 (highest observation within the range of U).
- There are no observations beyond L and U.

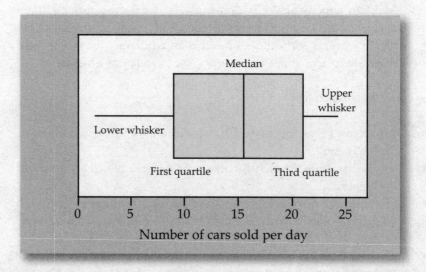

Figure 18: Boxplot of the number of cars sold per day

The longer, lower whisker and the longer, lower box indicate that the distribution of the number of cars sold per day has a slightly longer left tail, i.e., the distribution is slightly left-skewed. There are no outliers.

Example 13: Make a boxplot of the housing expenditure data given in the first example of this chapter (Table 1, page 100).

Solution: Compute summary measures as follows:

$$M = \$392 \text{ per month}$$

$$Q_1 = \$333.25 \text{ per month and } Q_3 = \$465 \text{ per month}$$

$$IQR = 465 - 333.25 = 131.75$$

$$L = Q_1 - 1.5IQR = 333.25 - 1.5(131.75) = 135.63$$

$$U = Q_3 + 1.5IQR = 465 + 1.5(131.75) = 662.63 \text{ (rounded up)}$$

Note that the lowest housing expenditure (\$255) is higher than L, so there are no outliers on the lower side. Also note that the highest housing expenditure (\$834) is larger than U. So there is at least one outlier on the higher side. The boxplot below identifies three outliers on the higher side. This means that there are three students with exceptionally high housing expenditures compared to the rest of the students. The distribution is right-skewed partly because of these outliers, though the longer right whisker indicates that the distribution would be right-skewed even without the outliers or if outliers fell within the range (Q3, U).

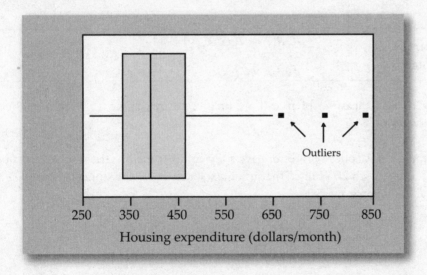

Figure 19: Boxplot of housing expenditure data

THE EFFECT OF CHANGING UNITS ON SUMMARY MEASURES

Let $X_1, X_2, \ldots, X_n$ be n observations. If we added a constant (a) to each observation or multiplied each observation by a constant (b, $b \neq 0$), then how will the summary measures change? The following chart shows the effect of such changes:

Summary Measure	$Y_i = X_i + a$	$Y_i = bX_i$
Mean	$\text{Mean}(Y) = \text{Mean}(X) + a$	$\text{Mean}(Y) = b\,\text{Mean}(X)$
Median	$\text{Median}(Y) = \text{Median}(X) + a$	$\text{Median}(Y) = b\,\text{Median}(X)$
Range	$\text{Range}(Y) = \text{Range}(X)$ *Range is unaffected.*	$\text{Range}(Y) = \lvert b \rvert\,\text{Range}(X)$
Standard Deviation	$\text{Standard deviation}(Y) = \text{Standard deviation}(X)$ *Standard deviation is unaffected.*	$\text{Standard deviation}(Y) = \lvert b \rvert\,\text{Standard deviation}(X)$
Quartiles	$\text{Quartiles}(Y) = \text{Quartiles}(X) + a$	$\text{Quartiles}(Y) = b\,\text{Quartiles}(X)$
Interquartile Range	$\text{IQR}(Y) = \text{IQR}(X)$ *IQR is unaffected.*	$\text{IQR}(Y) = \lvert b \rvert\,\text{IQR}(X)$

Note that all measures of spread are unaffected by adding a constant a to each observation.

Example 14: A college professor gave a test to his students. The test had five questions, each worth 20 points. The summary statistics for the students' scores on the test are as follows:

Summary Statistics for Scores	
Mean	62
Median	60
Range	45
Standard deviation	8
First quartile	48
Third quartile	71
Interquartile range	23

After grading the test, the professor realized that, because he had made a typographical error in question number 2, no student was able to answer the question. So he decided to adjust the students' scores by adding 20 points to each one. What will be the summary statistics for the new, adjusted scores?

Solution: Note that each student's score will increase by 20 points:

Summary Statistics for Adjusted Scores	
Mean	62 + 20 = 82
Median	60 + 20 = 80
Range	45 (unaffected)
Standard deviation	8 (unaffected)
First quartile	48 + 20 = 68
Third quartile	71+ 20 = 91
Interquartile range	23 (unaffected)

Example 15: The summary statistics for the property tax per property collected by one county are as follows:

Summary Statistics for Property Tax	
Mean	12,000
Median	8,000
Range	30,000
Standard deviation	5,000
First quartile	5,000
Third quartile	14,000
Interquartile range	9,000

This year, county residents voted to increase property taxes by 2 percent to support the local school system. What will be the summary statistics for the new, increased property taxes?

Solution: Note that each property owner will pay 2 percent more in taxes. So the new taxes will be:

new tax = 1.02 (old tax)

Summary Statistics for Increased Property Tax	
Mean	1.02 (12,000) = 12,240
Median	1.02 (8,000) = 8,160
Range	1.02 (30,000) = 30,600
Standard deviation	1.02 (5,000) = 5,100
First quartile	1.02 (5,000) = 5,100
Third quartile	1.02 (14,000) = 14,280
Interquartile range	1.02 (9,000) = 9,180

COMPARING DISTRIBUTIONS OF TWO OR MORE GROUPS

When comparing distributions of two or more groups, use the following criteria:

- Compare the centers of the distributions.
- Compare the spreads of the distributions. Consider the differences in the spread of data within each group as well as the differences between groups.
- Compare clusters of measurements and gaps in measurements.
- Compare outliers and any other unusual features.
- Compare the shapes of the distributions.

Example 16: A department store wants to compare the optical scanners it's currently using with some new scanners. Both models occasionally have trouble reading the bar codes on labels. The store manager decides to compare the number of reading errors made by the old scanners to the number of reading errors made by the new scanners. She selects a group of 50 items and runs them through each of the scanners 20 times and then records the number of errors made. The data is shown in the following table.

Scanner	Number of Reading Errors Per Group of 50 Items
New	2, 3, 3, 1, 2, 1, 2, 3, 1, 2, 2, 2, 4, 0, 1, 3, 2, 0, 2, 2
Old	6, 3, 4, 4, 6, 3, 5, 3, 1, 5, 3, 2, 5, 5, 4, 8, 4, 7, 3, 3

Display these data graphically so that the number of reading errors by the old and new scanners can be easily compared. Based on the examination of your graphical display, write a few sentences comparing the number of errors by the old and new scanners.

Solution: At least five graphs could be used here. The best is probably the boxplot because it shows the locations of the medians and quartiles most clearly.

1. **Parallel dotplots,** showing the errors made by both scanners. Parallel dotplots can be used to compare two or more data sets. Using the same scale, draw a dotplot for each data set. Label each line appropriately (see Figure 20).

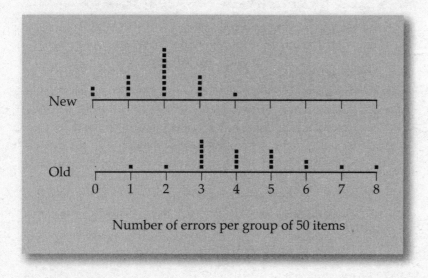

Figure 20: Parallel dotplots showing the number of errors by old and new scanners

2. **Parallel boxplots,** showing the errors made by both scanners. Parallel boxplots can also be used to compare two or more data sets. Using the same scale, draw a boxplot for each data set. Label each boxplot appropriately (see Figure 21).

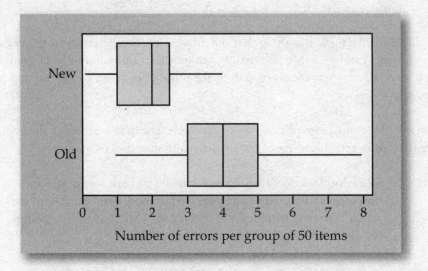

Figure 21: Parallel boxplots showing the number of errors by old and new scanners

3. **Back-to-back stemplots,** showing the errors made by both scanners, using the same stems. Back-to-back stemplots can *only* be used to compare two data sets. Put the common stems in the middle. On one side of the stems, make a stemplot for one data set. On the other side of the stems, make a stemplot for the other data set (see Figure 22).

Old Scanner		New Scanner
Leaves	Stems	Leaves
	0	00
0	1	0000
0	2	000000000
000000	3	0000
0000	4	0
0000	5	
00	6	
0	7	
0	8	

Figure 22: Back-to-back stemplots

4. **Two histograms,** showing the errors made by both scanners. Although not incorrect, this is not a great option. Be sure to use the same scale for both histograms; otherwise the comparison will not be valid. The problem with using two histograms is that we cannot lay one histogram over the other, because the bars of one graph may be partially or totally hidden behind the bars of the other. Therefore, we have to display the histograms vertically stacked (see Figure 23).

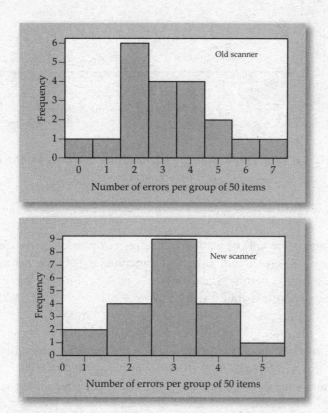

Figure 23: Stacked histograms showing the number of errors made by the old scanner and the new scanner

5. **Multiple frequency polygrams.** A **frequency polygram** is a graph showing the frequency of different values of a random variable. It is also known as a **line graph**. Basically, it can be drawn by connecting the midpoints of the tops of each bar of a histogram. Multiple frequency polygrams can be used to compare two or more data sets. Using the same scale, draw a line graph for each data set. Use different symbols and different types of lines to indicate different groups. Include the appropriate legend for correct identification (see Figure 24).

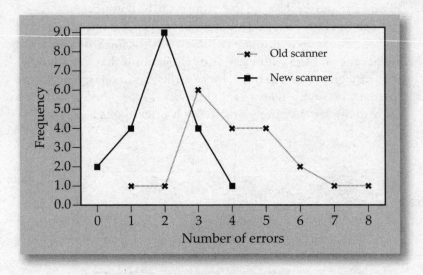

Figure 24: Line graph showing the number of errors by the old and new scanners

Examining any of these plots gives us the following information about the data:

- The distribution of the number of reading errors made by the old scanner is right-skewed, indicating that sometimes the old scanner makes a large number of errors. The distribution of the number of errors made by the new scanner is almost symmetric.

- The median number of errors made by the old scanner is about four, whereas those made by the new scanner is about two. So with the new scanner, 50 percent of the time, at most, two errors were made; whereas with the old scanner, 50 percent of the time more than four errors were made.

- The number of errors made by the old scanner ranged from one to eight, whereas the number of errors made by the new scanner ranged only from zero to four. The old scanner made at least one error in each run, whereas at times the new scanner read flawlessly. The old scanner shows a larger variation in the number of errors than the new scanner shows.

Examination of the parallel boxplots gives us the following additional information about the data:

- Although the *IQR* for both scanners is close, the longer whiskers on the boxplot for the old scanner, compared to the whiskers on the boxplot for the new scanner, indicate a larger variation in the number of errors made by the old scanner as compared to the variation in errors made by the new one.

- Although the distribution of errors made by the old scanner is right-skewed, there were no outliers detected in either boxplot.

EXPLORING BIVARIATE DATA

Bivariate data is data on two different variables collected from each item in a study.

We often want to investigate the relationship between two quantitative variables. If two different quantitative variables have a linear relation, then we can measure the strength of that relationship with **linear regression**, a popular and relatively simple method discussed below. For example, we might want to know the relation between:

- High school students' scores on the midterm and their scores on the final exam
- College students' SAT or ACT scores and their GPAs when they graduate
- The price of crude oil and the price of gasoline each month
- The daily temperature and the atmospheric pressure at a given location
- Advertising expenditure and either the number of items sold or amount of sales generated
- The weight of a car and its fuel efficiency

On the AP exam, there are two commonly used measures to summarize the relation between two variables. A **scatterplot** is a *graphical* summary measure. The **correlation coefficient** is a *numerical* summary measure.

Scatterplot

A **scatterplot** is used to describe the nature, degree, and direction of the relation between two variables x and y, where (x, y) gives a pair of measurements. Here's how to make one:

- Draw an x-axis and a y-axis.
- Scale the x-axis to accommodate the range of data for the first variable.
- Scale the y-axis to accommodate the range of data for the other variable.
- For each pair of measurements, mark the point on the graph where the (unmarked) lines of the x and y values cross.

Here's what a scatterplot can tell us about the two variables:

- **Shape:** A scatterplot tells us whether the nature of the relation between the two variables is linear or nonlinear. A linear relation is one that can be described well using a straight line (compare Figures 26 and 27 or 28).

- **Direction:** The scatterplot will show whether the *y*-value increases or decreases as the *x* increases, or that it changes direction. Specifically:
  - If a scatterplot shows an increasing or upward trend, then it indicates a *positive relation* between the two variables. For example, the relation between the heights of fathers and the heights of their sons is a positive relation: Taller fathers tend to have taller sons (see Figures 29 and 30).
  - If a scatterplot shows a decreasing or downward trend, then it indicates a *negative relation* between the two variables. For example, the relation between the weight of a car and its gas mileage is a negative relation: Heavier cars tend to get lower gas mileage (see Figures 31 and 32).

- **Strength of relationship:** If the trend of the data can be described with a line or a curve, then the spread of the data values around the line or curve describes the degree (or strength) of the relation between the two:
  - If a scatterplot shows fewer scattered points (i.e., points very close to the line or curve), then it indicates a *strong relationship* between the two variables (see Figures 29 and 31).
  - If a scatterplot shows more scattered points, then it indicates a *weaker relationship* between the two variables (see Figures 30 and 32).
  - If a scatterplot shows points scattered without any apparent pattern, then it indicates *no relationship* between the two variables (see Figure 25). The following scatterplots show various degrees of relation between the two variables.

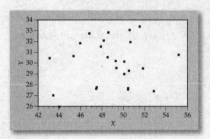

Figure 25: No relation between *x* and *y*

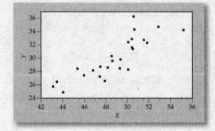

Figure 26: Linear relation between *x* and *y*

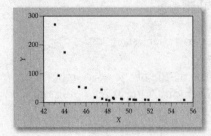

Figure 27: Nonlinear relation between *x* and *y*

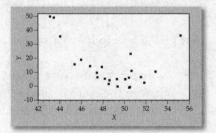

Figure 28: Nonlinear relation between *x* and *y*

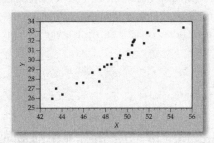

Figure 29: Strong positive linear relation between x and y

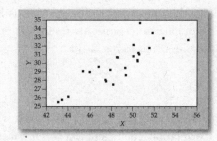

Figure 30: Weaker positive linear relation between x and y

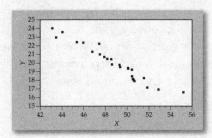

Figure 31: Strong negative linear relation between x and y

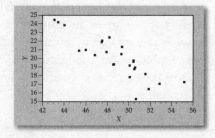

Figure 32: Weaker negative linear relation between x and y

Example 17: At the graduation ceremony of a large university, a random sample of 50 father–son pairs was selected, and the heights (in inches) of the fathers and sons were measured. Figure 33 is a scatterplot of the data collected.

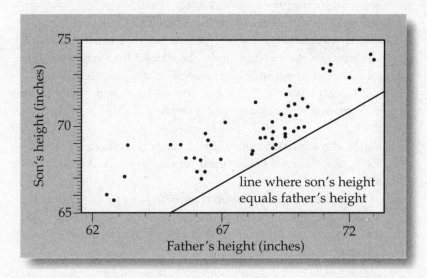

line where son's height equals father's height

Figure 33: Scatterplot of the heights of fathers and the heights of their sons

Notice from the plot that there is a positive relationship between the father's height and the son's height. The relation is fairly strong and linear. In general, taller fathers have taller sons; also, sons are taller than fathers. In this sample, every son is at least as tall as his father.

Correlation Coefficient

Correlation coefficients are *numerical* measures used to judge the linear relation between two variables. Note the word "linear." Correlation coefficients do not work well with nonlinear relationships.

Pearson's correlation coefficient (also known simply as "the correlation coefficient") is a numeric measure of the degree and direction of the linear relation between two quantitative variables. The Pearson's correlation coefficient between two variables x and y computed from a population is denoted by ρ (read as "rho"), whereas the correlation coefficient between two variables computed from a sample is denoted by r.

$$-1 \leq r \leq +1 \text{ always}$$

Here's what the correlation coefficient tells us:

- **Direction:** The positive or negative sign of the correlation coefficient describes the direction of the linear relation between the two variables.
  - A positive value of the correlation coefficient indicates a positive relation between x and y. This means that as x increases, y also increases linearly. For example, the relation between the heights of fathers and the heights of their sons is a positive relation. Taller fathers tend to have taller sons. A scatterplot of such data will show an increasing or upward linear trend.
  - A negative value of the correlation coefficient indicates a negative relation between x and y. This means that as x increases, y decreases linearly. For example, the relation between the weight of a car and its gas mileage is a negative relation. Heavier cars tend to get lower gas mileage. A scatterplot of such data will show a decreasing or downward linear trend.

- **Strength:** The numeric value of the correlation coefficient describes the strength (or degree) of the linear relation between the two variables:
  - If the value of the correlation coefficient is equal to +1, then it indicates a *perfect positive correlation* between two variables. In this case, all the points in a scatterplot would fall perfectly on an increasing line.

- If the value of the correlation coefficient is equal to –1, then it indicates a *perfect negative correlation* between the two variables. In this case, all the points in a scatterplot would fall perfectly on a decreasing line.

- If the value of the correlation coefficient is close to +1 or –1, then it indicates a *strong relationship* between two variables of interest. For example, if the correlation coefficient between x and y is 0.68, whereas the correlation coefficient between x and z is 0.82, then x and z have a stronger relationship than x and y.

- If the value of the correlation coefficient is close to 0, then it indicates a *weak relation* between the two variables. For example, if the correlation coefficient between x and y is –0.86, whereas the correlation coefficient between x and z is – 0.75, then x and y have a stronger relation than x and z.

- Values of the correlation coefficient that are farther from 0 indicate *stronger relationships*. For example, if the correlation coefficient between x and y is 0.68, whereas the correlation coefficient between x and z is – 0.75, then x and z have a stronger relationship than x and y. Note again that, unlike scatterplots, correlation coefficients do not show the shape of the relationship.

Correlation coefficients are usually computed using a calculator (see page 146) or by reading computer output from popular statistics programs. Formulas to find r are included on the AP exam formula sheet, but they are time-consuming.

Example 18: A sample of 12 father-and-son pairs were selected at random. The heights (in inches) of the selected father-son pairs are listed below:

Height (in Inches) of Father (x)	Height (in Inches) of Son (y)
66	66
68	67
66	65
66	67
67	68
67	65
67	67
68	70
69	70
70	70
71	72
73	74

Compute the correlation coefficient between the heights of the fathers and the heights of their sons. Interpret the computed value.

Solution: First, let's make a scatterplot to determine the nature of the relation between the two variables. Since a correlation coefficient only applies to linear relationships, we must make sure the scatterplot is linear. See Figure 34.

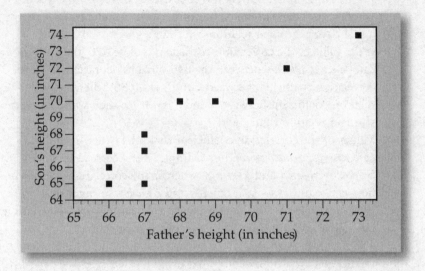

Figure 34: Scatterplot showing the heights of fathers and the heights of their sons

---

TI-83 or TI-84:

To make a scatterplot:
- Enter X-values into L_1
- Enter corresponding Y-values into L_2
- Choose **2nd → STAT PLOT → 1: Plot1**
- Turn the plot on by highlighting **On**
- Choose scatterplot by highlighting the picture of a scatterplot under Type
- Enter Xlist: L_1
- Enter Ylist: L_2
- Select type of marking from 3 available marks
- Choose **ZOOM → 9: ZoomStat**
- Use TRACE option to trace points in the scatterplot

The scatterplot shows a positive linear relation between the heights of the fathers and the heights of their sons. Now, let's compute the correlation coefficient.

There are $n = 12$ pairs of measurements.

TI-83 or TI-84:

To compute the correlation coefficient:
- Enter X-values into L_1
- Enter corresponding Y-values into L_2
- Choose **2nd** → **CATALOG** → **DiagnosticOn**

Note: This step is needed only the very first time. Once the diagnostics are turned on, omit this step.
- Choose **STAT** → **CALC** → **8: LinReg(a + bx)**
- Enter L_1, L_2. This will result in LinReg($a + bx$) L_1, L_2
- Don't forget the comma
- Press **ENTER**

This option will show a, b, r², and r for the regression line y = a + bx at r.

This gives $r = 0.9249$, so there is a very *strong positive linear relationship* between the heights of the fathers and the heights of their sons because r is very close to 1.

TI-83 or TI-84:

To get summary statistics for bivariate data:
- Enter X-values into L_1
- Enter corresponding Y-values into L_2
- Choose **STAT** → **CALC** → **2: 2-Var Stats**
- Enter L_1, L_2. This will result in 2-Var Stats L_1, L_2.
- Press **ENTER**
  This option will provide
  $\overline{X}$, ΣX, ΣX^2, S_X, σ_X, n
  $\overline{Y}$, ΣY, ΣY^2, S_Y, σ_Y
  ΣXY, min X, max X, min Y, max Y
  Use the up arrow and down arrow to scroll up and down the list.

In a scatterplot, when these bivariate data are plotted, or other bivariate data with

a linear relation, it shows a sort of elliptical cloud of points. Lengthwise, the cloud

is centered at $\overline{X}$ and spread approximately in the range of $(\overline{X} - 3s_x, \overline{X} + 3s_x)$.

Widthwise (or heightwise), the cloud is centered at $\overline{Y}$ and spread approximately in the range of $(\overline{Y} - 3s_y, \overline{Y} + 3s_y)$. The inclination of the cloud is determined by the correlation coefficient (or, equivalently, by the slope of the line, as discussed on the next page). The relation between slope of the line (b_1) and the correlation coefficient (r) is given by $b_1 = r\dfrac{S_y}{S_x}$.

Least-Squares Regression Line

Once we have established that the two variables are related to each other, we are often interested in estimating or quantifying the relation between the two variables. When one variable explains or causes the other, or when one is dependent on the other, estimating a linear regression model can be useful. Such an estimate can be useful for predicting the corresponding values of one variable for known values of the other variable.

A **linear regression model** or **linear regression equation** is an equation that gives a straight line relationship between two variables.

The linear relation between two variables is given by the following equation for the regression line

$$Y = \beta_0 + \beta_1 X + \varepsilon$$

where

- Y is the **dependent variable** or **response variable**.

- X is the **independent variable** or **explanatory variable**.

- β_0 is the **y-intercept**. It is the value of Y for $X = 0$.

- β_1 is the **slope** of the line. It gives the amount of change in Y for every unit change in X.

- ε is the random error. This general term accounts for everything besides what is accounted for by the predicted model, $Y = \beta_0 + \beta_1 X$. In the case of one point, the error or residual is represented by e, and it is the difference between the observed and predicted value. For example, suppose that, using some weather models, the weather station predicted that today's highest temperature would be 75 degrees Fahrenheit. At the end of the day, the highest temperature recorded was 78 degrees. Here, the predicted temperature is 75 degrees whereas the observed temperature is 78 degrees. The difference $78 - 75 = 3$ is the residual, e. In this case, the day's high temperature was underpredicted. The goal of the linear regression, then, is to reduce e to make the model predict the observed values as closely as possible.

The **predicted value** of Y for a given value of X is denoted by $\hat{y}$ (read as "y-hat"). It is computed using the estimated regression line

$$\hat{y} = a + bx$$

where $a = \hat{\beta}_0$ = the estimated y-intercept of the regression line and $b = \hat{\beta}_1$ = the estimated slope of the regression line.

Error or residual = $e = (y - \hat{y})$ = observed value of Y for a given value of X – predicted value of Y for a given value of X.

The **least-squares regression line** is a line that minimizes the sum of the squares of the residuals. It is also known as the line of best fit. The line of best fit will always pass through the point $(\overline{X}, \overline{Y})$.

The coefficient of determination measures the percent of variation in Y-values explained by the linear relation between X- and Y-values. In other words, it measures the percent of variation in Y-values attributable to the variation in X-values. It is denoted by R^2 (R-squared). It can be shown that, for a linear regression, R^2 is equal to the square of the Pearson's correlation coefficient. Note that $0 \le R^2 \le 1$ always.

Example 19: A random sample of 10 office assistants hired within the last six months was selected from a large company. Each assistant's experience (in months) at the time of hire and annual starting salary (in thousands of dollars) were recorded. The data is given in the table below:

Experience (in months)	Starting Salary (in 1,000 dollars)
5	28
12	34
2	24
0	19
2	24
10	32
5	25
1	20
10	29
5	26

(a) Compute the slope for the line of best fit. Interpret it.

(b) Compute the *y*-intercept of the line of best fit. Interpret it.

(c) Find the equation of the least-squares regression line to estimate starting salary using experience.

(d) Plot the line of best fit in a scatterplot.

(e) Predict the starting salary for an office assistant with six months of prior experience.

(f) What is the residual for the worker hired with 12 months experience?

(g) Compute the coefficient of determination. Interpret it.

Solution: In this example, note that the starting salary (in thousands of dollars) depends on the worker's experience (in months). It would make little sense to say that experience depended on starting salary! Therefore, starting salary is the *dependent,* or *response,* variable and experience is the *independent,* or *explanatory,* variable. There are 10 pairs of measurements. The scatterplot of the data is shown in Figure 35.

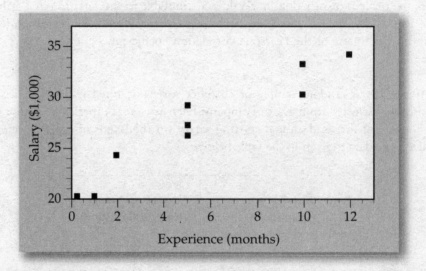

Figure 35: Scatterplot showing starting salary and experience of office assistants

The scatterplot shows that there is a *strong positive linear relationship* between the starting salary of office assistants and their prior experience.

From the data, compute: $n = 10$

TI-83 or TI-84:

To compute least-squares estimates of the slope (b), y-intercept (a), and coefficient of determination (r^2) for the line $y = a + bx$:

- Enter X-values into L_1
- Enter corresponding Y-values into L_2
- Choose **STAT → CALC → 8: LinReg(a + bx)**
- Enter L_1, L_2. This will display LinReg(a + bx) L_1, L_2
- Press **ENTER**

  This option will show a, b, r², r.

(a) Compute the estimated slope:

$\hat{\beta}_1 = b = \dfrac{SS_{xy}}{SS_{xx}} = \dfrac{171.8}{157.6} = 1.09$ is the estimated slope of the line of best fit.

For every month's additional experience at the time of hiring, the starting salary increases on the average by $1,090.

(b) Compute the estimated y-intercept:

$\hat{\beta}_0 = a = \overline{Y} - b\overline{X} = 26.1 - 1.09(5.2) = 20.432$ is the estimated y-intercept of the line of best fit.

The predicted starting salary of inexperienced (experience = 0 months) office assistants is $20,432.

(c) The equation of the least-squares regression line (or line of best fit) is: starting salary = 20.432 + 1.09 (experience)

(d) The scatterplot shown in Figure 36 shows the line of best fit superimposed on it.

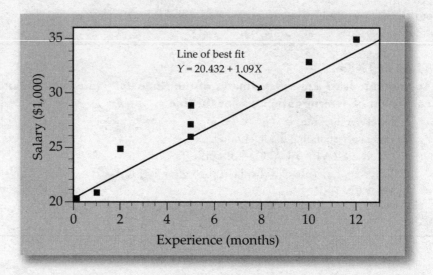

Figure 36: Line of best fit

(e) The office assistant has six months of prior experience. For X = six months: starting salary = 20.432 + 1.09(experience) = 20.432 + 1.09(6) = 26.972. The estimated starting salary for an office assistant with six months of prior experience is $26,972.

(f) The data show that an office assistant with 12 months of experience received $34,000 as a starting salary. The predicted salary is 20.432 + 1.09(12) = 33.512, i.e., $33,512. So, the residual = observed − predicted = 34,000 − 33,512 = 488. It means this office assistant received $488 more than the expected starting salary.

(g) The correlation coefficient is

$$r = \frac{SS_{xy}}{\sqrt{(SS_{xx})(SS_{yy})}} = \frac{171.8}{\sqrt{(157.6)(206.9)}} = 0.9514$$

So, the coefficient of determination = R^2 = $(0.9514)^2$ = 0.9052, i.e., 90.52%.

90.52 percent of the variation among starting salaries is attributable to prior experience. So there is still about 9.5 percent of variation among salaries that remains unexplained. It may be due to some other factors such as education, gender, the person the assistant is working for, etc.

Figure 37 shows the observed Y-value, the line of best fit, and the residual for one pair of values.

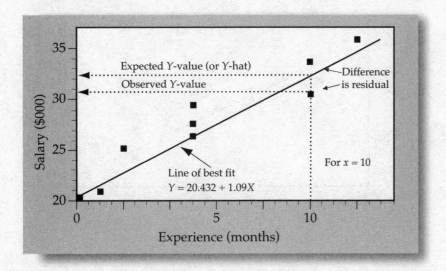

Figure 37: Plot showing observed and expected Y-values and the residual

---

TI-83 or TI-84:
To get a regression line superimposed on a scatterplot:
- Enter X-values into L_1
- Enter corresponding Y-values into L_2
- Choose **STAT → CALC → 8: LinReg(a + bx)**
- Enter L_1, L_2, Y_1. This will display: LinReg(a + bx) L_1,L_2,Y_1

To get Y_1, use the following sequence of commands.
- Choose **VARS → Y-VARS → 1: Function → 1: Y_1**
- Press **ENTER**
- Press **GRAPH**

Outliers and Influential Points

As discussed earlier, an **outlier** is an observation that is surprisingly different from the rest of the data—in other words, an observation that does not conform to the general trend. An **influential observation** is an observation that strongly affects a statistic. Some outliers are influential, others are not. If there is a considerable difference between the correlation coefficients computed with and without a specific observation, then that observation is influential. The same can be said about the line of best fit. If the estimates of the line of best fit change considerably when including or excluding a point, then that point is an influential observation.

Look at the following plots for examples of outlier points, shown in Figure 38.

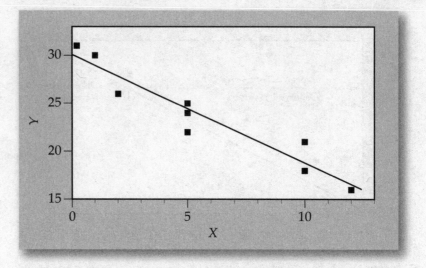

Figure 38: Scatterplot showing no outliers

This scatterplot shows no outliers. It demonstrates a strong negative linear relation between X and Y.

$$r = -0.951$$
$$R^2 = 0.905 \text{ or } 90.5\%$$

The line of best fit is $Y = 29.57 - 1.09X$

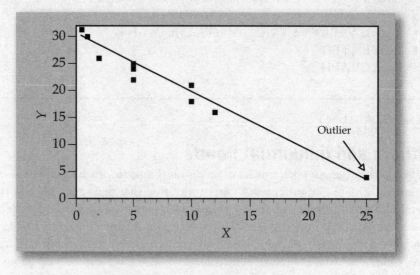

Figure 39: Scatterplot with an outlier

This scatterplot shows a very strong negative linear relation between X and Y. It also shows one outlier, which confirms the trend shown by the other observations. This outlier strengthens the relation between X and Y, but it is not an influential point because it does not change the parameter estimates.

$$r = -0.982$$
$$R^2 = 0.964 \text{ or } 96.4\%$$

The line of best fit is $Y = 29.31 - 1.03X$

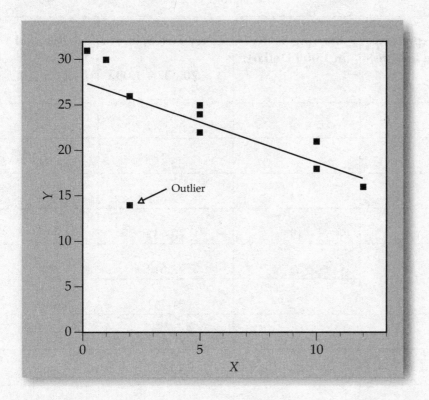

Figure 40: Scatterplot with an outlier

This scatterplot shows a strong negative linear relation between X and Y. But it also shows one outlier. This outlier weakens the strength of the relation between X and Y. It is an influential point, because it does considerably change the parameter estimates. R^2 is now much lower, the intercept is slightly lower, and the slope is much lower.

$$r = -0.643$$
$$R^2 = 0.414 \text{ or } 41.4\%$$

The line of best fit is $Y = 27.21 - 0.86X$

Residual Plots

A **residual plot** is a plot of residuals versus the predicted values of Y. This type of plot is used to assess the fit of the model. A residual plot should look random. If the residual plot shows any patterns or trends, it is an indication that the linear model is not appropriate.

Example 20: Refer to the earlier example of the office assistants. Compute the predicted values and the residual for each observed X-value.

Experience (in Months) X	Starting Salary (in 1,000 Dollars) Y	Predicted Salary $\hat{Y} = 20.432 + 1.09X$	Residual $e = Y - \hat{Y}$
5	28	25.882	2.118
12	34	33.512	0.488
2	24	22.612	1.388
0	19	20.432	−1.432
2	24	22.612	1.388
10	32	31.332	0.668
5	25	25.882	−0.882
1	20	21.522	−1.522
10	29	31.332	−2.332
5	26	25.882	0.118

TI-83 or TI-84: To get a residual plot
- Enter X values into L_1
- Enter corresponding Y-values into L_2
- Choose **STAT** → **CALC** → **8: LinReg(a + bx)**
- Enter L_1, L_2, Y_1. This will result in LinReg(a + bx) L_1, L_2, Y_1

To get Y_1, use the following sequence of commands:
- Choose **VARS** → **Y-VARS** → **1: Function** → **1: Y_1** Press **ENTER**

This will store the regression equation in Y_1.
- On TI-84, use LIST/NAMES and choose RESID.
- On TI-83, create a new column for residuals titled RESDL.
- Take the cursor to this new column title. This will allow you to define the column. Enter $L_2 - Y_1(L_1)$. This command will fill the column titled RESDL with residuals.
- Press **ENTER** to compute residuals for the above estimated line.

To plot the computed residuals (on both TI-83 and TI-84):
- Choose **Y =**
- In this screen, deselect regression equation \Y_1 by moving the cursor over the = symbol and pressing **ENTER**
- In this screen, set \Y_2 = 0
- Choose **2nd** → **STAT PLOT** → **1: Plot1**
- Turn Plot1 Off by highlighting **OFF** and pressing **ENTER**
- Choose **2nd** → **STAT PLOT** → **2: Plot2**
- Turn Plot2 On by highlighting **ON** and pressing **ENTER**
- Choose scatterplot by highlighting the picture of a scatterplot under Type and pressing **ENTER**
- Enter Xlist: L_1
- Enter Ylist: RESDL (*On a TI-84, enter LIST/NAMES/RESID here instead*)
- Select type of marking from the three available marks
- Choose **ZOOM** → **9: ZoomStat**
- Use **TRACE** option to trace points in the scatterplot

Transformations to Achieve Linearity

Always draw a scatterplot of the data to examine the nature of the relation between two variables. You should also examine the fit of the linear model using a residual plot. If either one of these plots indicates that the linear model might not be appropriate for the data, then there are two options available: You can either use **nonlinear models**, which are not tested on the AP exam, or use a **transformation** to achieve linearity. For example, if the data seems to have a relation of the nature $Y = aX^b$, then we can take the logarithm of both sides to get $\ln(Y) = \ln(a) + b\ln(X)$. This gives the equation of a straight line—in other words, a linear relation.

After the variables have been appropriately transformed, we can then use them to make a model. For example, we could take the natural log of all Y-values ($Z = \ln(Y)$) or the square root (square root is the most commonly applied power transformation) of all Y-values ($Z = \sqrt{Y}$). Then we would fit the model for Z as a function of X. When using a fitted model for predictions, remember to transform the predicted values back to the original scale using a reverse transformation. For example, when using the transformation $Z = \ln(Y)$ to get $\hat{Z} = a + bX$, you would need to use the reverse transformation of $\hat{Y} = e^{\hat{z}}$ for predictions. If using the transformation $Z = \sqrt{Y}$ to get $\hat{Z} = a + bX$, you would need to use the reverse transformation of $\hat{Y} = (\hat{Z})^2$ for predictions.

Here are some examples of transformations:

- The **log transformation** ($Z = \ln(Y)$) is used to linearize the regression model when the relationship between Y and X suggests a model with a consistently increasing slope.

- The **square root transformation** ($Z = \sqrt{Y} = Y^{\frac{1}{2}}$) is used when the spread of observations increases with the mean.

- The **reciprocal transformation** ($Z = \frac{1}{Y^1}$) is used to minimize the effect of large values of X.

- The **square transformation** ($Z = Y^2$) is used when the slope of the relation consistently decreases as the independent variable increases.

- The **power transformation** ($\ln(Y)$ and $\ln(X)$) is used if the relation between dependent and independent variables is modeled by $Y = aX^b$.

TI-83 or TI-84:
To use power transformation
This procedure will fit the model equation $Y = aX^b$ to the data using transformed values of $\ln(X)$ and $\ln(Y)$. In other words, the line $\ln(Y) = \ln(a) + b\ln(X)$ will be fitted to the data.
- Enter X-values into L_1
- Enter corresponding Y-values into L_2
- Choose **STAT → CALC → A: PwrReg**
- Enter L_1, L_2. This will display PwrReg L_1, L_2
- Press **ENTER**

TI-83 or TI-84:

To use logarithmic transformation

This procedure will fit the model equation $Y = a + b\ln(X)$ to the data using transformed values of $\ln(X)$ and Y. In other words, line $Y = a + b\ln(X)$ will be fitted to the data.

- Enter X-values into L_1
- Enter corresponding Y-values into L_2
- Choose **STAT → CALC → 9: LnReg**
- Enter L_1, L_2. This will display LnReg L_1, L_2
- Press **ENTER**

TI-83 or TI-84:

To use exponential transformation

This procedure will fit the model equation $Y = ab^X$ to the data using the X-values and the transformed values of $\ln(Y)$. In other words, the line $\ln(Y) = \ln(a) + X \ln(b)$ will be fitted to the data.

- Enter X-values into L_1
- Enter corresponding Y-values into L_2
- Choose **STAT → CALC → 0: ExpReg**
- Enter L_1, L_2. This will display ExpReg L_1, L_2
- Press **ENTER**

Example 21: A mathematics teacher is studying the relationship between the time children spend on computational drills and their scores on a particular standardized test. She divides students into 10 different groups. Each group spends a particular amount of time on computational drills. All students take the same standardized test after the computational drills. Their average score on the standardized test and the time they spent on computational drills are recorded in the following table.

Time (in Minutes)	Mean Score
25	45
30	56
50	68
60	87
75	89
80	96
100	105
110	112
125	118
130	126

Table 5: Average time and mean score

In this example, the scores on the standardized tests depend on the time spent on the computational drills. So time is the *independent* variable, and the score on the test is the *dependent* variable. A scatterplot and line of best fit of the data and the residual plot for a linear fit are shown in Figures 41 and 42.

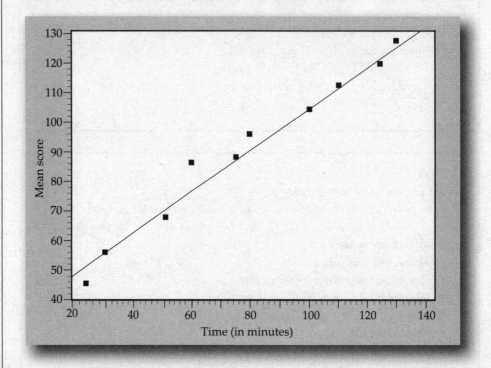

Figure 41: Scatterplot for time versus score

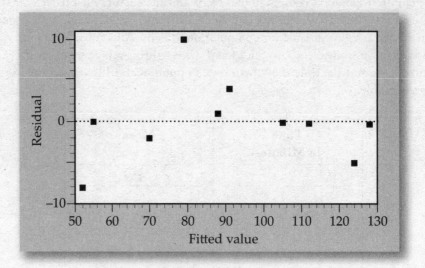

Figure 42: Residual plot for score versus time

Note that the scatterplot shows a slight curvature. Also, note that the residual plot shows a nonrandom pattern. The low and high fitted values have negative residuals, while moderate y-values have positive residuals, indicating that the line model is not a good fit for this data. Let's try a square root transformation. First, take the square root of the time. See Table 6.

Time (in Minutes)	$\sqrt{\text{Time}}$	Mean Score
25	5.0000	45
30	5.4772	56
50	7.0711	68
60	7.7460	87
75	8.6603	89
80	8.9443	96
100	10.0000	105
110	10.4881	112
125	11.1803	118
130	11.4018	126

Table 6: Transformed data

Now, let's make a scatterplot of score versus square root of time (see Figure 43). Also fit a line using square root of time as an independent variable and score as a dependent variable. Make a residual plot for the fit (see Figure 44).

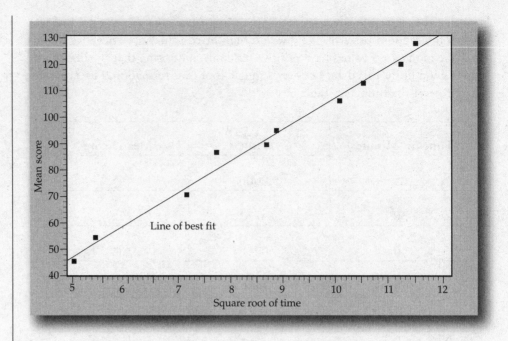

Figure 43: Scatterplot of transformed data

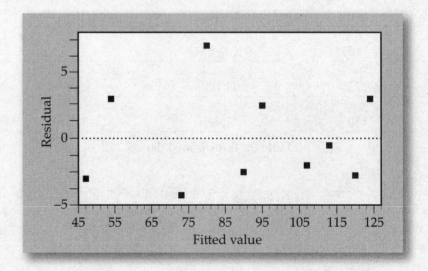

Figure 44: Residual plot for line fitted to transformed data

Now the scatterplot shows a very strong linear pattern. The residual plot shows no pattern, just randomly scattered residuals, which indicates that a line fit is good. The estimated line of best fit is

$$\text{score} = -11.2 + 11.8\sqrt{\text{time}}$$

with

$$R^2 = 0.984 \text{ or } 98.4\%$$

Suppose we are interested in predicting the mean score of students who do computational drills for 60 minutes. Then we would calculate:

$$\text{score} = -11.2 + 11.8 \sqrt{\text{time}} = -11.2 + 11.8 \sqrt{60} = 80.2$$

EXPLORING CATEGORICAL DATA: FREQUENCY TABLES

Remember that categorical data is data classified into different categories. We computed a frequency table for categorical data earlier in this chapter in the example regarding students' different types of housing. In that case, there was only one type of category used, namely, type of housing.

Data can also be classified into two categories simultaneously. For example:

- Students might be classified by gender (male or female) and their student status (freshman, sophomore, junior, or senior).
- Senators might be classified by party affiliation (Democrat or Republican) and their vote on a specific bill (yea or nay).
- Teachers might be classified by the type of college they belong to (Arts & Sciences, Engineering, Education, or Business) and their position (assistant professor, associate professor, or professor).
- Items produced by a factory might be classified by their batch number and their quality status (defective or nondefective).
- Car accidents might be classified by the number of vehicles involved and the cause of the accident.

Marginal and Joint Frequencies of Two-Way Tables

Suppose data is classified by two different criteria. If the classification criterion 1 has r categories and the classification criterion 2 has c categories, then the classification of data results in a table with r rows and c columns.

A table of data classified by r categories of classification criterion 1 and c categories of classification criterion 2 is known as an $r \times c$ **contingency table**.

Suppose 200 students were classified by gender and academic major. The data resulted in a 2 × 4 contingency table, shown in Table 7.

		Academic Major			
		Arts	Sciences	Engineering	Education
Gender	Female	35	15	5	25
	Male	10	40	50	20

Table 7: 2 × 4 contingency table

The table shows that:

- 35 female students are majoring in arts.
- 10 male students are majoring in arts.
- 15 female students are majoring in sciences.

The figures above are joint frequencies of respective categories. The **joint frequency** of two categories is the frequency with which two categories, one from each of the two classification criteria, occur together.

Let's compute row totals and column totals. See Table 8:

		Academic Major				Row Totals
		Arts	Sciences	Engineering	Education	
Gender	Female	35	15	5	25	80
	Male	10	40	50	20	120
Column Totals		45	55	55	45	200

Table 8: 2 × 4 contingency table with row and column totals

This table shows that:

- There are 80 female students in this study.
- There are 120 male students in this study.
- Out of the 200 students in this study, 45 are majoring in arts subjects.
- Out of the 200 students in this study, 55 are majoring in science subjects.
- Out of the 200 students in this study, 55 are majoring in engineering subjects.
- Out of the 200 students in this study, 45 are majoring in education subjects.

These row and column totals give the marginal frequencies for these two categories. The **marginal frequency** is the frequency with which each category occurs.

Conditional Relative Frequencies and Association

From the above contingency table we can see that:

- Among female students, $\frac{35}{80}$ or 43.75 percent are majoring in arts subjects. In other words, the conditional percentage of arts majors among female students is 43.75 percent.

- Among male students, $\frac{50}{120}$ or 41.67 percent are majoring in engineering subjects. In other words, the conditional percentage of engineering majors among male students is 41.67 percent.

- Among science majors, $\frac{15}{55}$ or 27.27 percent are females. In other words, the conditional percentage of female students among the science majors is 27.27 percent.

- Among education majors, $\frac{20}{45}$ or 44.44 percent are males. In other words, the conditional percentage of male students among the education majors is 44.44 percent.

The **conditional relative frequency** is the relative frequency of one category given that the other category has occurred. This frequency is used to determine whether there is an association between the two classification criteria. To measure the degree of relation between two quantitative variables, we use the concept of correlation, which we discussed earlier. On the other hand, to measure the degree of relation between two *categorical* variables, we use the concept of **association**.

If the data above shows a tendency for students of one particular gender to prefer a particular academic major, then we can say that there is *an association* between gender and academic major. If there is *no association* between the two classification criteria, then the expected number of measurements in a given cell of the contingency table is equal to:

$$\frac{(\text{row total})(\text{column total})}{\text{total number of measurements}}$$

For example, if there is not an association between gender and the academic major of students, then the expected number of female students majoring in sciences would be $\frac{(80)(55)}{200} = 22$. We can compare the expected frequency with the observed frequency to determine if there is an association between the two categories:

- For female students majoring in sciences:

  expected cell count = 22 > observed cell count = 15

  So we can say that there is a *negative association* between being female and majoring in science. In other words, fewer females tend to choose an academic major in the sciences than would be expected if there were no association between gender and academic major.

- For female students majoring in engineering:

  expected cell count = $\frac{(120)(55)}{200} = 33$ < observed cell count = 50

  So we can say that there is a *positive association* between being female and majoring in engineering. In other words, more females tend to choose an academic major in engineering than we would expect if there were no association between gender and academic major.

CHAPTER 4 REVIEW QUESTIONS

Multiple-Choice Questions
Answers can be found at the end of this section.

1. Which of the following is a qualitative variable?

    I. The mean income of teachers in Pennsylvania.
    II. The types of desserts available at a restaurant.
    III. The colors of cars in a parking lot.

    (A) I
    (B) II
    (C) III
    (D) I & II
    (E) II & III

2. Given the following frequency distribution of the colors of cars in a parking lot, what is the relative frequency of blue cars?

Color of Cars	Number of Cars with that Color
Red	36
White	27
Blue	45
Green	12
Black	30

    (A) 0.08
    (B) 0.18
    (C) 0.20
    (D) 0.24
    (E) 0.30

    $\dfrac{45}{tot}$

3. A researcher takes a sample of 3000 flowers and measures their heights. Which is the best way to represent the data?

    (A) bar chart
    (B) stemplot
    (C) histogram
    (D) pie chart
    (E) dotplot

4. Which of the following data sets has the largest standard deviation?

    (A) {1,4,7,10,13}
    (B) {1,1,3,5,5}
    (C) {1,3,5,7,9}
    (D) {1,2,3,4,5}
    (E) {1,1,1,1,1}

5. Which measure of center is best for skewed data?

    (A) mean
    (B) median
    (C) standard deviation
    (D) interquartile range
    (E) mode

6. Calculate the IQR for the following data.

1	3	13	7	6	11	5	2	9	3
16	2	4	8	9	11	11	1	6	3

    (A) 8
    (B) 13
    (C) 4
    (D) 15
    (E) 3

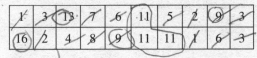

1,1,2,2,3,3,3,4,5,6,6,7,8,9,9

11,11,11,13,16.

21

3,10

7. A teacher grades her students' recent tests and computes the mean and median: 84 and 86, respectively. While going over the test, she realized her key had an error. To correct for it, she added 4 points to everyone's score. What are the new mean and median of the class?

    (A) Mean: 84; Median: 86
    (B) Mean: 88; Median: 86
    (C) Mean: 88; Median: 90
    (D) Mean: 84; Median: 90
    (E) Mean: 86; Median: 88

8. Which of the following does NOT show a positive correlation?

(A)

X	Y
0	4
1	8
2	12

(B)

X	Y
0	0
1	10
2	20

(C)

X	Y
0	0
1	1
2	2

(D)

X	Y
0	3
1	4
2	2

(E)

X	Y
0	0
1	2
2	6

9. Which of the following is an example of a categorical variable?

(A) mother's height in inches
(B) gross income in 2015
(C) favorite color
(D) high school GPA
(E) IQ

Free-Response Questions

10. A random sample of 10 students studying for the AP Statistics exam was taken from a large school. Each student's time studying for the class final (in hours) before the AP exam was recorded along with their scores (out of 100) on the exam. The data is presented in the table below:

Time Studied (hours)	2	10	6	8	5	4	8	7	4	2
Score	60	95	78	88	72	73	82	86	75	63

   a. Find the equations of the least square regression line to estimate scores using hours studied and interpret it.
   b. Predict the score of a student who studied 3 hours.
   c. Compute the coefficient of determination. Interpret it.

a. $\widehat{score} = 55.043 + 3.957 (\text{time studied})$

For every hour studied, the score increases by 3.957 points from 55.043, which represents a predicted score w/ no studying.

b. $\widehat{score} = 55.043 + 3.957(3)$
$\widehat{score} = 66.914 \approx 67$

c. $r^2 = 0.932$ This is the proportion of variability of the scores from the time studied.

11. The summary statistics for the number of inches of snow in Coldland for 116 years is shown below.

N	Mean	Median	St. Dev.	Min.	Max.	Q1	Q3
116	9.264	10.364	1.172	6.213	1.4578	8.746	12.379

   a. Describe a procedure that uses this information to determine whether there are outliers.
   b. Are there outliers? Justify using the procedure described in part (a).

a. Any value that is 1.5 IQR from the below the 1st quartile or above the 3rd quartile is an outlier.

CHAPTER 4 ANSWERS AND EXPLANATIONS

1. **E** A qualitative variable is a variable that is defined by a quality or feature of the data, not a numerical value. The mean income of teachers in Pennsylvania is a numerical value ($24,000, $12,500, $22,564.34, etc.), so it is quantitative. The types of desserts available at a restaurant will be a list of the kinds of desserts (ice cream, cake, pie, etc.), and cannot be described by numbers. The colors of cars in a parking lot will also be a list of the colors seen (red, blue, green, etc.), and cannot be described by numbers.

2. **E** The relative frequency is equal to the frequency of one case/total sample size. Therefore, Relative Frequency of Blue Cars $= \dfrac{45}{36+27+45+12+30} = \dfrac{45}{150} = 0.30$.

3. **C** The sample size is fairly large. For large sample sizes, histograms are a good representation of the data because you can see the patterns in the data, outliers, approximate center, and spread. There is too much data to be easily displayed on a stemplot or dot plot, and the data is continuous, not categorical, so neither a bar chart nor a pie chart would be appropriate.

4. **A** Standard deviation is a measure of the variation or the spread of the data, so you can quickly determine which data set has the largest standard deviation by examining which data set is the most spread out by comparing the ranges and how close the individual data points are to each other. This is only a shortcut for comparison and NOT an exact approach. Therefore, to know for sure you can use the formula for standard deviation of a population, $\sigma = \sqrt{\dfrac{\sum_{i=1}^{N}(X_i - \mu)^2}{N}}$, or the formula for standard deviation of a sample, $s = \sqrt{\dfrac{\sum_{i=1}^{N}(X_i - \bar{X})^2}{n-1}}$.

5. **B** Skewed data means that there is a shift in the data favoring one end, so the distribution has a "tail," The mean is influenced by "tails," i.e. one small or one large value can shift the mean toward that value. Median is located at the 50th percentile, so it divides the data in half. It is not affected by the actual values in each half, just that the data is split in half, so it is good for skewed data. The standard deviation and interquartile range are not measures of center; they are both measures of variation. The mode is neither a measure of center nor variation; it is simply the most frequently seen value.

6. **A** To determine the interequartile range (IQR), you must find the difference between the first and the third quartiles. First, arrange the data in order from smallest to largest: 1, 1, 2, 2, 3, 3, 3, 4, 5, 6, 6, 7, 8, 9, 9, 11, 11, 11, 13, 16. Next, determine the position of the value at the first and the third quartiles. The first quartile is at P_{25} and its position is at $l = \dfrac{(20+1)25}{100} = 5.25$. Similarly, the third quartile is at P_{75} and its position is at $l = \dfrac{(20+1)75}{100} = 15.75$. Therefore, you must determine the value at the 5.25th position beginning with the least value and the value at the 15.75th position beginning with the least value. At the 5th and 6th positions the values are both 3, so at the 5.25th position, the value is 3. At the 15th and 16th positions the values are both 11, so at the 15.75th position, the value is 11. Finally, the IQR is determine to be the difference between these two values. Thus, the IQR is 11 − 3 = 8.

7. **C** If you add a positive constant to every data point in a sample or population, then the measures of center (mean and median) will increase by the value of that constant, respectively. In this problem, every student had 4 points added to their score, so the mean and median each increased by four points.

8. **D** A positive correlation between two variables is present when two variables increase together or decrease together. Since we only have three data points of each set, we must assume that none are outliers and take each into consideration. Table A shows that each value of Y increases with each value of X. This is also true in tables B, C, and E. Table D has an initial increase in Y with X, but then Y decreases, so the correlation is not positive.

9. **C** In order to answer this question, you need to know the difference between categorical, or qualitative, or quantitative, or numerical variables. Here, since choices (A), (B), (D), and (E) are all numerical in nature, they can be eliminated. Favorite color, however, is qualitative in nature. For example, one's favorite color will be blue, black, or red, rather than a quantitative value. Thus, choice (C) is the correct answer.

10.   a.   Use your calculator to calculate the equation. By hand, use the equations:
$$\hat{y} = b_0 + b_1 x, \quad b_1 = \frac{\sum (x_i - \bar{x})(y_i - \bar{y})}{\sum (x_i - \bar{x})^2}, \text{ and } b_0 = \bar{y} - b_1 \bar{x}.$$ Use the data to calculate b_0 and b_1 and then plug those values into $\hat{y} = b_0 + b_1 x$. Either way, $b_1 = 3.957$ and $b_0 = 55.044$. Thus, the equation for the least-squares regression line is: score = 55.044 + 3.957 (time studied). This can be interpreted as: For every hour spent studying, a student's score will increase by 3.957 points above a score of 55.044 points (the score of someone who didn't study).

b. Use the least-squares regression line from part (a) and evaluate the equation when time studied = 3. So, score = 55.044 + 3.957(3) = 66.913. A student who studies three hours will score 66.913 points on the final exam.

c. The coefficient of determination is the square of the correlation coefficient. Therefore, you can use your calculator data or calculate r from the data: $r = \dfrac{1}{n-1}\sum\left(\dfrac{x_i - \bar{x}}{s_x}\right)\left(\dfrac{y_i - \bar{y}}{s_y}\right) = 0.9654$. Thus, $r^2 = 0.9321$. The statement to explain this could be: 93.21% of the variance among test scores is explained by the hours studied.

11. a. Using the Q_1 and Q_3 values, outliers can be calculated. Outliers are values that are less than L, where $L = Q_1 - 1.5 IQR$, or greater than U, where $U = Q_3 + 1.5 IQR$.

b. $L = 8.746 - 1.5(12.379 - 8.746) = 3.2965$

$U = 12.379 + 1.5(12.379 - 8.746) = 17.8285$

Because the minimum and maximum values are not less than L or greater than U, there are no outliers in this data set.

Chapter 5
Sampling and
Experimentation

PLANNING A STUDY

If you want to draw valid conclusions from a study, you must collect the data according to a well-developed plan. This plan must include the question or questions to be answered, as well as an appropriate method of data collection and analysis. This chapter discusses various techniques for planning a study. In the multiple-choice section, this topic appears in four to six out of 40 questions. In the free-response section, this topic usually appears in one out of six questions.

OVERVIEW OF METHODS OF DATA COLLECTION

Terms and Concepts

- A **population** is the entire group of individuals or items that we are interested in.

- A **frame** (or sampling frame) is a list of all members of the population—for example, a list of all account holders in a bank, a list of participants in the Boston Marathon in the year 2010, etc.

- A **sample** is the part of the population that is actually being examined.

- A **sample survey** is the process of collecting information from a sample. Information obtained from the sample is usually used to make inferences about population parameters.

- A **census** is the process of collecting information from all the units in a population. It is feasible to do a census if the population is small and the process of getting information does not destroy or modify units of the population. For example, if a school principal wants to know the educational background of the parents of all the children in his school, he can gather this information from every one of the school children. It is possible to do a census of a large population, as with the United States Census, but it requires a huge amount of work, time, and money.

As the following examples show, there are many situations in which a census is impossible or impractical:

- An advisor to a candidate for governor wants to determine how much support his candidate has in the state. Suppose the state has 4 million eligible voters. It would clearly be too time-consuming to contact each and every voter in this state, and even if it were accomplished, by the time the census was finished, the level of support for the candidate might have changed.

- Suppose an environmentalist is interested in determining the amount of toxins in a lake. Using a census would mean emptying the lake and testing all the water in the lake—obviously not a good way to gather information!

- A manufacturer of light bulbs is interested in determining the mean lifetime of 60-watt bulbs produced by his factory. Using a census would mean burning all the light bulbs produced in the factory and measuring their lifetimes. Again, a census would not be practical here.

Clearly, a census is often too costly or too time-consuming, and sometimes damaging to the population being studied. We usually have to take samples instead. How to get those samples is the subject of this chapter.

Experiments and Observational Studies

An **experiment** is a planned activity that results in measurements (data or observations). In an experiment, the experimenter *creates* differences in the variables involved in the study and then observes the effects of such differences on the resulting measurements. For example, suppose a team of engineers at an automotive factory runs cars at different predetermined and controlled speeds and then crashes the cars at a specific site. Then, the engineers measure the damage to the cars' bumpers. In this example, the team of engineers *creates* the differences in the environment by running the cars at different speeds. To sum up, in an experiment, the experimenter assigns a treatment to each subject rather than allowing subjects to make their own choices.

An **observational study** is an activity in which the experimenter *observes* the relationships among variables rather than creating them. For example, suppose an engineering student collects information from car accident reports filed by the local police department. The reports tell the student how fast the cars were traveling when the crashes occurred and how much damage was done to the cars' bumpers. In this example, the experimenter (the student) has no control over the speed of the car. The student observes the differences in speeds as recorded in the reports and the results of the crashes as measured by the amount of damage to the bumpers.

Experiments have some advantages, described below, but unfortunately, in some situations it is impossible, impractical, or unethical to conduct an experiment. Sometimes we must instead use an observational study. For example:

- To study the effect of smoking on people's lungs, an experiment would require that the experimenter assign one group of people to smoke and another group not to smoke. But it is clearly unethical to ask some people to smoke so that the damage to their lungs can be measured, and it may not be possible to force a smoker to quit.

- Certain inherited traits affect patients' reaction to medicine. However, it is not possible to create different genetic traits in different patients; they are born with those traits. An experiment in this situation would be impossible.

One of the problems with observational studies is that their results often cannot be generalized to a population because many observational studies use samples (such as volunteers or hospitalized patients) that aren't representative of the population of interest. These samples might simply be easiest to obtain. This problem can be solved by observing hospitalized as well as nonhospitalized patients. Another problem is that of **confounding factors**. Confounding occurs when the two variables of interest are related to a third variable instead of just to each other. For instance, in a study of elementary school children, taller students know more words. The confounding factor here is age; taller students are older, and older students know more words.

PLANNING AND CONDUCTING SURVEYS

Getting Samples

There are many methods of getting a sample from the population. Some sampling methods are better than others. **Biased sampling** methods result in values that are systematically different from the population values or systematically favor certain outcomes. **Judgmental sampling, samples of convenience,** and **volunteer samples** are some of the methods that generally result in biased outcomes. Sampling methods that are based on a probabilistic selection of samples, such as **simple random sampling**, generally result in unbiased outcomes.

Biased Samples

Judgmental sampling makes use of a nonrandom approach to determine which item of the population is to be selected in the sample. The approach is entirely based on the judgment of the person selecting the sample. For example, jury selection from an available pool of jurors is not a random process. Lawyers from both parties use their judgment to decide who shall be selected. The result may be a biased jury, i.e., a selection of jurors with specific opinions.

Using a **sample of convenience** is another method that can result in biased outcomes. Samples of convenience are easy to obtain. For example, suppose a real estate agent wants to estimate the mean selling price of houses in a Chicago suburb. To save time, he looks up the selling prices of houses sold in the last three months in the subdivision where he lives. Using his own subdivision may have saved him time, but the sample is not representative of all the houses in that suburb.

Volunteer samples, in which the subjects choose to be part of the sample, may also result in biased outcomes. For example, imagine that a local television station decides to do a survey about a possible tax increase to support the local school system. A telephone number is provided and respondents are asked to call and register their opinions by pressing 1 if they support the tax increase and 2 if they oppose it. The television station then counts the number of 1s and 2s to determine the degree of support for the tax increase. But the station may well have inadvertently introduced bias into the results. Only those who feel very strongly about the tax increase (either for or against) are likely to call the number and register their opinions, so the sample may not reflect the true feelings of the whole population.

Simple Random Sampling

Simple random sampling is a process of obtaining a sample from a population in which each member has an equal chance of being selected. In this type of sample there is no bias or preference for one individual over another. Simple random samples, also known as random samples, are obtained in two different ways:

1. **Sampling with replacement from a finite population.** An example is the process of selecting cards from a deck, provided that you return each card before the next is drawn. With this scheme, the chance of selection remains the same for all cards drawn—one out of 52. If you didn't replace the first card before drawing the second, then the chance of selecting a particular second card would be higher (one out of 51) than the chance of selecting the first one (one out of 52). When two cards are drawn with replacement, the probability of selecting two cards is $(1/52)(1/52) = 0.0003698$, and is the same regardless of the cards selected.

2. **Sampling without replacement from an infinite population** (or a population that is simply very large compared to the sample size)—for example, selecting two voters from a list of 200,000 registered voters in a city. Here the population size (200,000) is quite large compared to the sample size (two). Note that when you're sampling without replacement, the available population size decreases as you continue sampling, but because the population size is so large compared to the sample size, the change in the chance of a particular person getting selected is negligible for practical purposes. The chance of selecting the first voter is one out of 200,000 (that is, 0.000005). Because the sample is being selected without replacement, the chance of selecting the second voter increases slightly, to one out of 199,999 (that is 0.000005000025). But this isn't much of a difference. The chance of selecting two particular voters out of 200,000 *without* replacement is $(0.000005)(0.000005000025) = 2.5000125\text{E-}11$; whereas the chance of selecting the same two out of 200,000 *with* replacement is $(0.000005)(0.000005) = 2.5\text{E-}11$. So for all practical purposes, the chance of selection is the same.

How to Select a Simple Random Sample

To select a simple random sample from a population, we need to use some kind of chance mechanism. Here are some examples:

- Prizes offered at a baseball game. A portion of each ticket collected at the stadium entrance is put in a large box. About halfway through the game, all the ticket stubs in the box are mixed thoroughly. Then a pre-specified number of ticket stubs are picked from the box. The persons sitting in the selected seats (as identified by the ticket stubs) receive prizes.

- A teacher asks each student in a class of 40 to write his or her name on a separate (but identical) piece of paper and drop it in a box. The teacher then mixes thoroughly all the pieces in the box and selects one piece at random, without looking at the name. The student whose name appears on the selected piece of paper is designated as the class representative.

- A teacher wants to select about half of the students in the class for a project, so she asks each student to toss a coin. Those who toss "heads" are selected for the project.

- A kindergarten teacher wants to select five children to perform a song at the holiday party. The teacher puts two kinds of lollipops in a jar, five of them red and the rest green. He then asks each child to take one lollipop from the jar without looking at it. The five children that pick a red lollipop are selected to sing.

The same random result can be achieved by using random number tables. A portion of a random number table is given below:

96410	96335	55249	16141	61826	57992	21382	33971	12082	91970
26284	92797	33575	94150	40006	54881	13224	03812	70400	45585
75797	18618	90593	54825	64520	78493	92474	32268	07392	73286
48600	65342	08640	78370	10781	58660	77819	79678	67621	74961
82468	15036	79934	76903	48376	09162	51320	84504	39332	26922

To demonstrate the use of random number tables, let us again consider the example of the kindergarten teacher. He could number the children using two digit numbers: 01, 02, 03, ..., 50. He would then start anywhere in the random number table and read each pair of numbers sequentially (it doesn't matter whether he reads vertically or horizontally). But the teacher is selecting from only 50 children. So he should ignore 00 and the numbers from 51 to 99. Suppose he began at the fourth line. Then he would get 48, 60, 06, 53, 42, 08, 64, 07, and so on. The child numbered 48 would be selected. The number 60 in the sequence would be ignored. The next selected child would be number 06. Number 53 in the sequence would be ignored, and so on. As a result, children numbered 48, 06, 42, 08, and 07 would be selected to participate in the program.

Computer programs and calculators can generate random numbers.

TI-83 or TI-84: To generate random integers
- Choose **MATH** → **PRB** → **5: randInt(**

  Enter the range of numbers from which to select and the total number of random numbers to generate. Separate the three numbers by commas.

  This will result in: randInt(1, 50, 5)

  Note: The first and second numbers indicate the range of numbers from which to select, and the third number indicates the number of random numbers to generate. In this case, the calculator will generate five numbers between one and 50.

Other Methods of Random Sampling

Besides simple random sampling, there are other sampling procedures that make use of a random phenomenon to get a sample from a population:

- In a **systematic sampling** procedure, the first item is selected at random from the first k items in the frame, and then every k^{th} item is included in the sample. This method is popular among biologists, foresters, environmentalists, and marine scientists.

- In **stratified random sampling**, the population is divided into groups called *strata* (the singular is "stratum") and a simple random sample is selected from each stratum. Strata are homogeneous groups of population units—that is, units in a given stratum are similar in some characteristics, whereas those in different strata differ in those characteristics. For example, students in a university can be grouped into strata by their major. If a population is divided into homogeneous strata, then stratified sampling can be useful in reducing variation; that is, it can help make groups more similar and result in a more powerful test.

- In **proportional sampling**, the population is divided into groups called strata and a simple random sample of size proportional to the stratum size is selected from each stratum. The selection of members of Congress in the U.S. House of Representatives is a good example of proportional sampling; the U.S. Senate, on the other hand, is an example of stratified sampling.

- In **cluster sampling**, a population is divided into nonhomogeneous groups called clusters and a simple random sample is obtained from some clusters, but not necessarily all. In order to safely use cluster sampling, each cluster must be representative of the population as a whole.

BIAS IN SURVEYS

For a survey to produce reliable results, it must be properly designed and conducted. Samples should be selected using a proper randomization technique. A nonrandom selection will limit the generalizability of the results. Furthermore, interviewers should be trained in proper interviewing techniques. The attitude and behavior of the interviewer should not lead to any specific answers, because this would result in a biased outcome. Questions should be carefully worded, as the wording of a question can affect the response, and leading questions should be avoided.

Sampling error is a variation inherent in any survey. Even if a survey is repeated using the same sample size and the same questionnaires, the outcome will be different, if only slightly.

Sources of Bias in Surveys

A survey is biased if it systematically favors certain outcomes. The following are some sources of bias:

- **Response bias** is caused by the behavior of the interviewer or respondent. For example, if high school children are asked in the presence of their parents whether they've ever smoked a cigarette, then they are likely to deny smoking even if they have smoked. It is possible to reduce response bias by carefully training interviewers and supervising the interview process.

- **Nonresponse bias** occurs if the person selected for an interview cannot be contacted or refuses to answer.

- **Undercoverage bias** may occur if part of the population is left out of the selection process. For example, if you conduct a telephone survey, individuals without a telephone are left out of the selection process. In the United States, almost 70 percent of households have a telephone, so only a small percent of the population would be left out of a telephone survey. But in many African countries, less than 4 percent of households have telephones, and those that do are often affluent. A telephone survey there would give biased results. In every U.S. census, a certain percent of the population is missed due to undercoverage. This undercoverage tends to be higher in poorer sections of large cities.

- **Wording effect bias** may occur if confusing or leading questions are asked. For example, imagine an interviewer who says, "The American Dental Association recommends brushing your teeth three times a day. How often do you brush your teeth on a typical day?" The respondents may feel compelled to give an answer of three or more, even if they don't brush their teeth that often. So the responses are likely to be higher than the true average of the population. In this situation, the wording effect bias could be reduced or avoided by simply asking, "How often do you brush your teeth on a typical day?"

PLANNING AND CONDUCTING EXPERIMENTS

Terms and Concepts

- A **dependent** or a **response variable** is the variable to be measured in the experiment. An **independent** or **explanatory variable** is a variable that may explain the differences in responses. We are interested in studying the effect of independent variables on the dependent variables. For example, a dentist is interested in studying the duration of the effects of different amounts of anesthesia. In this case the "amount of anesthesia" is the *explanatory* variable and the "duration of the effect" is the *response* variable.

- An **experimental unit** is the smallest unit of the population to which a treatment is applied. In the above example, each patient receiving a dose of anesthesia is an experimental unit.

- A **confounding variable** is a variable whose effect on the response cannot be separated from the effect of the explanatory variable. In properly constructed experiments, an experimenter tries to control confounding variables. Confounding can be an even more serious problem in observational studies, because the experimenter has no control over the confounding variables. For example, if a new pain medication is tested on women with migraines and men with backaches, any measured differences in pain relief could be due to differences in sex or in the source of the pain. Sex and pain source are confounded.

- A **factor** is a variable whose effect on the response is of interest in the experiment. Factors are of two types: 1) **qualitative**—when studying the effect of education level (as defined by less than high school, high school, undergraduate, and graduate) on the achievement of children, the factor "education level" is a qualitative (or "categorical") factor; 2) **quantitative**—when studying the effect of a car's speed on its stopping distance, the factor "speed" is a quantitative variable. It is possible to redefine quantitative variables into categorical variables. For example, to study the effect of income level on spending power, we can categorize annual incomes by grouping them into less than $10,000, $10,000–$24,999, $25,000–$49,999, $50,000–$99,999, and $100,000 and above.

- **Levels** are the values of a factor used in the experiment. An experiment can have one or more factors. The number of levels used in the experiment may differ from factor to factor. **Treatments** are the factor-level combinations used in the experiment. If the experiment has only one factor, then all the levels of that factor are considered treatments of the experiment.

For example, suppose that there is only one medicine on the market for controlling anxiety, but then two pharmaceutical companies come up with new medicines. A doctor is interested in comparing the effectiveness of the current medicine with that of the two new medicines. Here, "anxiety-controlling medicine" is the only *factor* of interest. There are three *levels* of this medicine, which become three *treatments*, namely, current medicine, new medicine A, and new medicine B.

Now suppose the doctor also wants to determine the effect of two types of breathing exercises along with the medicines. Let us call the exercises Exec 1 and Exec 2. Now this experiment has two factors, one at three levels and one at two levels, as shown in the following table.

	Type of medicine		
Type of exercise	Current medicine	New medicine 1	New medicine 2
Exec 1	X	X	X
Exec 2	X	X	X

Then, as defined earlier, all the factor-level combinations become treatments.

So there are 3 × 2 = 6 treatments of interest to the doctor. They are the following:

1. Current medicine and Exec 1

2. New medicine A and Exec 1

3. New medicine B and Exec 1

4. Current medicine and Exec 2

5. New medicine A and Exec 2

6. New medicine B and Exec 2

- A **control group** is a group of experimental units similar to all the other experimental units except that it is not given any treatment. A control group is used to establish the baseline response expected from experimental units if no treatment is given. For example, the doctor from the example above might want to know what will happen to the anxiety level of patients if no treatment at all (medicine or breathing exercises) is prescribed.

- A **placebo group** is a control group that receives a placebo in experiments involving medicines. A placebo is a medicine that looks exactly like the real medicine but does not contain any active ingredients. The patients will not be able to tell the placebo and the real medicine apart by looking at them. People who do not receive any medicine sometimes have different responses from those who receive a placebo. It seems that just the comforting thought of taking medicine has some effect on patients, even when they are not receiving any active ingredients. In other words, belief in the presence or absence of an active ingredient can have an effect on a patient's reaction.

Single-Blind and Double-Blind Experiments

Similarly, it is possible that measurements will be biased if the person taking the measurements knows whether a patient received a placebo or not. **Blinding technique** is used in medical experiments to prevent such a bias. The blinding technique can be used in two different fashions: double blinding and single blinding. In a **single-blind experiment**, either the patient does not know which treatment he or she is receiving or the person measuring the patient's reaction does not know which treatment was given. In a **double-blind experiment,** both the patient and the person measuring the patient's reaction do not know which treatment the patient was given.

Double-blind experiments are preferred, but in certain situations they simply can't be conducted. For example, in an experiment designed to compare the drop in cholesterol level produced by a certain medication to that produced by going on a particular diet, the patients always know which treatment they are given. You can't hide from them the fact that they have been subjected to just a medication or to a new low-cholesterol diet! So a double-blind experiment would not be possible. But a single-blind experiment would be possible, because the lab technician measuring the patients' cholesterol level does not need to know which treatment the patients have been getting.

Randomization

The technique of randomization is used to average the effects of extraneous factors on responses. In other words, it balances the effects of factors you cannot see.

- If each experimental unit is supposed to receive only one treatment, then which experimental unit receives which treatment should be determined randomly. For example, in the experiment above that compares three anxiety-controlling medicines, the doctor should use some kind of randomization mechanism (such as one of the methods described earlier) to decide which participating patient should get each one of the three medicines.

- If each experimental unit is supposed to receive all treatments, then the order of treatments should be determined randomly for each experimental unit. Suppose the doctor is interested in comparing the effects of all three medicines on each patient. Then for each patient, the doctor should use some kind of randomization mechanism to decide the order in which the three medicines will be given. All participating patients will be given all three medicines with some washout period in between the administration of each medicine. But the order in which the three medicines are given will differ with each patient. Some will get current medicine first, then new medicine A, and then new medicine B. Others will get new medicine B first, then current medicine, and then new medicine A, and so on.

Blocking

The technique of **blocking** is used to control the effects of known factors—factors that you *can* see. A **block** is a group of homogeneous experimental units. Experimental units in a block are similar in certain characteristics, whereas those in different blocks differ in those characteristics. For example, a doctor might suspect that the effect of a certain medicine is different on women than on men. The doctor could then control this potentially confounding factor by separating patients into two groups by gender. There would then be two blocks, male and female. Blocking may reduce unwanted variation in responses, thus allowing the experimenter to see more clearly those differences in responses due to treatments. Essentially, blocking is another way of describing stratification.

Replication

Replication refers to the process of giving a certain treatment numerous times in an experiment or of applying it to a number of different experimental units. Replication reduces chance variation among results. It also allows us to estimate chance variation among results. In the example of comparing three medicines to control anxiety, suppose the doctor prescribes each of three medicines to only one patient each. If the responses of the three patients were different, then we would not know whether the differences were true effects of medicines or due just to chance. Could differences among the patients have led to differences in their responses? Yes, it is possible, but we could not know. What if the doctor were to prescribe each medicine to more than one patient? Each patient could receive one of three treatments selected at random. Then, on the average, the three groups of patients would likely be similar. As the differences among patients are averaged out, the effect of treatment differences will stand out.

Would all patients receiving the same treatment have the same responses? No, not likely. Then how can we explain the differences among the responses of patients receiving the same treatment? The differences are due simply to chance variation among results. Without replication, it would not be possible to estimate this chance variation.

Completely Randomized Design

In a completely randomized design, treatments are assigned randomly to all experimental units or experimental units are assigned randomly to all treatments. This design can compare any number of treatments. There are advantages in having an equal number of experimental units for each treatment, but this is not necessary.

Example 1: Suppose a doctor is interested in comparing an anxiety-controlling drug on the market now (let's call it "current medicine") with two new drugs ("new medicine A" and "new medicine B"). A group of patients from a local clinic is available for the experiment. Design an experiment to compare the effects of these three drugs.

Solution: In this experiment, there is one factor of interest with three levels.

- Factor of interest: anxiety-controlling medicines
- Number of levels: three
- Treatments: current medicine, new medicine A, and new medicine B
- Experimental unit: each patient
- Response variable: the anxiety level measured for each patient

Use the group of patients available from the local clinic and design the experiment as follows:

- Measure the anxiety level of each patient.
- Use a randomization scheme to divide the patients into three groups. For example, throw a six-sided die for each patient. If the numbers 1 or 2 show, then assign the patient to group 1; if the numbers 3 or 4 show, assign the patient to group 2; otherwise, assign to group 3. Or fill a jar with blue, red, and green beads, with the total number of beads equal to the total number of participating patients. Ask each patient to take out one bead without looking in the jar. If the patient selects a blue bead, assign that patient to group 1; if the patient selects a red bead, assign to group 2; if the patient selects a green bead, assign to group 3.
- Prescribe current medicine to all patients in group 1.
- Prescribe new medicine A to all patients in group 2.
- Prescribe new medicine B to all patients in group 3.
- After a designated time period, measure the anxiety level of each patient.
- Compare the results.

This scheme can also be described using the diagram shown in Figure 1.

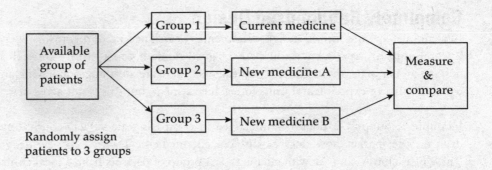

Figure 1: Schematic diagram of a completely randomized experiment

Randomized Block Design

If the treatments are the only systematic differences present in the experiment, then the completely randomized design is best for comparing the responses. But often there are other factors affecting responses. Unless they are controlled, the results will be biased. As we discussed earlier, one way to control the effects of known extraneous factors is to form groups of similar units called blocks. In a randomized block design, all experimental units are grouped by certain characteristics to form homogeneous blocks and then a completely randomized design is applied within each block. The blocking of experimental units allows the experimenter to remove systematic differences in responses due to a known factor and leads to more precise conclusions from the experiment.

If there are only two treatments to be compared in the presence of a blocking factor, then you should use a **randomized paired comparison design**. This can be designed in two different ways:

- Form two or more blocks of two experimental units each. Experimental units within each block should be matched by some relevant characteristics. Within each block, toss a coin to assign two treatments to the two experimental units randomly. In other words, both treatments will be applied within each block, with each experimental unit receiving only one treatment. Because both experimental units are similar to each other except for the treatment received, the differences in responses can be attributed to the differences in treatments. This type of experiment is called a **matched-pairs design**.

- Alternatively, each experimental unit can be used as its own block. Assign both treatments to each experimental unit, but in random order. To control the effect of the order of treatment, randomly determine the order. With each experimental unit, toss a coin to decide if the order of treatments should be treatment 1 → treatment 2 or treatment 2 → treatment 1. Because both treatments are assigned to the same experimental unit, the individual effects of experimental units are nullified, and the differences in responses can be attributed to the differences in treatments.

Example 2: Suppose a doctor wants to compare an anxiety-controlling drug currently on the market (current medicine) with two new drugs (new medicine A and new medicine B). A group of patients from a local clinic is available for the experiment. All three drugs are known to have different effects on men and women. Design an experiment to compare the effects of the three drugs.

Solution: In this experiment, there are two factors of interest: anxiety-controlling medicine and patient's gender. Of these two factors, anxiety-controlling medicine is a *treatment*, whereas patient's gender is a *blocking factor*. Patient responses may be different because of the treatment administered or because of the patient's gender. Separate the available group of patients by gender, so that block 1 consists only of men and block 2 only of women. Now, within each block all the patients are similar (same gender).

Measure the anxiety level of each participating patient. For each male patient, randomly assign one of the three treatments. For example, use a random number table to get one-digit random numbers. Assign numbers {1, 2, 3} to group 1, numbers {4, 5, 6} to group 2, numbers {7, 8, 9} to group 3, and ignore number 0. Then draw a random number for each patient. Separate the patients into three groups depending on the numbers they've drawn. Prescribe the current medicine to patients in group 1, new medicine A to patients in group 2, and new medicine B to patients in group 3. After a designated time, measure the anxiety level of each patient. Repeat this procedure for all female patients. When finished, compare the results. The schematic diagram shown in Figure 2 describes the design.

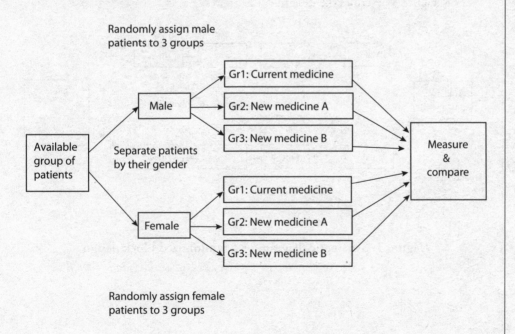

Figure 2: Schematic diagram of a randomized block design

Alternatively, the same experiment could be conducted as follows:

- Separate the available group of patients by gender so that block 1 consists only of men and block 2 only of women. Administer all three medicines to each patient one at a time, with a washout period in between. Determine the order in which the medicines are to be given using a randomization scheme. For example, use a random number table to get random one-digit numbers. Assign number 1 to the current medicine, number 2 to new medicine A, number 3 to new medicine B, and ignore numbers 0, 4, 5, 6, 7, 8, 9. Get two distinct random numbers for each patient to determine the order of medicines. For example, suppose the first patient draws {2, 1}. First, measure this patient's anxiety level. Next, give the patient new medicine A, and after a designated time, measure the patient's anxiety level. Then, after a washout period, measure the patient's anxiety level again, administer the current medicine, and afterward, measure the anxiety level. Again, after another washout period, measure the patient's anxiety level, administer <u>new</u> medicine B, and measure the anxiety level. The order of medicines given will differ for each patient, depending on the random numbers drawn. Compare the results for all three medicines, as well as for both genders.

- Here we have two sets of blocks. Gender defines one set of blocks and each patient becomes a block by itself. The schematic diagram shown in Figure 3 describes the design.

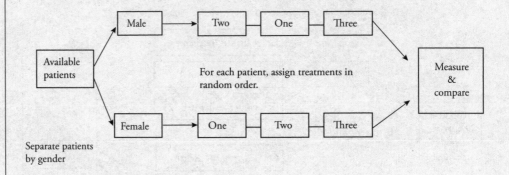

Figure 3: Schematic diagram of a randomized block design

Matched-Pairs Design

Example 3: A local sickle-cell association offers programs to educate people about sickle-cell anemia. The director of the association is interested in assessing the program's effect on the participants' knowledge about the disease.

(a) Design an experiment to assess the effectiveness of this educational program.

(b) Explain why this is a matched-pairs experiment.

Solution:

(a) Prepare a test consisting of questions about sickle-cell anemia. Select a random sample of participants enrolled in the program. At the beginning of the program, administer the test to all selected participants. Let's call this the *pre-test*. Record the results of the pre-test. Then, let all the participants complete the program. Afterward, administer the same test again. Let's call this the *post-test*. Record the results of the post-test. Finally, compare the results of the pre-test to the post-test.

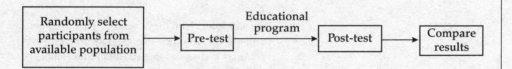

Figure 4: Schematic diagram of a matched-pairs design

(b) This is a matched-pairs design because the results of the two tests are matched by person. In this experiment, each participant's pre-test results are compared to the same participant's post-test results. A comparison of the pre-test results of one participant with the post-test results of another participant would be meaningless.

Dance party! Give yourself a study break with a dance party and maybe a cookie!

CHAPTER 5 REVIEW QUESTIONS

Multiple-Choice Questions
Answers can be found at the end of this section.

1. Which of the following is an appropriate sample for a study interested in the average interest rates on home loans form a national bank?

   (A) Less than one hundred loan rates from one branch in a town
   (B) Thousands of loan rates from all branches in the Midwest
   (C) All loan rates from all branches in one town and a random sample of loan rates from other area branches
   (D) A random sample of one thousand loan rates from one hundred randomly selected branches, nationally
   (E) Loan rates from ten of your neighbors who bank at the local branch

2. Which of the following is NOT a method of random sampling?

   (A) systematic
   (B) stratified
   (C) volunteer
   (D) proportional
   (E) cluster

3. If a study has three factors, each with three levels, how many treatments are there?

   (A) 6
   (B) 27
   (C) 5
   (D) 4
   (E) 10

4. A survey is administered to a random sample of participants. Which of the following does not describe a potential form of bias?

   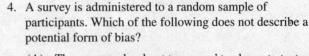

   (A) The survey asks about teenagers' tendency to text and drive and is administered in front of the teenagers' parents.
   (B) A small portion of the administered surveys are returned for analysis.
   (C) A study is meant to describe the behavior of high school students in general, but is only administered to girls.
   (D) The population of a high school is divided into nonhomogeneous groups and ten surveys are administered to a random sample from each cluster.
   (E) A question in the survey states, "Most teenagers know texting while driving is bad. How often do you text and drive?"

5. Suzy and John claim they each make the best chicken enchiladas. To test their claims, they each prepare enchiladas and served them to a random sample of friends. Those friends were then surveyed using the same questionnaire. Results were compared. Which of the following statements about the study is true? (Note: Suzy and John do not have the same friends in common.)

   (A) The results will generalize because the questionnaires were identical.
   (B) The samples were random so the results should not be biased.
   (C) The results of this study will definitively prove whose enchiladas are better.
   (D) There is a convenience sampling bias present for both Suzy and John.
   (E) The study was a single-blind design study.

6. A student is lobbying for a new robotics club to be established at her high school. The school newspaper conducts a survey of students to assess interest in such a club. What is the population of interest?

   (A) All faculty, staff, and students at the school
   (B) All students at the school
   (C) All high school students in the county
   (D) All students in the district
   (E) All freshman at the school

7. A study testing the effectiveness of a new antidepressant medication includes three groups: a group given the new antidepressant, a group given an antidepressant that has already been proven to be effective, and a group given an ineffective, non-medicated sugar pill. What is the best name for the group given the sugar pill?

   (A) placebo
   (B) control
   (C) experimental
   (D) treatment
   (E) block

8. Why is replication a good practice in experimental designs?

   (A) It "controls" the effects of known factors.
   (B) It eliminates chance variation.
   (C) It allows for causation to potentially be determined.
   (D) It makes a study random.
   (E) It allows for chance variation to be estimated.

9. What is an example of a non-biased sampling method?

   (A) A teacher selecting only students with last name starting with the letters P through Z to take a pop quiz
   (B) A teacher selecting only students with a current A or B grade in his class to take a pop quiz
   (C) A teacher picking 10 names out of a jar containing each name of the students in his class to take a pop quiz
   (D) A teacher selecting only students wearing long sleeves to take a pop quiz
   (E) A teacher asking the students sitting on the right side of his classroom to take a pop quiz.

Free-Response Questions

10. A scientist wants to determine which catalyst, A or B, will reduce the reaction times of three reactions (1, 2, and 3) most.

    a. Design an experiment to compare the effects of these catalysts.
    b. Is your experiment single-blind, double-blind, or neither?

11. A school psychologist is interested in showing whether or not stress about school can lead to poor grades in school. She interviews a random sample of 100 students from her district's schools (K-12) at the middle of the semester. She asks them how stressed they generally are on a scale from 1 to 10, 10 being the most stressed. Then, the psychologist compares the grades of these students at the end of the semester. After analyzing the data, she concludes that stress about school causes poor grades.

    a. Is this causal conclusion appropriate based on the design of the study? Why or why not?
    b. What are some flaws in the design? How are they flaws?
    c. Design an experiment that corrects these flaws.

a. No. since there is no treatment, assignment, there may be confounding lurking variable.

b. Only her school district.

CHAPTER 5 ANSWERS AND EXPLANATIONS

1. **D** Samples from a population should be randomly selected and representative of the population as a whole. The population is the interest rates on home loans nationally, so the sample should be nationally representative. Only (D) has a sample that is representative of the population.

2. **C** Volunteer samples are a form of biased samples since the subjects self-select their participation in the sample. The results can be biased as certain individuals can decide not to participate. The other options are all means of sampling a population randomly. For example, systematic sampling would be when a researcher selects every 5th name on a list for participation in a study. Stratified sampling would be dividing the population into strata or homogeneous groups (like boys and girls) and then randomly selecting participants from those groups. Proportional sampling would require the population to be divided into strata and the samples proportional to the size of the stratum size be selected (for example, 40% of the population is girls, so 40% of the sample is from the girls stratum). Finally, cluster sampling is when the population is divided into nonhomogeneous groups and then those clusters sampled (like when a teacher splits the classroom in half down the middle and randomly selects a sample from each half of the class—assuming the students are not seated to form strata.)

3. **B** The number of values you multiply together is equal to the number of factors in a study. Here, we have three factors, so we must multiply __ × __ × __. The values that go into each slot represent the number of levels for each factor. In this case, $3 \times 3 \times 3 = 27$.

	A	*B*	*C*
1	*A1*	*B1*	*C1*
2	*A2*	*B2*	*C2*
3	*A3*	*B3*	*C3*

4. **D** Choice (A) is an example of response bias; the students may not answer honestly in front of their parents. Choice (B) is an example of nonresponse bias; a portion of the population refused to answer. Choice (C) is an example of undercoverage bias; boys are completely left out of the sample! Choice (E) is an example of wording effect bias; students may feel obliged to respond in a way to make themselves look better, since they know the behavior is not favorable. Finally, choice (D) is a form of random sampling; it describes a cluster sampling procedure.

5. **D** Let's walk through each choice. Choice (A): The results will not generalize because the samples that tasted the two types of enchiladas were different. Choice (B): The samples were samples of convenience, which can be biased. Choice (C): The experiment cannot definitively prove anything for the reasons in (A), (B), and (E). Choice (E): Both the subjects and administrators knew who was in each group, so there was no blinding. Choice (D) is correct for the same reason (B) is incorrect; the samples were each individual's friends only.

6. **B**   The club is for the students in the high school, so all of them would be potential participants, and thus the population of interest. The faculty and staff at the school will not be participants, so they are not part of the population of interest. Students anywhere else in the district or county are not important to this one high school's students' interest. Finally, freshman are not listed as the only potential participants in the club.

7. **A**   A placebo group is a special form of a control group. It helps allow researchers to determine how effective a medication actually is versus the beneficial effects perceived from just taking a pill.

8. **E**   Replication within a design is beneficial because it allows researchers to determine whether the results for one participant (or group) are due to the treatment or due to characteristics of that participant (or group) or other factors. When multiple participants (or groups) are given a treatment, the variation due to chance or factors out of the researchers' control can be estimated.

9. **C**   A sample is considered non-biased if it is selected randomly, provides each individual with an equal chance of selection, and, therefore, represents the population. Choices (A), (B), and (D) can be eliminated because the teacher non-randomly selects students with particular characteristics, such as having a last name starting with a letter in the latter half of the alphabet, maintaining an A or B grade, or wearing long-sleeves in class. Eliminate choice (E) because the teacher non-randomly selects the right-side of the classroom to take the quiz. Therefore, the only answer that provides a scenario of random, non-biased sampling is (C), in which students are selected randomly from a jar.

10.
   a.   Example: Prepare 20 samples of each reaction (1, 2, and 3). Randomly assign each Catalyst A and B to 10 different samples of each reaction. For example, mix up the samples for each reaction 1, 2, and 3 and number the samples 1–20. Assign every odd numbered reaction to Catalyst A and any even numbered reaction to Catalyst B. Allow a lab technician to run the reactions using the catalysts and record the reaction times. This lab technician should not be involved in the assignment of catalysts to reactions. Finally, compare the results of the reaction times for each reaction under each catalyst.

   b.   The experiment is single-blind because the lab technician who records the results is not aware of which catalyst was used with each reaction sample. It is not a double-blind study because the reaction samples are not people, so they wouldn't know what catalyst they were receiving regardless. If the reactions were people it would still be single-blind because the patients would know which catalyst they were receiving.

11.
   a.   This causal conclusion is not appropriate because there are many factors that could have caused the poor grades in the students such as fatigue, not learning the material properly, missing class, etc. Also, this study was observational, not experimental, so causal conclusions cannot be drawn.

b. Here are a few examples:

1. The study is observational and not experimental, so causal conclusions cannot be drawn; all other potential causal factors were not controlled.

2. The sample is only drawn from the psychologist's district. This is a sample of convenience and cannot be generalized to students outside of the district.

3. There are different types of stress, and the psychologist didn't ask about them in her survey, so students may not be experiencing stress about school alone.

4. The psychologist is comparing students at multiple ages and grades against each other. These students are at different stages of development and may experience stress at varying rates due to age and workload.

5. She measures stress at the middle of the semester and grades at the end, but stress can change over time and a final grade is cumulative. So the time periods in question between the two variables are different.

c. In order to design an experiment that corrects the potential sources of error, it is necessary that the psychologist first utilize stratified random sampling to create groups based on grade level. Not only will random sampling improve the internal validity of the study, but it will also improve the external validity, and thus generalizability, of the study. At the beginning of the school year, the psychologist should administer a pre-test to assess the students' stress levels. At the end of the school year, the psychologist should administer an equivalent post-test to determine the students' stress levels. The psychologist can then compare the students' stress levels, based on grade, to determine whether stress increases during the school year.

Chapter 6
Anticipating
Patterns

PROBABILITY

Words referring to probability or chance are commonly used in conversation. For example, we often come across statements like these:

This chapter discusses how to use probability as a tool to judge the distribution of data under a given model. In the multiple-choice section, this topic appears in eight to 12 out of 40 questions. In the free-response section, this topic appears in one or two out of six questions.

- It is likely to rain today, so please take your umbrella with you.
- It was an easy test. I'll probably get an A on it.
- The Yankees have a much better chance of winning than the Mets.

Words like "probably," "likely," and "chance" carry similar meanings in conversation. They all convey uncertainty. By using probability, we can also make a numerical statement about uncertainty. For example, bank managers can never know exactly when their depositors will make a withdrawal or exactly how much they'll withdraw. Managers also know that though most loans they've granted will be paid back, some of them will result in defaults—but they can't know exactly which ones. In other words, a variety of outcomes is possible, and therefore bank managers can never know exactly how much money the bank will have at any given moment in the future. However, the bankers can use the rules of probability and their past experience to make a reasonable estimation, and then use that estimation when making business decisions.

What Is "Probability"?

Probability is a measure of the likelihood of an event. Consider a fair coin toss. What makes this coin toss "fair"? We call it fair if the coin's chance of showing heads when flipped is the same as its chance of showing tails—in other words, if there is a 50 percent chance of it showing heads and a 50 percent chance of it showing tails. Suppose we tossed the coin twice and got two heads. Does that mean this coin toss was not fair? What if we toss the coin three times? What do we expect to happen? Let's toss a coin 5, 10, 15, 20, 25, and more times and count the number of heads. Then we can calculate the probability of getting heads in a toss and plot that figure on a graph:

$$P(\text{Heads in a toss}) = \frac{\text{Number of heads}}{\text{Number of tosses}}$$

$$P(\text{Percent heads}) = \frac{\text{Number of heads}}{\text{Number of tosses}} \times 100$$

Table 1 lists the results of one such experiment, and the plot in Figure 1 shows them graphically.

Number of Tosses	Number of Heads	P(Heads)	Percent of Heads	Number of Tosses	Number of Heads	P(Heads)	Percent of Heads
2	0	0	0	35	17	0.48571	48.571
3	2	0.66667	66.667	40	18	0.45	45
4	3	0.75	75	45	18	0.4	40
5	5	1	100	50	23	0.46	46
6	3	0.5	50	60	32	0.53333	53.333
7	5	0.71429	71.429	70	29	0.41429	41.429
8	5	0.625	62.5	80	34	0.425	42.5
9	7	0.77778	77.778	90	48	0.53333	53.333
10	4	0.4	40	100	49	0.49	49
15	10	0.66667	66.667	150	74	0.49333	49.333
20	9	0.45	45	200	106	0.53	53
25	12	0.48	48	500	264	0.528	52.8
30	17	0.56667	56.667	1,000	508	0.508	50.8

Table 1: Number of heads shown in different numbers of tosses

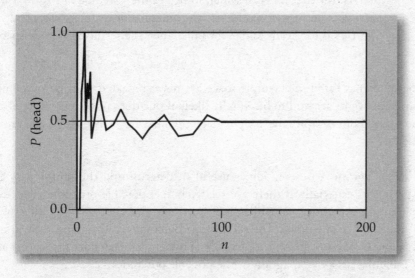

Figure 1: P(heads) estimated from different numbers of tosses

Notice that as the number of tosses increases, the percent of times that the coin lands on heads gets closer and closer to 50 percent. In other words, in the long run, the relative frequency of getting heads approaches 0.5, which is what we expected it to be. This relative frequency reflects the concept of probability. In fact, in the long run, the relative frequency of the occurrence of any specific event will always approach the expected value, also known as the probability. Random events are events that cannot be predicted in the short term, but do produce patterns (such as the 50/50 nature of a fair coin toss) in the long run.

Sample Space

Any process that results in an observation or an outcome is an experiment. An experiment may have more than one possible outcome. A set of all possible outcomes of an experiment is known as a **sample space**. It is generally denoted using the letter S.

- Tossing a coin will result in one of two possible outcomes, heads or tails. Therefore, the sample space of tossing a coin is

$$S = \{\text{Heads, Tails}\}$$

- Throwing a die will result in one of six possible outcomes. The resulting sample space is

$$S = \{1, 2, 3, 4, 5, 6\}$$

- Tossing two coins will result in one of four possible outcomes. We can indicate the outcome of each of the two tosses by using a pair of letters, the first letter of which indicates the outcome of tossing the first coin and the second letter the outcome of tossing the second coin. H is for heads and T for tails. Then the resulting sample space is

$$S = \{(H, H), (H, T), (T, H), (T, T)\}$$

The outcomes listed in a sample space are never repeated, and no outcome is left out. Two events are said to be equally likely if one does not occur more often than the other. For example, the six possible outcomes for a throw of a die are equally likely.

A **tree diagram** representation is useful in determining the sample space for an experiment, especially if there are relatively few possible outcomes. For example, imagine an experiment in which a die and a quarter are tossed together. What are all the possible outcomes? The six possible outcomes of throwing a die are 1, 2, 3, 4, 5, and 6. The two possible outcomes of tossing a quarter are heads (H) and tails (T). Figure 2 is a tree diagram of the possible outcomes:

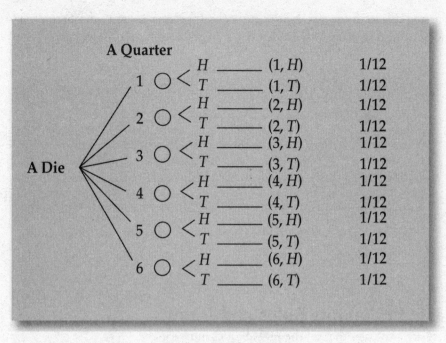

Figure 2: Tree diagram

Looking at the tree diagram, it is easy to see that the sample space is

$$S = \{(1, H), (2, H), (3, H), (4, H), (5, H), (6, H),$$

$$(1, T), (2, T), (3, T), (4, T), (5, T), (6, T)\}$$

The first number of each pair represents the outcome of throwing the die and the second represents the outcome of tossing the coin. All 12 outcomes are equally likely. Therefore, the probability of each outcome is $\dfrac{1}{12}$.

It is common practice to use capital letters to indicate events. For example, one may define

A = getting an even number when a die is thrown = {2, 4, 6}
B = getting two heads when two coins are tossed simultaneously = {(H, H)}

The probability of an event is generally denoted by a capital P followed by the name of the event in parentheses: P(the event). If all the events in a sample space are equally likely, then by using the concept of relative frequency, we can compute the probability of an event as

$$P(\text{An event}) = \frac{\text{Number of outcomes that lead to the event}}{\text{Total number of possible outcomes}}$$

Applying this to the events defined earlier—A (getting an even number in the toss of a die) and B (getting two heads when two coins are tossed)—we get:

- $P(A) = \dfrac{3}{6} = \dfrac{1}{2} = 0.5$. The probability of getting an even number when a six-sided die is thrown is 0.5. In other words, there is a 50 percent chance of getting an even number when a six-sided die is thrown.

- $P(B) = \dfrac{1}{4} = 0.25$. The probability of getting two heads when two coins are tossed simultaneously is 0.25. In other words, there is a 25 percent chance of getting two heads when two coins are tossed simultaneously.

Basic Probability Rules and Terms

There are two rules that all the probabilities must satisfy:

- **Rule 1:** For any event A, the probability of A is always greater than or equal to 0 and less than or equal to 1.

$$0 \leq P(A) \leq 1$$

- **Rule 2:** The sum of the probabilities for all possible outcomes in a sample space is always 1.

As a result, we can say the following:

- If an event can never occur, its probability is 0. Such an event is known as an **impossible event.**

- If an event must occur every time, its probability is 1. Such an event is known as a **sure event.**

The **odds in favor of an event** is a ratio of the probability of the occurrence of an event to the probability of the nonoccurrence of that event.

$$\text{Odds in favor of an event} = \frac{P(\text{Event } A \text{ occurs})}{P(\text{Event } A \text{ does not occur})}$$

or

$$P(\text{Event } A \text{ occurs}) : P(\text{Event } A \text{ does not occur})$$

Example 1: When tossing a die, what are the odds in favor of getting the number 2?

Solution: When tossing a die,

P(Getting the number 2) = $\frac{1}{6}$ and

P(Not getting the number 2) = P(Getting the numbers 1, 3, 4, 5, or 6) = $\frac{5}{6}$.

$$\frac{\frac{1}{6}}{\frac{5}{6}} \quad \frac{1}{5}$$

Thus, the odds in favor of getting the number 2 are $\frac{1}{6}$: $\frac{5}{6}$ or 1 to 5 (or 1:5).

More Terms

The Venn diagrams shown in Figures 3–6 illustrate some of the following terms. The rectangular box indicates the A' sample space. Circles indicate different events.

The **complement** of an event is the set of all possible outcomes in a sample space that does not lead to the event. The complement of an event A is denoted by A' (or A^C). See Figure 3.

Disjoint or **mutually exclusive events** are events that have no outcome in common. In other words, they cannot occur together. See Figure 4.

The **union** of events A and B is the set of all possible outcomes that lead to at least one of two events A and B. The union of events A and B is denoted by $(A \cup B)$ or (A or B). See Figure 5.

The **intersection** of events A and B is the set of all possible outcomes that lead to *both* events A and B. The intersection of events A and B is denoted by $(A \cap B)$ or (A and B). See Figure 6.

A **conditional event:** A given B is a set of outcomes for event A that occurs if B has occurred. It is indicated by $(A|B)$ and reads "A given B."

Two events A and B are considered **independent** if the occurrence of one event does not depend on the occurrence of the other.

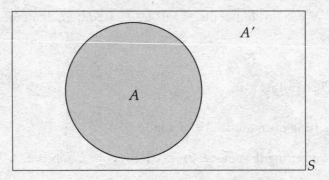

Figure 3: Event A and its complement

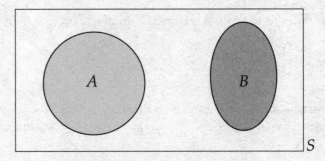

Figure 4: Disjoint events A and B

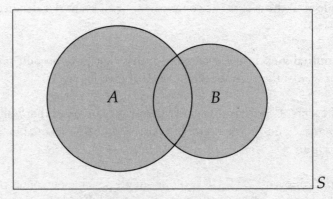

Figure 5: Union of events A and B

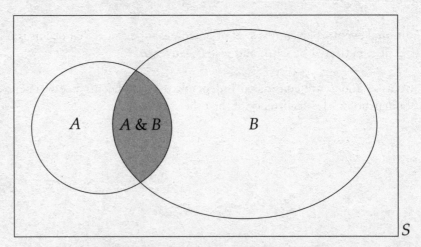

Figure 6: Intersection of events A and B

Independence versus Dependence

Imagine that you shuffle a standard deck of cards and then draw a card at random. The chance of your getting an ace is the same across all four suits (hearts, clubs, diamonds, and spades). In other words, the likelihood of your getting an ace does not depend on the suit of the card. So we can say that the events "getting an ace" and "getting a particular suit" are *independent*.

Now consider a doctor examining patients in an emergency room. The likelihood of a patient being diagnosed for a knee injury is higher if that patient is a football player, because football players are more likely to suffer knee injuries than non-football players. Therefore the event "knee injury" *depends* on the event "football player."

Example 2: The sample space for throwing a die is S = {1, 2, 3, 4, 5, 6}. Suppose events A, B, and C are defined as follows:

A = Getting an even number = {2, 4, 6}   2, 4, 6
B = Getting at least 5 = {5, 6}
C = Getting at most 3 = {1, 2, 3}

Find the probability of each of these events and its complement. Then, find the union, intersection, and conditional probability of each pair of events.

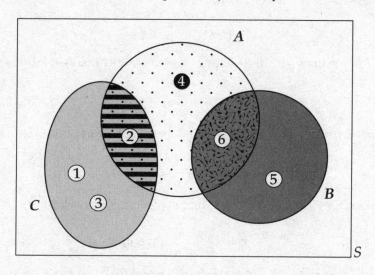

Figure 7: Venn diagram

Planning ahead? Don't miss *Cracking the GRE* and *Cracking the GMAT!*

Solution:

- **Probability:** $P(A) = \dfrac{3}{6} = 0.5$, $P(B) = \dfrac{2}{6} = 0.3\overline{3}$, and $P(C) = \dfrac{3}{6} = 0.5$

- **Complement:** A' = Getting an odd number = {1, 3, 5}

$$P(A') = \frac{3}{6} = 0.5 = 1 - P(A)$$

$B' =$ Getting a number less than 5 = {1, 2, 3, 4}

$$P(B') = \frac{4}{6} = 0.6\overline{6} = 1 - P(B)$$

$C' =$ Getting a number larger than 3 = {4, 5, 6}

$$P(C') = \frac{3}{6} = 0.5$$

- **Union:** $(A \cup B) =$ Getting an even number or a number greater than or equal to 5 or both.

$$= \{2, 4, 5, 6\}$$

$$P(A \cup B) = \frac{4}{6} = 0.6\overline{6}$$

$(A \cup C) =$ Getting an even number or a number less than or equal to 3 or both.

$$= \{1, 2, 3, 4, 6\}$$

$$P(A \cup C) = \frac{5}{6} = 0.83\overline{3}$$

$(B \cup C) =$ Getting a number that is at most 3 or at least 5 or both.

$$= \{1, 2, 3, 5, 6\}$$

$$P(B \cup C) = \frac{5}{6} = 0.83\overline{3}$$

- **Intersection:** $(A \cap B) =$ Getting an even number that is at least 5 = {6}

$$P(A \cap B) = \frac{1}{6} = 0.16\overline{6}$$

$(A \cap C) =$ Getting an even number that is at most 3 = {2}

$$P(A \cap C) = \frac{1}{6} = 0.16\overline{6}$$

$(B \cap C) =$ Getting a number that is at most 3 and at least 5 = { }

$$P(B \cap C) = \frac{0}{6} = 0.000$$

In other words, B and C are disjoint or mutually exclusive events.

- **Conditional event:** $(A \mid C) =$ Getting an even number given that the number is at most 3 = {2}

$$P(A \mid C) = \frac{1}{3} = 0.33$$

$(A \mid B) =$ Getting an even number given that the number is at least 5 = {6}

$$P(A \mid B) = \frac{1}{2} = 0.5$$

$(B|C)$ = Getting at least 5 given that the number is at most 3 = $\varnothing$

$$P(B \mid C) = 0$$

More Probability Rules

- **Complement:** The probability of the complement of an event A is given by

$$P(A') = 1 - P(A)$$

- **Union** (addition rule): The probability of the union of two events A and B is given by

$$P(A \cup B) = P(A) + P(B) - P(A \cap B)$$

If the events A and B are disjoint, then $P(A \cap B) = 0$, and

$$P(A \cup B) = P(A) + P(B)$$

- **Intersection** aka **Bayes Rule** (multiplication rule): For events A and B defined in a sample space S,

$$P(A \cap B) = P(A) \bullet P(B \mid A) = P(B) \bullet P(A \mid B)$$

- **Conditional probabilities:** The probability of A given B is

$$P(A \mid B) = \frac{P(A \cap B)}{P(B)}$$

- **Independence:** Two events A and B are independent if and only if

$$P(A \mid B) = P(A) \text{ and } P(B \mid A) = P(B)$$

In other words, two events A and B are independent if and only if

$$P(A \cap B) = P(A) \bullet P(B)$$

Example 3: Imagine that you shuffle a standard deck of 52 cards and draw a card at random.

Let

D = diamond	C = club
H = heart	S = spade
J = jack	Q = queen
K = king	1 = ace

Then $S = \{D1,\ldots, D10, DJ, DQ, DK, C1,\ldots, C10, CJ, CQ, CK, H1,\ldots, H10, HJ, HQ, HK, S1,\ldots, S10, SJ, SQ, SK\}$

Suppose we define the following events:
A = Getting an ace = $\{D1, C1, H1, S1\}$
B = Getting a diamond = $\{D1,\ldots, D10, DJ, DQ, DK\}$
C = Getting a club = $\{C1, \ldots C10, CJ, CQ, CK\}$

Then

- $P(A) = \dfrac{4}{52}$, $P(B) = \dfrac{13}{52}$, $P(C) = \dfrac{13}{52}$

- A' = Getting a non-ace card

$$P(A') = 1 - P(A) = 1 - \frac{4}{52} = \frac{48}{52}$$

- B' = Getting a non-diamond card

$$P(B') = 1 - P(B) = 1 - \frac{13}{52} = \frac{39}{52}$$

- $(A \cap B)$ = Getting an ace of diamonds = $\{D1\}$

$$P(A \cap B) = \frac{1}{52}$$

Events A and B are not disjoint, because an ace of diamonds ($D1$) is a common outcome for both the events.

- $(B \cap C)$ = Getting a card that is a club and a diamond = $\{\ \}$

$$P(B \cap C) = 0$$

The events B and C are disjoint, because no outcome is common to them. Each card in a deck belongs to only one suit.

- $(A \cup B)$ = Getting an ace or a diamond or both
$\{D1,\ldots, D10, DJ, DQ, DK, C1, H1, S1\}$

$$P(A \cup B) = \frac{16}{52}$$

Alternatively,

$$P(A \cup B) = P(A) + P(B) - P(A \cap B)$$

$$= \frac{4}{52} + \frac{13}{52} - \frac{1}{52}$$

$$= \frac{16}{52}$$

- $P(B \cup C)$ = Getting a diamond or a club or both
  = {D1,..., D10, DJ, DQ, DK, C1,..., C10, CJ, CQ, CK}

$$P(B \cup C) = \frac{26}{52}$$

Alternatively, because B and C are disjoint, $P(B \cap C) = 0$.
Therefore,

$$P(B \cup C) = P(B) + P(C)$$

$$= \frac{13}{52} + \frac{13}{52}$$

$$= \frac{26}{52}$$

- $(A \mid B)$ = Getting an ace given that a diamond has been drawn =
  {D1}

$$P(A \mid B) = \frac{1}{13}$$

Alternatively,

$$P(A \mid B) = \frac{P(A \cap B)}{P(B)} = \frac{1/52}{13/52} = \frac{1}{13}$$

Note that $P(A \mid B) = P(A)$. Therefore, events A and B are independent.

Example 4: Seventy-five percent of people who purchase hair dryers are female. Of these female purchasers of hair dryers, 30 percent are over 50 years old. What is the probability that a randomly selected hair dryer purchaser is a female over 50 years old?

$$\frac{3}{4} \times \frac{3}{10} = \frac{9}{40}$$

Solution: Let us define the events as follows:

W = The purchaser of a hair dryer is a female.
F = The purchaser of a hair dryer is over 50 years old.

It is known that $P(W) = 0.75$ and $P(F \mid W) = 0.30$.

Thus,

$$P(W \cap F) = P(F \mid W) \bullet P(W) = 0.30(0.75) = 0.225$$

There is a 22.5 percent chance that a randomly selected hair dryer purchaser is a female over 50 years old.

Example 5: Company I has 24 total employees that are classified as associates, partners, managers or entrepreneurs. There are 10 associates, six partners, five managers, and three entrepreneurs. There are three levels of experience within each of these classifications: entry, junior, or senior (i.e., an employee can be a junior associate, a senior manager, etc.). The percentages of Company I employees that are entry, junior, and senior level are 50.0 percent, 37.5 percent, and 12.5 percent, respectively. An employee from Company II needs to arrange a conference meeting with four employees from Company I.

(a) Find the probability that two of the people she meets with are senior managers.
(b) Find the probability that one is a junior partner and one is an entry entrepreneur.
(c) Find the probability that one is a senior associate and two are entry-level associates.

Solution. First we will define all of our variables so the solution to follow is logical and comprehensive.

$P(A)$ = probability that the employee of Company I is an associate = 10/24
$P(B)$ = probability that the employee of Company I is a manager = 5/24
$P(C)$ = probability that the employee of Company I is a partner = 6/24
$P(D)$ = probability that the employee of Company I is an entrepreneur = 3/24
$P(E)$ = probability that the employee of Company I is entry-level = 0.500
$P(F)$ = probability that the employee of Company I is junior-level = 0.375
$P(G)$ = probability that the employee of Company I is senior-level = 0.125

(a) The probability that the first employee she meets with is a senior manager is: $P(G \mid B) = (5/24) \cdot (0.125) = 0.026$. With one senior-level manager selected, $P(B)$ now becomes 4/23. The probability that the second employee she meets with is also a senior manager is: $P(G \mid BB) = (4/23) \cdot (0.125) = 0.022$. The total probability of meeting these criteria is: $P(B \text{ and } BB) = P(G \mid B) \cdot P(G \mid BB) = (0.026) \cdot (0.022) = 5.6 \times 10^{-4}$ or 0.056 percent.

(b) Analogous to part (a), $P(F \mid C) = (6/24) \cdot (0.375) = 0.094$. With one junior-level partner selected, we can calculate the probability that the second employee will be an entry-level entrepreneur: $P(E \mid D) = (3/23) \cdot (0.500) = 0.065$. The total probability of meeting these criteria is: $P(C \text{ and } D) = P(F \mid C) \cdot P(E \mid D) = (0.094) \cdot 0.065 = 6.11 \times 10^{-3}$ or 0.611 percent.

(c) Analogous to parts (a) and (b), $P(G \mid A) = (10/24) \cdot (0.125) = 0.052$. With one senior-level associate selected, we can calculate the probability that the second and third employees chosen will be entry-level associates: $P(E \mid AA) = (9/23) \cdot (0.500) = 0.196$ and

$P(E \mid AAA) = (8/22) \cdot (0.500) = 0.182$. The total probability of meeting these criteria is $P(A$ and AA and $AAA) = P(G \mid A) \cdot P(E \mid AA) \cdot P(E \mid AAA) = (0.052) \cdot (0.196) \cdot (0.182) = 1.9 \times 10^{-3}$ or 0.19 percent.

Example 6: An insurance agent knows that 70 percent of her customers carry adequate collision coverage. She also knows that of those who carry adequate coverage, 5 percent have been involved in accidents, and of those who do not carry adequate coverage, 12 percent have been involved in accidents. If one of her clients is involved in an auto accident, then what is the probability that the client does not have adequate collision coverage?

Solution: Let us define events as follows:

A = Client carries adequate coverage
B = Client is involved in an auto accident

We need to find $P(A' \mid B)$, which equals $\dfrac{P(A' \cap B)}{P(B)}$

It is known that

> $P(A)$ = Probability that a client carries adequate coverage = 0.70, therefore
> $P(A') = 1 - 0.70 = 0.30$
> $P(B \mid A)$ = Probability that a client carrying adequate coverage is involved in an auto accident = 0.05
> $P(B \mid A')$ = Probability that a client without enough coverage is involved in an auto accident = 0.12

First, let's work out the numerator. $P(A' \cap B)$, the probability that a client is not carrying enough insurance and gets involved in an auto accident.

$$P(A' \cap B) = P(B \mid A') \cdot P(A')$$

$$= 0.12(0.30)$$

$$= 0.036$$

Next, the denominator is the probability that a randomly selected client is involved in an auto accident

$$P(B) = P(B \cap A) + P(B \cap A') = P(B \mid A) \cdot P(A) + P(B \mid A') \cdot P(A')$$

$$= 0.05(0.70) + 0.12(1 - 0.70)$$

$$= 0.071$$

Therefore,

$$P(A' \mid B) = \frac{P(A' \cap B)}{P(B)} = \frac{0.036}{0.071} = 0.507$$

There is a 50.7 percent chance that this client does not carry adequate insurance.

An alternative method is to make a table of the possible combinations, and fill in the numbers as we can. We are given that

	Adequate coverage		Total
In accident	Yes	No	
Yes	0.05 • 0.70	0.12 • ???	
No			
Total	0.70		1.00

1.00 − 0.70 = 0.30, so

	Adequate coverage		Total
In accident	Yes	No	
Yes	0.05 • 0.70	0.12 • 0.30	
No			
Total	0.70	0.30	

Next, do the division to get

	Adequate coverage		Total
In accident	Yes	No	
Yes	0.035	0.036	
No			
Total	0.70	0.30	

Next, add across the accident–yes row, subtract in the columns, and get

	Adequate coverage		Total
In accident	Yes	No	
Yes	0.035	0.036	0.071
No	0.665	0.264	0.929
Total	0.70	0.30	1

The question asked the probability that a client does not have adequate coverage, given that he or she was in an accident. This is 0.036/0.071 = 0.507.

Example 7: The local Chamber of Commerce conducted a survey of 1,000 randomly selected shoppers at a mall. For all shoppers, gender of shopper and items shopping for was recorded. The data collected is summarized in the following table:

Gender	Shopping For			
	Clothing	Shoes	Other	Total
Male	75	25	150	250
Female	350	230	170	750
Total	425	255	320	1,000

If a shopper is selected at random from this mall,

(a) What is the probability that the shopper is a female?
(b) What is the probability that the shopper is shopping for shoes?
(c) What is the probability that the shopper is a female shopping for shoes?
(d) What is the probability that the shopper is shopping for shoes given that the shopper is a female?
(e) Are the events "female" and "shopping for shoes" disjoint?
(f) Are the events "female" and "shopping for shoes" independent?

Solution:

(a) What is the probability that the shopper is a female?

$$P = P(\text{Female}) = \frac{750}{1,000} = 0.75$$

(b) What is the probability that the shopper is shopping for shoes?

$$P = P(\text{Shopping for shoes}) = \frac{255}{1,000} = 0.255$$

(c) What is the probability that the shopper is a female shopping for shoes?

$$P = P(\text{Female} \cap \text{Shopping for shoes}) = \frac{230}{1,000} = 0.23$$

(d) What is the probability that the shopper is shopping for shoes given that the shopper is a female?

$$P = P(\text{Shopping for shoes} \mid \text{Female}) =$$

$$\frac{P(\text{Shopping for shoes} \cap \text{Female})}{P(\text{Female})} = \frac{0.23}{0.75}$$

$$= 0.3067$$

(e) Are the events "female" and "shopping for shoes" disjoint? There are 230 females shopping for shoes, or $P = P(\text{Female} \cap \text{Shopping for shoes}) = 0.23 \neq 0$. Therefore the events "female" and "shopping for shoes" are not disjoint.

(f) Are the events "female" and "shopping for shoes" independent? $P = P(\text{Shopping for shoes} \mid \text{Female}) = 0.3067$ and $P(\text{Shopping for shoes}) = 0.255$, which means $P(\text{Shopping for shoes} \mid \text{Female}) \neq P(\text{Shopping for shoes})$. Therefore, events "female" and "shopping for shoes" are not independent.

RANDOM VARIABLES AND THEIR PROBABILITY DISTRIBUTIONS

A **variable** is a quantity whose value varies from subject to subject. Examples include:

- Height (which varies from person to person)
- The number of e-mail messages you receive per day (which changes from day to day)
- The number of patients examined by a doctor per day (which changes from day to day)
- The number of home runs hit in a season by members of a baseball team (which varies from player to player)
- The hair color of students in a class (which varies from student to student)
- The altitude of an airplane in flight (which varies from minute to minute)

A **probability experiment** is an experiment whose possible outcomes may be known but whose exact outcome is a random event and cannot be predicted with certainty in advance. If the outcome of a probability experiment takes a numerical value, then the outcome is a **quantitative variable**. A **random variable** is an outcome of a probability experiment. Random variables are usually denoted using capital letters, such as X or Y. Sometimes two or more variables are denoted using the same letter but different subscripts, such as X_1 and X_2. Let us consider random variables with numeric outcomes.

There are two types of random variables, discrete and continuous:

- A **discrete random variable** is a quantitative variable that takes a countable number of values. The following are all discrete random variables:
  o the number of e-mail messages received per day
  o the number of home runs per batter
  o the number of red blood cells per sample of blood
  o the number of students present in class per day
  o the number of customers served by a bank teller per hour

  Note that between any two possible values of a discrete random variable, there is a countable number of possible values. You may receive 10 e-mail messages a day or 12 messages a day, but you can never receive 12.5 messages in one day, or 12.6324 messages.

- A **continuous random variable** is a quantitative variable that can take all the possible values in a given range. A person's weight is a good example. A person can weigh 150 pounds or 155 pounds or any weight between those two, including 151.5 pounds or 153.23487 pounds. Other examples of continuous random values are:
  o the altitude of a plane
  o the amount of rainfall in a city per day
  o the amount of gasoline pumped into a car's gas tank
  o the weight of a newborn baby
  o the amount of water flowing through a dam per hour

THE PROBABILITY DISTRIBUTIONS OF DISCRETE RANDOM VARIABLES

A **probability distribution of a discrete random variable** or a **discrete probability distribution** is a table, list, graph, or formula giving all possible values taken by a random variable and their corresponding probabilities.

Let X be a random variable taking values $x_1, x_2,..., x_n$ with respective probabilities $P(x_1), P(x_2),..., P(x_n)$. Then $\{(x_1, P(x_1)), (x_2, P(x_2)),..., (x_n, P(x_n))\}$ gives a valid probability distribution if:

- $0 \leq P(x_i) \leq 1$ for all $i = 1, 2,..., n$, and

- $\sum_{i=1}^{n} P(x_i) = 1$

A probability distribution is often given as a table. See below.

Random Variable	Probability
X	$P(X = x_i)$
x_1	$P(x_1)$
x_2	$P(x_2)$
x_3	$P(x_3)$
$\vdots$	$\vdots$
x_n	$P(x_n)$

Table 2: Probability distribution of a discrete random variable

Mean of a Discrete Random Variable

The mean (μ) of a discrete random variable X is also known as the **expected value**. It is denoted by $E(X)$ and is computed by multiplying each value of the random variable by its probability and then adding over the sample space.

$$\mu = E(X) = \sum_{i=1}^{n} x_i P(x_i)$$

Variance of a Discrete Random Variable

The variance of a discrete random variable is defined as the sum of the product of squared deviations of the values of the variable from the mean and the corresponding probabilities:

$$\sigma^2 = \sum_{i=1}^{n} \left(x_i - \mu\right)^2 P\left(x_i\right)$$

Remember that standard deviation is simply the square root of variance.

Example 8: Sophia was recently promoted to assistant manager at a small women's clothing store. One of her duties is to fill out order forms for women's shirts, which come in sizes 6, 7, 8, 9, 10, 11, and 12. She would like to determine how many shirts of each size to order. At first, she thought of ordering exactly the same number of shirts from each of the available sizes, but then she decided against doing that, because there might be a greater demand for certain sizes than for others. She looked up sales receipts from the past three months and summarized the information as follows:

Shirt Size	6	7	8	9	10	11	12
Number Sold	85	122	138	154	177	133	92

(a) Prepare a probability distribution of the number of shirts sold for each size.
(b) What is the probability that a randomly selected customer will request a shirt of size at least 11?
(c) Compute the expected shirt size of a random shopper and the standard deviation of the shirt size.
(d) If Sophia plans to order a total of 1,000 shirts, how many shirts of size 8 should she order?

Solution: (a) The total number of shirts sold is 901. Using this information, we can compute the probability of each shirt size being sold. For example, the probability of selling size 6 is 85/901 = 0.09. The random variable here (X) is the shirt size, and it takes values 6, 7, 8, 9, 10, 11, and 12. Both Table 3 and the graph in Figure 8 give the probability distribution of the number of shirts sold for each size.

Shirt Size	$P(x)$
6	0.09
7	0.14
8	0.15
9	0.17
10	0.20
11	0.15
12	0.10

Table 3: Probability distribution of shirt size

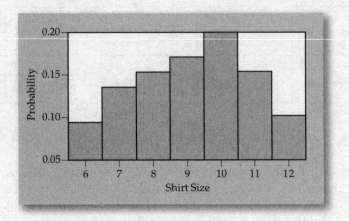

Figure 8: Probability distribution of shirt size

This probability distribution shows that 9 percent of the customers bought size 6 shirts, 14 percent bought size 7 shirts, and so on.

(b) P(A customer will request a shirt of size at least 11)

$\quad = P$(Shirt size = 11 or 12)

$\quad = P$(Shirt size = 11) + P(Shirt size = 12)

$\quad = 0.15 + 0.10$

$\quad = 0.25$

(c) The expected shirt size:

$\mu = E(x) = 6(0.09) + 7(0.14) + 8(0.15) + 9(0.17) + 10(0.20) +$
$11(0.15) + 12(0.10) = 9.09$

The standard deviation of shirt size:

$$\sigma = \sqrt{(6-9.09)^2 (0.09)+(7-9.09)^2 (0.14)+\ldots+(12-9.09)^2 (0.10)}$$

$$= \sqrt{3.24} = 1.80$$

(d) From the probability distribution, P(Shirt size = 8) = 0.15.
Therefore, she needs to order 1,000(0.15) = 150 shirts of size 8.

Combinations

A **combination** is the number of ways r items can be selected out of n items if the order of selection is *not* important. It is denoted by $\binom{n}{r}$, which reads as "n choose r," and is computed as

$$\binom{n}{r} = \frac{n!}{r!(n-r)!}$$

For any integer $n \geq 0$, $n!$, is read as "n factorial" and is computed as

$$n! = n(n-1)(n-2)(n-3)...3(2)1$$

For example, $3! = 3(2)1 = 6$ and $5! = 5(4)3(2)1 = 120$

Note that $0! = 1$ and $1! = 1$

Example 9: A teacher wants to choose two students to represent the class in a competition. She finds that there are five students in the class who meet the eligibility criteria: Calvin, Sung, Jan, Becky, and Antoine. Because all five are eligible, she decides to select two at random. In how many different ways can this teacher select two students out of five students?

Solution: This is a combination problem, because the order in which two students get selected does not matter. The following list gives all the possible ways in which two students can be selected from Calvin, Sung, Jan, Becky, and Antoine. Note that, because the order of selection is immaterial, selecting Calvin and Sung is the same as selecting Sung and Calvin.

1. Calvin and Sung	6. Sung and Becky
2. Calvin and Jan	7. Sung and Antoine
3. Calvin and Becky	8. Jan and Becky
4. Calvin and Antoine	9. Jan and Antoine
5. Sung and Jan	10. Becky and Antoine

There are 10 different ways to select two students out of five when the order of selection is not important. Using the combination function, we can find this number without having to list all the possibilities. The combination is as follows:

$$\binom{5}{2} = \frac{5!}{2!(5-2)!} = \frac{120}{2(6)} = 10$$

TI-83 or TI-84:
- Type the number 5 in the window
- Choose **MATH → PRB → 3: nCr**
- Type the number 2. This will result in 5 nCr 2
- Press **ENTER**

Example 10: In a bowling game, the pins are numbered 1 to 10, as shown:

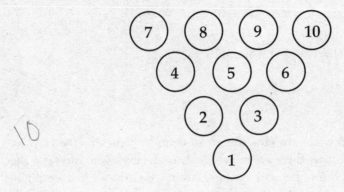

Figure 9

Suppose that following the first roll, three pins, arbitrarily located, are knocked down. In how many combinations can the remaining pins be standing after the first three have been knocked over?

Solution: The combination is as follows:

$$\binom{10}{3} = \frac{10}{3! \times 7!} = 120$$

Binomial Distribution

One example of a distribution of discrete random variables is the binomial distribution. A binomial distribution occurs in an experiment that possesses the following properties:

- There are n repeated trials
- All trials are identical and independent
- Each trial has two possible outcomes, in general known as "success" and "failure"

The binomial variable X:

$$X = \text{the number of successes in } n \text{ trials}$$

$$= 0, 1, 2, \ldots, n$$

$$P(x \text{ successes in } n \text{ trials}) = \binom{n}{x} p^x (1-p)^{n-x}$$

where $p = P$(success in a given trial).

Mean of a binomial random variable:

$$\mu = E(x) = np$$

Variance of a binomial random variable:

$$\sigma^2 = np(1 - p)$$

Some examples of binomial random variables:

- A quality control inspector takes a random sample of 20 items from a large lot, inspects each item, classifies each as defective or nondefective, and counts the number of defective items in the sample.
- A telephone survey asks 400 area residents, selected at random, if they support the new gasoline tax increase. The answers are recorded as "yes" or "no." The number of persons answering "yes" is counted.
- Consider families with three children. The number of girls out of the three children of each family is recorded.
- A certain medical procedure is performed on 15 patients who are not related to each other. The number of successful procedures is counted.
- A homeowner buys 20 azalea plants from a nursery. The number of plants that survive at the end of the year is counted.

The shape of the binomial distribution depends on the values of n and p. The distribution spreads from 0 to n. Figures 10–12 show different binomial distributions with $n = 10$.

For $n = 10$ and $p = 0.2$, the binomial distribution is right skewed with mean $\mu = 10(0.2) = 2$. In general, as p gets closer to 0 the binomial distribution becomes more right skewed. See Figure 10.

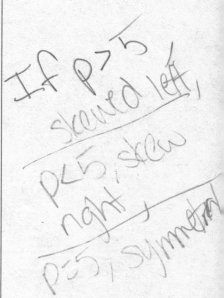

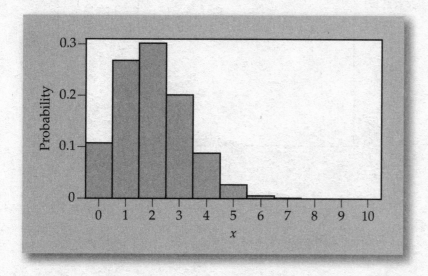

Figure 10: Binomial distribution with $n = 10$ and $p = 0.2$

For $p = 0.5$, the binomial distribution is symmetric with mean $\mu = 10(0.5) = 5$. See Figure 11.

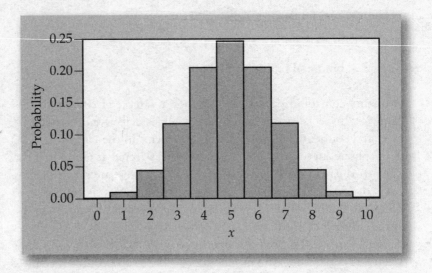

Figure 11: Binomial distribution with $n = 10$ and $p = 0.5$

For $p = 0.8$, the binomial distribution is left skewed with mean $\mu = 10(0.8) = 8$. In general, as p gets closer to 1, the binomial distribution becomes more left skewed. See Figure 12.

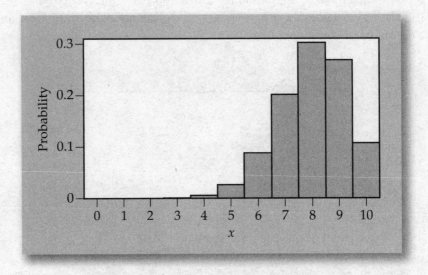

Figure 12: Binomial distribution with $n = 10$ and $p = 0.8$

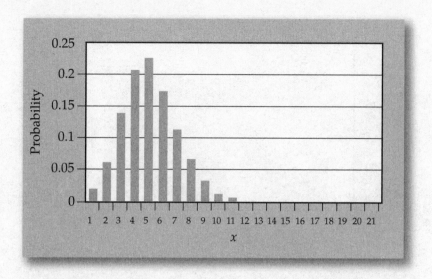

Figure 13: Binomial distribution with n = 20 and p = 0.2

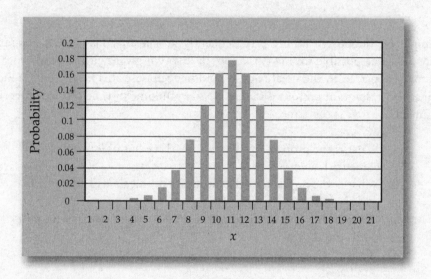

Figure 14: Binomial distribution with n = 20 and p = 0.5

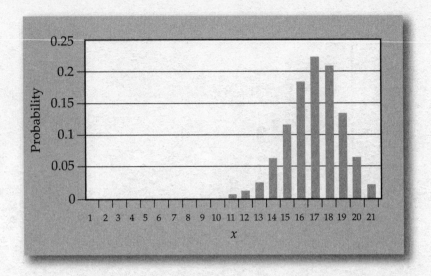

Figure 15: Binomial distribution with *n* = 20 and *p* = 0.8

Example 11: Suppose a family eats frequently at a nearby fast food restaurant. There are three possible toys (a car, a top, or a yo-yo) given with the kids' meals. The toys are placed in the meal bags at random. Suppose this family buys a kid's meal at this restaurant on four different days at random, and the chance of receiving any of the toys is the same.

(a) What is the probability that exactly three out of four meals will come with a yo-yo?

(b) What is the probability that at most two meals will come with a yo-yo?

(c) What is the probability of getting at least three yo-yos with four meals purchased?

(d) What is the expected number of yo-yos when four meals are purchased?

(e) Compute the standard deviation of the number of yo-yos when four meals are purchased.

Solution:

(a) Each kid's meal purchased is viewed as a trial with two possible outcomes, "yo-yo" or "no yo-yo." Let us consider getting a yo-yo as a success. Then:

$$p = P(\text{Getting a yo-yo with a meal}) = \frac{1}{3}.$$

Because 4 meals were purchased, there are 4 trials (*n* = 4). Then:

$$P(3 \text{ meals out of 4 with a yo-yo}) = \binom{4}{3}\left(\frac{1}{3}\right)^{3}\left(1-\frac{1}{3}\right)^{4-3} =$$

$$4(0.037)(0.667) = 0.0988$$

This is how you would get the probability with your calculator:

TI-83 or TI-84:
- Choose **2nd → DISTR → 0: binompdf(**
- Enter n, p, x values in that order separated by a comma.

$$\text{binompdf}(4,1/3,3)$$

- Press **ENTER**

(b) $P(\text{At most 2 meals with a yo-yo}) = P(0) + P(1) + P(2)$
This is a cumulative probability, $P(x \le 2)$:

$$P(\text{No yo-yo}) = P(x = 0) = \binom{4}{0}\left(\frac{1}{3}\right)^0\left(1-\frac{1}{3}\right)^{4-0} = 0.1975$$

$$P(\text{One yo-yo}) = P(x = 1) = \binom{4}{1}\left(\frac{1}{3}\right)^1\left(1-\frac{1}{3}\right)^{4-1} = 0.3951$$

$$P(\text{Two yo-yos})\ P(x = 2) = \binom{4}{2}\left(\frac{1}{3}\right)^2\left(1-\frac{1}{3}\right)^{4-2} = 0.2963$$

$$P(\text{At most 2 meals with a yo-yo}) = P(0) + P(1) + P(2)$$
$$= 0.1975 + 0.3951 + 0.2963$$
$$= 0.8889$$

Here's how you'd get this cumulative probability with your calculator:

TI-83 or TI-84:
- Choose **2nd → DISTR → A: binomcdf(**
- Enter n, p, x values in that order, separated by a comma.

$$\text{binomcdf}(4, 1/3, 2)$$

- Press **ENTER**

(c) $P(\text{At least 3 meals with a yo-yo}) = P(3) + P(4)$

$$= 0.0988 + \binom{4}{4}\left(\frac{1}{3}\right)^4\left(1-\frac{1}{3}\right)^{4-4}$$

$$= 0.0988 + 1\left(\frac{1}{3}\right)^4$$

$$= 0.0988 + 0.0123$$

$$= 0.1111$$

(d) $E(X) = np = 4\left(\frac{1}{3}\right) = \frac{4}{3} = 1.33$

On the average, we expect to get 1.33 yo-yos when four meals are purchased.

(e) Standard deviation is $\sigma = \sqrt{np(1-p)} = \sqrt{4\left(\frac{1}{3}\right)\left(1-\frac{1}{3}\right)} = 0.9428$

Simulating a Binomial Distribution

Let's simulate the situation in the previous example using a six-sided die. Designate the outcomes as follows:

- Getting a 1 or 2 on the die means getting a yo-yo with the meal. The probability of getting a number 1 or 2 is $\frac{2}{6} = \frac{1}{3}$.

- Getting one of the remaining numbers (3, 4, 5, or 6) means getting a different toy (not a yo-yo) with the meal. The probability of getting a 3, 4, 5, or 6 is $\frac{4}{6} = \frac{2}{3}$.

Because the family is purchasing four meals, roll the die four times. Each roll represents a meal purchased. Based on the outcome for each roll, determine the toy received with the meal using the above scheme. For example, imagine that the first set of four rolls resulted in the numbers (4, 3, 2, 6). This means that only the third meal came with a yo-yo, and the remaining three meals came with other toys. So from this set of four meals purchased, the family got only one yo-yo. Repeat this procedure (that of rolling the die four times and noting the number of yo-yos received out of four meals) 100 times. The results of one such simulation are listed below:

1, 1, 2, 1, 1, 1, 2, 1, 1, 1, 1, 2, 0, 0, 1, 0, 1, 1, 2, 1, 2, 0, 3, 1, 0,

0, 1, 3, 4, 1, 2, 1, 2, 2, 1, 0, 1, 1, 1, 0, 2, 2, 2, 0, 0, 1, 0, 3, 2, 2,

0, 1, 0, 1, 2, 1, 2, 1, 1, 0, 1, 1, 2, 1, 1, 2, 2, 3, 0, 2, 1, 2, 3, 2, 1,

1, 2, 0, 1, 3, 2, 1, 1, 1, 1, 1, 2, 1, 2, 2, 2, 2, 3, 1, 2, 2, 1, 1, 2, 1

This data shows that the first set of four meals resulted in getting one yo-yo, the second also resulted in one, the third resulted in two, and so on. The outcome zero means that the family got no yo-yos with the purchase of four meals; the number 4 means the family got a yo-yo with each of the four meals purchased. Now summarize the data as shown in Table 4:

Number of Meals out of 4 with a Yo-Yo	Simulated Count
0	16
1	45
2	31
3	7
4	1
Total	100

Table 4: Frequency distribution of number of meals with a yo-yo

Using these simulated results, we can estimate the probabilities and the expected value:

(a) *P*(Getting 3 meals with a yo-yo) = 7 out of 100 = 0.07
(b) *P*(Getting at most 2 meals with a yo-yo)
= *P*(0, 1, or 2 meals with a yo-yo)
= 92 out of 100
= 0.92
(c) *P*(Getting at least 3 meals with a yo-yo)
= *P*(3 or 4 meals with a yo-yo)
= 8 out of 100
= 0.08
(d) Expected number of yo-yos per 4 meals
= [0(16) + 1(45) + 2(31) + 3(7) + 4(1)]/100
= 132/100
= 1.32
Note that these numbers do not match the calculations in the previous section exactly, though they are close.

Geometric Distribution

Another example of a distribution of discrete random variables is the geometric distribution. The geometric distribution occurs in an experiment where repeated trials possess the following properties:

- The trials are repeated until the first success is observed.
- All trials are identical and independent.
- Each trial has two possible outcomes, in general known as "success" and "failure."

The geometric random variable X:

X = the number of trials required to obtain the first success = 0, 1, 2, …

$P(x$ trials needed until the first success is observed) = $(1 - p)^{x-1}p$

Mean of the geometric random variable:

$$\mu = E(X) = \frac{1}{p}$$

Variance of the geometric random variable:

$$\mu = Var(X) = \frac{1-p}{p^2}$$

Some examples of the geometric random variable:

- A worker opening oysters to look for pearls counts the number of oysters he has to open until he finds the first pearl.
- A supervisor at the end of an assembly line counts the number of non-defective items produced until he finds the first defective one.
- An electrician inspecting cable one yard at a time for defects counts the number of yards he inspects before he finds a defect.

Example 12: Let's go back to the example of the fast food restaurant. Again, there are three possible toys (a car, a top, a yo-yo) given with the kids' meals, and the toys are placed in the meal bags at random. Suppose the kid in the family has his heart set on getting a yo-yo, so the family will buy him kids' meals until they get one with a yo-yo in it.

    (a) Find the probability that the family will get its first yo-yo with the third meal.

    (b) Find the probability that the family will get its first yo-yo with the fifth meal.

    (c) What is the expected number of meals needed to get a yo-yo?

Solution: Each kid's meal purchased is viewed as a trial with two possible outcomes, "yo-yo" or "no yo-yo." Let us consider getting a yo-yo as a success. So,

$$p = P(\text{Getting a yo-yo with a meal}) = \frac{1}{3}$$

(a) P(Having to purchase exactly 3 meals before getting a yo-yo)

$= P(\text{No yo-yo in first 2 meals}) \, P(\text{Yo-yo with the 3rd meal})$

$= (1-p)(1-p)p$

$= (1-p)^2 p$

$= \left(1 - \frac{1}{3}\right)^2 \left(\frac{1}{3}\right)$

$= 0.148$

TI-83 or TI-84:

- Choose **2nd** → **DISTR** → **D: geometpdf(**
- Enter p, x values in that order separated by a comma.

$$\text{geometpdf } (1/3, 3)$$

- Press **ENTER**

(b) P(Having to purchase exactly 5 meals before getting a yo-yo)

$= (1-p)^4 p$

$= \left(1 - \frac{1}{3}\right)^4 \left(\frac{1}{3}\right)$

$= 0.0658$

(c) The expected number of meals to get a yo-yo

$$= E(X) = \frac{1}{p} = \frac{1}{\frac{1}{3}} = 3$$

Simulating a Geometric Distribution

Consider the earlier example of purchasing kids' meals. Let's simulate the situation using a six-sided die. Designate the outcomes as follows:

- Getting a 1 and 2 on the die means getting a yo-yo with the meal. The probability of getting a number 1 or 2 is $\frac{2}{6} = \frac{1}{3}$.

- Getting one of the remaining numbers (3, 4, 5, or 6) means getting a different toy (not a yo-yo) with the meal. The probability of getting a 3, 4, 5, or 6 is $\frac{4}{6} = \frac{2}{3}$.

Because the family will purchase meals till they get a yo-yo, roll the die until the number 1 or 2 shows. Each roll represents a meal purchased. Count the number of rolls it takes to get number 1 or 2. For example, the first set of rolls resulted in faces with numbers (4, 3, 6, 5, 6, 2). This means that the sixth meal came with a yo-yo, whereas the first five meals came with different (non-yo-yo) toys. So in this set, the family had to purchase six meals to get one yo-yo. Suppose the next set of rolls resulted in (5, 5, 1). In this case, the family had to purchase only three meals to get a yo-yo. Roll 100 of these sets. From each set, note the number of meals the family had to purchase to get a yo-yo. The results of one such simulation are listed below:

6, 3, 2, 1, 8, 1, 3, 3, 2, 2, 2, 1, 3, 1, 2, 1, 7, 2, 9, 1, 1, 2, 2, 2, 7,

6, 2, 1, 1, 2, 1, 3, 2, 1, 1, 4, 5, 1, 2, 5, 1, 2, 5, 5, 2, 1, 2, 3, 2, 2,

3, 2, 2, 1, 1, 2, 1, 3, 2, 4, 3, 1, 3, 2, 1, 4, 1, 2, 2, 1, 3, 2, 2, 1, 2,

3, 3, 4, 7, 1, 1, 3, 2, 1, 3, 4, 3, 3, 4, 1, 2, 1, 2, 1, 1, 1, 1, 2, 1, 1

This shows that the first set resulted in the family's purchasing six meals to get a yo-yo; the second time, it took the family three meals to get a yo-yo; the third time, it took the family just two meals. Now summarize the results as shown in Table 5 and Figure 16:

Number of Meals Purchased Before Getting a Yo-Yo	1	2	3	4	5	6	7	8	9
Simulated Count	34	32	17	6	4	2	3	1	1

Table 5: Frequency distribution of the number of meals purchased before getting a yo-yo

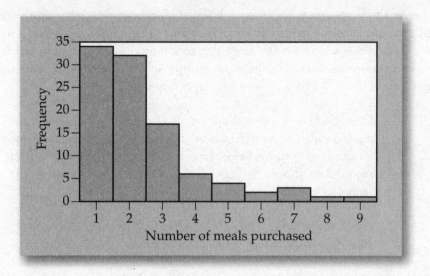

Figure 16: Frequency distribution of the number of meals purchased

Using these simulated results, we can estimate the following probabilities:

(a) P(Having to purchase 3 meals to get a yo-yo) = 17 out of 100 = 0.17.

(b) P(Having to purchase 5 meals to get a yo-yo) = 4 out of 100 = 0.04.

(c) Expected number of meals needed to get a yo-yo

= The mean number of meals needed to get a yo-yo

= [1(34) + 2(32) + 3(17) + 4(6) + 5(4) + 6(2) + 7(3) + 8(1) + 9(1)] / 100 = 2.43

On average, you would have to purchase 2.43 meals before you got a yo-yo.

Note again that these results do not match the calculations in the previous section exactly, though they are close.

Note on Binomial and Geometric Distributions

- In the binomial distribution, the number of trials (number of meals purchased) is fixed, and the number of successes (number of yo-yos received with a set of meals purchased) is a random event.

- In the geometric distribution, the number of successes (you need to get just one yo-yo) is fixed, but the number of trials required to get the success (the number of meals purchased before getting one yo-yo) is a random event.

Example 13: Suppose a large research hospital is interested in recruiting patients with a specific medical condition for an experiment. Overall, four in every 10 patients visiting this hospital suffer from this condition. The physician in charge of the project wants to determine the mean number of patients he needs to examine before he can identify two patients with this condition.

(a) Describe how you would use a table of random numbers to carry out a simulation for determining the number of patients the doctor needs to examine before he can identify two patients with the required condition. Include a description of what each digit will represent in your simulation.

(b) Use the random number table given below to show two runs of your simulation. Do this by marking up the table directly:

```
56085  31590  73956  27931  49899  68676  54570  95456  43655  46907
96254  15612  29355  61739  89226  18360  69722  46304  61735  10436
96880  54319  72584  10836  77289  74077  74042  27133  53459  66476
77295  82889  96136  17766  46568  31392  14120  64658  14620  90969
65508  98265  82101  29153  72906  68119  48288  16211  96864  90572
```

(c) Perform 100 runs of your simulation. Find the expected number of patients the doctor needs to interview before he finds two with the required condition.

Solution:

(a) With each patient, there are two possible outcomes: The patient either suffers from the condition or does not suffer from the condition. It is known that four out of every 10 patients visiting this hospital suffer from this condition. This means that the probability that a randomly selected patient will suffer from the condition is

$$\frac{4}{10} = 0.4$$

i.e., $p = 0.4$

Consider one-digit random numbers, 0 through 9. Designate numbers 1, 2, 3, 4 (any four will do) as patients with the condition and numbers 0, 5, 6, 7, 8, 9 (the remaining numbers) as patients without the condition. Start at the beginning of the first line of the random number chart. Each number represents a patient being examined. Classify each number as representing either "patient with condition" or "patient without condition." Stop when the second "patient with condition" is identified. Count the number of patients examined until two are found with the condition.

(b) Begin the first simulation in the first row and the second simulation in the second row.

56085   31590 73956 27931 49899 68676 54570 95456

96254 15612 29355 61739 89226 18360 69722 46304

The first run shows that a total of seven patients were examined before two with the condition were identified.

The second run shows that a total of five patients were examined before two with the specific condition were identified.

(c) The frequency distribution of a sample of 100 runs of the above-described simulation is shown in Table 6. Another simulation of 100 runs would result in slightly different counts, of course.

Number of Patients Examined to Find Two with the Condition	Simulated Count
2	39
3	27
4	15
5	7
6	6
7	3
8	1
9	2

Table 6: Frequency distribution of the number of patients examined to find two with the condition

E(Number of patients examined to identify 2 with the condition) = $[2(39) + 3(27) + 4(15) + 5(7) + 6(6) + 7(3) + 8(1) + 9(2)] / 100 = 3.37$

On the average, three to four patients will be examined to find two with the required condition.

THE PROBABILITY DISTRIBUTIONS OF CONTINUOUS RANDOM VARIABLES

Recall that a continuous random variable takes all possible values in a given range. For example:

- The distance traveled by a car using one gallon of gas
- Waiting time at the checkout counter of a grocery store
- The amount of water released through the Hoover Dam on a given day

Occasionally, when a discrete variable takes lots of values, it is treated as a continuous variable.

The probability distribution of a continuous random variable or **the continuous probability distribution** is a graph or a formula giving all possible values taken by a random variable and the corresponding probabilities. It is also known as the **density function.**

Let X be a continuous random variable taking values in the range (a, b). Then:

- The area under the density curve is equal to the probability.
- $P(L < X < U)$ = the area under the curve between L and U, where $a \leq L \leq U \leq b$.
- The total probability under the curve = 1.
- The probability that X takes a specific value is equal to 0, i.e., $P(X = x_0) = 0$.

The reason is that the probability of getting any x exactly is 0. For example, the chance of it raining exactly 3.00233221 inches in Rainy City is 0, but the chance of it raining between 3.00 and 3.01 inches is small but measurable.

The cumulative distribution function (CDF) of a random variable X is $P(X < x_0)$ for any $a < x_0 < b$. It is equal to 0 for any $x_0 < a$, and it is equal to 1 for any $x_0 > b$.

Example 14: The graph in Figure 17 gives the distribution of the yearly amount of rainfall in Rainy City.

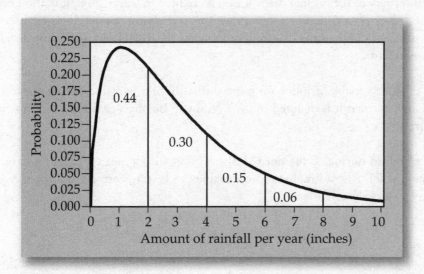

Figure 17: Probability distribution of amount of rainfall per year

In a randomly selected year,

  (a) What is the probability that Rainy City got more than eight inches of rain?
  (b) What is the probability that Rainy City got between two and six inches of rain?
  (c) What is the probability that Rainy City got exactly two inches of rain?
  (d) What is the probability that Rainy City got at most six inches of rain?

Solution: Let X = the amount of rain per year in Rainy City.

  (a) P(Rainy City got more than 8 inches of rain)
       = $P(X > 8) = 1 - P(X < 8) = 1 - [0.44 + 0.30 + 0.15 + 0.06] =$
       $1 - 0.95 = 0.05$
  (b) P(Rainy City got between 2 and 6 inches of rain)
       = $P(2 < X < 6) = 0.30 + 0.15 = 0.45$
  (c) P(Rainy City got exactly 2 inches of rain) = 0
  (d) P(Rainy City got at most 6 inches of rain)
       = $P(X \leq 6) = 0.44 + 0.30 = 0.15 = 0.89$

THE NORMAL DISTRIBUTION

The discovery of the normal distribution is credited to Carl Gauss. It is also known as the *bell curve* or *Gaussian distribution*. This is the most commonly used distribution in statistics because it closely approximates the distributions of many different measurements.

If a random variable X follows a normal distribution with mean μ and standard deviation σ, then it is denoted by $X \sim N(\mu, \sigma)$. The density function is shown in Figure 18.

The **standard normal** is the normal distribution with a mean of 0 and a standard deviation of 1. Any normal random variable can be transformed into the standard normal using the relation

$$Z = \frac{X - \mu}{\sigma}$$

which means $X \sim N(\mu, \sigma) \quad \Rightarrow \quad Z = \frac{X - \mu}{\sigma} \sim N(0, 1)$

and

$$Z \sim N(0, 1) \quad \Rightarrow \quad X = Z\sigma + \mu \sim N(\mu, \sigma)$$

The value of variable Z computed as $Z = \frac{X - \mu}{\sigma}$ for any specific value of X is known as the **z-score**. For example, suppose $X \sim N(10, 2)$. The z-score for $X = 12.5$ is then

$$Z = \frac{X - \mu}{\sigma} = \frac{12.5 - 10}{2} = 1.25$$

Properties of the Normal Distribution

The normal distribution has the following characteristics:

- It is continuous.
- It is symmetric around its mean.
- It is bell-shaped or mound-shaped.
- Mean = median = mode.
- The curve approaches the baseline (horizontal axis) on both sides of the mean without ever touching or crossing it.
- Nearly all of the distribution (99.73 percent) lies within three standard deviations of the mean.

- It has two inflection points: One at μ − σ and one at μ + σ. (Don't worry if you don't know what this means; it is from calculus and is not a topic on the AP exam.)
- The normal distribution is fully determined by two parameters, namely, mean and variance (or standard deviation).
- The location of the distribution on the number line depends on the mean of the distribution. See Figures 18 and 19.
- The shape of the distribution depends on the standard deviation. A normal distribution with a larger standard deviation is more spread out, while one with a smaller standard deviation is more tightly bunched. See Figure 19.

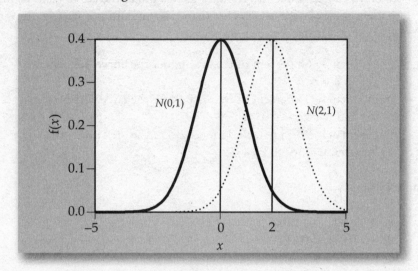

Figure 18: Normal distributions with different means 0 and 2 and standard deviations of 1

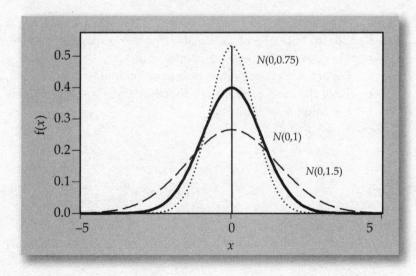

Figure 19: Normal distributions with means of 0 and standard deviations of 0.75, 1 and 1.5

Using the Normal Distribution Table

If the random variable X follows a normal distribution with mean μ and standard deviation σ, then the random variable $Z = \dfrac{X - \mu}{\sigma}$ follows a standard normal distribution, i.e., a normal distribution with mean 0 and standard deviation 1.

To find the area under the standard normal distribution—a normal distribution with mean 0 and standard deviation 1—you can simply look at the standard normal probability table, which is given to you on the AP exam and is also reprinted at the back of this book (Table A). To find the area under the curve (i.e., the probability) for any normal distribution other than the standard normal, we convert it to a standard normal using the formula above.

- Approximately 68 percent of the area under the curve lies between $\mu - \sigma$ and $\mu + \sigma$
- Approximately 95 percent of the area under the curve lies between $\mu - 2\sigma$ and $\mu + 2\sigma$
- Approximately 99.73 percent (almost all) of the area under the curve lies between $\mu - 3\sigma$ and $\mu + 3\sigma$

Example 15:

    (a) Find $P(Z < 1.27)$.
    (b) Find $P(Z < 0.82)$.
    (c) Find $P(0.82 < Z < 1.27)$.
    (d) Find $P(Z > 1.27)$.
    (e) Find the 95th percentile of the standard normal distribution.

Solution:

    (a) Refer to the normal probability table (Table A on pages 445–446).
- Go down to the row corresponding to 1.2
- Go across to the column corresponding to 0.07
- Read the number in the cross-section of the row for 1.2 and the column for 0.07
- It says that $P(Z < 1.27) = 0.8980$

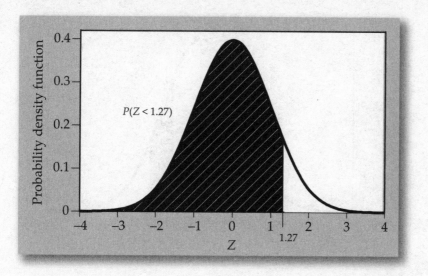

Figure 20: Shaded area under the standard normal distribution shows $P(Z < 1.27)$

TI-83 or TI-84:
- Choose **2nd → DISTR → 2: normalcdf(**
- Enter *lower bound, upper bound,* μ, and σ values in that order, separated by commas. The lower bound in this example should be negative infinity ($-\infty$). You can simulate ∞ and $-\infty$ by using any number beyond 5 standard deviations from the mean. This will display:

$$\text{normalcdf}(-5, 1.27, 0, 1)$$

- Press **ENTER**

(b) To find the $P(Z < 0.82)$, read the number in the cross-section of row for 0.8 and column for 0.02. We see that $P(Z < 0.82)$ = 0.7939.

(c) $P(0.82 < Z < 1.27) = P(Z < 1.27) - P(Z < 0.82)$
= 0.8980 - 0.7939
= 0.1041

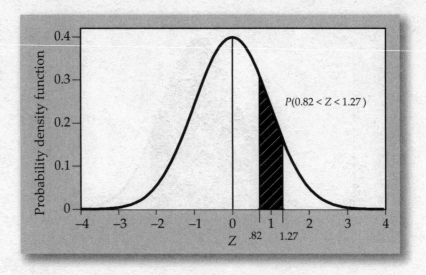

Figure 21: Shaded area under the standard normal distribution
shows $P(0.82 < Z < 1.27)$

TI-83 or TI-84:
- Choose **2nd** → **DISTR** → **2: normalcdf(**
- Enter *lower bound, upper bound,* μ, and σ values in that order separated by commas. This will display:

  normalcdf (0.82, 1.27, 0, 1)

- Press **ENTER**

(d) Because the area under the entire curve equals 1, the probability that Z is *greater* than a given number is 1 − (the probability that it is *less* than that number). See Figure 22.
$$P(Z > 1.27) = 1 - P(Z < 1.27)$$
$$= 1 - 0.8980$$
$$= 0.1020$$

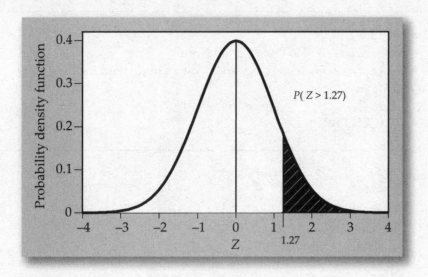

Figure 22: The darker shaded area under the standard normal distribution shows $P(Z > 1.27)$

(e) To find the 95th percentile means to find z_0 such that $P(Z < z_0) = 0.95$. To do this, we can simply use the table backward. Find the number closest to 0.95 among the probability values. Then we get $z_0 = 1.645$ (between 1.64 and 1.65).

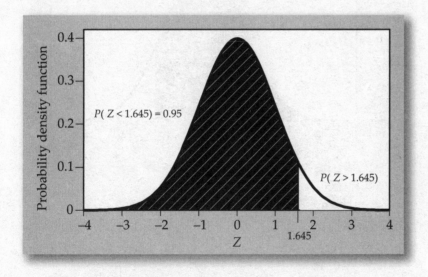

Figure 23: z-score such that $P(Z < z\text{-score}) = 0.95$

> **TI-83 or TI-84:**
> - Choose **2nd** → **DISTR** → **3: invNorm(**
> - Enter *probability below* z_0, μ, and σ values in that order separated by commas.
> $$\text{invNorm}(0.95, 0, 1)$$
> - Press **ENTER**

Example 16: Suppose $X \sim N(10, 2)$. Find

- (a) $P(X < 12.28)$
- (b) $P(6.72 < X < 12.28)$
- (c) Find x_0 such that $P(X > x_0) = 0.15$

Solution:

(a) $P(X < 12.28) = P\left(Z < \dfrac{12.28 - 10}{2} \right) = P(Z < 1.14) = 0.8729$

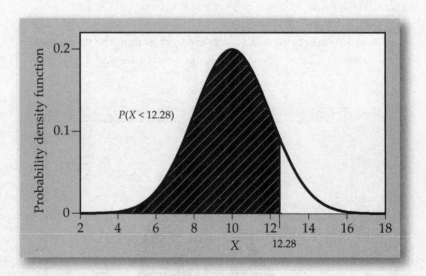

Figure 24: Shaded area shows $P(X < 12.28)$

$P(X < 12.28)$ is the same as $P(Z < 1.14)$ where $X \sim N(10, 2)$ and $Z \sim N(0, 1)$.

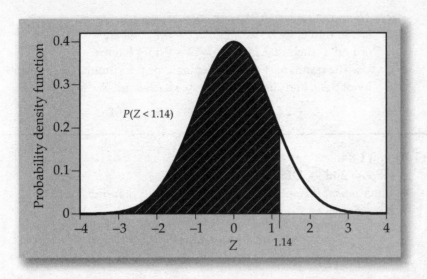

Figure 25: Shaded area shows $P(Z < 1.14)$

TI-83 or TI-84:
- Choose **2nd → DISTR → 2: normalcdf(**
- Enter *lower bound, upper bound*, μ, and σ values in that order separated by a comma. Simulate $-\infty$ for the lower bound by using any number beyond 5 standard deviations below the mean. This displays:

$$\text{normalcdf}(0, 12.28, 10, 2)$$

- Press **ENTER**

(b) $P(6.72 < X < 12.28) = P\left(\dfrac{6.72 - 10}{2} < Z < \dfrac{12.28 - 10}{2} \right)$

$= P(-1.64 < Z < 1.14)$

$= P(Z < 1.14) - P(Z < -1.64)$

$= 0.8729 - 0.0505$

$= 0.8224$

TI-83 or TI-84:
- Choose **2nd → DISTR → 2: normalcdf(**
- Enter *lower bound, upper bound*, μ, and σ values in that order separated by a comma. This displays:

$$\text{normalcdf}(6.72, 12.28, 10, 2)$$

- Press **ENTER**

(c) To find x_0 such that $P(X > x_0) = 0.15$,
i.e., to find z_0 such that $P(Z > z_0) = 0.15$, where $z_0 = \dfrac{x_0 - 10}{2}$
or find z_0 such that $P(Z < z_0) = 1 - 0.15 = 0.85$:
Use the standard normal table, look for the cumulative probability of 0.85, and then read the table backward. We get $z_0 = 1.04$

$$x_0 = 2z_0 + 10 = 2(1.04) + 10 = 12.08$$

TI-83 or TI-84:
- Choose **2nd** → **DISTR** → **3: invNorm(**
- Enter *probability below z_0,* μ, and σ values in that order, separated by a comma.

  invNorm(0.85, 10, 2)

- Press **ENTER**

The Normal Distribution as a Model For Measurements

The normal distribution is commonly used to describe a variety of measurements.

Example 17: At the end of the semester, a teacher determines the percent grade earned by students, taking into account all homework, test, and project scores. These student scores are normally distributed with a mean of 75 and a standard deviation of 8.

(a) If a 90-80-70-60 scheme is used to determine the letter grades of students, what percent of students earned an A?
(b) If a 90-80-70-60 scheme is used to determine the letter grades of students, what percent of students earned a B?
(c) If the teacher decides to give A's to the top 10 percent of the class, then what is the cutoff point for an A?
(d) If the teacher decides to give B's to the next 20 percent of the class, then what are the cutoff points for a B?

Solution: Remember that the grades are normally distributed with μ = 75 and σ = 8.

(a) In the 90-80-70-60 scheme, a grade of 90 or better earns an A. Compute $P(X \geq 90)$

$$P(X \geq 90) = P\left(Z \geq \frac{90 - 75}{8}\right) = P(Z \geq 1.875) = 1 - P(Z < 1.875) = 1 - 0.9696 = 0.0304$$

Therefore, 3.04 percent of the class got A's.

TI-83 or TI-84:
- Choose **2nd** → **DISTR** → **2: normalcdf(**
- Enter *lower bound, upper bound,* μ, and σ values in that order, separated by commas. Simulate an upper bound of ∞ by using any number beyond 5 standard deviations above the mean.

$$\text{normalcdf}(90, \ 130, \ 75, \ 8)$$

- Press **ENTER**

(**b**) In the 90-80-70-60 scheme, a grade of 80 or better but less than 90, earns a B.
Compute $P(80 \le X < 90)$

$$P(80 \le X < 90) = P\left(\frac{80-75}{8} \le Z < \frac{90-75}{8} \right)$$

$$= P(0.625 \le Z < 1.875)$$

$$= P(Z < 1.875) - P(Z - 0.625)$$

$$= 0.9696 - 0.7340$$

$$= 0.2356$$

Therefore, 23.56 percent of the class got B's.

TI-83 or TI-84:
- Choose **2nd** → **DISTR** → **2: normalcdf(**
- Enter *lower bound, upper bound,* μ, and σ values in that order, separated by commas.

$$\text{normalcdf}(80, \ 90, \ 75, \ 8)$$

- Press **ENTER**

(c) To find x_0 such that $P(X \ge x_0) = 0.10$, i.e. to find z_0 such that
$P(Z \ge z_0) = 0.10$, where $z_0 = \dfrac{x_0 - 75}{8}$ or find z_0 such that
$P(Z < z_0) = 1 - 0.10 = 0.90$: Use the standard normal table, look for
the cumulative probability of 0.90, and then read the table backward. We get $z_0 = 1.28$. $x_0 = 8z_0 + 75 = 8(1.28) + 75 = 85.24$.

(d) Similar to part (c), you must work backwards. The next 20 percent will be the range from the top 10 percent to the top 30 percent. The value at the top 10 percent was found in part (c), so follow those steps to determine the value at the top 30 percent mark. $P(Z < z_0) = 1 - 0.30 = 0.70$. From the standard normal table, we get $z_0 = 0.525$. $x_0 = 8z_0 + 75 = 8(0.525) + 75 = 79.2$. Therefore, the lower cutoff will be at 79.2 and the upper at 85.24.

COMBINING INDEPENDENT RANDOM VARIABLES

Sometimes we are interested in linear combinations of independent random variables. If we know the mean and the variance of two random variables, we can determine the mean and the variance of a linear combination of these variables. Suppose X is a random variable with mean μ_X and variance σ_X^2. Suppose Y is a random variablewith mean μ_Y and variance σ_Y^2. The two variables X and Y are independent.

Random Variable	Mean	Variance	
X	μ_X	σ_X^2	**Independent**
Y	μ_Y	σ_Y^2	

Now consider a linear combination of random variables $w = aX + bY$, where a and b are constants. Then $aX + bY$ is also a random variable, with mean $\mu_w = a\mu_X + b\mu_Y$ and variance $\sigma^2 w = a^2\sigma_X^2 + b^2\sigma_Y^2$. The following are specific cases:

Random Variable	Mean	Variance
aX	$a\mu_X$	$a^2\sigma_X^2$
$X + b$	$\mu_X + b$	σ_X^2
$aX + b$	$a\mu_X + b$	$a^2\sigma_X^2$
$X + Y$	$\mu_X + \mu_Y$	$\sigma_X^2 + \sigma_Y^2$
$X - Y$	$\mu_X - \mu_Y$	$\sigma_X^2 + \sigma_Y^2$
$aX + bY$	$a\mu_X + b\mu_Y$	$a^2\sigma_X^2 + b^2\sigma_Y^2$

If X and Y are normally distributed, then a linear combination of the two will also be normally distributed.

Example 18: A company markets 16-ounce bottles of jam. The mean amount of jam per bottle is 16 ounces, with a standard deviation of 0.1 ounces. The mean weight of the glass bottles holding the jam is five ounces, with a standard deviation of 0.5 ounces.

(a) What is the mean weight of a filled bottle?
(b) What is the standard deviation of the weight of a filled bottle?
(c) When shipped to stores, 12 random bottles are packed in each box. What is the mean and standard deviation of the weights of these random groupings of 12 bottles?
(d) The mean weight of the empty boxes is 50 ounces, with a standard deviation of four ounces. What is the mean weight and the standard deviation of the weights of the filled boxes?
(e) If the amount of jam per bottle, the weight of the bottles (with their lids), and the weight of the boxes are approximately normally distributed, what percent of boxes will weigh more than 320 ounces?

Solution: Let A = the amount of jam per bottle
B = the weight of the empty bottles (with lids)
C = the weight of a box packed with 12 filled bottles

It is known that

μ_A = 16 ounces, σ_A = 0.1 ounces, and
μ_B = 5 ounces, σ_B = 0.5 ounces.

(a) Let W = weight of a filled bottle = weight of bottle content + weight of a bottle (with its lid)
Therefore the mean weight of a filled bottle is

$$\mu_W = \mu_A + \mu_B = 16 + 5 = 21 \text{ ounces}$$

(b) The standard deviation of the weight of a filled bottle is

$$\sigma_W = \sqrt{\sigma_A^2 + \sigma_B^2} = \sqrt{0.1^2 + 0.5^2} = 0.5099 \approx 0.51 \text{ ounces}$$

Remember that you cannot add standard deviations, only variances.

(c) Twelve random bottles are grouped together. Let G = total weight of a group of 12 filled bottles.
The mean weight of the group = $\mu_G = 12\mu_W = 12(21) = 252$ ounces
The standard deviation of the weight of the group is

$$\sqrt{12^2 \sigma_W^2} = \sqrt{12^2 (0.51)^2} = 6.12 \text{ ounces}$$

(d) Let E = the weight of an empty box
C = the weight of a packed box = $G + E$
The mean weight of a packed box is $\mu_C = \mu_G + \mu_E = 252 + 50 = 302$ ounces

The standard deviation of the weights of the packed boxes is

$$\sigma_C = \sqrt{\sigma_G^2 + \sigma_E^2} = \sqrt{6.12^2 + 4^2} = 7.31 \text{ ounces}$$

(e) Because all weights are approximately normally distributed, $C \sim N(302, 7.31)$. Therefore,

$$P(C > 320) = P\left(Z > \frac{320 - 302}{7.31}\right) = P(Z > 2.46) = 1 - P(Z < 2.46) = 0.0069$$

Thus, 0.69 percent boxes will weigh more than 320 ounces.

SAMPLING DISTRIBUTIONS

Terms and Concepts

- A **parameter** is a numerical measure of a population. For example, a student's GPA is computed using grades from all his or her courses, therefore, GPA is a parameter.
- A **statistic** is a numerical measure of a sample. An example is the percent of votes received by a presidential candidate. Generally, not every eligible voter votes in a presidential election. Therefore, the president is elected based on the support received from a sample of the eligible voters, so the percent is a statistic. (If, however, every eligible voter does vote, then the percent of votes received would be a parameter.) A good mnemonic for this is that **p**arameter and **p**opulation both start with **p**, and **s**ampling and **s**tatistic both start with **s**.
- The **sampling distribution** is the probability distribution of a statistic. Different samples of the same size from the same population will result in different statistic values. Therefore, a statistic is a random variable. Any table, list, graph, or formula giving all possible values a statistic can take and their corresponding probabilities give a sampling distribution of that statistic.
- The **standard error** is the standard deviation of a statistic. Fun fact: Parameters are usually represented by Greek letters, statistics by Roman letters.

Central Limit Theorem

Regardless of the shape of the distribution of the population, if a large number of samples are taken from that population, then the distribution of the sample means will be approximately normal, with mean.

$$\mu_{\bar{X}} = \mu \text{ and standard deviation } \sigma_{\bar{X}} = \frac{\sigma}{\sqrt{n}}$$

Basically, the central limit theorem tells us the following:

Regardless of the shape of the population distribution, as the sample size n increases:

- The shape of the distribution of $\overline{X}$ becomes more symmetric and bell-shaped (more like a normal distribution).
- The center of the distribution of $\overline{X}$ remains at μ.
- The spread of the distribution of $\overline{X}$ decreases and the distribution becomes more peaked.

Sampling Distribution of a Sample Proportion

Consider a population with a proportion of successes (for example, "yes" answers to the question "Do you support the president's policies?") equal to p. Take a random sample of size n from this population and compute the sample proportion $\hat{p}$. Note that $\hat{p}$ estimates p. Different samples of size n will result in different $\hat{p}$ values. Therefore, $\hat{p}$ is a random variable. The probability of occurrence differs among the different $\hat{p}$ values. Some values of $\hat{p}$ are more likely to occur than others. All possible values of $\hat{p}$ along with their corresponding probabilities give the sampling distribution of $\hat{p}$. For a sufficiently large n, the sampling distribution of $\hat{p}$ is approximately normal, with mean

$$\mu_{\hat{p}} = p \text{ and standard deviation } \sigma_{\hat{p}} = \sqrt{\frac{p(1-p)}{n}}$$

Sampling Distribution of a Sample Mean

Consider a population with a mean equal to μ. Take a random sample of size n from this population and compute the sample mean $\overline{X}$. Note that $\overline{X}$ estimates μ. Different samples of size n will result in different $\overline{X}$ values. Therefore, $\overline{X}$ is a random variable. The probability of occurrence differs among the different $\overline{X}$ values. Some values of $\overline{X}$ are more likely to occur than others. All the possible values of $\overline{X}$ along with their corresponding probabilities give the sampling distribution of $\overline{X}$. For a sufficiently large n, the sampling distribution of $\overline{X}$ is approximately normal, with mean

$$\mu_{\overline{X}} = \mu \text{ and standard deviation } \sigma_{\overline{X}} = \frac{\sigma}{\sqrt{n}}$$

Sampling Distribution of a Difference Between Two Independent Sample Proportions

Consider two populations with proportions of successes equal to p_1 and p_2, respectively. Imagine that we want to find the difference in population proportions $(p_1 - p_2)$. Take independent random samples of sizes n_1 and n_2, respectively, from these populations and compute the respective sample proportions $\hat{p}_1$ and $\hat{p}_2$. Note that $(\hat{p}_1 - \hat{p}_2)$ estimates $(p_1 - p_2)$. Different samples of sizes n_1 and n_2 will result in different $(\hat{p}_1 - \hat{p}_2)$ values. Therefore, $(\hat{p}_1 - \hat{p}_2)$ is a random variable. The probability of occurrence differs among the different $(\hat{p}_1 - \hat{p}_2)$ values. Some values of $(\hat{p}_1 - \hat{p}_2)$ are more likely to occur than others. All the possible values of $(\hat{p}_1 - \hat{p}_2)$ along with their corresponding probabilities give the sampling distribution of $(\hat{p}_1 - \hat{p}_2)$. For sufficiently large sample sizes, the sampling distribution of $(\hat{p}_1 - \hat{p}_2)$ is approximately normal, with mean $\mu_{(\hat{p}_1 - \hat{p}_2)} = (p_1 - p_2)$ and standard deviation

$$\sigma_{(\hat{p}_1 - \hat{p}_2)} = \sqrt{\frac{p_1(1 - p_1)}{n_1} + \frac{p_2(1 - p_2)}{n_2}}$$

Example 19: The GPAs of graduating students at a large university are normally distributed, with a mean GPA of 2.8 and a standard deviation of 0.5. A random sample of 50 students is taken from all the graduating students.

(a) Find the probability that the mean GPA of the sampled students is above 3.0.

(b) Find the probability that the mean GPA of sampled students is between 2.7 and 3.0.

Solution: Sample size 50 is sufficiently large for us to assume approximate normality for the sampling distribution of $\overline{X}$ with $\mu_{\overline{X}} = 2.8$ and $\sigma_{\overline{X}} = \dfrac{0.5}{\sqrt{50}} = 0.071$. In other words, $X \sim N(2.8, 0.071)$ approximately.

(a) P(The mean GPA of the sampled students is above 3.0)

$$= P(\overline{X} > 3.0)$$

$$= P\left(Z > \frac{3.0 - 2.8}{0.071}\right)$$

$$= P(Z > 2.82)$$

$$= 0.0024$$

There is less than a 1 percent chance (0.24 percent) that the mean GPA of the 50 sampled students will exceed 3.0.

(b) *P*(The mean GPA of sampled students is between 2.7 and 3.0)

$$= P(2.7 < \bar{X} < 3.0)$$

$$= P\left(\frac{2.7 - 2.8}{0.071} < Z < \frac{3.0 - 2.8}{0.071} \right)$$

$$= P(-1.41 < Z < 2.82)$$

$$= 0.9183$$

There is almost a 92 percent chance that the mean GPA of the 50 sampled students will be between 2.7 and 3.0.

Sampling Distribution of a Difference Between Two Independent Sample Means

Consider two populations with means equal to μ_1 and μ_2, respectively. Imagine that we want to find the difference in population means $(\mu_1 - \mu_2)$. Take independent random samples of sizes n_1 and n_2, respectively, from these populations and compute the respective sample means $\bar{X}_1$ and $\bar{X}_2$. Note that $(\bar{X}_1 - \bar{X}_2)$ estimates $(\mu_1 - \mu_2)$. Different samples of size n_1 and n_2 will result in different $(\bar{X}_1 - \bar{X}_2)$ values. Therefore, $(\bar{X}_1 - \bar{X}_2)$ is a random variable. The probability of occurrence differs among the different $(\bar{X}_1 - \bar{X}_2)$ values. Some values of $(\bar{X}_1 - \bar{X}_2)$ are more likely to occur than others. All the possible values of $(\bar{X}_1 - \bar{X}_2)$, along with their corresponding probabilities, give the sampling distribution of $(\bar{X}_1 - \bar{X}_2)$. For sufficiently large n_1 and n_2, the sampling distribution of $(\bar{X}_1 - \bar{X}_2)$ is approximately normal with mean $\mu_{(\bar{X}_1 - \bar{X}_2)} = (\mu_1 - \mu_2)$ and standard deviation

$$\sigma_{(\bar{X}_1 - \bar{X}_2)} = \sqrt{\frac{\sigma_1^2}{n_1} + \frac{\sigma_2^2}{n_2}}$$

CHAPTER 6 REVIEW QUESTIONS

Multiple-Choice Questions

Answers can be found at the end of this section.

1. Sixty percent of chocolate desserts ordered at a restaurant are ordered by women. Of these women, seventy percent share their dessert. What is the probability that a randomly selected chocolate dessert was ordered by a woman who will share it?

   (A) 0.13
   (B) 0.18
   (C) 0.42
   (D) 0.45
   (E) 0.70

2. The average weight of dogs that come to a certain vet's office is 55.6 lbs, with a standard deviation of 2.2 lbs. If the weights are normally distributed, what percent of dogs weigh more than 60 lbs?

   (A) 66.8%
   (B) 47.2%
   (C) 33.4%
   (D) 15.9%
   (E) 2.28%

3. An intern goes to a coffee shop every day to buy four small coffees. Each cup contains a mean of 12 oz of coffee, with a standard deviation of 1.2 oz. The cups holding the coffee each have a mean weight of 2 oz, with a standard deviation of 0.1 oz. The intern carries the coffees in a carrier that has a mean weight of 8 oz, with a standard deviation of 0.5 oz. What is the standard deviation of the weight of the carrier holding four filled coffee cups?

   (A) 1.304 oz
   (B) 1.342 oz
   (C) 2.460 oz
   (D) 4.843 oz
   (E) 7.810 oz

4. Which of the following is FALSE about the central limit theorem?

   (A) As the sample size, n, increases the center of the distribution of $\overline{X}$ remains at μ.
   (B) It is only valid if the population distribution is normal.
   (C) The distribution of $\overline{X}$ becomes more peaked as n increases.
   (D) The sample distribution will be approximately normal as n increases.
   (E) As n increases, the spread of the distribution of $\overline{X}$ decreases

5. If you toss a fair coin seven times and get heads every time, then the eighth toss MUST be tails. Is this true?

   (A) Yes because there have been so many heads, there must be a tails next.
   (B) Yes, otherwise the coin is not really fair.
   (C) Yes, the law of large numbers says that half the tosses must be tails, so tails is overdue.
   (D) No, the next toss cannot be predicted with certainty from the previous tosses.
   (E) No, the coin is not really fair, so it could be heads again.

6. At a certain college, ten percent of freshmen enter without a major declared. Of those who enter with a major declared, twenty percent change it by the end of their second year. If the college admits 150 freshmen this year, how many will end their second year with the major they declared upon entry?

   (A) 12
   (B) 27
   (C) 108
   (D) 123
   (E) 147

7. At an ice cream shop, a sundae is made by selecting two flavors of ice cream and topping them with fudge, whipped cream, nuts, and a cherry. The available flavors of ice cream are chocolate, vanilla, strawberry, rocky road, chocolate chip cookie dough, and mint chip. How many different sundae combinations are possible?

(A) 2
(B) 15
(C) 24
(D) 120
(E) 720

8. The probability that Sue purchases a dress is $\frac{3}{5}$. If she does buy a dress, the probability that she buys shoes is $\frac{5}{8}$. If she does not buy a dress, the probability that she buys shoes is $\frac{1}{4}$. If you learn Sue bought shoes, what is the probability that she bought a dress?

(A) $\frac{1}{10}$
(B) $\frac{3}{8}$
(C) $\frac{19}{40}$
(D) $\frac{15}{19}$
(E) $\frac{19}{20}$

9. A math teacher and a history teacher each assigns her students a textbook for her class. A math text book has an average weight of 8.00 lbs with a standard deviation of 0.4lbs. A history textbook has an average weight of 6.00 lbs with a standard deviation of 0.2lbs.

What is the mean weight of both the textbooks?

(A) 8.00 lbs
(B) 14.00 lbs
(C) 10.00 lbs
(D) 6.00 lbs
(E) 12.00 lbs

10. Suzie receives a math textbook that weighs 7.6 lbs and a history textbook that weighs 6.2 lbs. On average, how many standard deviations from the norm are Suzie's textbooks?

(A) −2.0
(B) −1.0
(C) 0.0
(D) 1.0
(E) 2.0

Free-Response Questions

11. In a classroom, textbooks are distributed at the beginning of the bell and collected at the end. There are 15 books that are thoroughly mixed before every bell and, of those 15, 5 are missing a table of contents.

    a. If 10 books are selected. What is the probability that at most 2 of them are missing a table of contents?
    b. What is the probability that the first book missing a table of contents will be the seventh book selected?

    $a.$

12. A student is selecting between two new computers for the start of the school year. Computer A costs $550 plus $100 for a lifetime warranty. Computer B costs $600 plus $50 per repair over its lifetime. The student only expects the computer he buys to last 5 years before he upgrades. The table shows the probability of repairs required to Computer B over five years. Based on this information, what is the difference between the mean costs of Computer A (with the warranty) and Computer B?

Number of Repairs	0	1	2	3	4
Probability	0.40	0.25	0.20	0.10	0.05

CHAPTER 6 ANSWERS AND EXPLANATIONS

1. **C** $P(W)$ = The probability that a given chocolate dessert is ordered by a woman = 0.60 and $P(S \mid W)$ = The probability that the chocolate dessert ordered by a woman will be shared = 0.70. We are then asked to determine the intersection of these two events: $P(W \cap S) = P(W) \bullet P(S \mid W)$ = 0.60 • 0.70 = 0.42. Thus, the probability that an ordered chocolate dessert will be ordered by a woman who then shares it is 0.42.

2. **E** In order to find the percent of dogs weighing more than 60 lbs, we need to find the area under the normal curve that is greater than 60 lbs. Therefore, we must use a z-score: $P(X > 60) = (z > \dfrac{6 - 55.6}{2.2}) = P(z > 2) = 1 - 0.9772 = 0.0228$. (Use your calculator or the standard normal table to find the value at $z = 2$.) When you convert 0.0228 to a percentage, it is 2.28%.

3. **D** The carrier has a standard deviation of 0.5 oz. Each coffee has a standard deviation of 1.2 oz, but note that the carrier is holding four of them. There are also four cups in the carrier, each with a standard deviation of 0.1 oz. When combining standard deviations of random variables, remember you are initially combining their variances. The rules that apply here are: random variable aX has variance $a^2 \sigma_x^2$, where a is a constant. Further, random variable $X+Y$ has variance $\sigma_x^2 + \sigma_y^2$. Therefore, the variance of four coffees is $4^2(1.2)^2 = 23.04$. The variance of four cups is $4^2(0.1)^2 = 0.16$. Finally, the random variables' variances can be combined to the variance of four coffees, four cups and the carrier: $4^2(1.2)^2 + 4^2(0.1)^2 + 0.5^2 = 23.04 + 0.16 + 0.25 = 23.45$. Take the square root to get the standard deviation: $\sqrt{23.45} = 4.843$.

4. **B** The population can be normal or not for the central limit theorem to hold; the central limit theorem is not concerned with the distribution of the population. All of the other statements about the sample population are true under the central limit theorem.

5. **D** Each toss is an independent event, so the seven heads that came up before do not affect the eighth toss. Further, the law of large numbers says that as the number of trials increases, the percentage of hits will approach the expected value. In this case, as we increase the number of trials (and this means to the 100s–1000s range), the percentage of heads will approach the expected value, 0.5.

6. **C** 150 freshmen enter and 90% of them declare a major, so 135 declare a major. Of those 135, 80% end their second year with that major, so 108 don't change. Or, $P(D)$ = the probability of freshmen who do not declare and $P(D')$ = the probability who declare; $P(C)$ = the probability of those who declare who change it and $P(C')$ = the probability who do not change. This problem is interested in $P(D' \cap C') = P(D') \bullet P(C' \mid D') = 0.90 \bullet 0.80 = 0.72$. Since there are 150 freshmen, multiply the probability by the number of freshmen, 0.72 • 150 = 108.

7. **B** Be careful about what the question said. All sundaes are made by selecting two flavors of ice cream and are topped with a standard set of toppings, so the toppings do not affect the types of possible sundaes! The only thing that affects the types of sundaes available is the combinations of flavors selected. Recall the formula for calculating the number of combinations possible: $\binom{n}{r} = \dfrac{n!}{r!(n-r)!}$. In this problem $n = 6$ and $r = 2$, so $\binom{6}{2} = \dfrac{6!}{2!(6-2)!} = 15$.

8. **D** We are trying to find the conditional probability that a dress was bought given that shoes were bought. Start with a tree diagram:

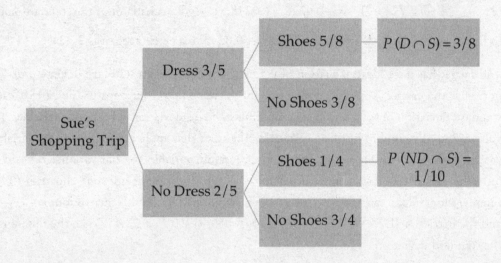

Now insert the values into the equation:

$$P(D|S) = \frac{P(D \cap S)}{P(S)} = \frac{3/8}{3/8 + 1/10} = \frac{3/8}{19/40} = \frac{15}{19}$$

9. **B** Here, the question is asking for the mean weight of both textbooks. Therefore, we need to find the sum of the average weight of each textbook. Accordingly, 8.00 lbs + 6.00 lbs = 14.00 lbs, and choice (B) is correct.

10. **C** There is a lot of information in this question, so take bite-sized pieces! First, you are told that Suzie receives a math textbook that weighs 7.6 lbs, or one standard deviation from the norm. Next, you are told that Suzie receives a history textbook that weighs 6.2 lbs, or one standard deviation from the norm. Finally, you need to calculate the average number of standard deviations Suzie's textbooks are from the norm. Thus, $\dfrac{1+1}{2} = 1$, and choice (C) is correct.

11.   a.   The probability of at most two books is the sum of the probability of 0 books, 1 book and

2 books and each of these probabilities are the probabilities of binomial random variables.

Therefore, you can use the general formula for the probability of a binomial random variable:

$\left(\dfrac{n}{x}\right)p^{x(1-p)n-x}$. Thus, $P(x=1)\left(\dfrac{15}{1}\right)\left(\dfrac{1}{3}\right)^{1}\left(1-\dfrac{1}{3}\right)^{15-1}=0.017127$, and

$P(x=2)=\left(\dfrac{15}{2}\right)\left(\dfrac{1}{3}\right)^{2}\left(1-\dfrac{1}{3}\right)^{15-2}=0.059946.$

Finally, $P(at\ most\ 2)=P(0)+P(1)+P(2)=0.00228+0.017127+0.059946=0.079357$.

b.   The probability that the first book is missing the table of contents is the seventh book is the probability of a geometric random variable with the general formula:

$P(x$ trials needed until the first success is observed$)=(1-p)^{x-1}p.$

Thus, $P(x=7)=\left(1-\dfrac{1}{3}\right)^{7-1}\left(\dfrac{1}{3}\right)=0.029264.$

12.   Computer A costs: $650

Computer B costs: $600 + expected cost of repairs

$\mu_{cost\ of\ repairs}=\$0(0.40)+\$50(0.25)+\$100(0.20)+\$150(0.10)+\$200(0.05)=\$57.50$

So, Computer B would be expected to cost $657.50.

The difference between the mean costs of A and B is $650 − $657.50 = −$7.50. Therefore, Computer B costs $7.50 more than Computer A.

Chapter 7
Statistical Inference

This chapter discusses the use of estimation and statistical inference in order to solve the types of problems you'll see on the AP Statistics Exam. In the multiple-choice section, this topic appears in 12 to 16 out of 40 questions. In the free-response section, this topic appears in two to three out of six questions.

CONFIRMING MODELS

Important information about a population of interest is often unknown, but we can take samples from the population and gather and summarize the information from the samples. Such summary statistics can then be used to

- estimate unknown population characteristics
- make inferences about unknown population characteristics

PARAMETERS AND STATISTICS

In a telephone survey conducted by a local newspaper, 400 randomly selected residents of a county on the Gulf of Mexico were asked, "Are you in favor of spending tax money on measures to prevent the erosion of private beaches?" The answers were recorded as "yes," "no," or "no opinion." The newspaper found that 76 percent of respondents were against spending tax money to support private beaches. This percentage, known as a statistic, was calculated from the information obtained from a random sample of county residents and not the entire population of that county. Still, it provides a reasonable estimate for the unknown parameter, namely, the percentage of *all* county residents who oppose such action.

- A **parameter** is a characteristic of a population. The following are all examples of parameters, i.e., numbers describing respective populations:
  - o the mean annual household income in the state of California
  - o the percentage of voters in favor of a certain presidential candidate in the state of Florida
  - o the variance of the amount of sugar per can of a specific brand of soda

- A **statistic** is a number computed from the sample. Generally, a statistic is used to estimate an unknown parameter and make an inference about it. The following are all examples of statistics:
  - o the mean annual household income computed from 500 randomly selected households in the state of California
  - o the percentage of voters in favor of a certain presidential candidate in a sample of 385 randomly selected voters in the state of Florida
  - o the variance of the amount of sugar per can of a specific brand of soda in 12 randomly selected cans

ESTIMATION

Generally, population characteristics (parameters) are unknown. To estimate them, we take samples from the population and use information from those samples to make our best guess. This procedure of guessing an unknown parameter value using the observed values from samples is known as an **estimation process**. A specific guess or value computed from a sample is known as an **estimate**.

To estimate the mean annual income per resident of Los Angeles County, we would probably use the mean annual income per resident of a random sample of residents of Los Angeles County. The sample mean would estimate the unknown population mean. Similarly, if we were interested in estimating the proportion of voters in favor of a candidate in the state of Louisiana, then we would use the proportion of voters in favor of this candidate from any random sample of voters from Louisiana. Again, the sample proportion would estimate the population proportion.

There are two estimation methods:

- **Point estimation** gives a single value as an estimate of the unknown parameter and makes no allowance for the uncertainty of the value's accuracy.
- **Interval estimation** recognizes the uncertainty of the estimate's accuracy and compensates for it by specifying a range of values around the estimate within which the population parameter may actually lie.

For example, Paul is planning a trip to Florida during his spring break. He collects information about the trip and prepares a budget. Using the collected information, he concludes, "This trip will cost me $1,000, give or take $100." Paul is expecting the cost of his trip to be somewhere between $900 and $1,100. Because he does not know all the exact costs for the different components of this trip, his estimation procedure does not guarantee that the actual cost of the trip will be within the estimated range, but still he believes that there is a very good chance that it will be within those limits. His estimated cost of $1,000 is a point estimate of the unknown cost of the trip. The range of $100 around the point estimate of the cost is known as the **margin of error**. The estimated range of cost ($900–$1,100) is an **interval estimate** of the cost of his trip.

POINT ESTIMATION

Consider a population with an unknown parameter θ (*theta*). Let $X_1, X_2,..., X_n$ be a random sample from this population. A point estimator of θ is a statistic computed from the sample to estimate the value of the unknown parameter. That means that θ is a function of $X_1, X_2,..., X_n$. Some examples are listed below:

- If θ is the unknown population mean μ, then the point estimate is $\overline{X}$. In other words, the sample mean $\overline{X}$ is an estimator for μ. It is computed from the sampled data as

$$\overline{X} = \frac{\left(X_1 + X_2 + \cdots + X_n\right)}{n}$$

For example, the mean family income computed from a random sample of families from Miami estimates the mean family income in Miami.

- If θ is the unknown population proportion p, then the point estimate is $\hat{p}$. In other words, the sample proportion $\hat{p}$ is an estimator for p. It is computed from the sampled data as

$$\hat{p} = \frac{\text{Number of favorable occurrences}}{\text{Sample size}}$$

For example, the proportion of children receiving free lunches obtained from a random sample of 100 children in a certain county's education system estimates the proportion of children receiving free lunches in the entire education system of that county.

- If θ is the unknown population variance σ^2, then the point estimate is S^2. The sample variance S^2 is an estimator for σ^2. It is computed from the sampled data as

$$S^2 = \frac{\sum_{i=1}^{n}\left(X_i - \overline{X}\right)^2}{n-1}$$

The variance in the fat content of 2 percent milk computed from 15 randomly selected gallons of milk estimates the variance in the fat content of all the 2 percent milk bottled by that dairy.

- If θ is the unknown difference in population means $(\mu_1 - \mu_2)$, then the point estimate is $(\overline{X}_1 - \overline{X}_2)$. The difference in sample means $(\overline{X}_1 - \overline{X}_2)$ is an estimator for $(\mu_1 - \mu_2)$. It is computed from the sampled data as $(\overline{X}_1 - \overline{X}_2) =$

$$\left(\overline{X}_1 - \overline{X}_2\right) = \left[\frac{\left(X_{11} + X_{12} + ... + X_{1n_1}\right)}{n_1}\right] - \left[\frac{\left(X_{21} + X_{22} + ... + X_{2n_2}\right)}{n_2}\right]$$

Note: Subscripts 11, 12, etc., indicate "one-one" (not 11) and "one-two" (not 12).

For example, if we are interested in estimating the difference in the mean lifespan of two brands of tires, then we could use the difference in the mean lifespan of randomly selected samples of these two brands of tires.

- If θ is the unknown difference in population proportions $(p_1 - p_2)$, then the point estimate is $(\hat{p}_1 - \hat{p}_2)$. The difference in sample proportions $(\hat{p}_1 - \hat{p}_2)$ is an estimator for $(p_1 - p_2)$.

It is computed from the sampled data as

$$(\hat{p}_1 - \hat{p}_2) =$$
$$\left[\frac{\text{Favorable occurences in sample 1}}{\text{Size of sample 1}} \right] - \left[\frac{\text{Favorable occurences in sample 2}}{\text{Size of sample 2}} \right]$$

For example, to estimate the difference in the proportion of women graduating with a degree in engineering at two major universities in Alabama, we could use the difference in those proportions computed from randomly selected samples of engineering students from each of these universities.

Sampling Distribution of a Statistic

As seen from these examples, the point estimate statistic is a function of random variables. Therefore, it is a random variable itself. Different samples will result in different estimates. How close or how far can these estimates be from the true value? We can answer this question by studying the distribution of the estimates. The **sampling distribution** of a statistic is the distribution of estimates (values taken by the statistic) from all possible samples of the same size from the same population.

Example 1: Suppose a student is interested in estimating p, the probability of getting heads when a penny is tossed. Suppose she tosses a penny 50 times and gets 24 heads. This sample of 50 tosses gives her an estimated probability ($\hat{p}$) of $\frac{24}{50} = 0.48$. So the student decides to see what happens if she repeats the experiment. The histogram and the table on the next two pages summarize the results of 100 such experiments, each of 50 tosses:

Estimated P(Heads)	Number of Samples Giving This Estimate	Estimated P(Heads)	Number of Samples Giving This Estimate
0.32	1	0.50	14
0.34	2	0.52	10
0.36	3	0.54	16
0.38	3	0.56	5
0.40	5	0.58	5
0.42	6	0.60	2
0.44	6	0.62	3
0.46	6	0.64	2
0.48	11	0.66	0

Table 1: Distribution of P(Heads) estimated from 50 tosses

Table 1 gives a sampling distribution of a certain statistic, i.e., the probability of getting heads as estimated from 50 tosses of a penny.

Although an estimator is a random variable, we would like to get estimates close to the actual value. Three criteria used to evaluate the quality of a point estimator are

- The center of the distribution of estimates as measured by the mean
- The spread of the distribution of estimates as measured by the standard deviation
- The shape of the distribution

Let us look at a histogram of the sampling distribution given in the above example. This will help us describe the center, spread, and shape of the sampling distribution. See Figure 1.

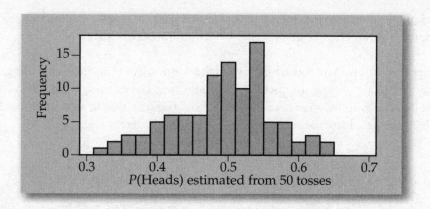

Figure 1: Sampling distribution of P(Heads) for a 2001 penny

- The estimates are distributed around 0.5.
- The estimates range from about 0.32 to 0.64.
- The sampling distribution is slightly left skewed.
- From the sampling distribution in Table 1, we can see that approximately 86 percent of the estimates are between 0.40 and 0.60.

Properties of a Statistic

The Center of a Statistic's Distribution

The property of **unbiasedness** refers to the idea that a statistic is expected to give values centered on the unknown parameter value. The bias of a statistic is defined as the difference between the estimated probability and the true value of the parameter being estimated. For example, in the case of the coin toss:

$$\text{Bias}(\hat{p}) = E(\hat{p}) - p$$

where $E(\hat{p})$ gives the mean of the sampling distribution of $\hat{p}$.

A statistic is unbiased if the mean of the sampling distribution of the statistic is equal to the true value of the parameter. Bias measures the average accuracy of a statistic. For an unbiased statistic, bias is equal to 0. A biased statistic has a systematic tendency to give estimates other than the actual value. In the case of the coin toss, $\text{Bias}(\hat{p}) = 0.493 - 0.48 = 0.013$, which is very close to zero, and thus a relatively unbiased statistic.

The Spread of a Statistic's Distribution

The property of **variability** refers to the degree of variation in a statistic's values. Suppose more than one unbiased statistic is available to estimate an unknown parameter. The statistic with a smaller variance (or standard deviation) is considered to be more efficient. Such a statistic is more likely to give values closer to the unknown parameter value—in other words, more precise estimates.

Whenever we estimate something, we make a guess. **Bias** indicates that our guess is systematically wrong. **Inefficiency** indicates that our guess is wrong unsystematically. The dotplots shown in Figure 2 show the true weight of an item and its weight estimated from repeated weighings on four different scales.

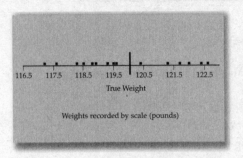

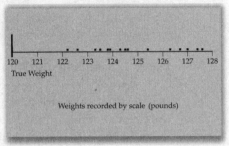

Scale A: Unbiased with large variability

Scale B: Biased with large variability

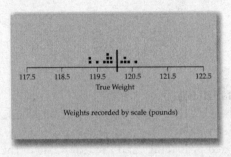

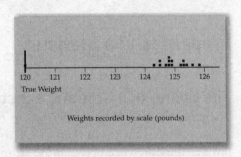

Scale C: Unbiased with small variability

Scale D: Biased with small variability

Figure 2: Properties of a statistic

Note that the weights measured using scales A and C are scattered around the true weight, whereas the weights measured using scales B and D are scattered around some value higher than the true weight. So the scales B and D have a tendency to systematically overweigh items. Therefore, scales B and D are biased, whereas scales A and C are unbiased.

The weights measured by scales A and B are spread more widely than the weights measured by scales C and D. Therefore, scales C and D are more efficient than scales A and B.

INTERVAL ESTIMATION AND THE CONFIDENCE INTERVAL

A point estimate provides some information. It is like a "best guess" of the answer. But we would also like to know how good our guess is. We have more confidence in some answers than in others. For example, you have a better idea of your own weight than of the weight of a classmate. You might guess 140 pounds for both yourself and your friend, but you would be more sure you were close to the exact number with yourself. In statistics, we talk about the goodness of an estimate using **confidence intervals** and **confidence levels**.

A confidence interval consists of two numbers between which we are reasonably certain our true parameter will fall. How certain? As certain as the confidence level we have chosen (typically 95 percent). More precisely, the confidence level means that in repeated sampling, a certain percentage of the intervals will contain the true parameter value.

The confidence interval can also be described in terms of margin of error (MOE). The MOE is the difference between the point estimate and the lower and upper confidence limits.

INFERENCE: TESTS OF SIGNIFICANCE

Statistical inference is the process of using information from a sample in order to answer a specific question or make a decision about the population parameter.

Example 2: Imagine that, last month, a statewide poll showed that 65 percent of state residents supported the governor. This week, a widely circulated newspaper reported that the governor had approved some shady financial deals. With the election approaching, the governor's advisors need to know what effect the news had on the governor's popularity. Specifically, has her support dropped from 65 percent as estimated by the last poll?

Solution: How can we answer this question? The best way is to take another random sample of state residents and estimate the governor's current statewide support by computing the percent of the sample still in favor of the governor. If this percentage is 65 percent or higher, then there is no evidence that the scandal had an adverse effect. If this percentage is lower than 65 percent, then the question is:

- How likely is it that this decrease is due to chance?

We need to make a decision about p, the population proportion, based on $\hat{p}$, the sample proportion.

- Suppose $P = 0.64$. How likely is such a change if P has not changed? What if $P = 0.63$? What if $P = 0.60$?

At what point do we cease considering the difference to be the result of a chance variation in the data and start believing that the governor's support has decreased? It all depends on the likelihood of our estimates. We can determine the likelihood by examining the probability that a specific sample result will occur assuming that the real statewide support for the governor has stayed at 0.65. If different samples of the same size are taken, then the estimated proportion $\hat{p}$ will change from sample to sample. Some values are more likely to occur than others. So we need to know which values are less likely to occur in a sample if the percent of support has remained unchanged. In other words, we need to know the sampling distribution of $\hat{p}$. Let's simulate it.

Assume that the proportion of voters supporting the governor is still 0.65. Then we can simulate the situation by drawing repeated samples of, say, size 500. Imagine that each sample gives a different proportion. For example, the first sample results in a $\hat{p} = 0.61$; the second sample results in a $\hat{p} = 0.63$; the third sample results in a $\hat{p} = 0.67$, and so on. A histogram of 1,000 of these estimated proportions is shown in Figure 3.

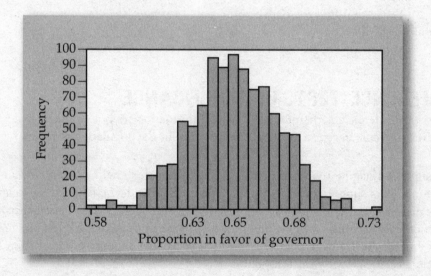

Figure 3: Frequency distribution of the estimated proportion of voters supporting the governor

This histogram shows that a sample proportion closer to 0.65 is most likely to occur, whereas values farther from 0.65 are increasingly less likely to occur. For example, from this simulated data we can estimate

- $P(\hat{p} \leq 0.63) = 0.177$. Note that to get this value, we have to add the frequency on the chart for $\hat{p} = 0.63$ to the frequencies for all $\hat{p}$ values lower than 0.63.

- $P(\hat{p} \leq 0.60) = 0.006$. Again, note that to get this value, we have to add the frequency on the chart for $\hat{p} = 0.60$ to the frequencies for all $\hat{p}$ values lower than 0.60.

You may have noticed that we said earlier that the probability of any exact result was zero, whereas here we have added the value for $\hat{p} = 0.60$ to frequencies for a lower $\hat{p}$. The reason is that here we are dealing with estimates that come from samples, not parameters that come from populations. In a sample of size n, there is a probability of getting any particular proportion, but in an infinite population, the probability of any exact value is 0.

Suppose our sample of 500 residents gives $\hat{p} = 0.60$. Our simulation results indicate that if 65 percent of the residents from the entire state still support the governor, then a sample of 500 is not very likely to give $\hat{p} = 0.60$ or lower. If we obtain a result of $\hat{p} = 0.60$, then we are likely to conclude that support for the governor has probably decreased.

Statistical inference is usually based on theoretical models for $\hat{p}$ or X, not on simulation. On the following pages, we will use the normal model and two others to determine if our sample result is unusual or not.

Testing a Hypothesis

The process described above of decision-making about the value of a population parameter using information collected from a random sample is known as **testing a hypothesis**.

A **statistical hypothesis** (the plural is "hypotheses") is a claim or a statement about a parameter value. A hypothesis is always a statement about a population characteristic and not about a sample. There are two types of hypotheses:

- The **null hypothesis** is a statement that is assumed to be true until proven otherwise. Sometimes it is described as the status quo statement about the parameter. The null hypothesis is denoted by H_0. It is a statement that formalizes the idea that "nothing is going on," i.e., that there is no difference between two groups or that the value for a single group has stayed the same.

- The **alternative hypothesis** is a statement about the parameter that must be true if the null hypothesis is false. Sometimes it is described as the research hypothesis. The alternative hypothesis is denoted by H_1 or H_a. It is the statement that we wish to prove.

In Example 2, we would define:

- H_0: $p \geq 0.65$ (The proportion of state residents in favor of the governor is still 0.65 or greater.) This can also be written as $p = 0.65$.
- H_a: $p < 0.65$ (The proportion of state residents in favor of the governor has dropped below 0.65.)

The goal is to determine whether the sample provides enough evidence for us to reject the null hypothesis. The evidence is in terms of the probability of the sample proportion occurring assuming the null hypothesis is true. From the sampled data, we compute a test statistic value and a *p*-value.

- The **test statistic** (*TS*) is a statistic computed from the sampled data and used in the process of testing a hypothesis. If we are using a normal model, the test statistic is the familiar *z*-score.

- The ***p*-value** is the probability that we would observe a test statistic value at least as extreme as the one computed from the sample if the null hypothesis were true. The *p*-value is the evidence we will use in deciding whether to reject the null hypothesis. A large *p*-value means our result is common if the null hypothesis is true, while a small *p*-value means that our result would be rare if the null hypothesis were true.

Using the information from the sample, we make one of the following decisions:

- The sample provides enough evidence to reject the null hypothesis and accept the alternative hypothesis (*p*-value < α); or

- Because of the lack of evidence, we do not reject the null hypothesis (*p*-value ≥ α). (Note that failing to *reject* the null hypothesis does not imply *accepting* the null hypothesis. No amount of evidence allows us to accept the null hypothesis.)

Possible Errors

Using the sampled data does not guarantee that our decision is correct. Because our decision is based on a sample and not on the entire population, it's possible for us to make the wrong decision because of random sampling variability. There are two types of errors we could make.

A **Type I error** is the error of rejecting the null hypothesis when it is true. The probability of a Type I error occurring is denoted by α.

A **Type II error** is the error of failing to reject the null hypothesis when it is false. The probability of Type II error is denoted by β.

For a given sample size, we cannot control both Type I and Type II errors. If we try to reduce one type of error, the other type of error will increase. Also, keep in mind that in certain tests, it's more important to reduce one type of error than the other. For example, when trying a defendant, the null hypothesis is that the defendant is not guilty. The legal system considers the Type I error (to reject the null hypothesis when the null hypothesis is true—in other words, to convict an innocent defendant) to be worse than the Type II error (to fail to reject the null when the alternative hypothesis is true—in other words, acquit a guilty defendant), because our judicial system believes that it's more important to protect an innocent person than to punish a guilty person. The only way to reduce the probability of both types of errors is to increase the sample size.

		True Situation	
		Null hypothesis is true	Alternative hypothesis is true
Decision	Fail to reject null hypothesis	<u>Correct decision</u> P(Correct decision) = $1 - \alpha$	<u>Type II error</u> P(Type II error) = β
	Reject null hypothesis	<u>Type I error</u> P(Type I error) = α	<u>Correct decision</u> P(Correct decision)= $1 - \beta$ = Power of the test

Table 2: Two types of errors

The power of the test for a test of fixed significance is the probability that the null hypothesis will be rejected when a particular alternative value of the parameter is true. For a specific alternative,

$$\text{Power of a test} = 1 - P(\text{Type II error})$$

A good test has a high power. Also note that:

- The power of a test increases as the sample size increases.
- The power of a test increases as the Type I error rate (α) increases.
- The power of a test increases as the effect size increases. The effect size is the size of the thing we are trying to measure.

Example 3: A pharmaceutical company claimed that its new medicine prevented the common cold. A government agency is investigating this claim. What decision might constitute a Type I error? A Type II error?

Solution: The null hypothesis is nearly always that nothing is happening. Here, an appropriate null hypothesis is that the medicine does not cure the common cold, and an appropriate alternate hypothesis is that it does prevent colds. A Type I error consists of saying that the null is false when, in fact, it is true. Therefore, if the government said that the medicine does prevent colds, it might be a Type I error (it might also be a correct statement). On the other hand, a Type II error consists of saying that the null is true when, in fact, it is false. Here, a statement that the medicine did not prevent colds might be a Type II error (again, it might be a correct statement).

Determining the Critical Value

The terms "too small" and "too large" are vague. How do we decide which values are too large and which are too small? The answer is simple: Values of the test statistic beyond the critical values are considered too large or too small. The critical value is determined based on how much risk of rejecting the true null hypothesis the investigator is willing to take. For example:

- In a **right-tailed test**, when the investigator is willing to take a 5 percent risk (i.e., $\alpha = 0.05$) of rejecting a true null hypothesis, the rejection region is formed by the largest values of the test statistic with a probability of occurrence totaling 0.05. In that case, the test statistic value above which 5 percent of the possible values are under the sampling distribution becomes the critical value.

- In a **two-tailed test**, when the investigator is willing to take a 5 percent risk of rejecting a true null hypothesis, the rejection region is formed by the largest and smallest values of the test statistic with a probability of occurrence totaling 0.05. Therefore, the entire rejection region is divided equally into two parts, one in the left tail and the other in the right tail. The size of each part of the rejection region equals $\alpha/2$ (here, 0.025). In this case, there are two critical values. The test statistic value below which the bottom 2.5 percent of the sampling distribution lies becomes one critical value, and the test statistic value above which the top 2.5 percent of the sampling distribution lies becomes the other critical value.

Making a decision based on a two-sided confidence interval is equivalent to testing a two-sided hypothesis in that a two-sided confidence interval gives a non-rejection region for a two-tailed test. Similarly, making a decision based on a one-sided confidence interval is equivalent to testing a one-sided hypothesis in that a one-sided confidence interval gives a non-rejection region for a one-tailed test. In other words, rejecting the null hypothesis when the test statistic falls *in the rejection region* is equivalent to rejecting the null hypothesis when the hypothesized parameter value falls *outside the confidence interval.*

The Rejection and Non-Rejection Regions

The entire set of the possible values of a test statistic can be divided into two regions: the rejection region and the non-rejection region. The **rejection region** (**RR**) is the set of test statistic values for which we should reject the null hypothesis. It is also known as the **critical region** (**CR**). The set of test statistic values for which we should fail to reject the null hypothesis is called the **non-rejection region**. The size of the rejection region is equal to α. The value of a test statistic that gives the boundary between the rejection and the non-rejection region is known as the **critical value** (**CV**). The critical value is shown as z^* or t^* on the AP Statistics Exam.

The location of the rejection region is determined by the nature of the alternative hypothesis, such as $\mu < 10$, $\mu > 10$, or $\mu \neq 10$. We can use three different types of tests, as defined by the location of the rejection region:

- **Left-tailed test:** In a left-tailed test, "too-small" values of the statistic as compared to the hypothesized parameter value lead to the rejection of the null hypothesis. Therefore, the entire rejection region falls in the left tail of the sampling distribution of the test statistic. For example, a brewery markets bottles labeled "net contents 12 oz." A consumer advocacy group suspects that the average content of the bottles is lower than that printed on the labels and decides to investigate. The group is interested in testing H_0: $\mu = 12$ oz. against H_a: $\mu < 12$ oz., where μ = the mean amount filled per bottle. This is a left-tailed test. Too-small values of the sample mean will result in the rejection of the null hypothesis and the acceptance of the alternative hypothesis. So the rejection region is located in the left tail of the sampling distribution, as shown in Figure 4.

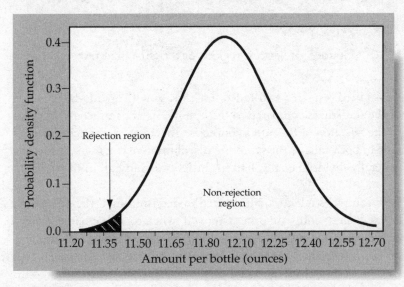

Figure 4: Rejection region for a left-tailed test

- **Right-tailed test:** In a right-tailed test, "too-large" values of the statistic as compared to the hypothesized parameter value lead to the rejection of the null hypothesis. Therefore, the entire rejection region falls in the right tail of the sampling distribution of the test statistic.

  For example, a manufacturer of steel beams used in construction claims that the breaking strength of its beams is at least 500 psi. The engineering firm interested in using these beams decides to check out the claim. The firm will use the beams only if the strength exceeds 500 psi. It is interested in testing H_0: μ = 500 psi against H_a: μ > 500 psi, where μ = the mean breaking strength of beams. This is a right-tailed test. Too-large values of the sample mean will result in the rejection of the null hypothesis and the acceptance of the alternative hypothesis. So, the rejection region is located in the right tail of the sampling distribution as shown in Figure 5.

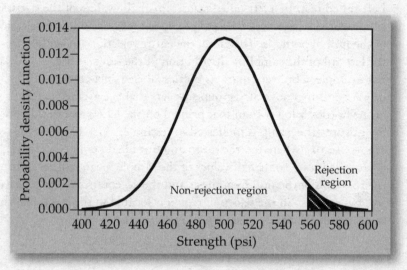

Figure 5: Rejection region for a right-tailed test

- **Two-tailed test:** In a two-tailed test, "too-small" or "too-large" values of the statistic as compared to the hypothesized parameter value lead to the rejection of the null hypothesis. Therefore, the rejection region falls in both tails of the sampling distribution of the test statistic. It's generally divided equally, half in the left tail and half in the right.

  For example, students are interested in determining if the new gold dollar is a fair coin—in other words, if, when tossed, it has a 50 percent chance of landing on heads and a 50 percent chance of landing on tails. To evaluate its fairness, the students decide to toss a gold dollar 100 times and count the number of heads. They are interested in testing H_0: p = 0.50, against H_a: $p \neq 0.50$, where p = the proportion of heads. This is a two-tailed test. Too-large or too-small proportions of heads in 100 tosses will result in the rejection of the null hypothesis and the acceptance of the alternative hypothesis. So the rejection region is located in both tails of the sampling distribution, half in the left and half in the right as shown in Figure 6.

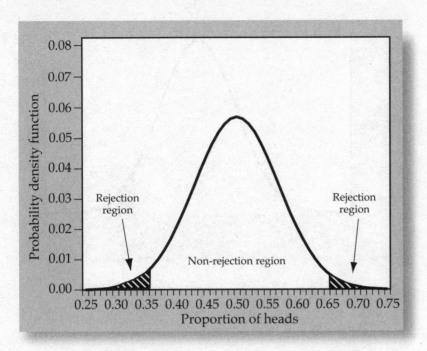

Figure 6: Rejection region for a two-tailed test

Determining Sample Size

Experimenters are often interested in determining the sample size needed to achieve certain reliable results. This helps the experimenter in planning the experiment and in budgeting its cost. The sample size needed to estimate the parameter within a specified margin of error and the required confidence level can be determined using the formula for the margin of error.

Note: When computing sample size, round up the numerical answer to attain the desired level of accuracy. For example, if the answer is 96.012, then we need at least 97 observations to attain the desired level of accuracy.

Finding Z_α

When determining sample size, you'll often need to find the value for the z-score Z_α, or z-(alpha). In most AP textbooks, the critical z-score is designated as z^*, which stands for the critical value for either a one- or two-tailed test. In this book, for increased clarity about the value of z^* for each test, we will use the designations Z_α and $Z_{\alpha/2}$. Z_α = the z-score such that the area under the standard normal distribution beyond the z-score is equal to α. As shown in Figure 7, Z_α is the number on the baseline. It is a z-score. The subscript α (of Z_α) gives the area in the right tail.

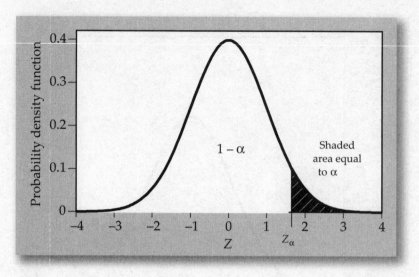

Figure 7: Graphical representation of Z_α

Example 4: Find $Z_{0.05}$ (z^* of a 5 percent rejection region in a one-tailed test).

Solution: As described earlier, $Z_{0.05}$ = the z-score such that the area under the standard normal distribution beyond the z-score is equal to 0.05. In other words, 95 percent of the area under the curve is to the left of $Z_{0.05}$. This makes $Z_{0.05}$ the 95th percentile. So, as shown in Figure 8, finding $Z_{0.05}$ is the same as finding the 95th percentile for the standard normal distribution.

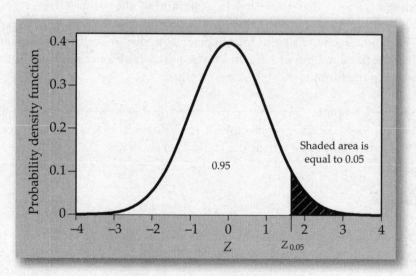

Figure 8: Graphical representation of $Z_{0.05}$

- **Finding $Z_{0.05}$ using the standard normal table:** Inside the body of the table, locate the number closest to 0.95. It is halfway between 0.9495 and 0.9505. Note that 0.9495 corresponds to the z-score 1.64 and 0.9505 corresponds to the z-score 1.65. So 0.95 corresponds to the z-score 1.645. In other words, $z^* = Z_{0.05} = 1.645$.

- Finding $Z_{0.05}$ using the TI-83 or TI-84: 2nd → DISTR → 3: inv-Norm(0.95)

This gives $z^* = Z_{0.05} = 1.6448$, which is approximately 1.645.

Example 5: For $\alpha = 0.05$, find $Z_{\alpha/2}$ (z^* of a 5 percent rejection region in a two-tailed test).

Solution: It is given that $\alpha = 0.05$, which means $\alpha/2 = 0.025$. So, as described earlier, $z^* = Z_{\alpha/2} = Z_{0.025} =$ the z-score such that the area under the standard normal distribution beyond the z-score is equal to 0.025.

Therefore, we are interested in finding the 97.5th percentile for the standard normal distribution.

- **Using the standard normal table:** Inside the body of the table, locate the number closest to 0.975. In this case, it is exactly equal to 0.9750 and corresponds to the z-score 1.96. So $z^* = Z_{0.025} = 1.96$.
- **Using the TI-83 or TI-84:** 2nd → DISTR → 3: invNorm(0.975)
  This gives $Z_{0.025} = 1.95996$, which can be rounded to 1.96.

Some of the commonly used z-scores and the corresponding tail probabilities are listed in Table 3.

α Area in the Right Tail of the Standard Normal Distribution	Z_α (z^* for one-tailed test)	$Z_{\alpha/2}$ (z^* for two-tailed test)
0.20	0.84	1.28
0.10	1.28	1.645
0.05	1.645	1.96
0.02	2.05	2.33
0.01	2.33	2.576

Table 3: z-scores associated with commonly used values of α

Determining the Sample Size to Estimate Population Mean μ

- The margin of error to estimate μ is $ME = Z_{\alpha/2}\left(\dfrac{\sigma}{\sqrt{n}}\right)$. First, determine the desired level of confidence and the margin of error. Then estimate n by equating the desired margin of error with this formula.

- We can estimate the required sample size as

$$n \geq \left(\frac{Z_{\alpha/2} \sigma}{ME} \right)^2$$

- If the population standard deviation is unknown, use the sample standard deviation in place of the population standard deviation.

Determining the Sample Size to Estimate Population Proportion p

- The maximum margin of error to estimate p is $Z_{\alpha/2} \sqrt{\frac{p(1-p)}{n}}$. First, determine the desired level of confidence and the margin of error. Then estimate n by equating the desired margin of error with this formula.

- If an estimate of p is available from past experiments, then estimate the required sample size as

$$n \geq \left(\frac{Z_{\alpha/2}}{ME} \right)^2 p(1-p)$$

- If no information about p is available, then use $p = \frac{1}{2}$ and estimate the required sample size as

$$n \geq \left(\frac{Z_{\alpha/2}}{2ME} \right)^2$$

This gives a conservative estimate for the sample size in the absence of any prior information about p.

- For a 95 percent confidence level, $z^* = Z_{\alpha/2} = 1.96 \cong 2.0$. By substituting this in the above formula, we get

$$n \geq \left(\frac{1}{ME} \right)^2$$

Note that, to cut the margin of error in half, the sample size needs to be quadrupled.

It can be seen from the above formulas that:

- Sample size increases as the desired margin of error decreases.
- Sample size increases as the required confidence level increases.
- Sample size increases as the standard deviation increases.

Example 6: A factory cans fresh pineapple in sugar syrup. The manager in charge is interested in estimating the average amount of sugar per can to within 2 mg of the true mean. From previous experiments, he knows that the standard deviation of the sugar content is approximately 15 mg. Each test of measuring the amount of sugar in a can costs $5.00. One thousand dollars have been budgeted for this experiment. Does the manager have enough funds to estimate the average amount of sugar per can with a 95 percent confidence?

Solution: The manager is interested in determining the sample size needed to estimate

μ = the mean amount of sugar per can.

Confidence level = $0.95 \Rightarrow \alpha = 0.05 \Rightarrow z^* = Z_{\alpha/2} = Z_{0.025} = 1.96$

The desired ME = 2 mg, and the standard deviation is 15 mg.

So the required sample size is

$$n \geq \left(\frac{Z_{\alpha/2}\sigma}{ME} \right)^2 = \left(\frac{1.96(15)}{2} \right)^2 = 216.09$$

The manager should sample at least 217 cans. It will cost him at least 217(5) = $1,085. Because he has a budget of $1,000, he does not have enough money.

Example 7: Officials at a large university want to estimate the proportion of students in favor of changing from a quarter system to a semester system. They would like the estimate to be within 0.04 of the true proportion with a 95 percent confidence level.

(a) Estimate the required sample size if no prior information is available.
(b) Assume that a similar poll was conducted two years ago. It resulted in 35 percent of the students favoring a change from the quarter system to the semester system. Estimate the required sample size.

Solution: The officials are interested in estimating p = the proportion of students in favor of changing from a quarter system to a semester system.

Confidence level = $0.95 \Rightarrow \alpha = 0.05 \Rightarrow z^* = Z_{\alpha/2} = Z_{0.025} = 1.96$

The desired ME = 0.04

(a) Because no prior information is available, use $\hat{p} = \dfrac{1}{2}$ to get a conservative estimate of the required sample size.

$$n \geq \left(\frac{Z_{\alpha/2}}{2\,ME}\right)^2 = \left(\frac{1.96}{2(0.04)}\right)^2 = 600.25$$

The university officials need to poll at least 601 students at random.

(b) Using information from the prior poll, we get $\hat{p} = 0.35$. Then the required sample size is

$$n \geq \left(\frac{Z_{\alpha/2}}{ME}\right)^2 \hat{p}\left(1 - \hat{p}\right) = \left(\frac{1.96}{0.04}\right)^2 (0.35)(1 - 0.35) = 546.23$$

The university officials need to poll at least 547 students at random.

ESTIMATION AND INFERENCE PROBLEMS

To do well on the AP Statistics Exam, you will need to be able to estimate and make inferences about the following parameters:

- Population proportion (p)
- Population mean (μ)
- The difference between two population proportions ($p_1 - p_2$)
- The difference between two population means ($\mu_1 - \mu_2$)
- The slope of the least-squares regression line (β_1)

In addition, you also need to know how to make inferences about categorical data. *Estimation procedures*, such as constructing confidence intervals, are used to estimate unknown population parameters; whereas *inference procedures*, such as testing hypotheses, are used for testing claims about unknown population parameters.

Below are the general steps you need in order to solve problems involving confidence intervals and the testing of hypotheses. All these steps are covered in detail later in this chapter. Before answering any estimation or inference problem, read the entire question carefully. Some problems may require you to use all the steps listed below, whereas others may require only a few.

Steps for Constructing a Confidence Interval

1. Set up the problem correctly.
   - Identify the parameter of interest—for example:
     - population proportion (p)
     - population mean (μ)
     - difference in population proportions ($p_1 - p_2$)
     - difference in population means ($\mu_1 - \mu_2$)
     - population mean of differences (μ_d)

   - Describe the parameter in the context of the problem. For example, write p = the proportion of voters in Iowa in favor of the governor's position, or μ_d = the mean difference in the cholesterol level of patients before and after taking the new medicine.

2. Identify the appropriate type of confidence interval and check its requirements.

   - Give the correct name or formula for the type of confidence interval you've selected. For example, to construct a confidence interval for p = the proportion of voters in Iowa in favor of the governor's position, you could write either

   (a) A large sample's z-interval for proportion, or
   (b) The confidence interval for p is constructed as

   $$\hat{p} \pm Z_{\alpha/2} \sqrt{\frac{\hat{p}(1-\hat{p})}{n}}$$

   - Check the requirements for the selected confidence interval. For example, to construct a confidence interval for p, ask yourself whether $n\hat{p} > 10$ and $n(1-\hat{p}) > 10$ (all requirements will be discussed in detail later in this chapter). Show your work. Just stating the assumptions or saying they are satisfied is not enough.

   Note: If you use the wrong type of confidence interval, then you will not get any credit for this part of the problem on the AP Statistics Exam!

3. Provide the correct mechanics to solve the problem.

   - Give the correct values obtained from statistical tables or your calculator. For example, for a 95 percent confidence interval for p, give $z^* = Z_{\alpha/2} = Z_{0.025} = 1.96$.

   - Compute the confidence interval correctly. Show you're plugging in the correct numbers for the formula you already gave in step 2. After you've computed the correct confidence interval, be sure to state it as (lower limit, upper limit).

4. State the correct conclusion in the context of the problem, using your confidence interval.

   For example, if your 95 percent interval for p is (0.62, 0.68), then write, "We are 95 percent confident that the proportion of voters in Iowa in favor of the governor's position is between 0.62 and 0.68."

Steps for Testing a Hypothesis

1. State a correct set of hypotheses.
   - State the null and alternative hypotheses correctly, defining any notation used.
   - State both hypotheses in the context of the problem. For example, write:
     (a) $H_0: p = 0.5$ against $H_a: p > 0.5$, where p = the proportion of voters in the state of Iowa in favor of the governor's position, or
     (b) $H_0: \mu_d = 0$ against $H_a: \mu_d > 0$, where μ_d = the mean difference in the cholesterol level of patients before and after taking the new medicine.
     Note: If you switch the null and alternative hypotheses around, you will lose all credit for this step on the AP Statistics Exam.

2. Identify the appropriate statistical test and check the appropriate requirements.
   - Give the correct name of the test, or give the correct symbol or formula for the test statistic. For example, to test for p as defined in step 1, write either:
     (a) Use a large samples z-test for proportion, or
     (b) The test statistic is $z = \dfrac{\hat{p} - p_0}{\sqrt{\dfrac{p_0(1 - p_0)}{n}}}$
   - Check the requirements for the selected test. (Use the same procedure as in step 3 of the estimation problem process above).
     Note: If you use the wrong statistical test (for example, if you use a paired t-test when an independent samples t-test is more appropriate), then you will not get any credit for this part of the problem on the AP Statistics Exam.

3. Provide the correct mechanics to solve the problem.
   - Give the correct numerical value of the test statistic. Be sure to show that you're plugging in the correct numbers into the formula you gave in step 2. For example, write:

   $$\text{Test statistic} = z = \frac{\hat{p} - p_0}{\sqrt{\dfrac{p_0(1 - p_0)}{n}}} = \frac{0.64 - 0.5}{\sqrt{\dfrac{0.5(1 - 0.5)}{250}}} = 4.43$$

- At this point there are two ways to do the problem: the *p*-value approach and the **rejection region approach** (again, both are described in detail later in this chapter). The *p*-value approach is generally the easier way to go if you're using a TI-83 or TI-84 calculator. The TEST option on the calculator will give the *p*-value. The rejection region is a bit more complicated, but it can be done just by using the tables supplied on the AP Statistics Exam—it does not require a calculator. Both approaches are equally acceptable to the AP graders. **Note:** Minor computational errors will not necessarily lower your score on this part of the AP Statistics Exam.

4. State the correct conclusion in the context of the problem using the results of your statistical test.

   - Use your test results from the earlier step to arrive at the conclusion, using either the *p*-value approach or the rejection region approach. State clearly the link between the conclusion and the test result. For example, write:
     (a) Because *p*-value = 0.0000047 < any reasonable α, we reject the null and accept the alternative hypothesis; or
     (b) Because the test statistic value 4.43 falls in the rejection region, we reject the null and accept the alternative hypothesis; or
     (c) Because the test statistic value 4.43 > 1.645, we reject the null and accept the alternative hypothesis.

   - Write the conclusion in the context of the problem, consistent with the defined hypotheses. In other words, do not stop after saying "reject" or "do not reject" the null hypothesis. For the above example, you should write the following: "There is significant evidence to suggest that the proportion of voters in Iowa in favor of the governor's position is more than 0.5."

ESTIMATION FOR AND INFERENCE ABOUT A POPULATION PROPORTION *p*

Newspapers, television stations, and manufacturers routinely use public opinion polls to estimate the proportion of a population in favor of a certain issue, candidate, or product.

Parameter of interest: Population proportion *p*

- Select a random sample of size *n*.
- Define what a "success" will be. For example, if you are interested in the proportion of pet owners in a neighborhood, define a "success" as owning a pet.

Note: If the rejection rule is applied incorrectly, you will not get any credit for this part of the problem on the AP Statistics Exam!

- Count the number of successes in your sample (x).

- The estimated proportion from the sample is $\hat{p} = \dfrac{x}{n}$. $\hat{p}$ is a point estimate of an unknown population proportion. Different random samples of size n from the same population will result in different sample proportions, giving different estimates. The distribution of the estimated proportions from all possible random samples of size n is the sampling distribution of $\hat{p}$.

- The mean of all possible sample proportions is p. Therefore $\hat{p}$ is an unbiased estimator of p.

- The standard deviation of the sampling distribution of $\hat{p}$ is $\sigma_{\hat{p}} = \sqrt{\dfrac{p(1-p)}{n}}$. When we use our sample proportion $\hat{p}$ in this formula, we refer to it as the standard error. Standard error $= \sqrt{\dfrac{\hat{p}(1-\hat{p})}{n}}$

- For a large n, the sampling distribution of $\hat{p}$ is approximately normally distributed. Therefore, for a large n, we can construct a z-interval or use a z-test. For a small n, we may need to use a different test, but these tests are not on the AP exam.

Estimating p using $(1 - \alpha)100\%$ confidence interval:
Large sample case: Construct a z-interval

Margin of Error: $z^*\sigma_{\hat{p}} = Z_{\alpha/2}\sqrt{\dfrac{\hat{p}(1-\hat{p})}{n}}$

Confidence Interval: $\hat{p} \pm Z_{\alpha/2}\sqrt{\dfrac{\hat{p}(1-\hat{p})}{n}}$

Example 8: Suppose a pollster needs to determine the proportion of adult Americans who favor universal health care. Of the 2,000 Americans surveyed, 1,355 respond in favor of universal health care.

(a) Find the true proportion of all adult Americans favoring universal health care according to this survey. Use a sample proportion point estimator.

(b) Assume it is binomial: either the respondents favor universal health care, or they do not. Find the standard deviation from point estimators. Assume the entire population surveyed is normally distributed.

Solution:

(a) The sample proportion point estimator is $\hat{p} = \dfrac{1355}{2000} = 0.678$.

This represents the true proportion of all adult Americans favoring universal health care. Those who do not favor it are represented by $\hat{q} = 1 - \hat{p} = 0.322$.

(b) σ = standard deviation of sample proportions =

$$\sqrt{\left(\hat{p} \times \dfrac{\hat{q}}{n}\right)} = \sqrt{\left(\dfrac{(0.678 \times 0.322)}{2000}\right)} = 0.010$$

Making an inference about the population proportion p:
Large sample case: Use a z-test.

H_0: $p = p_0$ (specified) H_a: $p > p_0$ or $\quad\ p < p_0$ or $\quad\ p \neq p_0$	$z = \dfrac{\hat{p} - p_0}{\sqrt{\dfrac{p_0(1 - p_0)}{n}}}$

	Rejection Rule	
Alternative hypothesis:	Rejection region approach:	p-value approach:
H_a: $p > p_0$ H_a: $p < p_0$ or H_a: $p \neq p_0$	Reject H_0 if $z > Z_\alpha$ $z < -Z_\alpha$ $z > Z_{\alpha/2}$ or $z < -Z_{\alpha/2}$	Reject H_0 if p-value $< \alpha$, where p-value $= P(Z > z)$ p-value $= P(Z < z)$ p-value $= P(Z > |z|) + P(Z < -|z|)$

Conditions:

(a) An independent random sample of size n is taken from the population.

(b) The sample size is large enough so that the distribution of $\hat{p}$ is approximately normal (see below).

Checking the normality condition (b):

If the following conditions are satisfied, then the sample size is large enough to assume that the distribution of $\hat{p}$ is approximately normal.

- $n\hat{p}$ and $n(1 - \hat{p}) > 10$ for an estimation problem, where $\hat{p}$ = sample proportion.
- $np_0 > 10$ and $n(1 - p_0) > 10$ for an inference problem, where p_0 = claimed proportion.

Example 9: 123 baseball games are played in a season, and your favorite team wins 83 games. The population proportion to win a baseball game is 77 percent. At a 5 percent significance level, test the claim that your favorite team wins 77 percent of the 123 games.

Solution: The population values for p and q are: $p = 0.77$ and $q = 0.23$

The point estimator sample proportions are:

$$\hat{p} = \frac{83}{123} = 0.67 \qquad \hat{q} = \frac{40}{123} = 0.33$$

The population proportion standard deviation is:

$$\sigma = \sqrt{p \cdot \frac{q}{n}} = \sqrt{\frac{(0.77 \times .23)}{123}} = 0.038$$

At 5 percent significance (95 percent confidence), the two-sided valued interval yields $z^* = z_\alpha = -1.96$.

$$H_0 \colon p = 0.77$$

$$H_a \colon p \text{ does not equal } 0.77$$

$$Z = \frac{p - p_0}{\sigma} = \frac{(0.67 - 0.77)}{0.038} = -2.63$$

Since $-2.63 < -1.96$, we reject the H_0 claim at 95 percent confidence. Unfortunately, your favorite team is not likely to win exactly 77 percent of their 123 games. But there is hope! Their win percentage may be smaller *or* larger than 77 percent.

Example 10: A large national bank randomly selected 300 checking accounts from all its checking accounts and found that 45 were overdrawn at least once in the past two years.

(a) Estimate the true proportion of checking accounts at this bank that were overdrawn at least once in the last two years, using a 95 percent confidence interval.

(b) The bank manager reported that the bank has a significantly lower percentage of overdrawn checking accounts compared to the nation as a whole. If 20 percent of accounts nationally are overdrawn, can we believe the bank manager's report?

Solution:

(a) Estimation:

Step 1: The bank is interested in estimating p = the true proportion of checking accounts overdrawn at least once in the last two years

Step 2: A random sample of $n = 300$ accounts was taken. Of the sampled accounts, $x = 45$ were overdrawn at least once in the last two years.

The sample proportion is $\hat{p} = \dfrac{x}{n} = \dfrac{45}{300} = 0.15$

Conditions:

(1) The accounts are independent because it is given that a random sample of accounts was taken and there are over 3,000 checking accounts at the bank.

(2) $n\hat{p} = 300(0.15) = 45 > 10$ and $n(1 - \hat{p}) = 300(1 - 0.15) = 255 > 10$. Therefore, the sample size is large enough to assume that the sampling distribution of $\hat{p}$ is approximately normal.

Both conditions are satisfied, so we can construct a large sample z-interval for proportion.

Step 3: To construct a 95 percent confidence interval, we use $\alpha = 0.05$. Therefore, as discussed in the section on "Finding Z_α," we can find $z^* = Z_{\frac{\alpha}{2}} = Z_{\frac{0.05}{2}} = Z_{0.025} = 1.96$.

The 95 percent $ME = Z_{\alpha/2}\sqrt{\dfrac{\hat{p}(1-\hat{p})}{n}} = 1.96\sqrt{\dfrac{0.15(1-0.15)}{300}} = 0.04$

So, $\hat{p} \pm ME \Rightarrow 0.15 \pm 0.04 \Rightarrow (0.11, 0.19)$

Therefore, a 95 percent confidence interval to estimate p is (0.11, 0.19).

Step 4: We are 95 percent confident that the true proportion of checking accounts at this bank that were overdrawn at least once in the last two years is between 0.11 and 0.19.

In other words, we are 95 percent confident that 11 percent to 19 percent of checking accounts at this bank were overdrawn at least once in the last two years.

```
TI-83 or TI-84:
• Choose STAT → TESTS → A: 1-PropZInt
• Enter appropriate values
    1-PropZInt
    X: 45
    n: 300
    C-Level: .95
    Calculate
• Highlight Calculate
• Press ENTER
```

(b) Inference:

Step 1: We are interested in making an inference about p = the true proportion of checking accounts at this bank overdrawn at least once in the last two years.

Nationally, 20 percent of checking accounts are overdrawn. The manager reported that $p < 0.20$. We are looking for evidence to support the manager's report. Therefore, use $p_0 = 0.20$ and define the null and alternative hypotheses as $H_0: p \geq 0.20$ (the proportion of overdrawn accounts at this bank is the same as the national proportion, or higher) and $H_a: p < 0.20$ (the proportion of overdrawn accounts at this bank is lower than the national proportion).

Step 2: A random sample of $n = 300$ accounts was taken.

Of the sampled accounts, $x = 45$ were overdrawn at least once in the last two years.

The sample proportion is

$$\hat{p} = \frac{x}{n} = \frac{45}{300} = 0.15$$

Conditions:

(a) It is given that a random sample of accounts was taken.
(b) $np_0 = 300\,(0.20) = 60 > 10$ and $n(1 - p_0) = 300(1 - 0.20) = 240 > 10$.

Therefore, the sample size is large enough to assume that the sampling distribution of $\hat{p}$ is approximately normal.

The conditions are satisfied, so we can use a large sample z-test for proportion.

Step 3: The alternative hypothesis indicates that this is a left-tailed test. Suppose we are willing to take a 5 percent risk of rejecting the true null hypothesis. In this case, $\alpha = 0.05$.

Using the _p_-value approach: The rejection rule is "Reject H_0 if _p_-value < 0.05."

Compute the test statistic value as

$$z = \frac{\hat{p} - p_0}{\sqrt{\dfrac{p_0\left(1 - p_0\right)}{n}}} = \frac{0.15 - 0.20}{\sqrt{\dfrac{0.20(1 - 0.20)}{300}}} = \frac{-0.05}{0.023} = -2.165$$

Compute the _p_-value using either the standard normal table or the TI-83 or TI-84.

- Using the standard normal table: The probability corresponding to the _z_-score of $-2.165 \approx -2.17$ is 0.015.
- Using the TI-83 or TI-84: **2nd → DISTR → 2:normalcdf(–5000, –2.165, 0, 1)**. This gives the figure 0.01519, which can be rounded to 0.015. Therefore, value $P(Z < -2.165) = 0.015$. See Figure 9.

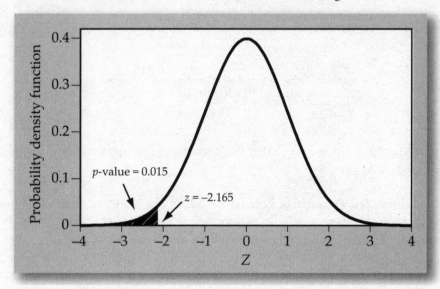

Figure 9: _p_-value approach

Using the rejection region approach:

The rejection rule is "Reject H_0 if $z < z^* = -Z_\alpha = -Z_{0.05} = -1.645$."

The graph in Figure 10 shows the rejection region.

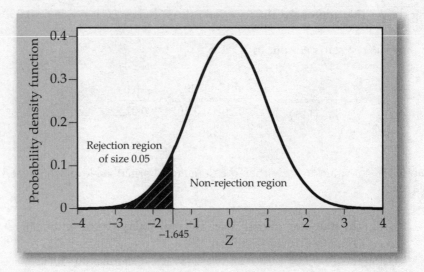

Figure 10: Rejection region and non-rejection region

Compute the test statistic value as

$$z = \frac{\hat{p} - p_0}{\sqrt{\dfrac{p_0\left(1 - p_0\right)}{n}}} = \frac{0.15 - 0.20}{\sqrt{\dfrac{0.20\left(1 - 0.20\right)}{300}}} = \frac{-0.05}{0.023} = -2.165$$

Step 4: Make a decision using either the rejection region approach or the *p*-value approach as follows:

The rejection region approach: Because $z = -2.165$, which is less than -1.645 (or because, from the above graph, we can see that the z falls in the rejection region), we should reject the null hypothesis and accept the alternative hypothesis.

The *p*-value approach: Because *p*-value = 0.015, which is less than 0.05, we should reject the null hypothesis and accept the alternative hypothesis.

Now state the conclusion in the context of the problem: At a 5 percent risk of error, we can conclude that the data provides sufficient evidence to support the manager's report that the bank's proportion of overdrawn accounts is lower than the national proportion.

TI-83 or TI-84:

- Choose STAT → TESTS → 5: 1-PropZTest
- Enter appropriate values

  1-PropZTest

  p_0: 0.20

  x: 45

  n: 300

  prop ≠ p_0 < p_0 > p_0 Choose option < p_0

  Calculate Draw
- Press **ENTER**
- Choose **Calculate**
- Press **ENTER**

Student's *t*-Distribution

The *t*-distribution is different from the normal distribution. We use it when making estimates of, or inferences about, a population mean, the difference between two population means, or the slope of a regression line with a small sample.

The *t*-distribution can be described as follows: Consider a sample of size *n* taken from a normally distributed population with unknown mean μ and unknown standard deviation σ. Then the unknown population standard deviation is estimated using the sample standard deviation *s*. The statistic $t = \dfrac{\bar{x} - \mu}{s/\sqrt{n}}$ is computed from the sample. Different samples of size *n* will result in different values for the statistic. William Gosset, while working for the Guinness brewery, discovered the sampling distribution that the above statistic follows. He published his results under the pen name "Student." Since then, this sampling distribution has been known as student's *t*-distribution.

The characteristics of the *t*-distribution include the following:

- It's a continuous distribution.
- Its mean is 0.
- It's symmetric about its mean.
- It's bell shaped.

- Its shape depends on a parameter, called **degrees of freedom**, denoted by *df*. For smaller degrees of freedom, the distribution is more spread out, whereas as degrees of freedom increase, the distribution becomes more compact. In other words, as the degrees of freedom increase, the standard deviation of the *t*-distribution decreases.
- It approaches the standard normal distribution as the degrees of freedom increase.
- It has a larger standard deviation than the standard normal distribution. In other words, it has thicker tails than the standard normal distribution. As the degrees of freedom increase, the standard deviation of the *t*-distribution approaches 1.

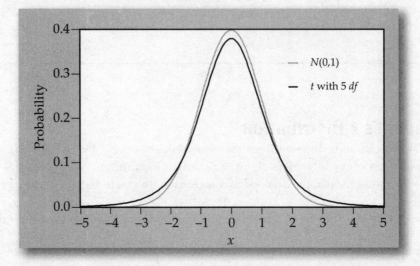

Figure 11: Comparison of standard normal and *t*-distribution

How to Read the t Table

The critical *t*-value (t^*) is the value of *t* required to achieve a certain upper tail probability. On the table for *t*-distribution critical values, the degrees of freedom (*df*) are listed in the leftmost column, the confidence levels (*C*) are listed across the bottom, and the corresponding upper tail probability (*p*) for each confidence level is listed across the top of the table.

- Determine the required degrees of freedom *df*. There are different formulas for degrees of freedom depending on which test or confidence interval you're using.
- Determine the area in the right tail of the distribution, namely the upper tail probability.
- In the *t* table, go down to the row that corresponds to the degrees of freedom, and then go across to the column that corresponds to the tail probability. Read the number in the cross-section of the selected row and column.

Example 11: (a) Find t^* for tail probability 0.05 and 8 degrees of freedom.
(b) Find t^* for tail probability 0.01 and 15 degrees of freedom.

Solution:

(a) We are interested in finding t^* for tail probability 0.05 and 8 degrees of freedom. This means we need to find the t score for a t-distribution with 8 degrees of freedom such that the area to the right of this t score is equal to 0.05. So read the number in the cross-section of the row corresponding to $df = 8$ and the column corresponding to $p = 0.05$. $t^* = 1.860$.

(b) We are interested in finding t^* for tail probability 0.01 and 15 degrees of freedom. This means we need to find the t score for a t-distribution with 15 degrees of freedom such that the area to the right of this t score is equal to 0.01. So read the number in the cross-section of the row corresponding to $df = 15$ and the column corresponding to $p = 0.01$. $t^* = 2.602$.

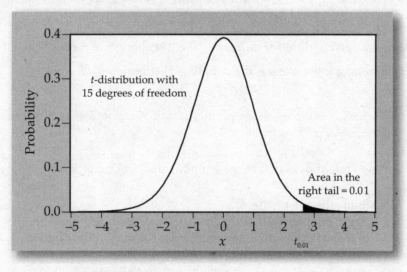

Figure 12: Finding the t score for a specified area in the right tail

ESTIMATION FOR AND INFERENCE ABOUT A POPULATION MEAN μ

Another important parameter is population mean. Here are some examples of the usefulness of a mean:

- Manufacturers are often interested in estimating the mean amount of a product per box filled by a filling machine, the mean amount of time spent by robots per assembly of a specific number of units, etc.

- The Department of Education might be interested in the mean amount of money per child spent by the state on education, the mean amount of time spent by parents on volunteer activities in their children's schools, etc.
- Local television stations might be interested in the mean amount of time viewers spend watching a particular station.

Parameter of interest: Population mean μ

- Select a random sample of size n.
- For each item or subject in the sample, measure the numerical characteristic of interest, X.

$$\text{Sample: } (x_1, x_2, x_3, ..., x_n)$$

- Compute the sample mean $\bar{x} = \dfrac{\sum x_i}{n}$ and sample standard deviation s.

This sample mean $\bar{x}$ is a point estimate of the unknown population mean. Different random samples of size n from the same population will result in different sample means, giving different estimates. The distribution of means from all possible random samples of size n is the sampling distribution of $\bar{x}$.

- The mean of all possible sample means is μ. Therefore $\bar{x}$ is an unbiased estimator of μ.

- The standard deviation of the sampling distribution of $\bar{x}$ is $\sigma_{\bar{X}} = \dfrac{\sigma}{\sqrt{n}}$.

- Sampling distribution of $\bar{x}$:
  o If the population is normally distributed and the population standard deviation is known, then the sampling distribution of $\bar{x}$ is also a **normal distribution**.
  o If the population is normally distributed and the population standard deviation is unknown, then the sampling distribution of $\bar{x}$ is a **t-distribution** with $(n - 1)$ degrees of freedom.

To construct a confidence interval or make an inference using a normal (z) or a t-distribution, decide between a normal and a t-distribution using the following scheme:

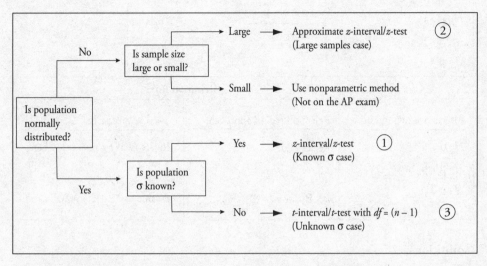

Figure 13: Scheme for selecting t- or z-interval for estimation of and inference about sample mean

In most cases on the AP exam, if the problem is about a mean or a difference of two means, you will use ③, the t-test.

① Z-Interval or Z-Test: Known Standard Deviation Case

This case is unusual because if we are trying to estimate the population mean, we probably don't know the population standard deviation. The population standard deviation σ is known, and the population is normally distributed.

> **Estimating μ using $(1 - \alpha)$100% confidence interval:**
> Known standard deviation case:
>
> Construct a z-interval
>
> Confidence Interval: $\bar{x} \pm z^* \dfrac{\sigma}{\sqrt{n}}$

> **Making an inference about the population mean μ:**
> Known standard deviation case: Use a z-test.
>
> | | |
> |---|---|
> | $H_0: \mu = \mu_0$
 $H_a: \mu > \mu_0$ or
 $\quad \mu < \mu_0$ or
 $\quad \mu \neq \mu_0$ | $z = \dfrac{\bar{x} - \mu_0}{\sigma / \sqrt{n}}$ |

	Rejection Rule	
Alternative hypothesis:	Rejection region approach:	p-value approach:
$H_a: \mu > \mu_0$ $H_a: \mu < \mu_0$ or $H_a: \mu \neq \mu_0$	Reject H_0 if $z > Z_\alpha$ $z < -Z_\alpha$ $z > Z_{\alpha/2}$ or $z < -Z_{\alpha/2}$	Reject H_0 if p-value $< \alpha$, where p-value $= P(Z > z)$ p-value $= P(Z < z)$ p-value $= P(Z > |z|) + P(Z < -|z|)$

Conditions:

(a) The subjects are independent, which is satisfied if a random sample is taken from the population and the sample size n is less than 10 percent of the population.

(b) The sampled population is normally distributed.

Checking the normality condition:

- Make a dotplot or a stem-and-leaf plot for the sample. Ask yourself whether the distribution is fairly symmetric and bell-shaped, without any outliers. In other words, ask yourself whether the distribution resembles the normal distribution. Alternatively, use a normal probability plot.

② Approximate Z-Interval or Z-Test: Large Sample Case

The population distribution σ is unknown, but the sample is large. If σ is unknown then estimate it using the sample standard deviation s.

> **Estimating μ using $(1 - \alpha)100\%$ confidence interval:**
> Unknown standard deviation case:
>
> Construct an approximate z-interval
>
> Confidence Interval: $\quad \bar{x} \pm z^* \dfrac{\sigma}{\sqrt{n}}$

Making an inference about the population mean μ:
Large sample case: Use an approximate z-test.

H_0: $\mu = \mu_0$ (specified)

H_a: $\mu > \mu_0$ or

$\quad$ $\mu < \mu_0$ or

$\quad$ $\mu \neq \mu_0$

$$z = \frac{\bar{x} - \mu_0}{\sigma / \sqrt{n}}$$

	Rejection Rule	
Alternative hypothesis:	Rejection region approach:	p-value approach:
H_a: $\mu > \mu_0$ H_a: $\mu < \mu_0$ or H_a: $\mu \neq \mu_0$	Reject H_0 if $z > Z_\alpha$ $z < -Z_\alpha$ $z > Z_{\alpha/2}$ or $z < -Z_{\alpha/2}$	Reject H_0 if p-value $< \alpha$, where p-value $= P(Z > z)$ p-value $= P(Z < z)$ p-value $= P(Z > |z|) + P(Z < -|z|)$

Conditions:

(a) The subjects are independent, which is satisfied if a random sample is taken from the population and the sample size n is less than 10 percent of the population.

(b) The sample size is large enough to apply the central limit theorem and get an approximate normal distribution for the sample mean.

Checking the sample size condition:

There is no fixed value that determines if a sample size is large or small; this depends on the shape of the sampled population. If there are no outliers, and the population distribution is not extremely skewed, then $n \geq 30$ is large enough to get approximately normal sampling distribution of $\bar{X}$.

③ t-Interval or t-Test

The population distribution is normal, but the population standard deviation σ is unknown. Estimate σ using the sample standard deviation s.

Estimating μ using $(1 - \alpha)100\%$ confidence interval:
Construct a t-interval with $df = (n - 1)$ degrees of freedom

$$\text{Confidence Interval:} \quad \bar{x} \pm t^* \frac{s}{\sqrt{n}}$$

	Making an inference about the population mean μ:
	Unknown variance case: Use a t-test with $df(n-1)$ degrees of freedom.

H_0: $\mu = \mu_0$ (specified)

H_a: $\mu > \mu_0$ or

   $\mu < \mu_0$ or

   $\mu \neq \mu_0$

$$t = \frac{\bar{x} - \mu_0}{s/\sqrt{n}}$$

	Rejection Rule	
Alternative hypothesis:	Rejection region approach:	p-value approach:
H_a: $\mu > \mu_0$	Reject H_0 if	Reject H_0 if p-value $< \alpha$, where
H_a: $\mu < \mu_0$	$t > t_\alpha(df)$	p-value $= P(t(df) > t)$
H_a: $\mu \neq \mu_0$	$t < -t_\alpha(df)$	p-value $= P(t(df) < t)$
	$t > t_{\alpha/2}(df)$ or $t < -t_{\alpha/2}(df)$	p-value $= P(t(df) > |t|) + P(t(df) < -|t|)$

Conditions:

(a) The subjects are independent, which is satisfied if a random sample is taken from the population and the sample size n is less than 10 percent of the population.

(b) The sampled population is normally distributed.

Checking the normality condition:

- Make a dotplot or a stem-and-leaf plot for the sample. Ask yourself whether the shape of the distribution is fairly symmetric and bell-shaped, without any outliers. In other words, ask yourself whether the distribution resembles the normal distribution. Alternatively, use a normal probability plot.

Example 12: A company that manufactures bicycles receives steel rods in large shipments from a supplier. From past experience, the bicycle company manager knows that $\sigma = 0.12$ inches (approximately) and that the lengths are approximately normally distributed. The manager takes a random sample of 10 rods. The lengths of the sampled rods in inches are as follows:

11.90, 11.94, 12.05, 12.07, 11.97, 12.01, 12.08, 12.05, 12.12, 12.14

(a) The manager wants to estimate the mean length of the latest shipment of rods using a 90 percent confidence interval. Help this manager construct a confidence interval and then interpret it.

(b) The company needs rods with a length of 12 inches in order to assemble the bikes properly. Because too-large and too-small rods are unsuitable, shipments not meeting the requirement are sent back to the supplier. Help this manager determine whether the shipment should be accepted or rejected.

Solution: (Remember that this is an unusual example because we usually do not know the population standard deviation.)

Step 1: (a) The manager is interested in estimating μ = true mean length of rods received in the latest shipment.

Step 2: A random sample of $n = 10$ rods was taken.

For each sampled rod, x = the length of the rod in inches.

It is given that the population standard deviation is σ = 0.12 inches.

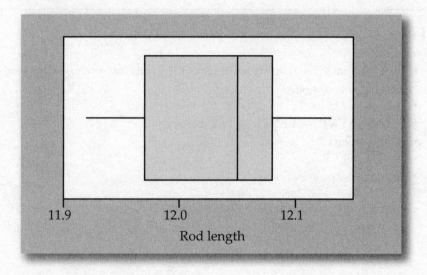

Figure 14: Distribution of rod lengths

Conditions:

(1) The rods are independent because it is given that a random sample of rods was taken from the shipment and 10 < 10% of the large shipment of rods.
(2) It is also given that the lengths of the rods are approximately normally distributed. The conditions are therefore satisfied and the population standard deviation is known. So this is a known standard deviation case, and we can use a z-interval to estimate the population mean.

Step 3: To construct a 90 percent confidence interval, we need α = 0.10. Therefore

$$z^* = Z_{\alpha/2} = Z_{0.10/2} = Z_{0.05} = 1.645$$

The sample mean is $\bar{x} = \dfrac{\sum x}{n} = \dfrac{120.33}{10} = 12.033$ inches.

The 90 percent $ME = z^* \dfrac{\sigma}{\sqrt{n}} = 1.645\left(\dfrac{0.12}{\sqrt{10}}\right) = 0.0624$

$\bar{x} \pm ME \Rightarrow 12.033 \pm 0.0624 \Rightarrow (11.9706,\ 12.0954)$

Therefore, the 90 percent confidence interval to estimate μ is (11.97, 12.10) inches.

Step 4: We are 90 percent confident that the true mean length of rods from this shipment is between 11.97 and 12.10 inches.

TI-83 or TI-84:

Using the data

If the actual measurements (the lengths of the rods, for example) are available, then use this option.

- Enter data in list L_1
- Choose **STAT** $\rightarrow$ **TESTS** $\rightarrow$ **7: ZInterval**
- Choose **Data**
- Press **ENTER**
- Enter appropriate values

    ZInterval

    Input: Data Stats

    σ : 0.12

    List: L_1

    Freq: 1

    C-Level: .90

    Calculate

- Highlight **Calculate**
- Press **ENTER**

> **TI-83 or TI-84:**
> **Using summary statistics**
> If the actual measurements are not available, but the sample mean and the
> population standard deviation are available, then use this option.
> - Choose **STAT → TESTS → 7: ZInterval**
> - Choose **Stats**
> - Press **ENTER**
> - Enter appropriate values
>   ZInterval
>   Input: Data Stats
> σ : 0.12
> $\bar{x}$: 12.033
>   n: 10
>   C-Level: .90
>   Calculate
> - Highlight **Calculate**
> - Press **ENTER**

(b) Making an inference about the mean.

Step 1: μ = the true mean length of rods received in the latest shipment.

The manager is interested in making an inference about the mean length of the rods in this shipment—in other words, he wants to test

$$H_0: \mu = 12 \text{ inches (accept the shipment)}$$

against H_a: $\mu \neq 12$ inches (reject the shipment)

Step 2: A random sample of $n = 10$ rods was taken.

For each sampled rod, x = the length of the rod measured in inches.

It is given that the population standard deviation $\sigma = 0.12$ inches.

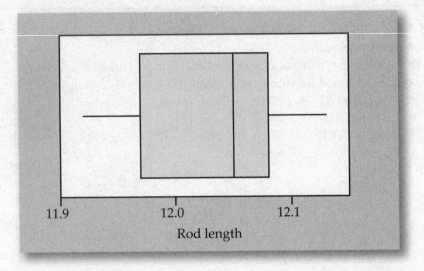

Figure 15: Distribution of rod lengths

Conditions: It is given that a random sample of rods is taken from the shipment. It is also given that the lengths are approximately normally distributed. The conditions are satisfied and the population standard deviation is known. So this is a known standard deviation case, and we can use a *z*-test for mean.

Step 3: Let's use $\alpha = 0.10$. $z^* = Z_{\alpha/2} = Z_{0.10/2} = Z_{0.05} = 1.645$

The rejection rule is:

- Reject the null hypothesis if *p*-value < 0.10 [using a *p*-value approach].

- Reject the null hypothesis if $z > 1.645$ or if $z < -1.645$ (using the rejection region approach).

The sample mean is $\bar{x} = 12.033$ inches.

$$z = \frac{\bar{x} - \mu_0}{\sigma / \sqrt{n}} = \frac{12.033 - 12}{0.12 / \sqrt{10}} = 0.87$$

p-value = $P(Z > 0.87) + P(Z < -0.87) = 0.3843$

Step 4: Because *p*-value = 0.3843 > 0.10 (or if using the rejection region approach, because $-1.645 < z < 1.6450$), we do not reject the null hypothesis. The manager should not reject the shipment. Note that *p*-value = 0.3843 indicates that if the manager rejects the shipment, then there is a 38.43 percent chance that he is rejecting a shipment that meets specifications. Because the manager is only willing to take a 10 percent risk of rejecting the true null hypothesis, he must not reject the shipment.

TI-83 or TI-84:

Using the data

If the actual measurements are available, then use this option.

- Enter data in list L_1
- Choose STAT → TESTS → 1: Z-Test
- Choose **Data**
- Press **ENTER**
- Enter appropriate values

    Z-Test

    Input: Data Stats

    μ_0: 12

    σ: 0.12

    List: L_1

    Freq: 1

    $\mu : \neq \mu_0 < \mu_0 > \mu_0$ Choose option $\neq \mu_0$

Calculate Draw

- Press **ENTER**
- Choose **Calculate**
- Press **ENTER**

TI-83 or TI-84:

Using summary statistics

If the actual measurements are not available, but the sample mean and the population standard deviation are available, then use this option.

- Choose STAT → TESTS → 1: Z-Test
- Choose **Stats**
- Press **ENTER**
- Enter appropriate values

    Z-Test

    Input: Data Stats

    μ_0: 12

    σ : 0.12

    $\bar{x}$: 12.033

    n: 10

    $\mu : \neq \mu_0 < \mu_0 > \mu_0$ (Choose option $\neq \mu_0$)

Calculate Draw

- Press **ENTER**
- Choose **Calculate**
- Press **ENTER**

Example 13: Consider a vending machine that is supposed to dispense eight ounces of a soft drink. A random sample of 20 cups taken over a one-week period contained the following amounts in ounces:

8.1	7.7	7.9	8.0	7.7	7.8	7.9	8.0	7.6	7.9
8.0	7.9	7.6	7.5	8.1	7.8	7.8	7.9	8.2	7.5

(a) Estimate the true mean amount dispensed by the machine using a 95 percent confidence level.

(b) Is there significant evidence to conclude that the machine is dispensing less than eight ounces?

Solution:

(a) Estimation:

Step 1: We are interested in estimating μ = the true mean amount of soft drink per cup dispensed by the machine.

Step 2: A random sample of $n = 20$ cups was taken.

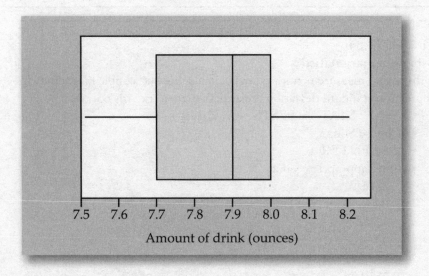

Figure 16: Boxplot of amount of drink dispensed per cup

Conditions:

(1) It is given that a random sample of cups was examined. Because the cups were filled over a period of one week, we can assume that the amounts filled are independent.

(2) Let's use a boxplot to summarize the data (see Figure 16). There are no outliers, and the distributions are fairly symmetric. Therefore, the above plot shows that it is reasonable to assume that the amounts dispensed per cup by the machine are approximately normally distributed.

The amount of soft drink dispensed per cup is approximately normally distributed, but the population standard deviation of the distribution of the amount of drink per cup is unknown. Therefore, we should construct a *t*-interval for the mean.

Step 3: Compute the sample mean and sample standard deviation using the formulas we already learned in Chapter 4.

$$\bar{x} = 7.845 \text{ and } s = 0.1986$$

With a sample of size 20, the degrees of freedom = 20 – 1 = 19.

To construct a 95 percent confidence interval, use $\alpha = 0.05$. Using the *t*-table for 19 degrees of freedom we get

$$t^* = t_{\alpha/2}(19) = t_{0.05/2}(19) = t_{0.025}(19) = 2.093$$

$$95 \text{ percent } ME = t_{0.025}(19)\left(\frac{s}{\sqrt{n}}\right) = 2.093\left(\frac{0.1986}{\sqrt{20}}\right) = 0.0929 \text{ ounces}$$

$$\bar{x} \pm ME \Rightarrow 7.845 \pm 0.0929 \Rightarrow (7.752, 7.938)$$

The 95 percent confidence interval to estimate μ is (7.75, 7.94).

Step 4: Interpretation.

- We are 95 percent confident that the true mean amount dispensed by the machine is between 7.75 ounces and 7.94 ounces.
- We are 95 percent confident that our best estimate of 7.845 ounces is within 0.0929 ounces of the true mean amount dispensed by the machine.

TI-83 or TI-84:
Using the data
If the actual measurements are available, then use this option:
- Enter the data into L_1
- Choose **STAT** → **TESTS** → **8: TInterval**
- Choose **Data**
- Press **ENTER**
- Enter the appropriate values
    TInterval
    Inpt: Data Stats
    List: L_1
    Freq: 1
    C-Level: .95
    Calculate
- Highlight **Calculate**
- Press **ENTER**

```
TI-83 or TI-84:
Using summary statistics
If the actual measurements are not available, but the sample mean and
sample standard deviation are available, then use this option:
• Choose STAT → TESTS → 8: TInterval
• Choose Stats
• Press ENTER
• Enter the appropriate values
      TInterval
      Inpt: Data  Stats
      x̄: 7.845
      Sx: 0.1986
      n: 20
      C-Level: .95
      Calculate
• Highlight Calculate
• Press ENTER
```

(b) Inference:

Step 1: We are interested in testing the hypothesis about

$\mu \geq$ The true mean amount of soft drink dispensed by the machine.

H_0: μ = 8 ounces (The true mean amount of soft drink dispensed by the machine is eight ounces.)

H_a: μ < 8 ounces (The true mean amount of soft drink dispensed by the machine is less than eight ounces.)

Step 2: A random sample of n = 20 cups was taken.

Conditions:

(1) It is given that a random sample of cups filled was examined.
(2) Let's use a histogram and boxplot to summarize the data. The amount of soft drink dispensed per cup is approximately normally distributed, but the population standard deviation of the distribution of the amount of soft drink per cup is unknown. Therefore, we should use a t-test for the mean.

Step 3: Compute the sample mean and sample standard deviation using the formulas already learned in Chapter 4.

$$\bar{x} = 7.845 \text{ and } s = 0.1986$$

With a sample of size 20, df = 20 − 1 = 19

Suppose we use $\alpha = 0.05$. Then, using a t-table for 19 degrees of freedom, we get $t^* = t_\alpha(19) = t_{0.05}(19) = 1.73$

So the rejection rule is to reject the null hypothesis and accept the alternative hypothesis if:

- $t < -1.73$ (rejection region approach)
- p-value < 0.05 (p-value approach)
  Compute the test statistic (and p-value if using p-value approach)

$$t = \frac{(\bar{x} - \mu_0)}{s/\sqrt{n}} = \frac{(7.845 - 8.000)}{0.1986/\sqrt{20}} = -3.49$$

$$p\text{-value} = P(t < -3.49) = 0.0012$$

Step 4: Write a conclusion.

- Using the **p-value approach:** Because p-value $= 0.0012 < \alpha = 0.05$, we should reject the null hypothesis and accept the alternative hypothesis.
- Using the **rejection region approach:** Because $t = -3.49 < -1.73$ (in other words, the test statistic falls in the rejection region), we should reject the null hypothesis and accept the alternative hypothesis.

Conclusion: At the 5 percent level of significance, there is sufficient evidence to conclude that the true mean amount dispensed by the machine is less than eight ounces.

TI-83 or TI-84:
Using the data
If the actual measurements are available, then use this option:
- Enter the data into L_1
- Choose **STAT** → **TESTS** → **2: T-Test**
- Choose option **Data**
- Press **ENTER**
- Enter appropriate values
      T-Test
      Input: Data Stats
      μ_0: 8.0
      List: L_1
      Freq: 1
      $\mu : \neq \mu_0 \quad < \mu_0 \quad > \mu_0$ (Choose option $< \mu_0$)
      Calculate Draw
- Press **ENTER**
- Choose option **Calculate**
- Press **ENTER**

TI-83 or TI-84:

Using summary statistics

If the actual measurements are not available, but the sample mean and sample standard deviation are available, then use this option:

- Choose **STAT** → **TESTS** → **2: T-Test**
- Choose option **Stats**
- Press **ENTER**
- Enter appropriate values

   T-Test
   Input: Data Stats
   μ_0: 8.0
   $\bar{x}$: 7.845
   Sx: 0.1986
   n: 20
   μ_0: $\neq \mu_0$ $< \mu_0$ $> \mu_0$ (Choose option $< \mu_0$)
   Calculate Draw

- Press **ENTER**
- Highlight **Calculate**
- Press **ENTER**

Example 14: A spring water bottling plant fills bottles labeled 12 ounces. The floor supervisor noticed that in the past couple of days the plant had had several bottles overflow during the filling process. Suspecting that the mean filling-process amount had increased, he took a random sample of 40 bottles from those filled in the last eight-hour shift and measured the contents of each selected bottle (in ounces). The amounts are as follows:

13.19	12.87	12.20	11.97	12.05	12.68	12.41	13.30
12.89	12.23	12.39	13.13	12.74	13.17	12.40	11.97
12.39	12.67	12.07	13.37	12.74	12.26	12.47	12.16
12.24	12.86	12.11	12.60	12.03	12.19	12.92	12.35
12.53	12.30	12.64	12.52	13.22	12.84	13.09	12.20

(a) Estimate the filling-process mean using a 90 percent confidence interval.

(b) Is there significant evidence to support the supervisor's suspicions? Justify your answer using statistical evidence.

Solution:

(a) Estimating the filling-process mean:

Step 1: The supervisor is interested in estimating

μ = the true mean amount of spring water filled per bottle (in ounces).

Step 2: A random sample of n = 40 bottles was taken.

For each sampled bottle, x = the amount of water measured in ounces.

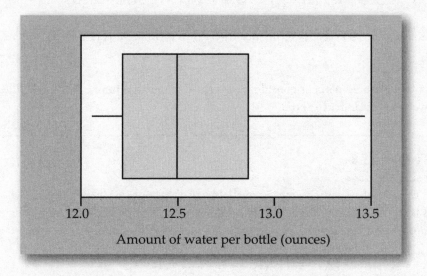

Figure 17: Boxplot of the amount of water filled per bottle

Conditions:

(1) It is given that a random sample of bottles was taken from those filled in the last eight-hour shift.
(2) A boxplot of the data (see Figure 17) shows no outliers. We do not know the distribution of the amount filled per bottle, but the sample size is large enough that we can apply the central limit theorem and assume that $\bar{x}$ is approximately normally distributed. Therefore, we can use a z-interval to estimate the population mean.

Step 3: To construct a 90 percent confidence interval, we need α = 0.10. Therefore,

$$z^* = Z_{\alpha/2} = Z_{0.10/2} = Z_{0.05} = 1.645$$

The sample mean $\bar{x} = \dfrac{502.36}{40} = 12.559$ oz.

The sample standard deviation is

$$s = \sqrt{\frac{6315.52 - \left(502.36^2 / 40\right)}{40 - 1}} = 0.405 \text{ oz.}$$

Then

$$90 \text{ percent } ME = Z_{\alpha/2} \frac{s}{\sqrt{n}} = 1.645 \frac{0.405}{\sqrt{40}} = 0.105 \text{ oz.}$$

$$\text{So, } \bar{x} \pm ME \Rightarrow 12.559 \pm 0.105 \Rightarrow (12.454, 12.664).$$

Therefore, the 90 percent confidence interval to estimate μ is (12.45, 12.66) oz.

Step 4: We are 90 percent confident that the true mean amount per bottle filled is between 12.45 and 12.66 oz.

TI-83 or TI-84:
Using the data
If the actual measurements are available, use this option. If the sample size is large and the population standard deviation is unknown, then input the sample standard deviation (s) for the population standard deviation (σ).
- Enter data in list L_1
- Choose **STAT → TESTS → 7: ZInterval**
- Choose option **Data**
- Press **ENTER**
- Enter the appropriate values
    Zinterval
    Input: Data Stats
    σ : 0.405
    List: L_1
    Freq: 1
    C-Level: .90
    Calculate
- Highlight **Calculate**
- Press **ENTER**

TI-83 or TI-84:

Using summary statistics

If the actual measurements are not available, but the mean of a large sample and the population standard deviation are available, then use this option. If the sample size is large and the population standard deviation is unknown, then input the sample standard deviation (s) for the population standard deviation (σ).

- Choose **STAT $\rightarrow$ TESTS $\rightarrow$ 7: ZInterval**
- Choose option **Stats**
- Press **ENTER**
- Enter the appropriate values
    ZInterval
    Input: Data Stats
    σ: 0.405
    $\bar{x}$: 12.559
    n: 40
    C-Level: .90
    Calculate
- Highlight **Calculate**
- Press **ENTER**

(b) The supervisor is interested in determining whether the filling-process mean has increased.

Step 1: The filling-process mean is

μ = true mean amount of spring water filled per bottle (in ounces).

To decide whether the filling-process mean has increased, the supervisor will test

H_0: μ = 12 oz. (The plant is still filling on the average 12 oz. per bottle.)

H_a: μ > 12 oz. (On the average, the plant is filling more than 12 oz. per bottle.)

Step 2: A random sample of n = 40 bottles was taken.

For each sampled bottle, x = the amount of water per bottle measured in ounces.

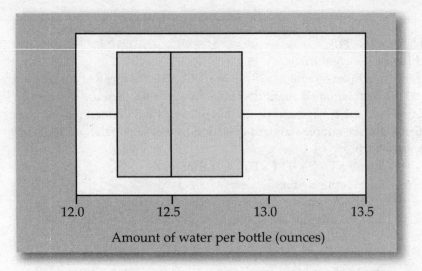

Figure 18: Boxplot of the amount of water filled per bottle

Conditions:

(1) It is given that a random sample of bottles was taken from the bottles filled in the last eight-hour shift.
(2) A boxplot of the data (Figure 18) shows no outliers. We do not know the distribution of the amount filled per bottle, but the sample size is large enough that we can apply the central limit theorem and assume that $\bar{x}$ is approximately normally distributed. Therefore, we can use a z-test to make an inference about the filling-process mean.

Step 3: Suppose we use $\alpha = 0.05$. Then

$$z^* = Z_\alpha = Z_{0.05} = 1.645$$

The sample mean is $\bar{x} = 12.559$ oz and the sample standard deviation is $s = 0.405$ oz.

The rejection rule is "Reject the null hypothesis if p-value < 0.05" (or, "reject the null hypothesis if $z > 1.645$," if using a rejection region approach).

Compute the test statistic value (and compute the p-value, if using a p-value approach).

$$z = \frac{x - \mu_0}{s / \sqrt{n}} = \frac{12.559 - 12}{0.405 / \sqrt{40}} = 8.74$$

$$p\text{-value} = P(Z > 8.74) = \text{almost } 0$$

Step 4: Because the p-value < 0.05 (or $z = 8.74 > 1.645$), reject the null hypothesis and accept the alternative hypothesis. At a 5 percent risk of rejecting the true null hypothesis, we can conclude that the filling-process mean has increased.

TI-83 or TI-84:

Using the data

If the actual measurements are available, use this option. If the sample size is large and the population standard deviation is unknown, then input the sample standard deviation (s) for the population standard deviation (σ).

- Enter data in list L_1
- Choose **STAT → TESTS → 1: Z-Test**
- Choose option **Data**
- Press **ENTER**
- Enter appropriate values
  Zinterval
  Input: Data Stats
  μ_0: 12
  σ: 0.405
  List: L_1
  Freq: 1
  $\mu: \neq \mu_0$ $< \mu_0$ $> \mu_0$ (Highlight option $> \mu_0$)
  Calculate Draw
- Press **ENTER**
- Choose option **Calculate**
- Press **ENTER**

TI-83 or TI-84:

Using summary statistics

If the actual measurements are not available, but the mean of a large sample and the population standard deviation are available, then use this option. If the population standard deviation is unknown, then use the sample standard deviation to estimate the population standard deviation.

- Choose **STAT → TESTS → 1: Z-Test**
- Choose option **Stats**
- Press **ENTER**
- Enter appropriate values
  Z-Test
  Input: Data Stats
  μ_0: 12
  σ : 0.405
  $\bar{x}$: 12.559
  n: 40
  $\mu : \neq \mu_0$ $< \mu_0$ $> \mu_0$ (Highlight option $> \mu_0$)
  Calculate Draw
- Press **ENTER**
- Choose option **Calculate**
- Press **ENTER**

ESTIMATION OF AND INFERENCE ABOUT THE DIFFERENCE IN POPULATION PROPORTIONS $(p_1 - p_2)$

Large Samples Case

Often we are interested in comparing proportions from two different populations. For example:

- Comparing the proportion of residents of Mobile County in favor of using tax money to rebuild private beaches to the proportion of residents of Baldwin County in favor of the same proposal
- Comparing the proportion of Florida residents who support the patient's bill of rights to that of Texas residents who support the bill
- Comparing the proportion of Visa cardholders assessed late-payment penalties to that of MasterCard cardholders assessed late-payment penalties

Let

$$p_1 = \text{the proportion of interest in population 1}$$

$$p_2 = \text{the proportion of interest in population 2}$$

In the situations described above, we are interested in estimating the difference between two population proportions.

Parameter of interest: Difference between two population proportions $(p_1 - p_2)$

- Select a random sample of size n_1 from population 1.
- Select a random sample of size n_2 from population 2.
- Be sure to select the two samples independently of each other.
- For each item or subject in the sample, note the presence or absence of the specific criteria of interest.
- Count the number of subjects meeting required criteria (x_1) from sample 1.
- Count the number of subjects meeting required criteria (x_2) from sample 2.

- The estimated proportion from sample 1 is $\hat{p}_1 = \dfrac{x_1}{n_1}$

- The estimated proportion from sample 2 is $\hat{p}_2 = \dfrac{x_2}{n_2}$

$\hat{p}_1$ and $\hat{p}_2$, respectively, provide point estimates of the unknown population proportions p_1 and p_2. The difference $(\hat{p}_1 - \hat{p}_2)$ gives a point estimate of $(p_1 - p_2)$. Different random samples of the same size from the same population will result in different sample proportions, giving different estimates. Therefore, the difference $(\hat{p}_1 - \hat{p}_2)$ is a random variable. The distribution of estimated differences from all possible random samples of sizes n_1 and n_2 is the sampling distribution of $(\hat{p}_1 - \hat{p}_2)$.

- The mean of the sampling distribution of $(\hat{p}_1 - \hat{p}_2)$ is $(p_1 - p_2)$.
  Therefore, $(\hat{p}_1 - \hat{p}_2)$ is an unbiased estimator of $(p_1 - p_2)$.

- The standard deviation of the sampling distribution of $(\hat{p}_1 - \hat{p}_2)$ is

$$\sigma_{(\hat{p}_1 - \hat{p}_2)} = \sqrt{\frac{p_1(1 - p_1)}{n_1} + \frac{p_2(1 - p_2)}{n_2}}$$

- For large sample sizes, the sampling distribution of $(\hat{p}_1 - \hat{p}_2)$ is approximately normally distributed.

Estimating $(p_1 - p_2)$ using $(1 - \alpha)100\%$ confidence interval:
Large samples case: Construct a z-interval

     Margin of Error:

$$Z_{\alpha/2} s_{(\hat{p}_1 - \hat{p}_2)} = Z_{\alpha/2} \sqrt{\frac{\hat{p}_1(1 - \hat{p}_1)}{n_1} + \frac{\hat{p}_2(1 - \hat{p}_2)}{n_2}}$$

    Confidence Interval:

$$(\hat{p}_1 - \hat{p}_2) \pm Z_{\alpha/2} \sqrt{\frac{\hat{p}_1(1 - \hat{p}_1)}{n_1} + \frac{\hat{p}_2(1 - \hat{p}_2)}{n_2}}$$

Making an inference about the difference in population proportions ($\hat{p}_1 - \hat{p}_2$):
Large samples case: Use a z-test.

H_0: $p_1 - p_2 = D_0$ (D_0 is "pooled $\hat{p}$")

H_a: $p_1 - p_2 > D_0$ or
$\quad\ p_1 - p_2 < D_0$ or
$\quad\ p_1 - p_2 \neq D_0$

$$z = \frac{(\hat{p}_1 - \hat{p}_2) - D_0}{\sqrt{\hat{p}_c\,(1 - \hat{p}_c)\left(\dfrac{1}{n_1} + \dfrac{1}{n_2}\right)}} \qquad \text{where} \quad \hat{p}_c = \frac{x_1 + x_2}{n_1 + n_2}$$

	Rejection Rule	
Alternative hypothesis:	Rejection region approach:	p-value approach:
H_a: $p_1 - p_2 > D_0$ H_a: $p_1 - p_2 < D_0$ H_a: $p_1 - p_2 \neq D_0$	Reject H_0 if $z > Z_\alpha$ $z < -Z_\alpha$ $z > Z_{\alpha/2}$ or $z < -Z_{\alpha/2}$	Reject H_0 if p-value $< \alpha$, where p-value $= P(Z > z)$ p-value $= P(Z < z)$ p-value $= P(Z > |z|) + P(Z < -|z|)$

Conditions:

(a) Random samples are taken from both the populations.
(b) The samples are taken independently.
(c) Both sample sizes are large enough that the distribution of $(\hat{p}_1 - \hat{p}_2)$ is approximately normal.

Note that when constructing a confidence interval, the separate sample proportions are used to calculate the standard deviation and to check the normality condition. When making an inference, the pooled or common $\hat{p}$ is used to calculate the standard deviation and check the normality condition.

Checking the normality condition:

If $n_1\hat{p}_1 > 10$, $n_1(1 - \hat{p}_1) > 10$, $n_2\hat{p}_2 > 10$, and $n_2(1 - \hat{p}_2) > 10$, then it is reasonable to assume that the distribution of $(\hat{p}_1 - \hat{p}_2)$ is approximately normal.

Example 15: A large manufacturer of jeans has two factories, one in Mexico and one in the Philippines. At the end of the assembly lines, each finished pair of jeans is inspected for quality and classified as either good or defective. The business manager wants to compare the proportion of defective jeans produced by the two factories. From one day's production, he randomly selects 500 pairs of jeans from the factory in Mexico and finds 25 defective. Similarly, he randomly selects 350 pairs of jeans from the factory in the Philippines and finds 27 defective. Estimate the difference in the proportion of defective jeans produced by the two factories, using a 98 percent confidence interval.

Solution:

Step 1: The business manager wants to estimate $(p_1 - p_2)$, where

p_1 = The true proportion of defective jeans manufactured at the plant in Mexico.

p_2 = The true proportion of defective jeans manufactured at the plant in the Philippines.

Step 2: A random sample of $n_1 = 500$ pairs of jeans was taken from the plant in Mexico.

Of the sampled jeans, $x_1 = 25$ were defective.

The sample proportion is $\hat{p}_1 = \dfrac{x_1}{n_1} = \dfrac{25}{500} = 0.05$

A random sample of $n_2 = 350$ pairs of jeans was taken from the plant in the Philippines.

Of the sampled jeans, $x_2 = 27$ were defective.

The sample proportion is $\hat{p}_2 = \dfrac{x_2}{n_2} = \dfrac{27}{350} = 0.077$

Conditions:

(a) It is given that random samples of jeans were taken. It is reasonable to assume that both samples were taken independently.

(b) $n_1 \hat{p}_1 = 500(0.05) = 25 > 10$ and $n_1(1 - \hat{p}_1) = 500(1 - 0.05) = 475 > 10$. $n_2 \hat{p}_2 = 350(0.077) = 27 > 10$ and $n_2(1 - \hat{p}_2) = 350(1 - 0.077) = 323 > 10$. Therefore the sample sizes are large enough that we can assume that the sampling distribution of $(\hat{p}_1 - \hat{p}_2)$ is approximately normal.

The conditions are satisfied and we can therefore use a large-samples z-interval for difference in proportions.

Step 3: To construct a 98 percent confidence interval, we use $\alpha = 0.02$

$$z^* = Z_{\alpha/2} = Z_{0.02/2} = Z_{0.01} = 2.33$$

$$(\hat{p}_1 - \hat{p}_2) = 0.05 - 0.077 = -0.027$$

$$98\% \ ME = Z_{\alpha/2}\sqrt{\frac{\hat{p}_1(1-\hat{p}_1)}{n_1} + \frac{\hat{p}_2(1-\hat{p}_2)}{n_2}}$$

$$= 2.33\sqrt{\frac{0.05(1-0.05)}{500} + \frac{0.077(1-0.077)}{350}}$$

$$= 0.04$$

$$(\hat{p}_1 - \hat{p}_2) \pm ME \Rightarrow -0.027 \pm 0.04 \Rightarrow (-0.067, 0.013)$$

Therefore, a 98 percent confidence interval to estimate $(p_1 - p_2)$ is $(-0.067, 0.013)$.

Step 4: We are 98 percent confident that the difference between the proportion of defective jeans produced by the plant in Mexico and the proportion of defective jeans produced by the plant in the Philippines is between -0.067 and 0.013. Because 0 falls in this interval, we cannot conclude that $p_1 - p_2 \neq 0$. In other words, there is no significant difference between the proportion of defective jeans produced by the factory in Mexico and the proportion produced by the factory in the Philippines.

TI-83 or TI-84:
- Choose **STAT** → **TESTS** → **B: 2-PropZInt**
- Enter appropriate values
  2-PropZInt
  x1: 25
  n1: 500
  x2: 27
  n2: 350
  C-Level: .98
  Calculate
- Highlight **Calculate**
- Press **ENTER**

ESTIMATION OF AND INFERENCE ABOUT THE DIFFERENCE IN POPULATION MEANS ($\mu_1 - \mu_2$)

We are often interested in comparing the means of two different populations. For example:

- Comparing the mean lifetimes of two comparable brands of tires
- Comparing the mean costs of education at two state universities
- Comparing the mean grades of students taught using two different methods

- Comparing the mean number of asthma attacks per month before and after patients are given a new medication
- Comparing the mean cost of long distance calls per minute using two different companies

In each of the above examples, we want to compare the means of two populations. To make such a comparison, we need to take a random sample from each of the two populations and compare their sample means. But notice that, in some cases, the two samples are independent, whereas in others the samples are dependent. By *dependence*, we mean that there is some kind of matching involved between the first sample and the second sample. Data collected from independent samples is analyzed differently from data collected from dependent samples:

- **Independent samples.** To compare the effect of two different teaching methods (traditional and new) on students' grades, take a group of students with similar educational backgrounds. Assign these students randomly to one of two different groups. Teach the students in group 1 using the traditional method and those in group 2 using the new method. At the end of the course, give the same exam to both groups and measure the students' grades. In this situation, there is no specific matching between the students in one group and the students in the other group. So the two samples are independent or unpaired.

- **Dependent samples.** To measure the effectiveness of a new diet, select a group of patients and measure their cholesterol levels before starting on a new diet. Then measure the cholesterol levels of the same patients after they've been put on the diet for three months. In this situation, note that there is a specific match between the "before diet" cholesterol level sample and the "after diet" cholesterol level sample. Both samples are taken from the same patients. It does not make sense to compare the "before diet" cholesterol level for Bob with the "after diet" cholesterol level for Ann. Dependence does not necessarily mean taking measurements on the same item or person, however.

Case of Independent or Unpaired Samples

Two samples are considered independent if the selection of one sample has no bearing on the selection of the other sample. For example, to compare the lifetime of Goodyear tires to the lifetime of Firestone tires, we could select a sample of tires from Goodyear's production line and a sample from Firestone's. Which tires get selected in one sample has no connection to which tires get selected in the other sample.

Here, we will let

μ_1 = The mean of population 1, and σ_1 = the standard deviation of population 1.

μ_2 = The mean of population 2, and σ_2 = the standard deviation of population 2.

Suppose we are interested in estimating the difference between two population means. Parameter of interest: Difference between two population means ($\mu_1 - \mu_2$).

- Select a random sample of size n_1 from population 1.
- Select a random sample of size n_2 from population 2.
- Select the two samples independently of each other.
- For each selected item, measure the specific variable of interest. Let $x_{11}, x_{12}, ..., x_{1n_1}$ be the measurements from the first sample and $x_{21}, x_{22}, ..., x_{2n_2}$ be the measurements from the second sample.
- Compute both sample means.

- The mean of sample 1 is $\bar{x}_1 = \dfrac{\sum\limits_{i=1}^{n_1} x_{1i}}{n_1}$. The mean of sample 2 is $\bar{x}_2 = \dfrac{\sum\limits_{i=1}^{n_2} x_{2i}}{n_2}$. Note that $\bar{x}_1$ estimates μ_1 and $\bar{x}_2$ estimates μ_2. The difference $(\bar{x}_1 - \bar{x}_2)$ gives a point estimate of the difference $(\mu_1 - \mu_2)$. Different random samples of the same size from the same population will result in different sample means, giving different estimates. Therefore, the difference $(\bar{x}_1 - \bar{x}_2)$ is a random variable. The distribution of the estimated differences in sample means from all possible random and independent samples of sizes n_1 and n_2 is the sampling distribution of $(\bar{x}_1 - \bar{x}_2)$.

- The mean of the sampling distribution of $(\bar{x}_1 - \bar{x}_2)$ is $(\mu_1 - \mu_2)$. Therefore $(\bar{x}_1 - \bar{x}_2)$ is an unbiased estimator of $(\mu_1 - \mu_2)$.

- Because the samples were taken independently, the standard deviation of the sampling distribution of $(\bar{x}_1 - \bar{x}_2)$ is

$$\sigma_{(\bar{x}_1 - \bar{x}_2)} = \sqrt{\dfrac{\sigma_1^2}{n_1} + \dfrac{\sigma_2^2}{n_2}}$$

- Note the following about the sampling distribution of $(\bar{x}_1 - \bar{x}_2)$:
  If both the populations are normally distributed and the population standard deviations are known, then the sampling distribution of $(\bar{x}_1 - \bar{x}_2)$ is also a **normal distribution**.

If both the populations are normally distributed and the population standard deviations are unknown but equal, then the sampling distribution of $(\bar{x}_1 - \bar{x}_2)$ is a *t*-distribution with $(n_1 + n_2 - 2)$ degrees of freedom.

If both the populations are normally distributed, and the population standard deviations are unknown and unequal, then the sampling distribution of $(\bar{x}_1 - \bar{x}_2)$ is an approximate *t*-distribution with degrees of freedom equal to

$$df = \frac{\left(\dfrac{s_1^2}{n_1} + \dfrac{s_2^2}{n_2}\right)^2}{\dfrac{\left(s_1^2/n_1\right)^2}{n_1 - 1} + \dfrac{\left(s_2^2/n^2\right)^2}{n_2 - 1}}$$

In most cases, this formula gives a fractional value for the required degrees of freedom. We would therefore need computers or calculators to find the true corresponding *t* values. When using tables, use the next smallest degree of freedom to the calculated *df*. For example, if the above formula gives degrees of freedom equal to 17.35, then use 17 degrees of freedom in the *t*-distribution table.

You do not need to memorize this (or any other) formula; you will be provided with all of the formulas you need. This calculation can be done on your calculator. On the TI-83 or TI-84, use the 2 Samp T-Int function from the STATS-Tests menu.

If both the sample sizes are large, then according to the central limit theorem, the sampling distribution of $(\bar{x}_1 - \bar{x}_2)$ is approximately **normal**, regardless of the population distributions.

• To construct a confidence interval using a normal or a *t*-distribution, decide between the two distributions using the scheme shown in Figure 19.

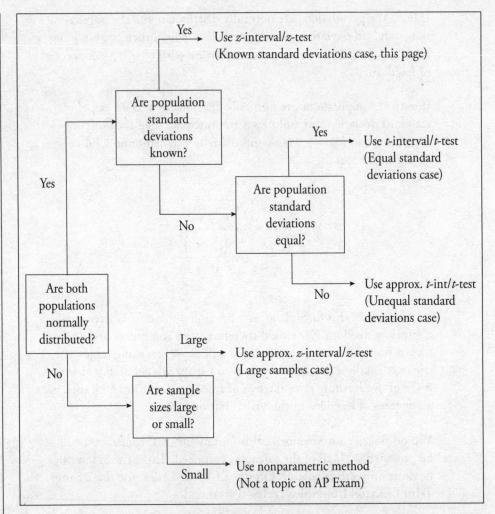

Figure 19: Scheme for selecting a confidence interval or test for difference of population means

Known Standard Deviations Case

The two population standard deviations σ_1 and σ_2 are known, and both populations are normally distributed. Again, this case is unusual. If we want to estimate the difference in means, we most likely do not know the standard deviations.

Estimating $(\mu_1 - \mu_2)$ using $(1 - \alpha)100\%$ confidence interval:

Known standard deviations case: Construct a z-interval

Margin of Error: $Z_{\alpha/2}\, \sigma_{(\bar{x}_1 - \bar{x}_2)} = Z_{\alpha/2} \sqrt{\dfrac{\sigma_1^2}{n_1} + \dfrac{\sigma_2^2}{n_2}}$

Confidence Interval: $(\bar{x}_1 - \bar{x}_2) \pm Z_{\alpha/2} \sqrt{\dfrac{\sigma_1^2}{n_1} + \dfrac{\sigma_2^2}{n_2}}$

Making an inference about the difference in population means ($\mu_1 - \mu_2$):
Known standard deviations case: Use a z-test.

$H_0: \mu_1 - \mu_2 = D_0$ (D_0 is specified)

$H_a: \mu_1 - \mu_2 > D_0$ or

$\quad \mu_1 - \mu_2 < D_0$ or

$\quad \mu_1 - \mu_2 \neq D_0$

$\quad D_0$ is specified difference

$$ z = \frac{\left(\bar{x}_1 - \bar{x}_2 \right) - D_0}{\sqrt{\dfrac{\sigma_1^2}{n_1} + \dfrac{\sigma_2^2}{n_2}}} $$

	Rejection Rule	
Alternative hypothesis:	Rejection region approach:	*p*-value approach:
$H_a: \mu_1 - \mu_2 > D_0$	Reject H_0 if	Reject H_0 if *p*-value $< \alpha$, where
$H_a: \mu_1 - \mu_2 < D_0$	$z > Z_\alpha$	*p*-value $= P(Z > z)$
$H_a: \mu_1 - \mu_2 \neq D_0$	$z < -Z_\alpha$	*p*-value $= P(Z < z)$
	$z > Z_{\alpha/2}$ or $z < -Z_{\alpha/2}$	*p*-value $= P(Z > |z|) + P(Z < -|z|)$

Conditions:

    (a) Random samples are taken from both the populations.
    (b) The samples are taken independently.
    (c) The sampled populations are normally distributed.

Checking the normality condition:

Make a dotplot or stem-and-leaf plot for each sample. Ask yourself whether each distribution is fairly symmetric and bell-shaped, without any outliers. In other words, ask yourself whether the distribution resembles the normal distribution. Alternatively, use a normal probability plot. There are more formal tests, but they are not topics on the AP exam.

Large Samples Case

Both samples are large.

If the population standard deviations (σ_1 and σ_2) are unknown, estimate them using the sample standard deviations (s_1 and s_2 respectively).

Estimating $(\mu_1 - \mu_2)$ using $(1 - \alpha)100\%$ confidence interval:
Large samples case: Construct a z-interval

Margin of Error: $\quad Z_{\alpha/2} s_{x_1 - x_2} = Z_{\alpha/2} \sqrt{\dfrac{s_1^2}{n_1} + \dfrac{s_2^2}{n_2}}$

Confidence Interval: $\quad \left(x_1 - x_2\right) \pm Z_{\alpha/2} \sqrt{\dfrac{s_1^2}{n_1} + \dfrac{s_2^2}{n_2}}$

Making an inference about the difference in population means $\quad (\mu_1 - \mu_2)$:
Large samples case: Use a z-test.

$H_0: \mu_1 - \mu_2 = D_0 \;\; (D_0 \text{ is specified})$
$H_a: \mu_1 - \mu_2 > D_0$ or
$\quad \mu_1 - \mu_2 < D_0$ or
$\quad \mu_1 - \mu_2 \neq D_0$
$(D_0 \text{ is specified difference})$

$$z = \dfrac{(\bar{x}_1 - \bar{x}_2) - D_0}{\sqrt{\dfrac{\sigma_1^2}{n_1} + \dfrac{\sigma_2^2}{n_2}}}$$

	Rejection Rule	
Alternative hypothesis:	Rejection region approach:	p-value approach:
$H_a: \mu_1 - \mu_2 > D_0$	Reject H_0 if	Reject H_0 if p-value $< \alpha$, where
$H_a: \mu_1 - \mu_2 < D_0$	$z > Z_\alpha$	p-value $= P(Z > z)$
$H_a: \mu_1 - \mu_2 \neq D_0$	$z < -Z_\alpha$	p-value $= P(Z < z)$
	$z > Z_{\alpha/2}$ or $z < -Z_{\alpha/2}$	p-value $= P(Z > |z|) + P(Z < -|z|)$

Conditions:

(a) Random samples are taken from both populations.
(b) The samples are taken independently.
(c) The samples are large enough that the distribution for $(\bar{x}_1 - \bar{x}_2)$ is approximately normal.

Checking the normality condition:

There is no unique value that determines in general if a sample size is large or small; this depends on the shape of the distribution of the sampled population. If there are no outliers and the population distributions are not extremely skewed, then $n_1 \geq 30$ and $n_2 \geq 30$ are large enough to get approximately normal sampling distributions for $\bar{x}_1$ and $\bar{x}_2$, and consequently that for $(x_1 - x_2)$.

Equal Standard Deviations Case

Two population standard deviations σ_1 and σ_2 are unknown, but are assumed to be equal. Let's say $\sigma_1 = \sigma_2 = \sigma$. Compute sample standard deviations from each sample. Let s_1 be the standard deviation computed from sample 1 and s_2 be the standard deviation computed from sample 2. We know that s_1 estimates σ_1 and s_2 estimates σ_2. But remember that $\sigma_1 = \sigma_2 = \sigma$. So we have two estimates (s_1 and s_2) for one unknown quantity σ. By pooling information from both samples, we can get an improved estimate of σ. The pooled estimate of σ is computed as

$$s_p = \sqrt{\frac{(n_1 - 1)s_1^2 + (n_2 - 1)s_2^2}{n_1 + n_2 - 2}}$$

Estimating $(\mu_1 - \mu_2)$ **using** $(1 - \alpha)100\%$ **confidence interval:**

Equal variances case: Construct a t-interval with df degrees of freedom, where $df = (n_1 + n_2 - 2)$.

Margin of Error: $t_{\alpha/2}\left(df\right)s_{(\bar{x}_1 - \bar{x}_2)} = t_{\alpha/2}\left(df\right)s_p\sqrt{\dfrac{1}{n_1} + \dfrac{1}{n_2}}$

Where $s_p = \sqrt{\dfrac{(n_1 - 1)s_1^2 + (n_2 - 1)s_2^2}{n_1 + n_2 - 2}}$

Confidence Interval: $\left(\bar{x}_1 - \bar{x}_2\right) \pm t_{\alpha/2}\left(df\right)s_p\sqrt{\dfrac{1}{n_1} + \dfrac{1}{n_2}}$

Making an inference about the difference in population means $(\mu_1 - \mu_2)$:
Equal standard deviations case: Use a t-test with $df = (n_1 + n_2 - 2)$ degrees of freedom.

$H_0: \mu_1 - \mu_2 = D_0$ (specified difference) $H_a: \mu_1 - \mu_2 > D_0$ or $\quad \mu_1 - \mu_2 < D_0$ or $\quad \mu_1 - \mu_2 \neq D_0$	$t = \dfrac{(\bar{x}_1 - \bar{x}_2) - D_0}{s_p\sqrt{\dfrac{1}{n_1} + \dfrac{1}{n_2}}}$ where $s_p = \sqrt{\dfrac{(n_1 - 1)s_1^2 + (n_2 - 1)s_2^2}{(n_1 + n_2) - 2}}$

Rejection Rule		
Alternative hypothesis:	Rejection region approach:	p-value approach:
$H_a: \mu_1 - \mu_2 > D_0$	Reject H_0 if	Reject H_0 if p-value $< \alpha$, where
$H_a: \mu_1 - \mu_2 < D_0$	$t > t_\alpha(df)$	p-value $= P(t(df) > t)$
$H_a: \mu_1 - \mu_2 \neq D_0$	$t < -t_\alpha(df)$	p-value $= P(t(df) < t)$
	$t > t_{\alpha/2}(df)$ or $t < -t_{\alpha/2}(df)$	p-value $= P(t(df) > |t|) + P(t(df) < -|t|)$

Conditions:

    (a) Random samples are taken from both the populations.
    (b) The samples are taken independently.
    (c) The sampled populations are normally distributed.
    (d) The population standard deviations are equal ($\sigma_1 = \sigma_2$).

Checking the normality condition:

Make a dotplot, histogram, or stem-and-leaf plot for each sample. Ask yourself whether each distribution is fairly symmetric and bell-shaped, without any outliers. In other words, ask yourself whether both the distributions resemble the normal distribution. Alternatively, use a normal probability plot.

Checking the condition of equal standard deviations:

Make dotplots or histograms and visually compare the spread of the measurements. If they are fairly comparable, without any outliers, then it is reasonable to assume that the standard deviations are equal. Alternatively, use a two-tailed *F*-test for equality of standard deviations (you may have learned how to do this in your statistics class, but it is not a topic on the AP exam).

Unknown Standard Deviations Case

Two population standard deviations σ_1 and σ_2 are unknown. Estimate the unknown population standard deviations using the sample standard deviations s_1 and s_2 respectively.

Estimating $(\mu_1 - \mu_2)$ **using** $(1 - \alpha)100\%$ **confidence interval:**

Unequal standard deviations case: Construct a *t*-interval with

$$df = \frac{\left(\dfrac{s_1^2}{n_1} + \dfrac{s_2^2}{n_2}\right)^2}{\dfrac{\left(s_1^2/n_1\right)^2}{n_1 - 1} + \dfrac{\left(s_2^2/n^2\right)^2}{n_2 - 1}} \quad \text{degrees of freedom}$$

Margin of Error: $t_{\alpha/2}(df)\, s_{(\bar{x}_1 - \bar{x}_2)} = t_{\alpha/2}(df)\sqrt{\dfrac{s_1^2}{n_1} + \dfrac{s_2^2}{n_2}}$

Confidence Interval: $(\bar{x}_1 - \bar{x}_2) \pm t_{\alpha/2}(df)\sqrt{\dfrac{s_1^2}{n_1} + \dfrac{s_2^2}{n_2}}$

On the TI-83 or TI-84, *df* can be obtained using the 2 samp *t*-int function under the STATS-Tests menu.

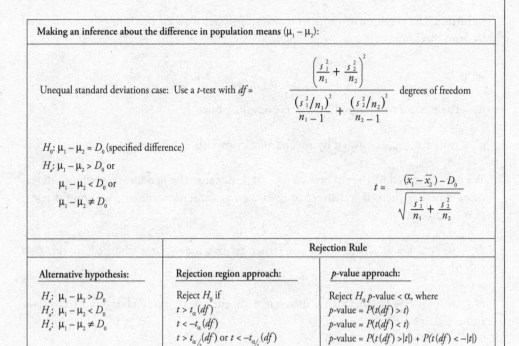

Making an inference about the difference in population means ($\mu_1 - \mu_2$):

Unequal standard deviations case: Use a *t*-test with $df = \dfrac{\left(\dfrac{s_1^2}{n_1} + \dfrac{s_2^2}{n_2}\right)^2}{\dfrac{\left(s_1^2/n_1\right)^2}{n_1 - 1} + \dfrac{\left(s_2^2/n_2\right)^2}{n_2 - 1}}$ degrees of freedom

$H_0: \mu_1 - \mu_2 = D_0$ (specified difference)

$H_a: \mu_1 - \mu_2 > D_0$ or

$\quad \mu_1 - \mu_2 < D_0$ or

$\quad \mu_1 - \mu_2 \neq D_0$

$$t = \frac{(\overline{x}_1 - \overline{x}_2) - D_0}{\sqrt{\dfrac{s_1^2}{n_1} + \dfrac{s_2^2}{n_2}}}$$

	Rejection Rule	
Alternative hypothesis:	**Rejection region approach:**	**p-value approach:**
$H_a: \mu_1 - \mu_2 > D_0$	Reject H_0 if	Reject H_0 p-value $< \alpha$, where
$H_a: \mu_1 - \mu_2 < D_0$	$t > t_\alpha(df)$	p-value $= P(t(df) > t)$
$H_a: \mu_1 - \mu_2 \neq D_0$	$t < -t_\alpha(df)$	p-value $= P(t(df) < t)$
	$t > t_{\alpha/2}(df)$ or $t < -t_{\alpha/2}(df)$	p-value $= P(t(df) > |t|) + P(t(df) < -|t|)$

Conditions:

(a) Random samples are taken from both the populations.

(b) The samples are taken independently.

(c) The sampled populations are normally distributed.

Checking the normality condition:

Make a dotplot or stem-and-leaf plot for each sample. Ask yourself whether the shape of each distribution is fairly symmetric and bell-shaped, without any outliers. In other words, ask yourself whether each distribution resembles the normal distribution. Alternatively, use a normal probability plot.

Checking the condition of unequal standard deviations:

In most cases, if the ratio of sample variances is larger than 4, then it is safe to assume that the standard deviations are unequal. Alternatively, use a two-tailed *F*-test for equality of standard deviations (you may have learned how to do this in your statistics class, but it is not a topic on the AP exam).

Example 16: An economist wants to compare the hourly rates charged by automobile mechanics in two suburbs. She randomly selects auto repair facilities from both suburbs and records their hourly rates (in dollars). The data are as follows:

Suburb 1: 40.0   38.0   38.0   37.0   36.0   39.0   41.5   38.0   39.5   37.5   35.0   40.0

Suburb 2: 35.0   37.0   31.0   39.0   31.5   35.0   32.5   34.0   39.0   36.0

Is there sufficient evidence to indicate a difference in the mean hourly rates for these two suburbs?

Solution: The economist wants to make an inference about the hourly rates charged by auto mechanics.

Step 1: Let

μ_1 = the mean rate charged by mechanics in suburb 1

μ_2 = the mean rate charged by mechanics in suburb 2

We are interested in the difference $(\mu_1 - \mu_2)$. Because the economist wants to determine whether there is a difference in the two population means, we should use a two-tailed test.

H_0: $(\mu_1 - \mu_2) = 0$ (there is no difference in the mean rates charged in the two suburbs)

H_a: $(\mu_1 - \mu_2) \neq 0$ (there is a difference in the mean rates charged in the two suburbs)

Step 2: The sample sizes n_1 = 12 and n_2 = 10 are both small. Let us plot both the samples.

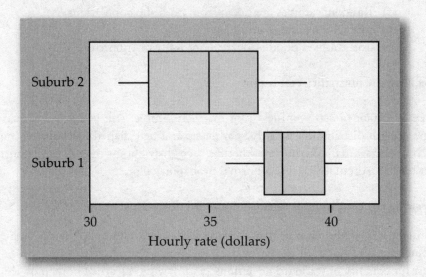

Figure 20: Boxplots of mechanics' hourly rates

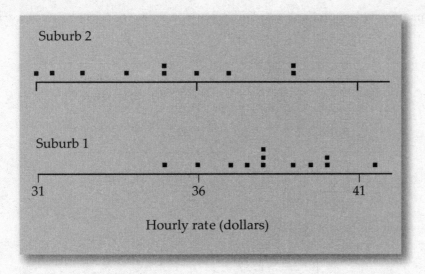

Figure 21: Parallel dotplots showing distribution of hourly rates

Conditions:

(a) It is given that random samples of auto repair facilities were obtained.

(b) There is no reason for the selection of facilities in one suburb to have any bearing on the selection of facilities in another suburb. Therefore, it is reasonable to assume that the samples were selected independently of each other.

(c) The graphs in Figures 20 and 21 show that the distributions of hourly rates are fairly symmetric, with no outliers. It is reasonable to assume that both the populations are approximately normally distributed.

All the conditions for a *t*-test are satisfied. Even though the population standard deviations are unknown, the dotplots show a similar spread for both samples, so it is reasonable to assume equal population standard deviations and to use an equal standard deviations *t*-test.

Step 3: Suppose we use a 5 percent level of significance. The degrees of freedom

$$df = 12 + 10 - 2 = 20 \text{ and } t^* = t_{\alpha/2}(df) = t_{0.025}(20) = 2.086$$

The rejection rule is "reject the null hypothesis if *p*-value < 0.05" (or, if using the rejection region approach, "reject the null hypothesis if $t < -2.086$ or $t > 2.086$").

Compute sample means and standard deviations, using the formulas we've learned before:

	n	Average	Standard Deviation
Suburb 1	12	38.29	1.83
Suburb 2	10	35.0	2.84

The pooled estimate of the standard deviation is

$$s_p = \sqrt{\frac{(12-1)1.83^2 + (10-1)2.84^2}{12+10-2}} = 2.34$$

Compute the test statistic value (and the p-value, if using the p-value approach).

$$t = \frac{(\bar{x}_1 - \bar{x}_2) - 0}{s_p\sqrt{\left(\frac{1}{n_1} + \frac{1}{n_2}\right)}} = \frac{38.29 - 35.00}{2.34\sqrt{\left(\frac{1}{12} + \frac{1}{10}\right)}} = 3.29$$

$$p\text{-value} = P(t(20) < -3.29) + P(t(20) > 3.29) = 0.0037$$

Step 4: Because p-value = 0.0037 < 0.05 (or, if using the rejection region approach, since the test statistic, $t = 3.29$, falls in the rejection region, or $t = 3.29 > 2.086$), we should reject the null hypothesis and accept the alternative hypothesis.

Because there is less than a 5 percent risk of making the wrong decision, we can conclude that there is a significant difference in the mean hourly charges in the two suburbs.

Because $\bar{x}_1 > \bar{x}_2$ we can say that the mean rates charged in suburb 1 are higher than the mean rates charged in suburb 2.

TI-83 or TI-84:

Inference using data

If the actual measurements are available, use this option:

- Enter data in 2 columns, say Suburb 1 in L_1 and Suburb 2 in L_2
- **Choose STAT → TESTS → 4: 2-SampTTest**
- Press **ENTER**
- Choose option **Data**
- Press **ENTER**
- Enter appropriate values

  2-SampTTest

  Input: Data   Stats

  List1: L_1

  List2: L_2

  Freq1: 1

  Freq2: 1

  $\mu_1: \neq \mu_2$ $<\mu_2$ $>\mu_2$ (Choose option $\neq \mu_2$)
- Press **ENTER**

  Pooled: No   Yes   (Select Yes or No)
- Press **ENTER**

  Calculate   Draw
- Choose option **Calculate**
- Press **ENTER**

Note:

- For equal standard deviation case choose
  Pooled: Yes
- For unequal standard deviation case choose
  Pooled: No

TI-83 or TI-84:

Estimation using data

If the actual measurements are available, use this option:

- Enter data in 2 columns, say Suburb 1 in L_1 and Suburb 2 in L_2
- **Choose STAT → TESTS → 0: 2-SampTInt**
- Press **ENTER**
- Choose option **Data**
- Press **ENTER**
- Enter appropriate values

  2-SampTInt

  Input: Data   Stats

  List1: L_1

  List2: L_2

  Freq1: 1

  Freq2: 1

  C-Level: .95

  Pooled: No   Yes   (Select No or Yes)

- Press **ENTER**

  Calculate

- Highlight **Calculate**
- Press **ENTER**

Note:

- For equal standard deviation case choose
  Pooled: Yes
- For unequal standard deviation case choose
  Pooled: No

Example 17: Students in a course at a large university felt that using a calculator would give them an advantage on an exam. Their instructor decided to check it out. Because she was teaching two of the 18 sections of this course and students were assigned randomly to different sections, she decided to allow one section to use calculators on the test and not the other. The students' scores on the test are approximately normally distributed. The average class scores and variances of the class scores are as follows:

	n	Class Average	Class Variance
Calculators	23	80.7	49.5
No Calculators	22	78.9	60.4

Is it advantageous for students to use calculators on the test? Justify using statistical evidence.

Solution: The instructor wants to compare two population means, namely, the mean test score of students using a calculator and the mean test score of students not using a calculator.

Step 1: Let

μ_1 = the mean score of students using a calculator

μ_2 = the mean score of students not using a calculator

We are interested in making an inference about $(\mu_1 - \mu_2)$.

H_0: $\mu_1 = \mu_2$ or $\mu_1 - \mu_2 = 0$

(There's no difference between the mean scores of the two groups.)

H_a: $\mu_1 > \mu_2$ or $\mu_1 - \mu_2 > 0$

(The mean score of the students using a calculator is higher than the mean score of students not using a calculator.)

Step 2: It is given that the students are assigned randomly to different sections. So it is reasonable to assume that the selected students are random, independent samples of all students taking this course. Also, it is given that the scores are approximately normally distributed.

The sample variances are fairly close to each other, and we can assume that the unknown population variances (and hence, their standard deviations) are equal. We can use the equal standard deviations t-test with $df = 23 + 22 - 2 = 43$ degrees of freedom. Let's use a 5 percent error rate.

Step 3: The rejection rule is to "reject null if p-value < 0.05" (or, if using the rejection region approach, "reject null if $t > 1.681$").

The pooled estimate of the standard deviation is

$$s_p = \sqrt{\frac{(23-1)49.5 + (22-1)60.4}{23+22-2}} = 7.40$$

Compute the test statistic value (and p-value if using p-value approach).

$$t = \frac{(\bar{x}_1 - \bar{x}_2) - 0}{s_p\sqrt{\left(\frac{1}{n_1} + \frac{1}{n_2}\right)}} = \frac{80.7 - 78.9}{7.40\sqrt{\left(\frac{1}{23} + \frac{1}{22}\right)}} = 0.815$$

p-value = $P(t(43) > 0.815) = 0.2097$

If it were not reasonable to assume equal population variances, then we could use the unequal variances t-test with

$$v = \frac{\left(\dfrac{s_1^2}{n_1} + \dfrac{s_2^2}{n_2}\right)^2}{\dfrac{\left(s_1^2/n_1\right)^2}{n_1 - 1} + \dfrac{\left(s_2^2/n_2\right)^2}{n_2 - 1}} = \frac{\left(\dfrac{49.5}{23} + \dfrac{60.4}{22}\right)^2}{\dfrac{\left(49.5/23\right)^2}{23 - 1} + \dfrac{\left(60.4/22\right)^2}{22 - 1}} = 42.12$$

where v is the symbol for degrees of freedom.

Again, use a 5 percent error rate. The rejection rule is to "reject null if p-value < 0.05"

(or, if using the rejection region approach, reject null if TS > 1.682).

Compute the test statistic value (and p-value if using p-value approach).

$$t = \frac{\left(\bar{x}_1 - \bar{x}_2\right) - 0}{\sqrt{\left(\dfrac{s_1^2}{n_1} + \dfrac{s_2^2}{n_2}\right)}} = \frac{80.7 - 78.9}{\sqrt{\left(\dfrac{49.5}{23} + \dfrac{60.4}{22}\right)}} = 0.813$$

p-value = $P(t(42.12) > 0.813) = 0.2103$

Step 4: Because, in either case, the p-value > 0.05 (or the t falls in the non-rejection region), we do not reject the null hypothesis. At a 5 percent risk, we can conclude that there is insufficient evidence to suggest that the use of calculators improves the mean student grade.

TI-83 or TI-84:

Inference using summary statistics

If the actual measurements are not available, but the sample means and sample standard deviations are available, then use this option.

- Choose STAT → TESTS → 4: 2-SampTTest
- Press **ENTER**
- Choose option **Stats**
- Press **ENTER**
- Enter appropriate values

    2-SampTTest
    Input: Data   Stats
    $\bar{x}1$: 80.7
    Sx1: $\sqrt{49.5}$
    n1: 23
    $\bar{x}2$: 78.9
    Sx2: $\sqrt{60.4}$
    n2: 22
    μ_1: $\neq \mu_2$ $<\mu_2$ $>\mu_2$ (Select option $> \mu_2$)

- Press **ENTER**

    Pooled: No   Yes   (Select Yes or No)

- Press **ENTER**

    Calculate   Draw

- Choose option **Calculate**
- Press **ENTER**

Note:

- For equal standard deviations case choose
    Pooled: Yes
- For unequal standard deviations case choose
    Pooled: No

TI-83 or TI-84:

Estimation using summary statistic

If the actual measurements are not available, but the sample means and sample standard deviations are available, then use this option:

- Choose **STAT** → **TESTS** → **0: 2-SampTInt**
- Press **ENTER**
- Choose option **Stats**
- Press **ENTER**
- Enter appropriate values

    2-SampTInt

    Input: Data   Stats

    $\bar{x}1$: 80.7

    Sx1: $\sqrt{49.5}$

    n1: 23

    $\bar{x}2$: 78.9

    Sx2: $\sqrt{60.4}$

    n2: 22

    C-Level: .95

    Pooled: No   Yes   (Choose No)

    Calculate

- Highlight **Calculate**
- Press **ENTER**

Example 18: A student waiting tables at a restaurant near a university in Chicago felt that customers tend to tip female waiters better than they tip male waiters. To confirm his suspicion, he contacted 50 female students and 75 male students who waited tables at different restaurants near the university and asked them to keep a record of tips received for one week. At the end of the week, he compiled the data in terms of the mean amount of tips received per hour worked by each student and summarized the data as follows:

	n	Average	Standard Deviation
Females	50	15.50	4.25
Males	75	12.25	3.20

(a) Estimate the difference in the mean amount of tips received hourly by female and male waiters. Use $\alpha = 0.10$.

(b) Does this data provide evidence to justify the student's suspicions?

(c) Would you do anything differently in this experiment if you repeated it? Why?

Solution:

(a) We are interested in the difference in the mean amount of tips received by female and male waiters.

Step 1: Let

μ_1 = The mean amount of tips received by female waiters per hour

μ_2 = The mean amount of tips received by male waiters per hour

We are interested in estimating

$(\mu_1 - \mu_2)$ = the difference in the mean amount of tips received by female and male waiters.

Step 2: The sample sizes are large enough that we can apply the central limit theorem and use a z-interval. Let us assume that

- There are no outliers in the data. (Because there is no data available, we cannot check.)
- All male and female waiters were selected randomly and independently.

Step 3: Using $\alpha = 0.10$, we get $z^* = Z_{\alpha/2} = 1.645$. The population standard deviations are unknown, so we estimate them using the sample standard deviations.

$$\text{The 90 percent } ME = Z_{\alpha/2}\sqrt{\frac{s_1^2}{n_1} + \frac{s_2^2}{n_2}} = 1.645\sqrt{\frac{4.25^2}{50} + \frac{3.20^2}{75}} = 1.16$$

$$(\bar{x}_1 - \bar{x}_2) \pm ME \Rightarrow (15.50 - 12.25) \pm 1.16 \Rightarrow (2.09, 4.41)$$

The 90 percent confidence interval to estimate $(\mu_1 - \mu_2)$ is (2.09, 4.41) dollars.

Step 4: We are 90 percent confident that the difference in mean amounts of tips received per hour by female and male waiters is between $2.09 and $4.41.

(b) Refer to the confidence interval constructed in part (a). Note that the interval does not contain zero. Therefore, at a 10 percent risk, we can conclude that there is a significant difference in the mean amount of tips received by female and male waiters.

Also note that the entire interval for $(\mu_1 - \mu_2)$ lies above 0. So, we can conclude that $(\mu_1 - \mu_2) > 0$. In other words, the mean amount of tips received by female waiters is significantly higher than the mean amount of tips received by male waiters.

Alternatively, we could test

$$H_0: (\mu_1 - \mu_2) < 0$$

(Female waiters do not receive higher tips on average than male waiters.)

$$H_a: (\mu_1 - \mu_2) > 0$$

(Female waiters receive on the average higher tips than male waiters.)

The large-samples z-test results in $z = 4.60$, p-value = 0.000002 (almost 0).

For this p-value, we should reject the null for any reasonable level of significance and conclude that there is evidence to support the student's suspicions. The data suggests that, on average, female waiters tend to receive higher tips than male waiters.

(c) A better way to do the study would be to take a random sample of waiters, regardless of whether or not they're students. It is not clear if these samples were selected at random. Because only student waiters were included in the experiment, the results will only be applicable to student waiters at this particular university, rather than all male and female waiters.

Case of Dependent or Paired Samples

Sometimes it's either not possible to take independent samples, or the results from the independent samples are insufficient to answer the questions at hand. For example, when checking the effectiveness of a certain weight loss program, you need to measure and compare the weights of the same participants before starting the program and after completing the program. Comparison of Bill's "before" weight with Leslie's "after" weight is meaningless. We need to compare Bill's "before" and "after" program weights, and Leslie's "before" and "after" weights. Therefore, we have to use dependent or paired measurements.

Pairing or matching does not necessarily mean taking both measurements on the same subject. For example, suppose we are interested in comparing two different brands of calculators (say, TI and HP) in terms of ease of computation. If we did some computations on TI calculators and some other computations on HP calculators, then it's possible that some of the differences in the ease of computation would be due to the differences in the types of computations performed. The responses would not be comparable. The best way to perform this experiment would be to do the same type of computations on both calculators, and to do each calculation in random order, to avoid giving any specific calculator the advantage of the practice effect. This would result in the matching or pairing of samples. The samples would therefore not be independent. Is this a problem? No. It just means that the data would need to be analyzed differently.

Some of the ways in which pairing or matching can be achieved are the following:

- Take both measurements on the same subject, such as we discussed in the diet example above.
- Use naturally occurring pairs (such as twins, or husbands and wives) and assign the two subjects in each pair to two different groups, using some kind of randomization scheme. Then take measurements on both groups and compare.
- Match subjects by some characteristics, the effect of which might otherwise obscure the difference in responses. For example, to compare the effects of two headache medicines, we could match patients by their ages, because the effect of the medicine may differ depending on the patient's age. Two patients in the same age group could each be given a different medicine and then the medicine's effects could be compared. The age effect would not then be confounded with the medicine effect.

Let μ_X be the mean of one population and μ_Y be the mean of the other. Each of the members of the X-population is paired in some way with each of the members of the Y-population. We are interested in the differences $(X - Y)$. Parameter of interest: Population mean of differences μ_d.

Here, $\mu_d = \mu_X - \mu_Y$, but this case differs from that of the two-samples cases described earlier in that the two populations are not independent, so the responses or measurements of the subjects will not be independent either.

- Select a random sample of size n items (or n pairs of items).
- For each selected item, measure the characteristic of interest, resulting in a sample of pairs of measurements.
  Sample: (x_1, y_1), (x_2, y_2), (x_3, y_3),..., (x_n, y_n)

- Compute the differences $d_1 = x_i - y_i$, $i=1, 2,..., n$. Note that the two-sample case reduces to a one-sample case.
- Compute the mean difference and the standard deviation of the differences

$$\bar{d} = \frac{\sum d_i}{n} \text{ and } s_d = \sqrt{\frac{\sum (d_i - \bar{d})^2}{n-1}}$$

This sample mean $\bar{d}$ is a point estimate of the unknown population mean μ_d. Different random samples of size n from the same population will result in different sample means, giving different estimates. The distribution of means from all possible random samples of n differences is the sampling distribution of $\bar{d}$.

- The mean of all possible sample means is $\mu_{\bar{d}}$. Therefore $\bar{d}$ is an unbiased estimator of μ_d.

- The standard deviation of the sampling distribution of $\bar{d}$ is $\sigma_{\bar{d}} = \dfrac{\sigma_d}{\sqrt{n}}$, where σ_d is the standard deviation of the population of differences.

- If the population of differences is normally distributed and the population standard deviation σ_d is unknown, then the sampling distribution of $\bar{d}$ is a t-distribution with $(n-1)$ degrees of freedom.

Estimating μ_d using $(1-\alpha)100\%$ confidence interval:

Construct a t-interval with $df = (n-1)$ degrees of freedom

Margin of Error: $\quad t_{\alpha/2}(df)S_{\bar{d}} = t_{\alpha/2}(df)\dfrac{s_d}{\sqrt{n}}$

Confidence Interval: $\quad \bar{d} \pm t_{\alpha/2}(df)\dfrac{s_d}{\sqrt{n}}$

Making an inference about the difference in population means μ_d:
Use a t-test with $df = (n-1)$ degrees of freedom.

H_0: $\mu_d = \mu_0$ (Specified Difference)
H_a: $\mu_d > \mu_0$ or
$\quad \mu_d < \mu_0$ or
$\quad \mu_d \neq \mu_0$

$$t = \dfrac{\bar{d} - \mu_0}{s_d/\sqrt{n}}$$

Alternative hypothesis:	Rejection region approach:	p-value approach:
		Rejection Rule
H_a: $\mu_d > \mu_0$	Reject H_0 if	Reject H_0 if p-value $< \alpha$, where
H_a: $\mu_d < \mu_0$ or	$t > t_\alpha(df)$	p-value $= P(t(df) > t)$
H_a: $\mu_d \neq \mu_0$	$t < -t_\alpha(df)$	p-value $= P(t(df) < t)$
	$t > t_{\alpha/2}(df)$ or $t < -t_{\alpha/2}(df)$	p-value $=$
		$P(t(df) > |t|) + P(t(df) < -|t|)$

Conditions:

(a) A random sample of differences is taken from the population differences.

(b) The sampled population of differences is normally distributed.

Checking the normality condition:

Make a dotplot or stem-and-leaf plot for the sample of differences $(d_1, d_2, \ldots d_n)$. Ask yourself whether the distribution is fairly symmetric and bell-shaped, without any outliers. In other words, ask yourself whether the distribution of differences resembles the normal distribution. Alternatively, use a normal probability plot. The AP Exam may or may not tell you that the distribution of differences is normal.

Example 19: Workers at a factory asked their supervisor to provide music during their shift. The supervisor wanted to know whether the music really helped improve the workers' performance. Because all the workers were assigned to different rooms at random, the supervisor randomly selected one room. For one week, he provided music in this room, and for one week, he provided none. He flipped a coin to determine which week to provide music. Afterward, he recorded the productivity of the workers, using the average number of items assembled per day:

Worker	1	2	3	4	5	6	7	8	9	10
With Music	29.38	31.53	27.45	27.76	29.31	27.69	29.07	27.48	29.83	28.96
Without Music	24.55	25.59	23.17	24.71	25.26	24.88	24.34	26.13	25.57	26.63

(a) Estimate the difference between the workers' performance in the presence of music and their performance in the absence of music using a 95 percent level of confidence.
(b) Does music improve the performance of workers as measured by the mean number of items assembled per day? Give statistical evidence.

Solution:

(a) Estimation.

Step 1: Let X = the performance with music

Y = the performance without music

μ_x = the mean performance with music

μ_y = the mean performance without music

We are interested in $\mu_d = \mu_x - \mu_y$ = the mean difference in performance.

Step 2: Because the performances "with music" and "without music" are measured on the same group of workers, this is a dependent samples case. The specific person's effect on the performance will be nullified when we look at the differences.

Define difference $d = X - Y$. Compute the differences in the performance of each worker.

Worker	1	2	3	4	5	6	7	8	9	10
With Music	29.38	31.53	27.45	27.76	29.31	27.69	29.07	27.48	29.83	28.96
Without Music	24.55	25.59	23.17	24.71	25.26	24.88	24.34	26.13	25.57	26.63
Difference	4.83	5.94	4.28	3.05	4.05	2.81	4.73	1.35	4.26	2.33

Plot the differences. (See Figure 22) Please note that the differences were rounded to the nearest whole number.

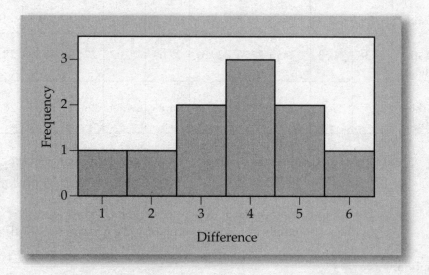

Figure 22: Histogram of the differences in performance

Conditions:

(1) It is given that a random sample of one room was taken. Because the workers are randomly assigned to different rooms, workers in the selected room where the sample was taken can be assumed to be a random sample of all workers at this factory.

(2) A histogram of the differences shows that there are no outliers and its shape suggests it is reasonable to assume that the differences in performance are approximately normally distributed.

Because the population standard deviation of the differences is unknown, we should construct a t-interval for the mean.

Step 3: Now the two-sample problem has been reduced to a one-sample problem. Compute the sample mean and standard deviation of the differences.

$$\bar{d} = 3.763 \text{ items per day, and } s_d = 1.362 \text{ items per day}$$

With a sample of size 10, degrees of freedom = $10 - 1 = 9$

To construct a 95 percent confidence interval, use $\alpha = 0.05$. Using a t-table for 9 degrees of freedom we get

$$t^* = t_{\alpha/2}(9) = t_{0.05/2}(9) = t_{0.025}(9) = 2.262$$

The 95 percent $ME = t_{0.025}(9)\left(\frac{s_d}{\sqrt{n}}\right) = 2.262\left(\frac{1.362}{\sqrt{10}}\right) = 0.974 \text{ items/day}$

$$\bar{d} \pm ME \Rightarrow 3.763 \pm 0.974 \Rightarrow (2.789, 4.737)$$

The 95 percent confidence interval to estimate μ_d is (2.79, 4.74).

Step 4: Interpretation:

We are 95 percent confident that the true mean difference in performance is between 2.79 and 4.74 items per day. We are 95 percent confident that our best estimate of the difference, 3.763 items per day, is worth 0.974 items of the true mean difference in performance.

Note that the confidence interval falls entirely above zero. Therefore, we can conclude that the mean difference in performance is significant and that the mean number of items produced per day with music is higher than the mean number produced without music.

```
TI-83 or TI-84:
Using data
   • Enter the data into two lists, "with music" in L₁, and "without
       music" in L₂
   • Move cursor to the column labeled L₃
   • Type L₁ – L₂
   • Press ENTER (all the differences should appear in list L₃)
   • Choose STAT → TESTS → 8: TInterval
   • Highlight Data
   • Press ENTER
   • Enter appropriate values
           TInterval
           Input: Data  Stats
           List: L₃
           Freq: 1
           C-Level: .95
           Calculate
   • Highlight Calculate
   • Press ENTER
```

(b) Inference.

Step 1: We are interested in testing a hypothesis about

μ_d = The true mean difference in performance of workers as measured by the number of items assembled per day = mean with music – mean without music.

H_0: $\mu_d = 0$ (There is no difference in the performance of workers with and without music.)

H_a: $\mu_d > 0$ (Music improves performance, i.e., the mean performance is better with music than without music.)

Step 2: A random sample of $n = 10$ workers was taken.

Because the performances "with music" and "without music" were measured on the same group of workers, this is a dependent-samples case. The specific person's effect on the performance will be nullified when we look at the differences.

Define difference $d = X - Y$. Compute the differences in the performance of each worker.

Worker	1	2	3	4	5	6	7	8	9	10
With Music	29.38	31.53	27.45	27.76	29.31	27.69	29.07	27.48	29.83	28.96
Without Music	24.55	25.59	23.17	24.71	25.26	24.88	24.34	26.13	25.57	26.63
Difference	4.83	5.94	4.28	3.05	4.05	2.81	4.73	1.35	4.26	2.33

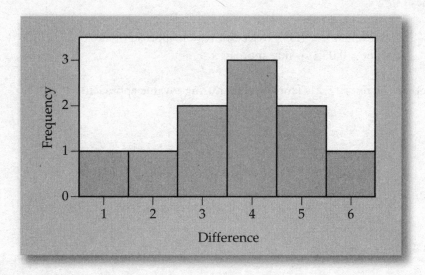

Figure 23: Histogram of difference in performance
(Note: Differences were rounded to the nearest whole number)

Conditions:

(1) It is given that a random sample of one room was taken. Because the workers are randomly assigned to different rooms, workers in the selected room can be assumed to be a random sample of all workers at this factory.

(2) A histogram of differences (see Figure 23) shows that there are no outliers, and its shape suggests it is reasonable to assume that the differences in performance are approximately normally distributed.

Because the population standard deviation of the differences is unknown, we should use a *t*-test for the mean.

Step 3: Now the two-sample problem has been reduced to a one-sample problem. Compute the sample mean and standard deviation of the differences.

$$\bar{d} = 3.763 \text{ items per day, and } s_d = 1.362$$

With a sample of size 10, degrees of freedom = $10 - 1 = 9$

Suppose we use $\alpha = 0.05$. Then, using the t-table for 9 degrees of freedom, we get

$$t^* = t_\alpha(9) = t_{0.05}(9) = 1.833$$

The rejection rule is to reject the null hypothesis and accept the alternative hypothesis if

- $t < -1.833$ or $t > 1.833$ (rejection region approach)
- p-value < 0.05 (p-value approach)

Compute the test statistic (and p-value if using p-value approach)

$$t = \frac{\left(\bar{d} - \mu_0\right)}{s_d \Big/ \sqrt{n}} = \frac{(3.763 - 0)}{1.362 \Big/ \sqrt{10}} = 8.737$$

$$p\text{-value} = P(t > 8.737) = \text{almost } 0$$

Step 4: Write conclusion.

- Using p-value approach:
  Because the p-value is almost 0, for any reasonable α we should reject the null hypothesis and accept the alternative hypothesis.
- Using the rejection region approach:
  Because $t = 8.737 > 1.833$ (or the test statistic falls in the rejection region), we should reject the null hypothesis and accept the alternative hypothesis.

Conclusion: At a 5 percent level of significance, there is sufficient evidence to conclude that the performance of workers has improved in the presence of music.

TI-83 or TI-84:

Using data

- Enter the data into two lists, "with music" in L_1, and "without music" in L_2
- Move cursor to the column labeled L_3
- Type $L_1 - L_2$
- Press **ENTER** (all the differences should appear in list L_3)
- Choose **STAT** → **TESTS** → **2: T-Test**
- Choose option **Data**
- Press **ENTER**
- Enter appropriate values
  T-Test
  Input: Data Stats
  μ_0: 0
  List: L_3
  Freq: 1
  μ: $\neq \mu_0$ $< \mu_0$ $> \mu_0$ (Choose option $> \mu_0$)
- Press **ENTER**
  Calculate Draw
- Choose option **Calculate**
- Press **ENTER**

MAKING AN INFERENCE USING CATEGORICAL DATA

A categorical variable is a variable that classifies the outcomes of an experiment into different categories. These categories can be numerical or nonnumerical. For example:

- A teacher classifies students according to the student status (freshman, sophomore, junior, and senior).
- A biologist classifies crossbred varieties of flowers according to the color of petals (white, red, or pink).
- A doctor classifies patients by sex (male, female).
- A factory classifies each item produced by its status (good, minor defect, major defect).
- A postal worker classifies letters by the state of the addressee (AL, … WA).
- To issue tax rebates in 2001, the Internal Revenue Service divided taxpayers according to the last two digits of their social security numbers (00, 01, … 99). This grouping was used to determine in which week each taxpayer would receive a check.

Suppose there are k different groups into which the measurements are categorized. These groups are typically referred to as cells. The **observed frequency** is the number of measurements from one experiment falling into that particular cell. The observed counts of cells, 1 through k, are denoted by $O_1, O_2,..., O_k$. If n observations are taken in one experiment, then

$$O_1 + O_2 + \cdots + O_k = n$$

Often, we devise a theory about the distribution of measurements into different categories, and we wish to check out our theory by conducting an experiment. The **expected frequency** is the number of measurements expected to fall into that cell according to our theory. The expected counts for cells 1 through k are denoted by $E_1, E_2,..., E_k$ and

$$E_1 + E_2 + \cdots + E_k = n$$

For example, a biologist might suspect that when two varieties of a flowering plant are crossbred, the result would be 20, 30, and 50 percent of the plants bearing white, red, and pink flowers, respectively. Then, to check her theory, the biologist might crossbreed and grow, say, 150 plants and classify each one by the resulting color of flowers that it produces. Suppose the experiment results in 28 plants bearing white flowers, 46 bearing red, and 76 bearing pink. In this case, 28, 46, and 76 are the observed counts. The theoretical proportions of 20, 30, and 50 percent lead to the expected counts in 150 plants as 30 bearing white flowers, 45 bearing red, and 75 bearing pink.

The question of interest here is whether the observed counts seem to agree with the expected counts, or how likely the observed counts would be if the truth were really described by the expected counts. The test statistic value that determines the extent of agreement between the observed and expected counts is computed as

$$\chi^2 = \sum_{\text{all cells}} \frac{(O_i - E_i)^2}{E_i}$$

The smaller the value of the test statistic, the higher the agreement between the expected and observed counts. Larger values of the test statistic indicate more discrepancy between the observed and expected counts. This test statistic follows an approximate χ^2 (chi-square) distribution.

The Chi-Square Distribution

Another commonly used sampling distribution, besides the t-distribution and the standard normal, is the χ^2 (or "chi-square") distribution. This distribution is commonly observed when we use inferential procedures for categorical data. It has the following properties:

- It is a continuous distribution.
- It is a distribution of the sums of squared normal random variables. So the chi-square variable takes only positive values.
- It is a right-skewed distribution.
- The shape of the chi-square distribution, like that of the t-distribution, depends on its degrees of freedom (df). Figure 24 shows how the shape of the distribution changes with the degrees of freedom.
- The mean of the chi-square distribution = df. Note, in Figure 24, that the center of the distribution shifts to the right as degrees of freedom increase.
- The standard deviation of the chi-square distribution = $\sqrt{2\,df}$.

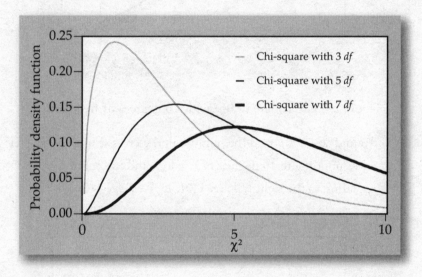

Figure 24: Chi-square distribution for different degrees of freedom

Reading a Chi-Square Table

χ_α^2: A chi-square value such that the area to the right under the distribution is equal to α.

- To find $\chi_{0.05}^2$ with 10 degrees of freedom from the table, go down to the row corresponding to 10 degrees of freedom and then go across to the column corresponding to the right-tail area 0.05. Read the number in the cross section of the row for 10 degrees of freedom and the column for right-tail area 0.05. It gives $\chi_{0.05}^2(10) = 18.3$.

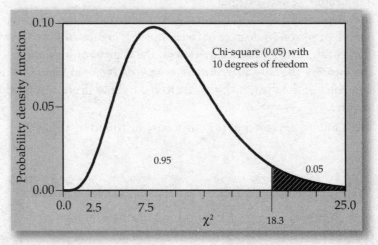

Figure 25: Chi-square (0.05) with 10 degrees of freedom

- To find $\chi_{0.01}^2(10)$, read the number in the cross section of the row corresponding to 10 degrees of freedom and the column corresponding to the right-tail area 0.01. It gives $\chi_{0.01}^2(10) = 23.21$.

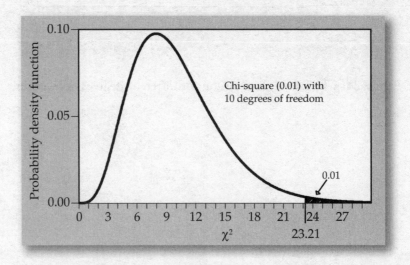

Figure 26: Chi-square (0.01) with 10 degrees of freedom

The Test of Goodness-of-Fit

This test is used to check whether the observed data counts confirm the expected distribution of counts into different categories. Read the problem carefully to determine the expected proportion for each category. For example, if there are five categories and the problem states that each category is equally likely, then the expected proportion for each is $\frac{1}{5}$ or 0.20.

- Suppose the population is divided into k different categories.
- Take a random sample of size n from the population of interest.
- Classify each selected item of the sample into one of the k categories.
- Count the number of items in each category. These are the observed counts, $O_1, O_2,..., O_k$.
- To get each expected count, multiply the sample size n by the proportion for that cell.

- Compute the test statistic $\chi^2 = \sum_{\text{all cells}} \frac{(O_i - E_i)^2}{E_i}$

- For a sufficiently large random sample, the distribution of the test statistic is approximately a chi-square with $df = (k - 1)$ degrees of freedom.

χ^2 **Test of Goodness-of-Fit:**

Use a chi-square test with $df = (k - 1)$ degrees of freedom.

H_0: The population is divided into k categories in the following proportions: $p_1, p_2,..., p_k$. ($p_1 + p_2 + ... + p_k = 1$ and $0 < p_i < 1$, for all $i = 1, 2,..., k$)

H_a: The population is divided into k categories in proportions that differ from $p_1, p_2,..., p_k$.

The rejection rule: Reject the null hypothesis if

- $TS > \chi^2 (df)$ (using the rejection region approach)
- p-value $< \alpha$, where p-value $= P(\chi^2(df) > TS)$ (using the p-value approach)

Conditions:

- (a) Data are counts, not percentages or averages.
- (b) A random sample of size n is taken.
- (c) The sample size n is large enough to get an approximate chi-square distribution for the test statistic.

Checking the condition of a large n:

If all expected counts are at least 5 ($E_i \geq 5$) then we have a large enough sample to use a chi-square approximation. If some cells have $E_i < 5$, then such cells should be combined with other adjoining cells in a logical manner to satisfy the requirement of expected counts, or, if no such combining is possible, exact tests may be used, but they are not a topic on the AP exam.

Example 20: An accounting firm in Mississippi has clients from various states. The chief accountant knew that last year the firm had the following distribution of clients from different states:

State of Residence	Mississippi	Alabama	Louisiana	Arkansas	Florida	Tennessee
Proportion of Clients	0.60	0.15	0.15	0.04	0.03	0.03

But the accountant thought that the distribution had changed this year. So he took a random sample of 400 clients and classified them according to their state of residence. The summarized data is as follows:

State of Residence	Mississippi	Alabama	Louisiana	Arkansas	Florida	Tennessee
Number of Clients	200	87	68	27	8	10

What does the data suggest? Is the distribution of clients the same as last year or has it changed?

Solution: The clients are classified by their state of residence, which is a categorical variable.

Step 1: We are interested in testing

H_0: The proportion of clients from Mississippi, Alabama, Louisiana, Arkansas, Florida, and Tennessee is the same this year as last year.

H_a: This year, at least two proportions have changed from those of last year.

Step 2: Use a chi-square test of goodness-of-fit. Compute the expected counts as $400p_i$, where p_i is the proportion of clients from the ith state. For example, last year, 60 percent of clients were from Mississippi. If the proportions this year are the same, then out of 400, 60 percent of clients—i.e., $400(0.60) = 240$ clients—should be from Mississippi.

State of Residence	Mississippi	Alabama	Louisiana	Arkansas	Florida	Tennessee
Observed Number of Clients (O_i)	200	87	68	27	8	10
Expected Number of Clients (E_i)	240	60	60	16	12	12

A random sample of clients was selected. All the expected counts are higher than five. Therefore, it is reasonable to use the chi-square test.

Step 3: The firm's clients are from six different states. So for $k = 6$, we get

$df = k - 1 = 5$ degrees of freedom. Suppose we use 0.05-level of significance.

The rejection rule is to "reject the null hypothesis if p-value < 0.05" (or, if using rejection region approach, "reject the null hypothesis if $TS > \chi^2_{0.05}(5) = 11.1$").

$$\chi^2 = \sum_{i=1}^{6} \frac{(O_i - E_i)^2}{E_i}$$

$$= \frac{(200-240)^2}{240} + \frac{(87-60)^2}{60} + \frac{(68-60)^2}{60} + \frac{(27-16)^2}{16} + \frac{(8-12)^2}{12} + \frac{(10-12)^2}{12}$$

$$= 6.67 + 12.15 + 1.07 + 7.56 + 1.33 + 0.33$$

$$= 29.11$$

The p-value = $P(\chi^2(5) > 29.11)$ = .000022, which is almost 0.

Step 4: Because p-value = 0.000022 < 0.05 (or $TS = 29.11 > 11.1$, if using the rejection region approach), we should reject the null hypothesis and accept the alternative hypothesis. The p-value indicates that if this year's proportion of clients had remained the same as last year's, then the probability of observing the test statistic value of 29.11 or higher is 0.000022. Therefore, we can conclude that the data suggests that the proportions have changed from those of last year.

TI-83 or TI-84:
- Clear lists L_1, L_2, and L_3
- Enter the observed counts in L_1
- Enter the expected counts in L_2
- Define list L_3 to be $(L_1 - L_2)^2/L_2$
  Bring the cursor to the list heading L_3
  Type $(L_1 - L_2)^2/L_2$
- Press **ENTER**
- Choose **2nd** $\rightarrow$ **LIST** $\rightarrow$ **MATH 5: sum(**
- Press **ENTER**
- Type (L_3) to give
  $\text{sum}(L_3)$
- Press **ENTER**

To compute the *p*-value:

Use the chi-square *CDF* from the distribution menu to compute the area between the *TS* value (given by the sum command as described above) and infinity (simulated using some large number).
- Choose **2nd** $\rightarrow$ **DISTR** $\rightarrow$ **7: χ^2 cdf**
- Press **ENTER**
- Type 29.11, 1E50, 5) to give
  χ^2 cdf(29.11, 1E50, 5)
  (Enter *TS*, simulated ∞, and *df* separated by commas)
- Press **ENTER**

Example 21: A nursery ships plants by truck in trays of 12 plants each. At the end of one such journey, 100 randomly selected trays were inspected and the number of plants in each tray that did not survive the journey was counted. The data was recorded as follows:

Number of Plants That Did Not Survive the Journey	0	1	2	3	4
Number of Trays	31	44	15	8	2

Is the binomial distribution an appropriate model to determine the chance of a single plant surviving?

Solution: There are 12 plants per tray, i.e., $n = 12$ trials. There is a total of $12 \times 100 = 1{,}200$ plants. Associated with each plant are two possible outcomes, namely, "surviving the journey" and "not surviving the journey." If we define success as "not surviving the journey," then the probability of success associated with each plant is estimated as follows:

Out of 1,200 plants inspected, $(31(0) + 44(1) + 15(2) + 8(3) + 4(2)) = 106$ did not survive the journey. So the estimated probability of not surviving the journey = $\hat{p} = 106/1{,}200 = 0.088$.

Step 1: Here we are interested in testing the following hypotheses:

H_0: A binomial distribution with $n = 12$ and $p = 0.088$ is not an appropriate model to describe this data.

H_a: A binomial distribution with $n = 12$ and $p = 0.088$ is an appropriate model to describe this data.

Step 2: We can use the chi-square goodness-of-fit test to check the appropriateness of the binomial distribution to describe the data above. Assuming that the null hypothesis is true (i.e., assuming that the data comes from a binomial population with $n = 12$, and $p = 0.088$), compute the likelihood of 0, 1, 2, 3, etc., plants not surviving the journey. For example:

$$P(X = 2 \text{ did not survive the journey}) = \binom{12}{2}0.088^2(1 - 0.088)^{10} = 0.2034$$

Number of Plants That Did Not Survive the Journey (x)	0	1	2	3	4	5 or more
$P(X = x)$	0.3311	0.3834	0.2034	0.0654	0.0142	0.0025

$$P(X \geq 5) = 1 - [P(X = 0) + P(X = 1) + \cdots + P(X = 4)]$$

Using these probabilities, compute the expected number of trays with the number of plants not surviving the journey equal to 0, 1, 2, etc., as $100 \times P(x)$. This gives the expected counts as follows:

Number of Plants That Did Not Survive the Journey (x)	0	1	2	3	4	5 or more
$P(X = x)$	0.3311	0.3834	0.2034	0.0654	0.0142	0.0025
Expected Counts	33.11	38.34	20.34	6.54	1.42	0.25

Because the expected counts for the last two categories are less than five, the chi-square test cannot be applied successfully. So let us combine the last three cells (this combination makes sense—three or more is a reasonable category) to give the expected counts as follows:

Number of Plants That Did Not Survive the Journey (x)	0	1	2	3 or more
Observed Counts (O_i)	31	44	15	10
Expected Counts (E_i)	33.11	38.34	20.34	8.21

All the expected counts are larger than five, and all trays were selected at random. So, the conditions for the chi-square test are satisfied.

Step 3: With four categories in the table, degrees of freedom = df = 3. If we are willing to take a 5 percent risk of rejecting the true null hypothesis, then the rejection rule is "reject the null hypothesis if p-value < 0.05" (or if using the rejection region approach, "reject the null hypothesis if the $TS > \chi^2_{0.05}(3) = 7.81$").

Compute the test statistic value (and p-value if using a p-value approach).

$$\chi^2 = \sum_{i=1}^{4} \frac{(O_i - E_i)^2}{E_i}$$

$$= \frac{(31-33.11)^2}{33.11} + \frac{(44-38.34)^2}{38.34} + \frac{(15-20.34)^2}{20.34} + \frac{(10-8.21)^2}{8.21}$$

$$= 2.76$$

The p-value = $P(\chi^2(3) > 2.76) = 0.4301$

Step 4: Because p-value $= 0.4301 > 0.05$ (or since $TS = 2.76 < \chi^2_{0.05}(3) = 7.81$), we fail to reject the null hypothesis. So, we can conclude that there is insufficient evidence against the null hypothesis. In other words, it is reasonable to assume that the data follows a binomial model with $n = 12$ and $p = 0.088$.

Contingency Tables

In many experiments, data is classified by two different criteria, each criterion with two or more categories. Such a classification of data results in a table with two or more rows and two or more columns, where rows represent categories of one factor and columns represent categories of the other factor. For example, students might be classified by sex and academic major, athletes by athletic specialty (track, football, gymnastics, etc.) and the type of injury sustained, or patients classified by sex and race.

An $r \times c$ contingency table is an arrangement of data into a table with r rows and c columns, creating a total of rc cells.

Test of Independence

Often, scientists are interested in determining whether two different categorical variables are independent or dependent. For example, television stations might want to know whether the type of program a viewer watches is associated with his or her sex, sociologists might want to know whether children's behavior patterns are associated with the marital status of parents, and marine biologists might want to know whether the behavior patterns of dolphins are associated with the time of year.

- Identify two factors of interest and their categories.
- Take a random sample of n items from the population of interest.
- Determine the category of each of two factors to which each item in the sample belongs.
- Summarize the observed data into an $r \times c$ contingency table, where
  r = the number of rows = the number of categories of interest for factor 1
  c = the number of columns = the number of categories of interest for factor 2

- Count the number of items in each cell. These are the observed counts O_{ij} ($i = 1, 2,..., r$, and $j = 1, 2,..., c$).

		Columns				Row Total R_i
		1	2	...	c	
Rows	1	O_{11}	O_{12}	...	O_{1c}	R_1
	2	O_{21}	O_{22}	...	O_{2c}	R_2
	.	.	.	.	.	.
	.	.	.	.	.	.
	.	.	.	.	.	.
	r	O_{r1}	O_{r2}	...	O_{rc}	R_r
Column Totals C_j		C_1	C_2	...	C_c	n

Table 4: $r \times c$ **contingency table of observed counts**

- Compute the row totals and the column totals. Note that the sum of the row totals and the sum of the column totals is n. This is a good way to check your math.
- If the two factors of interest are independent, then

P(A randomly selected item belongs to the $(i, j)^{th}$ cell)

$= P$(It belongs to the ith category of factor 1) $\times P$ (It belongs to the jth category of factor 2)

Therefore, out of n observations, the $(i, j)^{th}$ cell is expected to contain

$$E_{ij} = \frac{R_i C_j}{n} \quad \text{observations.}$$

In other words, find the expected value for each cell using $\dfrac{\text{(row total)(column total)}}{\text{grand total}}$.

Compute the expected counts for all cells and place them in parentheses next to the observed counts.

		Columns				Row Total R_i
		1	2	...	c	
Rows	1	$O_{11}(E_{11})$	$O_{12}(E_{12})$	...	$O_{1c}(E_{1c})$	R_1
	2	$O_{21}(E_{21})$	$O_{22}(E_{22})$	...	$O_{2c}(E_{2c})$	R_2
	.	.	.		.	.
	.	.	.		.	.
	.	.	.		.	.
	r	$O_{r1}(E_{r1})$	$O_{r2}(E_{r2})$	...	$O_{rc}(E_{rc})$	R_r
Column Totals C_j		C_1	C_2	...	C_c	n

Table 5: $r \times c$ contingency table of observed and (expected) counts

- Compute the test statistic value as

$$\chi^2 = \sum_{j=1}^{c}\sum_{i=1}^{r}\frac{\left(O_{ij} - E_{ij}\right)^2}{E_{ij}}$$

- For a sufficiently large n, the test statistic follows a chi-square distribution with $df = (r - 1)(c - 1)$ degrees of freedom.

χ^2 **Test of Independence:**

Use a chi-square test with $df = (r-1)(c-1)$ degrees of freedom.

H_0: The two factors of interest are independent. Or, there is no association between two factors of interest. (This should always be the null hypothesis.)

H_a: Two factors of interest are not independent. Or, there is an association between two factors of interest.

$$\chi^2 = \sum_{j=1}^{c} \sum_{i=1}^{r} \frac{\left(O_{ij} - E_{ij}\right)^2}{E_{ij}}$$

$$\text{where } E_{ij} = \frac{R_i C_j}{n}$$

The rejection rule: Reject the null hypothesis if

- $\chi^2 > \chi^2(df)$ (using the rejection region approach)
- p-value $< \alpha$, where p-value $= P(\chi^2(df) > TS)$ (using the p-value approach)

Conditions:

(a) Data are counts, not percentages or averages.
(b) A random sample of size n is taken.
(c) The sample size n is large enough to get an approximate chi-square distribution for the test statistic.

Checking the assumption of a large n:

If all expected counts are at least five, then we have a large enough sample to use the chi-square approximation. If some cells have $E_i < 5$, then the corresponding rows and/or columns should be combined with other rows and/or columns in a logical manner to satisfy the requirement of expected counts.

Example 22: The State Department of Education wanted to see whether there is any connection between the education level of fathers and sons. A random sample of 1,000 father-son pairs was selected from the available census data for the state of Alabama, and the level of education for both father and son was recorded as "less than high school (< HS)," "high school (HS)," or "more than high school (> HS)." The resulting data is summarized in the following table:

		Father's Education Level		
		<HS	HS	>HS
Son's Education Level	<HS	120	80	25
	HS	210	170	60
	>HS	110	140	85

Does this data provide significant evidence of an association between a father's education level and his son's education level?

Solution:

Step 1:

H_0: There is no association between a father's education level and his son's education level.

H_a: There is an association between a father's education level and his son's education level.

Or

H_0: A father's education level and his son's education level are independent.

H_a: A father's education level and his son's education level are not independent.

Step 2: Use a chi-square test for independence. Compute all row totals and column totals. Then compute the expected cell counts as

$$\text{Expected count for a cell} = \frac{(\text{Row total})(\text{Column total})}{\text{Grand total}}$$

Below is a table of observed and expected counts, with the expected counts in parentheses.

		Father's Education Level			
		<HS	HS	>HS	Total
Son's Education Level	<HS	120 (99.0)	80 (87.8)	25 (38.3)	225
	HS	210 (193.6)	170 (171.6)	60 (74.8)	440
	>HS	110 (147.4)	140 (130.7)	85 (57.0)	335
	Total	440	390	170	1000

All expected counts are greater than or equal to five, and the sample was chosen randomly. So the chi-square test of independence is appropriate.

Step 3: This is a 3×3 contingency table. So the degrees of freedom = $(3 - 1)(3 - 1)$ = 4. Suppose we use $\alpha = 0.05$. The rejection rule is "reject null if p-value $< \alpha$" (or if using the rejection region approach, "reject null if $TS > \chi^2_{0.05}(4) = 9.49$").

Compute the test statistic (and p-value if using the p-value approach).

$$TS = \sum_{i=1}^{3} \sum_{j=1}^{3} \frac{\left(O_{ij} - E_{ij}\right)^2}{E_{ij}}$$

$$= \frac{(120 - 99)^2}{99} + \frac{(80 - 87.8)^2}{87.8} + \cdots + \frac{(85 - 57)^2}{57}$$

$$= 38.03576$$

p-value = $P(\chi^2 > 38.03576) = 0.00000011 \approx 0$

Step 4: Because the p-value is too small for any reasonable level of significance (or since $TS = 38.036 > 9.49$, if using the rejection region approach), we should reject the null hypothesis and accept the alternative hypothesis. There is significant evidence to conclude that there is an association between a father's education level and his son's education level.

TI-83 or TI-84:

- Choose **MATRX** → **EDIT**
- Select 1: [A]
- Press **ENTER**
- $3 \triangleright \triangleright 3$
- Press **ENTER**
- Enter observed counts in a 3×3 matrix
- Choose **STAT** → **TESTS** → **C: χ^2 - Test**
- Press **ENTER**

    χ^2 - Test

    Observed: [A]

    Expected: [B]

    Calculate   Draw

- Choose option **Calculate**
- Press **ENTER**

To get the expected counts:

- Choose **MATRX** → **EDIT**
- Select 2: [B]
- Press **ENTER**

Test for Homogeneity of Proportions

To compare two or more populations, we use the chi-square test for homogeneity of proportions, which is an extension of the large-samples z-test for the difference of two independent proportions $(p_1 - p_2)$. In the chi-square test, independent samples are taken from two or more populations of interest. When comparing only two population proportions, the two-tailed z-test gives the same results as the chi-square test. The procedure for the test of homogeneity of proportions is similar to the procedure for the test of independence, except for one criterion. In the test of homogeneity, because the samples are taken from different populations of interest, row or column totals are fixed in the resulting contingency table.

- Identify k populations of interest, for which we are interested in comparing the proportions $p_1, p_2,..., p_k$, where p_i is the proportion for ith population of interest $0 < p_i < 1$ $(i = 1, 2,..., k)$.
- We want to make an inference about the equality of $p_1, p_2,..., p_k$.
- Take a random sample from each population of interest. Take the samples independently. Let the sample sizes be equal to $n_1, n_2,...,n_k$ respectively, from k populations. The total number of observations is $n = n_1 + n_2 + \cdots + n_k$.

- Count the number of items in favor of and against the criterion of interest from each sample. These are the observed counts.
- Summarize the observed data into a $k \times 2$ contingency table, where in each row, the number in the first column indicates the number in favor and the number in the second column indicates the number against the criterion of interest in that sample.
- The row totals are equal to the sample sizes, i.e.,

$$R_i = n_i \; (i = 1, 2,..., k)$$

- Compute the column totals

$$C_j = \sum_{i=1}^{k} O_{ji} \, , j = 1, 2$$

Note that

$$\sum_{i=1}^{k} R_i = \sum_{j=1}^{2} C_j = n$$

- If all k population proportions are equal, then the expected count in each cell of the table (in favor of and against the criterion in each sample) can be computed as

$$E_{ij} = \frac{R_i C_j}{n}$$

So compute the expected counts for all cells.

- Compute the test statistic value as

$$\chi^2 = \sum_{j=1}^{2} \sum_{i=1}^{k} \frac{\left(O_{ij} - E_{ij}\right)^2}{E_{ij}} \;\; (i = 1, 2,..., k \text{ and } j = 1, 2)$$

- For a sufficiently large n, the test statistic follows a chi-square distribution with $df = (k - 1)$ degrees of freedom.

χ^2 Test for homogeneity of proportions:

Use a chi-square test with $df = (k - 1)$ degrees of freedom.

H_0: $p_1 = p_2 = \ldots = p_k$, i.e., all population proportions are equal (this should always be the null hypothesis).

H_a: At least two population proportions are different.

$$\chi^2 = \sum_{j=1}^{2} \sum_{i=1}^{k} \frac{\left(O_{ij} - E_{ij}\right)^2}{E_{ij}}$$

$$\text{where } E_{ij} = \frac{R_i C_j}{n}$$

The rejection rule: Reject the null hypothesis if

- $TS > \chi^2 \,(df)$ (using the rejection region approach)
- p-value $< \alpha$, where p-value $= P(\chi^2(df) > TS)$ (using the p-value approach)

Assumptions:

(a) Each sample is selected at random from the population.
(b) All samples are taken independently of each other.
(c) The sample size n is large enough to get an approximate chi-square distribution for the test statistic.

Checking the assumption of a large n:

If all expected counts are at least five, then we have a large enough sample to use the chi-square approximation.

Example 23: On the campus of a large boarding school, students are housed in Alpha, Beta, Gamma, and Delta dormitories according to their grade levels (9, 10, 11, and 12, respectively). The school officials had heard several complaints about the food services for the dormitories but felt that the complaints differed across the four dormitories. To get student input, a random sample of students was selected from each dormitory (100 students each from Alpha and Beta dormitories, and 75 students each from Gamma and Delta dormitories). Each selected student was asked, "Are the current food services in your dormitory satisfactory?" The answers were recorded as "satisfactory" or "not satisfactory." The results were summarized as follows:

	Satisfactory	Sample Size
Alpha	78	100
Beta	72	100
Gamma	49	75
Delta	44	75

Is there significant evidence to indicate whether the proportion of students satisfied with the current food services differs in different dormitories?

Solution: Here we are interested in comparing four proportions:

p_1 = The proportion of students from Alpha dormitory satisfied with the food services.

p_2 = The proportion of students from Beta dormitory satisfied with the food services.

p_3 = The proportion of students from Gamma dormitory satisfied with the food services.

p_4 = The proportion of students from Delta dormitory satisfied with the food services.

Step 1: Define the null and alternative hypotheses as follows:

H_0: $p_1 = p_2 = p_3 = p_4$, i.e., the proportion of students satisfied with the food services is the same across all four dormitories.

H_a: At least two dormitories differ in the proportion of students satisfied with the food services.

Step 2: Use a chi-square test of homogeneity of proportions.

Complete the table of observed counts (add a "Not Satisfactory" column) and then compute the column totals.

	Satisfactory	Not Satisfactory	Row Totals $(R_i = n_i)$
Alpha	78	22	100
Beta	72	28	100
Gamma	49	26	75
Delta	44	31	75
Column Total (C_j)	243	107	$n = 350$

Compute the expected counts as

$$E_{ij} = \frac{R_i C_j}{n}$$

For example:

The expected number of students satisfied with the food services from

the Alpha dormitory $= \frac{(100)(243)}{350} = 69.43$

The following table shows the observed and expected counts, with the expected counts in parentheses:

	Satisfactory	Not Satisfactory
Alpha	78 (69.429)	22 (30.571)
Beta	72 (69.429)	28 (30.571)
Gamma	49 (52.071)	26 (22.929)
Delta	44 (52.071)	31 (22.929)

All the students were selected at random. All four samples were taken independently of each other. All the cell counts are larger than five. Therefore, the conditions for the chi-square test of homogeneity are satisfied.

Step 3: Suppose we are using a 5 percent level of significance. With $k = 4$ population proportions to compare, the degrees of freedom = $df = 3$. The rejection rule is "reject the null hypothesis if p-value < 0.05" (or if using the rejection region approach, "reject the null hypothesis if $TS > \chi^2_{0.05}(3) = 7.81$").

Compute the test statistic (and the p-value if using the p-value approach).

$$\chi^2 = \sum_{j=1}^{c} \sum_{i=1}^{r} \frac{\left(O_{ij} - E_{ij}\right)^2}{E_{ij}}$$

$$= \frac{(78 - 69.429)^2}{69.429} + \frac{(22 - 30.571)^2}{30.571} + \cdots + \frac{(31 - 22.929)^2}{22.929}$$

$$= 8.45$$

$$p\text{-value} = P(\chi^2 > 8.45) = 0.037$$

Step 4: Because p-value = 0.037 < 0.05 (or if using the rejection region approach, because $\chi^2 = 8.45 > 7.81$), we should reject the null hypothesis and conclude that at least two dormitories differ in terms of the proportion of students satisfied with the current food services.

Inference for the Slope of a Least-Squares Line

It's common practice to estimate the relation between correlated variables and use the estimated relation to predict a response for a given value of an independent variable. Some examples of such estimates are:

- Car manufacturers estimating the mean miles per gallon given by a model of a car from the weight of the car
- Real estate agents estimating the price of a house using the age and/or the location of the house
- Colleges estimating the grade point average of prospective students at graduation using their scores on college entrance examinations
- Crime labs using the dimensions of bones to estimate the age of a victim

A linear relation between two variables X (the **independent** or **explanatory** variable) and Y (the **dependent** or **response** variable) is a relation described by a line. Suppose the true linear relation between X and Y is given by

$$Y = \beta_0 + \beta_1 X + \varepsilon, \text{ where}$$

$$\beta_0 = Y\text{-intercept of the line}$$

$$\beta_1 = \text{slope of the line}$$

$$\varepsilon = \text{random error}$$

Here, β_0 and β_1 are population parameters.

Using the **least-squares regression technique**, the slope and the Y-intercept, respectively, can be estimated from n pairs of measurements as

$$b_1 = r\frac{s_y}{s_x} \text{ and } b_0 = \overline{y} - b_1\overline{x}$$

The sample statistics b_0 and b_1 estimate β_0 and β_1.

The **error (residual)** is the difference between the observed response and the response predicted by the estimated regression line, i.e., $e = (y - \hat{y})$, where $\hat{y} = b_0 + b_1x$. The standard deviation of all the error terms in the sample is denoted by s_e.

- Note that this quantity, the standard deviation of the residuals, is often designated in computer output of linear regression problems.

Then the question that arises is: Is there a significant relationship between Y and X? In other words: Does Y depend significantly on X? Or: Does X provide a significant amount of prediction of Y?

If the slope of the line of true relation is zero—i.e., if the relation between Y and X is a horizontal line—then there is no relation between Y and X. A line of slope zero gives the same value for Y regardless of the value of X. In other words, the value of Y does not depend on the value of X. The scatterplot of such population data will show a cloud of measurements with no specific direction; however, in a sample, this may not be true. Even for a population with $\beta_1 = 0$, the slope estimated from the sample (and not computed from the whole population) will not necessarily be equal to zero because of the sampling variation involved. If the estimated slope is non-zero, then the following questions arise:

- Is $b_1 \neq 0$ because the slope of true relation is non-zero, i.e., $\beta_1 \neq 0$?
  OR
- Is $b_1 \neq 0$ just because of sampling variation, when in fact $\beta_1 = 0$?

How much variation among b_1 values can be explained away as a chance variation? That can be determined using the sampling distribution of b_1. To check the likelihood of b_1 from a population with a specified β_1 (of zero or non-zero value), use the **t-test for slope**.

- Take a random sample of n pairs of observations from the population of interest, or take a random sample of n objects from the population, and make a pair of measurements on each selected object.

$$(x_1, y_1), (x_2, y_2),...,(x_n, y_n)$$

- Assume that random variables X and Y are linearly related. Make a scatterplot of the n pairs of observations. A quick review of the scatterplot will indicate whether an assumption of linear relation between X and Y is reasonable.
- If the assumption of linear relation is reasonable, then estimate the slope of the line of best fit (also known as "the least-squares regression line").

$$b_1 = \frac{n\sum xy - \left(\sum x\right)\left(\sum y\right)}{n\sum x^2 - \left(\sum x\right)^2}$$

- Different random samples of size n will result in different estimates for b_1. If for any fixed value of X, the responses are normally distributed with the same standard deviation σ, then the sampling distribution of b_1 is also a normal distribution with a mean of β_1 and a standard deviation given by σ_{β_1}:

Because the standard deviation of errors σ_ε is unknown, estimate it using S_{b_1}. Then the ratio b/S_{b_1} follows a t-distribution with $df = (n-2)$ degrees of freedom.

Estimating β_1 using $(1-\alpha)100\%$ confidence interval:

Construct a t-interval with $df = (n-2)$ degrees of freedom.

Margin of Error: $t^* s_{b_1}$

Confidence Interval: $b_1 \pm t^* s_{b_1}$

Making an inference about the slope (β_1) of a regression line:
Use a t-test with $df = (n-2)$ degrees of freedom.

H_0: $\beta_1 = 0$ (or other specified slope)		
H_a: $\beta_1 > 0$ or $\quad\quad \beta_1 < 0$ or $\quad\quad \beta_1 \neq 0$	$t = \dfrac{b_1 - \beta_1}{s_{b_1}}$	

	Rejection Rule	
Alternative hypothesis:	Rejection region approach:	p-value approach:
H_a: $\beta_1 > 0$ (or other specified slope) H_a: $\beta_1 < 0$ H_a: $\beta_1 \neq 0$	Reject H_0 if $t > t_\alpha(df)$ $t < -t_\alpha(df)$ $t > t_{\alpha/2}(df)$ or $t < -t_{\alpha/2}(df)$	Reject H_0 if p-value $< \alpha$, where p-value $= P(t(df) > t)$ p-value $= P(t(df) < t)$ p-value $=$ $P(t(df) > |t|) + P(t(df) < -|t|)$

Conditions:

  (a) A random sample of n pairs is obtained.
  (b) The residuals (errors) are normally distributed.
  (c) The mean error is 0.
  (d) The standard deviation of errors, σ_ε, is the same for all values of X.
  (e) The residuals are independent.

Checking the conditions:

  (a) From the description of the experiment, determine if it is reasonable to assume that the sample was randomly selected from the population of interest.
  (b) Make a boxplot or stem-and-leaf plot of the residuals. If the distribution is fairly symmetric and bell shaped, then it is reasonable to assume that the errors are normally distributed. Alternatively, use a normal probability plot to make the decision.
  (c) Plot the errors to get a residual plot. If all the errors are evenly scattered around 0, then it is reasonable to assume that the mean is 0.
  (d) If the residual plot shows a somewhat similar spread of errors across all values of X, then it is reasonable to assume a constant standard deviation.
  (e) If the residual plot shows no specific trends or patterns, it is reasonable to assume that the errors are independent.

Example 24: Some of the members of the faculty of the College of Education believe that reading performance is related to the point size of the letters in the document read. A group of randomly selected students were given a test. They were asked to read certain passages in different point sizes on a computer. The letter sizes were randomized. The average time (in minutes) required for the subjects to read the passages was determined. The data is given in the following table:

Letter Size (in Points)	7	8	9	10	11	12	13	14
Average Reading Time (in Minutes)	7.10	7.14	6.50	6.78	6.44	6.94	6.30	6.46

The regression analysis performed on the data by a computer gave the following results:

Predictor	Coef	StDev	T	P
Constant	7.6700	0.4225	18.15	0.000
Letter size	−0.09167	0.03931	−2.33	0.058

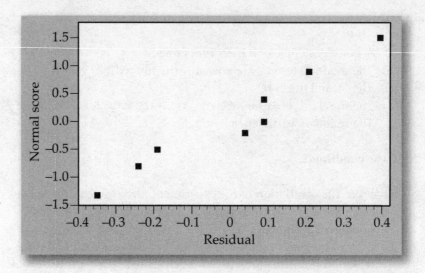

Figure 27: Normal probability plot for residuals

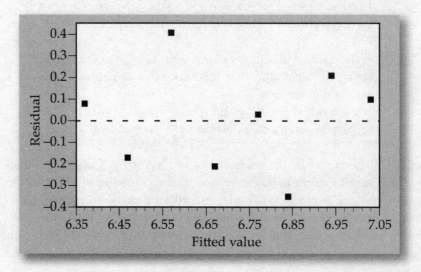

Figure 28: Residual plot

Is there a significant relation between the letter point size and the reading performance as measured by average reading time?

Solution:

Step 1: The faculty are interested in determining whether average reading time depends on the point size of the letter. So test

H_0: There is no relation between average reading time and letter size, or $\beta_1 = 0$.

H_a: There is a relation between average reading time and letter size, or $\beta_1 \neq 0$.

Step 2: Use the t-test for slope (or a t-test for correlation coefficient).

(a) A random sample of students was used.

(b) The normal probability plot in Figure 27 shows a fairly linear pattern. So it is reasonable to assume that the distribution of residuals is normal.

(c) The residual plot in Figure 28 shows that the residuals are scattered around 0. It is reasonable to assume that the mean is 0.

(d) The residual plot shows a somewhat similar spread of errors across all values of X. It is reasonable to assume a constant standard deviation.

(e) The residual plot shows no specific trends or patterns. It is reasonable to assume that the errors are independent.

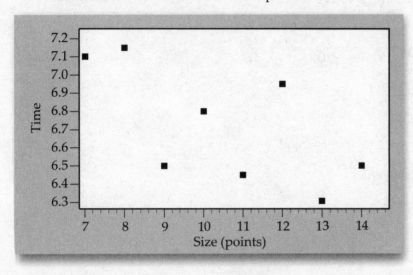

Figure 29: Scatterplot of reading time versus letter size

This scatterplot shown in Figure 29 indicates a slightly downward trend. It is reasonable to assume that a linear relation exists between the reading time and the letter point size.

Step 3: With $n = 8$ pairs of measurements, degrees of freedom $= n - 2 = 6$. Suppose we use $\alpha = 0.10$, then

$$t^* = t_{\alpha/2}\left(df\right) = t_{0.10/2}\left(6\right) = t_{0.05}(6) = 1.943$$

The rejection rule is to "reject null if p-value < 0.10" (or "reject null if $t > 1.943$ or $t < -1.943$," if using the rejection region approach).

From the results of the regression analysis provided we get

$$b_1 = -0.092, \ t = \frac{b_1}{S_{b_1}} = \frac{-0.092}{0.03931} = -2.33 \text{ and } p\text{-value} = 0.058$$

Step 4: Because the p-value $= 0.058 < 0.10$ (or, if using the rejection region approach, $t = -2.33$, which falls in the rejection region), reject the null hypothesis and accept the alternative hypothesis. At a 10 percent error rate, we can conclude that there is a linear relation between letter size and reading performance.

REVIEW OF FORMULAS ON THE EXAM:

I. Descriptive Statistics

$$\bar{x} = \frac{\sum x_i}{n}$$

$$s_x = \sqrt{\frac{1}{n-1}\sum(x_i - \bar{x})^2}$$

$$s_p = \sqrt{\frac{(n_1 - 1)s_1^2 + (n_2 - 1)s_2^2}{(n_1 - 1) + (n_2 - 1)}}$$

$$\hat{y} = b_0 + b_1 x$$

$$b_1 = \frac{\sum(x_i - \bar{x})(y_i - \bar{y})}{\sum(x_i - \bar{x})^2}$$

$$b_0 = \bar{y} - b_1 \bar{x}$$

$$r = \frac{1}{n-1}\sum\left(\frac{x_i - \bar{x}}{s_x}\right)\left(\frac{y_i - \bar{y}}{s_y}\right)$$

$$b_1 = r\frac{s_y}{s_x}$$

$$s_{b_1} = \frac{\sqrt{\dfrac{\sum(y_i - \hat{y}_i)^2}{n-2}}}{\sqrt{\sum(x_i - \bar{x})^2}}$$

II. Probability

$$P(A \cup B) = P(A) + P(B) - P(A \cap B)$$

$$P(A|B) = \frac{P(A \cap B)}{P(B)}$$

$$E(X) = \mu_x = \sum x_i p_i$$

$$Var(X) = \sigma_x^2 = \sum (x_i - \mu_x)^2 p_i$$

If X has a binomial distribution with parameters n and p, then:

$$P(X = k) = \binom{n}{k} p^k (1 - p)^{n-k}$$

$$\mu_x = np$$

$$\sigma_x = \sqrt{np(1 - p)}$$

$$\mu_{\hat{p}} = p$$

$$\sigma_{\hat{p}} = \sqrt{\frac{p(1 - p)}{n}}$$

If $\bar{x}$ is the mean of a random sample of size n from an infinite population with mean μ and standard deviation σ, then:

$$\mu_{\bar{x}} = \mu$$

$$\sigma_{\bar{x}} = \frac{\sigma}{\sqrt{n}}$$

III. Inferential Statistics

Standardized test statistic: $\dfrac{\text{statistic} - \text{parameter}}{\text{standard deviation of statistic}}$

Confidence interval: statistic $\pm$ (critical value) $\cdot$ (standard deviation of statistic)

Single-Sample

Statistic	Standard Deviation of Statistic
Sample Mean	$\dfrac{\sigma}{\sqrt{n}}$
Sample Proportion	$\sqrt{\dfrac{p(1-p)}{n}}$

Two-Sample

Statistic	Standard Deviation of Statistic
Difference of sample means	$\sqrt{\dfrac{\sigma_1^2}{n_1} + \dfrac{\sigma_2^2}{n_2}}$ Special case when $\sigma_1 = \sigma_2$ $\sigma\sqrt{\dfrac{1}{n_1} + \dfrac{1}{n_2}}$
Difference of sample proportions	$\sqrt{\dfrac{p_1(1-p_1)}{n_1} + \dfrac{p_2(1-p_2)}{n_2}}$ Special case when $p_1 = p_2$ $\sqrt{p(1-p)}\ \sqrt{\dfrac{1}{n_1} + \dfrac{1}{n_2}}$

Chi-square test statistic $= \sum \dfrac{(\text{observed} - \text{expected})^2}{\text{expected}}$

It's a nice day! Take a walk! Stop and smell the flowers!

CHAPTER 7 REVIEW QUESTIONS

Multiple-Choice Questions

Answers can be found at the end of this section.

1. A researcher wants to determine if a new cat food leads to an increased mean weight in cats. Which of the following are the correct null and alternative hypotheses?

    (A) $H_0: \mu_1 < \mu_2$; $H_a: \mu_1 = \mu_2$
    (B) $H_0: \mu_1 = \mu_2$; $H_a: \mu_1 < \mu_2$
    (C) $H_0: \mu_1 > \mu_2$; $H_a: \mu_1 = \mu_2$
    (D) $H_0: \mu_1 = \mu_2$; $H_a: \mu_1 > \mu_2$
    (E) $H_0: \mu_1 \leq \mu_2$; $H_a: \mu_1 = \mu_2$

    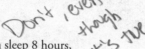 *Don't even though it's true*

2. Given the null hypothesis that all children sleep 8 hours, which of the following is a Type I error?

    (A) Claiming all children do not sleep 8 hours, when, in fact, they do.
    (B) Failing to reject the claim that all children sleep 8 hours when that statement is not true.
    (C) Claiming all children sleep 8 hours when it is true.
    (D) Claiming all children do not sleep 8 hours when it is true.
    (E) Claiming all children sleep 8 hours.

3. A grocer would like to determine the proportion of milk cartons that have expired within 0.05 of the true proportion with a 95% confidence interval. What is the minimum required sample size?

    (A) 300
    (B) 383
    (C) 384
    (D) 385
    (E) 400

    $0.05 = z_{\frac{1}{2}} + 95\% \sqrt{\dfrac{\frac{1}{2} \cdot \frac{1}{2}}{n}}$ $\left(\dfrac{ME}{95^0}\right)^2$

4. Which of the following is FALSE about the power of a test?

    (A) It increases as the sample size increases. T
    (B) It increases as the Type I error rate increases.
    (C) It is directly calculated from the error of rejecting the null hypothesis when the hypothesis is true.
    (D) It increases as the effect size increases. T
    (E) It increases as β decreases. T

5. A 90 percent confidence interval is computed from data to estimate the mean age of summer camp attendees at a local camp. The interval is (4.6 years, 6.3 years). Which of the following is a correct statement based on this interval?

    (A) 90 percent of the attendees' ages fall between 4.6 and 6.3 years.
    (B) There is a 5% probability that no attendee was less than 4.6 years old.
    (C) There is a 90% chance that another sample of attendees will get an interval of 4.6 to 6.3 years.
    (D) 90% of the population was sampled and their ages fell between 4.6 and 6.3 years.
    (E) There is a 10% probability that the mean age of attendees is not between 4.6 and 6.3 years.

6. Which test is appropriate for analyzing categorical data?

    (A) z-test
    (B) 2 sample t-test
    (C) chi-square test
    (D) 1-sample t-test
    (E) a nonparametric test

7. When using the rejection region approach, when is it appropriate to reject the null hypothesis?

    (A) The p-value of the test statistic is less than α.
    (B) The test statistic falls within the rejection region, as determined by α. ✓
    (C) The test statistic falls outside of the rejection region, as determined by α.
    (D) The p-value of the test statistic is greater than α.
    (E) The test statistic is less than α.

8. Which of the following is NOT a similarity between the t-distribution and the standard normal distribution?

    (A) Both depend on degrees of freedom.
    (B) Both distribution means are zero.
    (C) Both are continuous distributions.
    (D) Both are bell shaped.
    (E) Both are symmetric about the mean.

9. The probability of it raining when it is cloudy outside is 0.7. The probability it is cloudy outside is 0.5. What is the probability it is both cloudy and raining?

    (A) 0.4
    (B) 0.15
    (C) 0.5
    (D) 0.2
    (E) 0.35

$$\frac{1}{2} \cdot \frac{7}{10} \qquad \frac{7}{20}$$

Free-Response Questions

10. A researcher wants to see if there is a connection between a mother's career field type and a daughter's career field type. A random sample of 500 mother-daughter pairs were selected from a large metropolis and the results are shown in the table below.

		Mother's Career Field		
		Fine Arts	STEM	Social Sciences
Daughter's Career Field	Fine Arts	72	15	24
	STEM	20	99	64
	Social Sciences	44	73	89

Does this data provide significant evidence of an association between the mother's career field type and her daughter's career field type?

11. A fruit distributor ships cases of oranges to grocery stores nationally. The distributor takes a random sample of 10 cases shipped over the course of a month. The weights are as follows: 26.3 lbs; 27.5 lbs; 25.6 lbs; 26.8 lbs; 24.9 lbs; 24.2 lbs; 25.7 lbs; 25.3 lbs; 23.8 lbs; 25.5 lbs.

   a. Estimate the mean weight of the latest shipment of orange cases using a 95% confidence interval and interpret it.
   b. The mean weight should be 25 lbs/case. Should the shipment be accepted or rejected?

CHAPTER 7 ANSWERS AND EXPLANATIONS

1. **B** The null hypothesis typically is in the form of "no change." In this case, the null hypothesis would state that the mean weight of cats before eating the food, μ_1, is the same as the mean weight of cats after eating the food, μ_2. The alternative hypothesis will be what the researcher wants to test, in this case, that the new food increases the mean weight of cats or the original mean weight of the cats is less than those cats' mean weight after they eat the food. These two hypotheses would be written as: $H_0: \mu_1 = \mu_2$; $H_a: \mu_1 < \mu_2$.

2. **A** A Type I error is the error that the null hypothesis is rejected when it is true. In this case, the null hypothesis states that children sleep 8 hours, so if someone claims that children do not sleep 8 hours when they really do, that is a Type I error, as in choice (A). Note that a Type II error, in contrast, is failing to reject the null hypothesis when the alternative hypothesis is true. In this example, the Type II error is choice (B).

3. **D** In order to determine the sample size required to estimate a population proportion, use the formula: $n \geq \left(\dfrac{Z_{\alpha/2}}{ME}\right)^2 p(1-p)$. However, if an estimate of p from past experiments is not available, as in this case, use this formula: $n \geq \left(\dfrac{Z_{\alpha/2}}{2ME}\right)^2$. The ME is how far off from the true proportion we are willing to be, in this case, 0.05. $Z_{\alpha/2}$ is equal to the z-score for a certain percentage, $\alpha/2$. In this case, since we want a 95% confidence interval, $\alpha = 0.05$. Since the confidence interval is two-tailed, we take $\alpha/2 = 0.025$. The z-score for $\alpha/2 = 1.96$. (See standard normal table or use your calculator.) Finally, plug this information into the inequality for n: $n \geq \left(\dfrac{1.96}{2(0.05)}\right)^2$, $n \geq 384.16$. We need the minimum number of cartons, so we need a whole number. Because the minimum value for n is a decimal, we must round up to 385.

4. **C** Power of a test $= 1 - P$ (Type II error). Choice (C) is describing a Type I error, which is not directly related to the calculation of the power of a test, although it does influence the power. All other answer choices are correct.

5. **E** A confidence interval describes the mean of the population the sample is drawn from. For a 90% confidence interval, there is a 90 percent probability that the interval contains the mean of the population. Conversely, there is a 10 percent probability that the mean of the population is not contained within the interval.

6. **C** A chi-square test is a test for making inferences about categorical data. The other tests are tests for continuous data. Nonparametric tests are not tested on the AP, so you wouldn't be expected to know what that is for (although you may remember that it is an option for continuous data in certain situations).

7. **B** The rejection region approach states that the null hypothesis should be rejected if the test statistic (z, t, etc.) falls within the rejection region which is determined by α. The p-value approach states that the null hypothesis should be rejected if the p-value of the test statistic is less than α.

8. **A** The t-distribution depends on the degrees of freedom that affect the spread of the data. Thus, as the degrees of freedom increase, the standard deviation of the t-distribution decreases. Another distinction is that the standard deviation of the t-distribution is greater than that of the standard normal distribution, but it approaches 1 as the degrees of freedom increase. The other features are shared by the two distributions.

9. **E** For this question, let $P(A) = 0.7$, the probability of it raining when cloudy, and $P(B) = 0.5$, the probability it is cloudy. Here, you need to calculate $P(A \text{ and } B)$, which requires you to multiply the two probabilities together. Thus, $P(A \text{ and } B) = 0.7 \cdot 0.5 = 0.35$, or choice (E).

10. The following are the two hypotheses. H_0: There is no association between a mother's career field type and her daughter's career field type. H_a: There is an association between a mother's career field type and her daughter's career field type.

To test these hypotheses, use a chi-square test for independence. Select an α level, for example 0.05.

Compute the row totals, column totals, and expected cell counts using the formula:

$$\text{Expected cell count for a cell} = \frac{(Row\,total)(Column\,total)}{Grand\,total}$$

		Mother's Career Field			
		Fine Arts	**STEM**	**Social Sciences**	**Total**
Daughter's Career Field	**Fine Arts**	72 (30.2)	15 (41.5)	24 (39.3)	111
	STEM	20 (49.8)	99 (68.4)	64 (64.8)	183
	Social Sciences	44 (56.0)	73 (77.0)	89 (72.9)	206
	Total	136	187	177	500

Check the conditions: 1. The data are counts. 2. The sample is random. 3. The sample is large enough because every cell's expected count is greater than 5.

Calculate the degrees of freedom using: $df = (r - 1)(c - 1) = (3 - 1)(3 - 1) = 4$. Between this and the α level above, the rejection rule is "reject the null if $p < 0.05$" or, for the rejection region approach, "reject the null if TS $> \chi^2_{0.05}(4) = 9.49$."

Compute the test statistic and p-value: $TS = \sum_{i=1}^{3} \sum_{j=1}^{3} \frac{(O_{ij} - E_{ij})^2}{E_{ij}} = \frac{(72 - 30.2)^2}{30.2} + \frac{(20 - 49.8)^2}{49.8} +$

$\frac{(44 - 56.0)^2}{56.0} + \frac{(15 - 41.5)^2}{41.5} + \frac{(99 - 68.4)^2}{68.4} + \frac{(73 - 77.0)^2}{77.0} + \frac{(24 - 39.3)^2}{39.3} + \frac{(64 - 64.8)^2}{64.8} +$

$\frac{(89 - 72.9)^2}{72.9} = 118.6$ and $p - \text{value} = P(x2 > 118.6) \approx 0$

Because the p-value is less than 0.05, or, by the rejection region approach, TS $= 118.6 > 9.49$, the null hypothesis should be rejected and the alternative hypothesis can be accepted. In other words, there is significant evidence to conclude that there is an association between a mother's career field type and a daughter's career field type.

11.　　a.　The statistic of interest is an estimate of μ = the true weight of a case of oranges shipped. A random sample of 10 cases was shipped. Check the conditions: 1. The sample is given to be random and we can assume they are independent because the cases were shipped over the course of a month. 2. A boxplot of the data (not shown) does not show any outliers and appears to be quite symmetric, so it is safe to assume that the weights of the cases are normally distributed.

Since the population standard deviation is unknown—though we can assume a normal distribution—a t-interval for the mean is required.

Compute the sample mean and standard deviation: $x = 25.56$ lbs and $s = 1.1217$ lbs.

Compute the degrees of freedom: $df = n - 1 = 10 - 1 = 9$. Since we are constructing a

95% confidence interval, $\alpha = 0.05$. From here, use the t-table for 9 degrees of freedom to

calculate the critical t-value: $t^* = \frac{t_\alpha}{2}(9) = t_{0.05}(9) = t_{0.025}(9) = 2.262$. Then, the 95 percent

$ME = t_{0.025}(9)\left(\frac{s}{\sqrt{n}}\right) = 2.262\left(\frac{1.1217}{\sqrt{10}}\right) = 0.8024$ lbs. Thus, the confidence interval is found:

$x \pm ME = 25.56 \pm 0.8024 \rightarrow (24.758, 26.362)$.

In other words, we are 95 percent confident that the true mean weight of a case of oranges shipped is between 24.748 lbs and 26.362 lbs.

b.　Now, we are going to make an inference, thus test a hypothesis: H_0: $\mu = 25$ lbs (accept the shipment) and H_a: $\mu \neq 25$ lbs (reject the shipment).

The conditions met from part (a) are still valid. As are the degrees of freedom, t*, and the α value.

The rejection rules are either to reject the null if p-value < 0.05 or reject the null if $t > 2.262$ or if $t < -2.262$.

Next, compute the test statistic: $t = \dfrac{(\bar{x} - \mu_0)}{s / \sqrt{2}} = \dfrac{25.56 - 25.00}{1.1217 / \sqrt{10}} = 1.579$ and the p-value: p-value $= P(t < 1.579) = 0.1488$.

Because $p > 0.05$ or because $-2.262 < t < 2.262$, we fail to reject the null hypothesis. Therefore, the distributor should not reject the shipment.

Part VI
Practice Test 2

- Practice Test 2
- Practice Test 2: Answers and Explanations

Practice Test 2

AP® Statistics Exam

SECTION I: Multiple-Choice Questions

DO NOT OPEN THIS BOOKLET UNTIL YOU ARE TOLD TO DO SO.

<table>
<tr><td>

At a Glance

Total Time
1 hour and 30 minutes
Number of Questions
40
Percent of Total Grade
50%
Writing Instrument
Pen required

</td><td>

Instructions

Section I of this exam contains **40 multiple-choice questions. Fill in only the ovals for numbers 1 through 40 on your answer sheet.**

Indicate all of your answers to the multiple-choice questions on the answer sheet. No credit will be given for anything written in this exam booklet, but you may use the booklet for notes or scratch work. After you have decided which of the suggested answers is best, completely fill in the corresponding oval on the answer sheet. Give only one answer to each question. If you change an answer, be sure that the previous mark is erased completely. Here is a sample question and answer.

</td></tr>
</table>

Sample Question   Sample Answer

Omaha is a   

(A) state
(B) city
(C) country
(D) continent
(E) village

Use your time effectively, working as quickly as you can without losing accuracy. Do not spend too much time on any one question. Go on to other questions and come back to the ones you have not answered if you have time. It is not expected that everyone will know the answers to all of the multiple-choice questions.

About Guessing

Many candidates wonder whether or not to guess the answers to questions about which they are not certain. Multiple–choice scores are based on the number of questions answered correctly. Points are not deducted for incorrect answers, and no points are awarded for unanswered questions. Because points are not deducted for incorrect answers, you are encouraged to answer all multiple-choice questions. On any questions you do not know the answer to, you should eliminate as many choices as you can, and then select the best answer among the remaining choices.

Once you have checked your answers, remember to return to page 4 and respond to the Reflect questions.

STATISTICS
SECTION I
Time—1 hour and 30 minutes
Number of questions—40
Percent of total grade—50

Directions: Solve each of the following problems, using the available space for scratchwork. Decide which is the best of the choices given and fill in the corresponding oval on the answer sheet. No credit will be given for anything written in the test book. Do not spend too much time on any one problem.

1. Fifty oranges of one variety were selected at random and weighed. A 95 percent confidence interval computed from the sample weights to estimate the mean weight of oranges of this variety is (7.58, 8.72) ounces. Which of the following statements is true with respect to the confidence level used?

   (A) In repeated samplings of the same size, 95 percent of the intervals constructed will contain the true mean weight of the oranges of this variety.

   (B) In repeated samplings of the same size, 95 percent of the intervals constructed will contain the sampled mean weight of the oranges.

   (C) Ninety-five percent of the oranges in this sample weigh between 7.58 and 8.72 ounces.

   (D) Ninety-five percent of the oranges of this variety weigh between 7.58 and 8.72 ounces.

   (E) There is a 95 percent chance that the mean weight of another sample of 50 oranges from this variety will be between 7.58 and 8.72 ounces.

2. In the jury pool available for this week, 30 percent of potential jurors are women. A particular trial requires that, out of a jury of 12, at least three are women. If a jury of 12 is to be selected at random from the pool, what is the probability it meets the requirements of this trial?

   (A) 0.168

   (B) 0.843

   (C) 0.915

   (D) 0.949

   (E) The answer cannot be determined without knowing the size of the jury pool.

GO ON TO THE NEXT PAGE.

3. The mean daily demand for bread at a popular bakery is 2,500 loaves, with a standard deviation of 225 loaves. Every morning the bakery bakes 3,000 loaves. What is the probability that today it will run out of bread? Assume that the mean daily demand for bread at this bakery is normally distributed.

(A) 0.8333
(B) 0.1667
(C) 0.9869
(D) 0.0132
(E) 0.0900

$$\frac{3000 - 2500}{225}$$

4. A medicine is known to produce side effects in one in five patients taking it. Suppose a doctor prescribes the medicine to four unrelated patients. What is the probability that none of the patients will develop side effects?

(A) 0.8000
(B) 0.4096
(C) 0.2500
(D) 0.2000
(E) 0.0016

binomialpdf(4,0.2,0)

GO ON TO THE NEXT PAGE.

5. An automobile service station performs oil changes and tire replacements, as well as other services. Sixty percent of its customers request an oil change, 30 percent request tire replacements, and 10 percent request both. A customer requests an oil change. What is the probability this customer does not request tire replacements?

(A) 0.420

(B) 0.500

(C) 0.700

(D) 0.833

(E) 0.857

[Handwritten: Actuallly 50% & 30%]

$$\frac{0.5}{0.5+0.1}$$

[Handwritten: 0.6 b/c 10% both]

$$\frac{0.6}{0.6+0.10}$$

---

6. The following boxplot summarizes the prices of books at a bookstore.

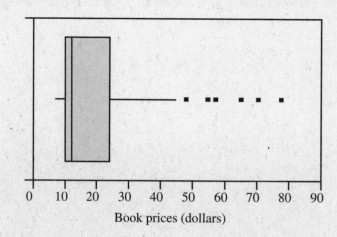

Book prices (dollars)

Which of the following is true about the prices of books at this store?

(A) This store carries more books priced above the mean than below the mean.

(B) This store carries more books priced below the mean than above the mean.

(C) This store carries about the same number of books at different prices in the entire price range.

(D) The mean price of books at this store is the same as the median price of books.

(E) The mean price of books at this store is lower than the median price of books.

GO ON TO THE NEXT PAGE.

7. Random variable X is normally distributed, with a mean of 25 and a standard deviation of 4. Which of the following is the approximate interquartile range for this distribution?

   (A) $25.00 - 22.30 = 2.70$
   (B) $27.70 - 22.30 = 5.40$
   (C) $27.70 \div 22.30 = 1.24$
   (D) $2.00(4.00) = 8.00$
   (E) $37.00 - 13.00 = 24.00$

---

8. An experiment was designed to test the effects of three different types of paint on the durability of wooden toys. Because boys and girls tend to play differently with toys, a randomly selected group of children was divided into two groups by sex. Which of the following statements about this experiment is true?

   (A) There are three types of paint and two sex groups, giving a total of six treatment combinations in this experiment.
   (B) Type of paint is a blocking factor.
   (C) Sex is a blocking factor.
   (D) This is a completely randomized design.
   (E) This is a matched-pairs design in which one boy and one girl are matched by age to form a pair.

GO ON TO THE NEXT PAGE.

9. The following graph summarizes data collected on annual rainfall in two cities for the past 150 years.

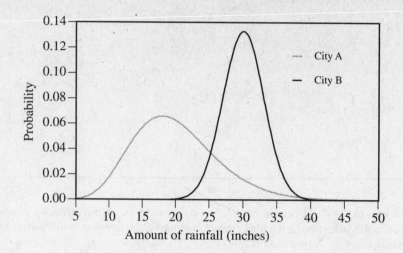

Which of the following conclusions can be made from this graph?

(A) The cities have different mean annual rainfalls, but the range of their annual rainfalls is approximately the same.

(B) On average, City B gets more rain than City A, but it has a smaller range of annual rainfall.

(C) On average, City B gets more rain than City A, and it has a larger range of annual rainfall.

(D) On average, City A gets more rain than City B, but it has a smaller range of annual rainfall.

(E) On average, City A gets more rain than City B, and it has a larger range of annual rainfall.

10. According to the Central Limit Theorem, regardless of the population distribution, the sample mean $\bar{X}$ is approximately normally distributed with $\mu_{\bar{x}} = \mu_x$ and $\sigma_{\bar{x}} = \dfrac{\sigma_x}{\sqrt{n}}$,

(A) provided that a large number of random samples of the same size are selected from the population

(B) provided that a large random sample of size n is taken from the population

(C) provided that the population median is equal to the population mean

(D) provided that the sample size does not exceed 30

(E) It is always true. No other condition is required.

GO ON TO THE NEXT PAGE.

11. Which of the following is a discrete random variable?

    (A) The number of times a student guesses the answers to questions on a certain test
    (B) The amount of gasoline purchased by a customer
    (C) The amount of mercury found in fish caught in the Gulf of Mexico
    (D) The height of water-oak trees
    (E) The time elapsed until the first field goal at home football games

---

12. A random sample of 300 shoppers was selected to estimate the proportion of customers satisfied with the floor displays of merchandise throughout the store. What is the maximum margin of error if a 90 percent confidence interval is to be constructed?

    (A) 0.0033
    (B) 0.0475
    (C) 0.0566
    (D) 0.0949
    (E) 0.1132

$$1.645\sqrt{\frac{0.5^2}{300}}$$

GO ON TO THE NEXT PAGE.

13. Which of the following statements correctly describes the relation between a t-distribution and a standard normal distribution?

   (A)   The standard normal distribution is centered at zero, whereas the t-distribution is centered at $(n-1)$.

   (B)   As the sample size increases, the difference between the t-distribution and the standard normal distribution increases.

   (C)   The standard normal is just another name for the t-distribution.

   (D)   The standard normal distribution has a larger standard deviation than the t-distribution.

   (E)   The t-distribution has a larger standard deviation than the standard normal distribution.

---

14. Researchers are concerned that the mean clutch size (number of eggs per nest) of robin's eggs in a particular forest has decreased from the mean of 4.8 eggs measured 10 years ago. They plan to send out teams to locate and count the number of eggs in 50 different nests, and then perform a hypothesis test to determine if their concerns are well-founded. What is the most appropriate test to perform in this situation?

   (A)   A one-tailed t-test on one population mean.

   (B)   A one-tailed t-test on the difference between two independent population means.

   (C)   A one-tailed t-test on the mean difference between ordered pairs.

   (D)   A one-tailed z-test on a population proportion.

   (E)   A chi-squared test on independence between two variables.

GO ON TO THE NEXT PAGE.

15. Scores on the take-home part of a test are approximately normally distributed, with a mean of 40 and a standard deviation of 3. Scores on the in-class part of the same test are also approximately normally distributed, with a mean of 34 and a standard deviation of 6. The final score on the test is the sum of the score on the take-home part and the score on the in-class part. What are the mean and standard deviation of the final test scores?

   (A)   Mean 74 and standard deviation 4.50

   (B)   Mean 37 and standard deviation 6.71

   (C)   Mean 37 and standard deviation 4.50

   (D)   Mean 74 and standard deviation 6.71

   (E)   Mean 74 and standard deviation 3.00

74

$3^2 + 6^2$

16. On a boxplot, an observation is classified as an outlier if

   (A)   it is smaller than $\bar{X} - 3S$ or larger than $\bar{X} + 3S$

   (B)   it is larger than $\bar{X} - 3S$ and smaller than $\bar{X} + 3S$

   (C)   it is smaller than Q_1 or larger than Q_3

   (D)   it is smaller than $Q_1 - 1.5IQR$ or larger than $Q_3 + 1.5IQR$

   (E)   it is larger than $Q_1 - 1.5IQR$ and smaller than $Q_3 + 1.5IQR$

GO ON TO THE NEXT PAGE.

17. The following cumulative graph gives the electricity demand of a certain town.

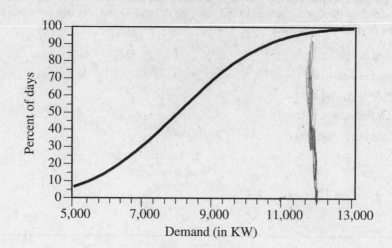

The power plant that provides electricity to this town is capable of generating 12,000 kW daily. On what percent of days will the power plant not be able to meet the demand for electricity?

(A) About 3 percent

(B) About 60 percent

(C) About 80 percent

(D) About 92 percent

(E) About 97 percent

GO ON TO THE NEXT PAGE.

18. Sixty pairs of measurements were taken at random to estimate the relation between variables X and Y. A least-squares regression line was fitted to the collected data. The resulting residual plot is as follows:

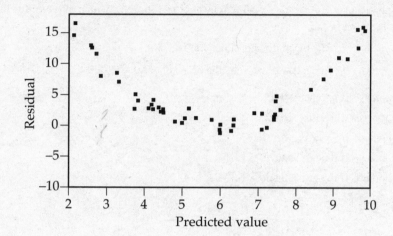

Which of the following conclusions is appropriate?

(A)   A line is an appropriate model to describe the relation between X and Y.

(B)   A line is not an appropriate model to describe the relation between X and Y.

(C)   The assumption of normality of errors has been violated.

(D)   The assumption of constant sample standard deviations has been violated.

(E)   The variables X and Y are not related at all.

GO ON TO THE NEXT PAGE.

19. A consumer awareness group has received several complaints that the price of an asthma medicine has significantly increased in recent years. Two years ago, the mean price for this medicine was estimated to be $78.00, and the price at different pharmacies was approximately normally distributed. The group decides to select 10 pharmacies at random and record the price of the medicine at each of the pharmacies. Assuming a 5 percent level of significance, which of the following decision rules should be used to test the hypotheses below?

H_0: The mean price of medicine is $78.00.

H_a: The mean price of medicine is higher than $78.00.

(A) Reject the null hypothesis if p-value ≥ 0.05.

(B) Reject the null hypothesis if p-value ≥ 0.025.

(C) Reject the null hypothesis if $\bar{X} > 78.00$.

(D) Reject the null hypothesis if the test statistic > 1.812.

(E) Reject the null hypothesis if the test statistic > 1.833.

use t-table 1.645 cal   x − 78

---

20. A team of engineers at the research center of a car manufacturer performs crash tests to determine the proportion of times the cars' airbags fail to operate in a crash. With the airbag system's new modified design, the team expected to reduce the failed proportion to below last year's proportion of 0.08. They decided to test H_0: $p = 0.08$ versus H_a: $p < 0.08$, where p = the proportion of failed airbags during crash tests. If 300 crashes performed in the lab resulted in 18 failures, which of the following is the test statistic for this test?

(A) $z = \dfrac{0.06 - 0.08}{\sqrt{\dfrac{0.08(1 - 0.08)}{300}}}$

(B) $z = \dfrac{0.06 - 0.08}{\sqrt{\dfrac{0.06(1 - 0.06)}{300}}}$

(C) $z = \dfrac{0.06 - 0.08}{\sqrt{300(0.08)(1 - 0.08)}}$

(D) $z = \dfrac{0.06 - 0.08}{\sqrt{300(0.06)(1 - 0.06)}}$

(E) $z = \dfrac{0.06 - 0.08}{\sqrt{\dfrac{0.06(1 - 0.08)}{300}}}$

GO ON TO THE NEXT PAGE.

21. A farmer wants to know whether a new fertilizer has increased the mean weight of his apples. With the old fertilizer, the mean weight was 4.0 ounces per apple. The farmer decides to test $H_0: \mu = 4.0$ ounces versus $H_a: \mu > 4.0$ ounces, at a 5 percent level of significance, where μ = the mean weight of apples using the new fertilizer. The weights of apples are approximately normally distributed. The farmer takes a random sample of 16 apples and computes a mean of 4.3 ounces and a standard deviation of 0.6 ounces. Which of the following gives the p-value for this test?

(A) $P(Z > 2)$

(B) $P(Z < 2)$

(C) $P(t > 2)$ with 15 degrees of freedom

(D) $P(t < 2)$ with 15 degrees of freedom

(E) $P(t > 2)$ with 16 degrees of freedom

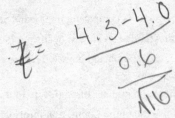

22. Tina's science fair project was to estimate the mean amount of chemicals in her city's water supply. At first, she had decided to use a random sample of 15 observations. But her teacher asked her to take 35 observations. The mean and standard deviation from 35 observations turned out to be approximately the same as those from 15 observations. Is there any advantage in using 35 observations instead of 15 observations?

(A) There is no advantage. Because the mean and the standard deviation are about the same, the confidence interval computed using 35 observations should be approximately the same as that computed using 15 observations.

(B) There is no advantage. In fact, the 20 extra observations will increase the likelihood of error.

(C) There is no advantage. Because she took 35 observations instead of 15 observations, the confidence interval using 35 observations will be wider than that using 15 observations.

(D) There is some advantage. Because she took 35 observations instead of 15 observations, the confidence interval using 35 observations will be narrower than that using 15 observations.

(E) There is some advantage. With 35 observations, she will be able to compute an exact z-confidence interval instead of an approximate t-confidence interval.

GO ON TO THE NEXT PAGE.

23. The Hardcore Construction Company has two offices, one in Atlanta and one in New Orleans. Fifteen engineers work in the Atlanta office, and 14 engineers work in the New Orleans office. The business manager decided to use a 2-sample *t*-test to compare the mean salaries of engineers in the two offices. Because there were only 15 engineers in one office and 14 engineers in the other, he used the salaries of all the engineers in the computation. Is the 2-sample *t*-test an appropriate inferential technique in this situation?

    (A) Yes, because he is comparing the means of two small groups.

    (B) Yes. Both Atlanta and New Orleans are large cities, so the salaries are comparable.

    (C) Yes. Because Atlanta and New Orleans are about 500 miles apart, the two groups of engineers can be assumed to be independent.

    (D) No, because the number of engineers in the two offices is different.

    (E) No, because the entire population information was used from both offices. Because no samples were taken, a *t*-test should not be used.

---

24. The distribution of salaries of a county school system with 4,752 employees is known to be right skewed, with the superintendent's salary an outlier on the higher side. A random sample of 20 employees was taken and their salaries recorded. A 95 percent *t*-confidence interval for the mean salary of the county school system employees is ($15,360, $32,470). The *t*-confidence interval is not appropriate in this situation because

    (A) the sample size is too small compared to the number of employees in the system to give a fair representation

    (B) the skewed salary distribution tells us that assumption of normality of the sampled population will not be satisfied

    (C) the population standard deviation of the salaries of employees of this county school system is not known

    (D) the teacher salaries are not negotiable, but the superintendent's salary is negotiable, so the superintendent's salary should be excluded from the population sampled

    (E) the salaries depend on the number of years of experience, which is not taken into account here

Don't care abt. how it compares

GO ON TO THE NEXT PAGE.

25. A random sample of families was taken in order to estimate the relation between fertility and level of education (measured in number of years). A confidence interval needs to be constructed for the slope of the regression line. The social worker in charge of the project is debating whether to use a 90 percent or a 95 percent confidence interval. Which of the following statements about the length of these intervals is true?

   (A) The 95 percent confidence interval will be wider than the 90 percent confidence interval.

   (B) The 95 percent confidence interval will be narrower than the 90 percent confidence interval.

   (C) Both intervals will be of the same length, because they are computed from the same sample.

   (D) The length of the confidence interval will depend on the sample size, not on the confidence level.

   (E) The length of the confidence interval will depend on the sample standard deviation, not on the confidence level.

26. An insurance agent is successful in selling a life insurance policy to 20 percent of the customers he contacts. He decides to construct a simulation to estimate the mean number of customers he needs to contact before being able to sell a policy. Which of the following schemes should he use to do the simulation?

   (A) Assign numbers 0, 1 to successfully selling a policy to a customer and numbers 2, 3, 4, 5, 6, 7, 8, 9 to failing to sell a policy to a customer.

   (B) Assign numbers 0, 1 to successfully selling a policy to a customer and numbers 2, 3, 4 to failing to sell a policy to a customer.

   (C) Assign number 0 to successfully selling a policy to a customer and number 1 to failing to sell a policy to a customer.

   (D) Assign numbers 0, 1, 2, 3, 4 to successfully selling a policy to a customer and numbers 5, 6, 7, 8, 9 to failing to sell a policy to a customer.

   (E) Assign number 20 to successfully selling a policy to a customer and numbers 1, 3, 5, 7, 9, 11, 13, 15, 17, 19 to failing to sell a policy to a customer.

GO ON TO THE NEXT PAGE.

27. The mean height of adult men is 70 inches, with a standard deviation of four inches. The mean height of adult women is 66 inches, with a standard deviation of three inches. Between a man with a height of 74 inches and a woman with a height of 70 inches, who is more unusually tall within his or her respective sex?

    (A) It cannot be determined, because the mean heights for the two groups are different.

    (B) It cannot be determined, because the standard deviations of the heights for the two groups are different.

    (C) The man, because he is 74 inches tall and the woman is only 70 inches tall.

    (D) Both should be considered equally tall, because both of them are four inches taller than the average height of their respective sex groups.

    (E) The woman, because her height is 1.33 standard deviations above the mean height of all women, whereas the man's height is only one standard deviation above the mean height of all men.

---

28. The amount of rainfall per month in a certain city is approximately normally distributed, with a mean of six inches and a standard deviation of 1.6 inches. Which of the following is the highest amount of rainfall, in inches, this city could have this month for the month to be among the 10 percent driest months the city has seen?

    (A) 8.05

    (B) 7.60

    (C) 3.95

    (D) 3.37

    (E) 2.28

GO ON TO THE NEXT PAGE.

29. A large city was interested in annexing part of the surrounding county. In a survey conducted by the local newspaper, 58 percent of respondents said they were against the annexation. During the actual vote, not all eligible voters voted, but 56 percent of the respondents voted against the annexation. Which of the following best describes the difference in the percentages obtained from the newspaper poll and the vote itself?

   (A)   It is an example of nonresponse bias, the systematic tendency of individuals with particular characteristics to refuse to answer a survey question.

   (B)   It is the systematic difference between a statistic and parameter caused by the nonrandom selection of surveyed persons.

   (C)   It is the difference between the same statistics computed from two different samples.

   (D)   It is the difference between the statistic and the truth due to use of a random sample.

   (E)   It was caused by the large number of newspaper subscribers in the county.

---

30. In a clinical trial, 30 sickle cell anemia patients are randomly assigned to two groups. One group receives the currently marketed medicine, and the other group receives an experimental medicine. Each week, patients report to the clinic where blood tests are conducted. The lab technician is unaware of the kind of medicine the patient is taking. This design can be described as

   (A)   a completely randomized design, with the currently marketed medicine and the experimental medicine as two treatments

   (B)   a matched-pairs design, with the currently marketed medicine and the experimental medicine forming a pair

   (C)   a randomized block design, with the currently marketed medicine and the experimental medicine as two blocks

   (D)   a randomized block design, with the currently marketed medicine and the experimental medicine as two treatments

   (E)   a stratified design with two strata, patients with sickle cell disease forming one stratum and those without sickle cell disease forming the other stratum

GO ON TO THE NEXT PAGE.

31. The registrar's office at a university has noticed that a large number of students fail to report a change of address. The registrar decides to take a random sample of 150 students from the current directory of students and determine the number of students with the correct addresses on record. He then uses this information to construct a 95 percent confidence interval. Which of the following statements must be true?

(A) The true proportion of students at this university with the correct address on record is within the confidence interval constructed.

(B) Ninety-five percent of students at this university have the correct address on record.

(C) The true proportion of students at this university with the correct addresses on record is within the confidence interval 95 percent of the time.

(D) The sample proportion of students at this university with the correct address on record is within the confidence interval 95 percent of the time.

(E) The sample proportion of students at this university with the correct address on record is within the confidence interval.

---

32. In which of the following situations is a binomial model <u>not</u> an appropriate model to describe the outcome?

(A) The number of heads in three tosses of a coin

(B) The number of rainy days in a given week

(C) The number of girls in a family of five children

(D) The number of students present in a class of 22

(E) The number of defective computer monitors out of seven purchased

GO ON TO THE NEXT PAGE.

33. Which of the following statements about any two events A and B is true?

    (A) $P(A \cup B)$ implies events A and B are independent.

    (B) $P(A \cup B) = 1$ implies events A and B are mutually exclusive.

    (C) $P(A \cap B) = 0$ implies events A and B are independent.

    (D) $P(A \cap B) = 0$ implies events A and B are mutually exclusive.

    (E) $P(A \cap B) = P(A) - P(B)$ implies A and B are equally likely events.

34. A newspaper reporter examined police reports of accidents during the past 12 months to collect data about the speed of a car and its stopping distance. The reporter then constructed a scatterplot and computed a correlation coefficient to show the relation between a car's speed and its stopping distance. This is an example of

    (A) a double-blind study

    (B) a single-blind study

    (C) a study involving no blinding at all

    (D) an observational study

    (E) a well-designed experiment

GO ON TO THE NEXT PAGE.

35. A company with offices in five different countries is interested in estimating the proportion of its employees in favor of banning smoking on the office premises. It is known that the views of people from different countries on issues like smoking tend to vary due to the influence of different local social structures. Which of the following is an appropriate sampling technique to use in this situation, and why?

    (A) Stratified sample, because the population is divided into five strata—namely, five offices in five different countries

    (B) Cluster sample, because the population is divided into five clusters—namely, five offices in five different countries

    (C) Simple random sample, because this is the simplest sampling method

    (D) Simple random sample, because this is the only method that gives unbiased results

    (E) Simple random sample, because this is the only method for which inferential techniques are available

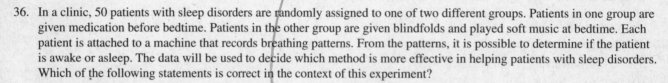

36. In a clinic, 50 patients with sleep disorders are randomly assigned to one of two different groups. Patients in one group are given medication before bedtime. Patients in the other group are given blindfolds and played soft music at bedtime. Each patient is attached to a machine that records breathing patterns. From the patterns, it is possible to determine if the patient is awake or asleep. The data will be used to decide which method is more effective in helping patients with sleep disorders. Which of the following statements is correct in the context of this experiment?

    (A) It is not possible for this experiment to be single-blind or double-blind, because human subjects are involved.

    (B) This is only a single-blind experiment because the experimenters did not include a control group that received neither medication nor a blindfold and soft music.

    (C) This is only a single-blind experiment because patients will know which treatment they are receiving, although the examining doctor might not.

    (D) This is a double-blind experiment because the experimenters could prevent both groups of patients from knowing what sort of treatment the other group is receiving.

    (E) This is a double-blind experiment because the patients were divided into the two treatment groups randomly.

GO ON TO THE NEXT PAGE.

37. Data were collected on two variables X and Y and a least-squares regression line was fitted to the data. The estimated equation for this data is $y = -2.29 + 1.70x$. One point has $x = 5$, $y = 6$. What is the residual for this point?

    (A) 7.91
    (B) 6.21
    (C) 0.21
    (D) -0.21
    (E) -2.91

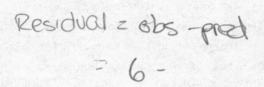

Residual = obs - pred
= 6 -

38. The relation between studying time, h (in hours) and expected grade on a final exam (0–100) in a random sample of students in math class was found to be

    $$\text{Grade} = 50.25 + 10.2(h)$$

    How will a student's expected grade be affected if she studies for two hours?

    (A) Her grade will go up by 40.05 points.
    (B) Her grade will go up by 20.4 points.
    (C) Her grade will remain unchanged.
    (D) Her grade will go down by 10.2 points.
    (E) It cannot be determined from the information given.

GO ON TO THE NEXT PAGE.

39. A group of scientists wanted to estimate the proportion of geese returning to the same site for the next breeding season. Suppose they decided to increase the sample size from 200 to 2,000. How will this affect the distribution of the sample proportion?

    (A) The distribution of the sample proportion will be more spread out.

    (B) The distribution of the sample proportion will be less spread out. ✓

    (C) The spread of the distribution of the sample proportion will remain unaffected.

    (D) The distribution of the sample proportion will more closely resemble the binomial distribution.

    (E) The distribution of the sample proportion will more closely resemble the chi-square distribution.

---

40. A company has 400 employees. Their mean income is $20,500, and the standard deviation of their incomes is $3,750. The distribution of incomes is normally distributed. How many of the 400 employees do you expect to have an income of between $13,000 and $28,000?

    (A) 50
    (B) 100
    (C) 200
    (D) 390
    (E) 400

$$\frac{-20500}{3750}$$

2   2

.0228   .9773

97.5% of data

END OF SECTION I

STATISTICS
SECTION II
Time—1 hour and 30 minutes
Number of questions—6
Percent of total grade—50

Part A
Questions 1–5
Spend about 60 minutes on this part of the exam.
Percent of Section II grade—75

Show all your work. Indicate clearly the methods you use, because you will be graded on the correctness of your method as well as on the accuracy of your results and explanation.

1. A short-term parking facility allows cars to be parked for a maximum of four hours. For any fraction of an hour a car is parked, the facility charges for the full hour. For example, if a person parks at this facility for one hour and 25 minutes, then the person is charged for two full hours. The probability distribution of the parking time at this short-term parking facility, as measured in full hours, is as follows:

Hours	1	2	3	4
Probability	0.15	0.25	0.45	0.15

(a) What is the mean parking time charged for in this facility?

$$\bar{x} = (1)(0.15) + 2(0.25) + 3(0.45) + 4(0.15)$$

$$\boxed{\bar{x} = 2.6}$$

GO ON TO THE NEXT PAGE.

(b) The facility charges \$3.00 for the first hour of parking and \$2.50 per hour thereafter. Let X be the parking fee charged for a car parked in this facility. In the table below, give the probability distribution function for X.

x	$P(X = x)$
3	0.15
5.5	0.25
8.0	0.45
10.5	0.15

(c) Determine the mean and standard deviation of the parking fee charged for a car parked at this facility.

$$\bar{X} = 3(0.15) + 5.5(0.25) + 8(0.45) + 10.5(0.15)$$

$$SD = \sqrt{\frac{1}{4-1}}$$

(d) The parking facility offers a monthly parking permit, which allows a car to park without paying the hourly parking fee for an entire month. This permit costs \$100. The driver of a cab parks his cab for one hour or less in the facility 80 percent of times he parks there, and he never parks in the facility for over two hours. What is the minimum number of times in a month he would need to park in this facility in order for the monthly parking permit to <u>cost less than</u> his expected cost for paying the hourly rate?

$$.80(x)(3) + 0.2(x)(5.5) = 100$$

$$2.4x + 1.1x = 100$$

$$3.5x = 100$$

$$x \approx 28.57$$

$$\boxed{x = 29 \text{ days}}$$

GO ON TO THE NEXT PAGE.

2. Scientists have suspected that animals, when deficient in certain chemicals, tend to ingest natural resources that have high concentrations of those chemicals to offset the deficiency. In a study, scientists drained saliva from the parotid gland of sheep in order to make them sodium deficient. Then they offered these sheep a solution of sodium bicarbonate and measured the sheep's sodium intake. The sodium deficiency and the sodium intake, both measured in millimoles, are recorded as follows:

Sodium Deficit (in millimoles)	Sodium Intake (in millimoles)
100	110
200	180
570	610
850	790
700	750
425	390
375	420
325	380
450	300
850	790

The summary statistics and the regression output for this data are as follows:

Variable	N	Mean	Median	StDev	Q1	Q3
Deficit	10	484.5	437.5	256.4	293.7	737.5
Intake	10	472.0	405.0	250.0	270.0	760.0

Predictor	Coef	StDev	T	P
Constant	15.55	47.94	0.32	0.754
Deficit	0.94211	0.08843	10.65	0.000

GO ON TO THE NEXT PAGE.

(a) Does a line appear to be a reasonable model for this data? Explain your answer.

(b) State and interpret the slope in terms of the problem.

(c) Estimate the correlation between sodium deficit and sodium intake. Interpret your answer in the context of this problem.

(d) Estimate the amount of a sheep's sodium intake if the sheep is found to be deficient in sodium by 800 millimoles.

GO ON TO THE NEXT PAGE.

3. A university offers degrees in the following four areas:

   - Arts and Sciences (A&S)

   - Engineering (Eng)

   - Business and Management (B&M)

   - Computer Science (Comp)

Incoming freshmen apply for majors in A&S, Eng, B&M, and Comp in a ratio of approximately 5:6:6:8, but many students change their major during the course of study. The university officials are interested in determining whether the distribution of majors among graduating students differs from that of incoming students. They took a random sample of 200 graduating students and classified them according to their majors. The distribution of graduating students in this sample is given in the table below.

	Major			
	A&S	Eng	B&M	Comp
Number of Students	60	30	60	50

Is the distribution of majors among graduating students different from that of incoming students? Provide statistical justification for your answer.

$$\chi^2 = \frac{(60-40)^2}{40} + \frac{(30-48)^2}{48} + \frac{(60-48)^2}{48} + \frac{(50-64)^2}{64}$$

GO ON TO THE NEXT PAGE.

4. An education professor is interested in getting students involved in a tutoring program for area schools. The participating students are paid through a grant from the city. This year, the city has agreed to provide funds to support three students in this program. The professor has found that about four out of five students he interviews are not willing to participate in the program due to other commitments.

(a) Describe how you would use a random number table to carry out simulations to determine the number of students the professor needs to interview to fill the three spots in the tutoring program. Describe what each random number represents in your simulation.

(b) Run two trials of your simulation. Use the random number table provided to illustrate your simulation.

25211	75049	70678	24646	96329	63547	37255	51013	25211	75049
97077	82384	33078	59574	34916	09422	85700	74202	97077	82384
82641	66179	30341	40674	51778	97680	84707	88808	82641	66179
60675	60254	16308	70130	29610	27658	94288	88752	60675	60254
53860	97861	34625	85190	38477	60503	34561	04360	53860	97861

GO ON TO THE NEXT PAGE.

(c) Suppose the professor did 100 simulations to estimate the number of students that he needs to interview to find three students willing to work for the tutoring program. The results of the simulations are shown below.

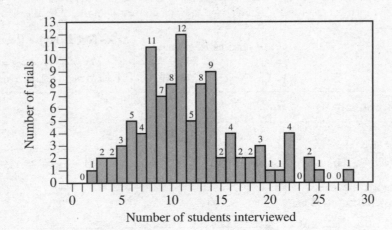

Estimate the probability that the professor has to interview more than 20 students before he finds three willing to work for the tutoring program.

GO ON TO THE NEXT PAGE.

5. A resident at a medical college was interested in showing that exercising regularly helps reduce cholesterol levels. Over a period of one month, he selected a random sample of 50 patients who came to his clinic for their annual physical examination. He asked the patients if they exercised regularly, and noted down the answers as "Exercises regularly" or "Does not exercise regularly." He also recorded their current cholesterol levels and their cholesterol levels from the previous year's physical examination, as noted in their medical records. He summarized the data on their cholesterol levels as shown in the table below.

	Exercises Regularly		Does Not Exercise Regularly	
	Last Year	This Year	Last Year	This Year
Number of Patients	18	18	32	32
Mean	223.80	189.75	268.35	265.53
Standard Deviation	15.88	18.77	32.81	28.17
Difference in Mean Cholesterol Levels (Last Year – This Year)	34.05		2.82	

(a) The resident included the following in his report:

"On the average, the group that exercises regularly has experienced a larger decrease in cholesterol level as compared to the group that does not exercise regularly. Because the observed difference is considerably large, we can conclude that exercising regularly reduces cholesterol level."

Why is such a causal conclusion not warranted by this data? Explain your answer.

(b) Design an experiment that will allow the resident to draw such a conclusion.

END OF PART A

STATISTICS
SECTION II
Part B
Question 6
Spend about 30 minutes on this part of the exam.
Percent of Section II grade—25

6. Pam and Dave decided to buy a small house and move out of their apartment. After looking around, they decided that they both liked two neighborhoods, Sunshine Estates and Pinewoods Estates, and they wanted to buy a house in one of those two neighborhoods if they could afford it. Their real estate agent selected a random sample of houses sold in the last 12 months from each neighborhood and found out how much the houses sold for. The summary statistics for the selling prices (in $1,000) of houses in both neighborhoods are as follows:

	Sunshine Estates	Pinewoods Estates
Sample Size	14	15
Mean Selling Price	113.357	124.333
Standard Deviation of Selling Price	3.296	14.181
Minimum Selling Price	107.000	97.000
1st Quartile Selling Price	111.000	112.000
Median Selling Price	113.500	121.000
3rd Quartile Selling Price	116.000	133.000
Maximum Selling Price	119.000	149.000

(a) Make parallel boxplots to compare the selling prices of houses in Sunshine Estates and Pinewoods Estates. Write a few sentences describing the selling prices in these two neighborhoods.

GO ON TO THE NEXT PAGE.

(b) Assume the selling prices of houses in these two neighborhoods are normally distributed. Construct a 95 percent confidence interval to compare the mean prices in the two neighborhoods. Interpret your interval.

(c) Pam and Dave decide that they could afford to spend $120,000 on their new house. What percent of houses in Sunshine Estates are within their budget?

(d) In which neighborhood are they more likely to find a house within their budget? Justify your answer.

(e) Using the information available, can we support the assumption that the prices of the houses are distributed normally? Explain your answer.

STOP

END OF EXAM

Practice Test 2:
Answers and
Explanations

PRACTICE TEST 2 ANSWER KEY

1.	A	21.	C
2.	E	22.	D
3.	D	23.	E
4.	B	24.	B
5.	D	25.	A
6.	B	26.	A
7.	B	27.	E
8.	C	28.	C
9.	B	29.	C
10.	B	30.	A
11.	A	31.	E
12.	B	32.	B
13.	E	33.	D
14.	A	34.	D
15.	D	35.	A
16.	D	36.	C
17.	A	37.	D
18.	B	38.	B
19.	E	39.	B
20.	A	40.	D

PRACTICE TEST 2 EXPLANATIONS

Section I—Multiple-Choice

1. **A** Note that this question asks for an interpretation of the confidence *level* and not of the confidence *interval*. The example uses a confidence level of 0.95. This means that if lots of random samples of 50 oranges are taken and a 95 percent confidence interval is constructed from each selected sample, then 95 percent of those confidence intervals constructed will contain the true mean weight of the oranges of this variety.

2. **E** We cannot use a binomial model unless we know that the probability of drawing a woman for the pool is nearly constant. However, since we are drawing 12 jurors without replacement, this is not necessarily true unless the jury pool is very large (at least 120).

3. **D** It is given that the demand for bread is $N(2{,}500, 225)$. We need to find the probability that the demand will exceed the supply. If 3,000 loaves are available today, compute

    $P(\text{Demand for bread} > 3000)$

    $= P\left(Z > \dfrac{3000 - 2500}{225} \right)$

    $= P(Z > 2.22)$

    $= 1 - 0.9868$

    $= 0.0132$

    (Hint: On the TI-83 or TI-84, use the normalcdf function from the DISTR menu, or use Table A, $z = 2.22$.)

4. **B** This is a binomial situation. Because four patients are trying the medicine, that means there are four trials. The probability that a patient will develop side effects is one out of five, i.e., $1/5 = 0.20$. The probability that a patient will not develop side effects $= 4/5 = 0.80$. So the probability that none of the four patients will develop side effects is $P(0) = \dbinom{4}{0}\left(\dfrac{1}{5}\right)^{0}\left(\dfrac{4}{5}\right)^{4} = 1 \times 1 \times 0.80^4 = 0.80^4 = 0.4096$

    (Hint: On the TI-83 or TI-84, use the binompdf function from the DISTR menu.)

5. **D** A Venn diagram is useful for this question. The overlap between the circles represents the 10 percent of customers who request both services. Since a total of 60 percent of customers request an oil change, the other part of the O circle must be 50 percent; likewise the other part of the T circle must be 20 percent. Finally, since 50 percent + 20 percent + 10 percent = 80 percent, the remaining 20% of customers request neither of these services.

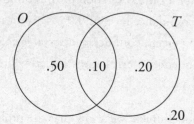

We are asked to compute the conditional probability P (no tire replacement|oil change). By the conditional probability formula, P (no tire replacement|oil change) =

$$\frac{P \text{ (no tire replacement} \cap \text{oil change)}}{P \text{ (oil change)}} = \frac{0.50}{0.60} = 0.833$$

6. **B** This boxplot is highly right-skewed. The book prices range from about $8 to $80, but the median price is around $12. This means that 50 percent of the books are priced around $12 or lower. Even the third quartile is around $25, which means that about 75 percent of the books are priced at $25 or below. When a distribution is right-skewed, the mean is above the median, and therefore, more books are below the mean than above it.

7. **B** The first quartile of the distribution is Q_1 such that $P(X < Q_1) = 0.25$. Thus

$$Q_1 = 25 - Z_{0.25}(4) = 25 - 0.675(4) = 22.32$$

The third quartile of the distribution is Q_3 such that

$$P(X < Q_3) = 0.75 \text{ or } P(X > Q_3) = 0.25$$

Thus

$$Q_3 = 25 + Z_{0.25}(4) = 25 + 0.675(4) = 27.68$$

Therefore, the interquartile range = $Q_3 - Q_1 = 27.68 - 22.32 = 5.36$

(Hint: On the TI-83 or TI-84, use invNorm function from DISTR menu.)

An easier method of getting the answer is to first note that a range is always the difference between two numbers, thus eliminating (C) and (D). Next, note that, for a normally distributed variable, the two numbers must surround the mean, thus eliminating (A). Finally, recall that, for a normally distributed variable, nearly all of the distribution (over 99 percent) is within three standard deviations—but the answer calls for an interquartile range, which is 50 percent. Choice (E) is three standard deviations on either side of the mean; it cannot be right, so the answer must be (B).

8. **C** In this experiment, sex is a blocking factor and the three different types of paint make up three treatments. Children are divided into two groups by sex. There is no matching by age involved. The experiment is therefore a randomized block design, not a completely randomized design.

9. **B** The approximate range of annual rainfall for City A is five to 45 inches, with a mean of approximately 23 inches. The approximate range of annual rainfall for City B is 20 to 40 inches, with a mean of approximately 30 inches. This means that, on the average, City B gets more rain than City A, but the range for City A is larger than that for City B.

10. **B** The central limit theorem is applicable to samples of large size.

11. **A** A discrete variable takes only a countable number of values. The number of test questions a student guesses the answers to is a random variable with possible values 0, 1, 2, ... n, where n is the number of questions on the test.

12. **B** For a 90 percent confidence interval, $Z_{\alpha/2} = Z_{0.05} = 1.645$. Because $\hat{p}$ is not given, use $\hat{p} = \frac{1}{2} = 0.5$. The maximum 90 percent margin of error is

$$Z_{\alpha/2}\sqrt{\frac{\hat{p}(1-\hat{p})}{n}} = 1.645\sqrt{\frac{0.5(1-0.5)}{300}} = 0.0475$$

(Hint: On the TI-83 or TI-84, use the invNorm function from the DISTR menu or the 1-propZInt function from the STAT → TESTS menu, or look in the body of Table A of $1 - 0.05 = 0.95$, which is midway between $z = 1.64$ and $z = 1.65$.)

13. **E** The t-distribution has a larger standard deviation than the standard normal distribution and is also centered at zero. As sample size increases, the difference between the t-distribution and the standard normal distribution decreases.

14. **A** Choice (C) is wrong because we do not have paired data. Choice (D) is wrong because we are concerned about a population mean, not a population proportion. Choice (E) is not appropriate because the data is not categorical if the counts of clutch sizes were being grouped based on frequency. For example, if the researchers counted and recorded the number of clutches with one egg, with two eggs, with three, etc., then the data would be categorical. Choice (B) is incorrect because a test on the difference between two independent population means is appropriate when we have independent samples from two different populations; we have only one sample here, and we are comparing it to a previously determined value. Thus, (A) is correct.

15. **D** It is given that take-home grades ~ $N(40, 3)$ and in-class grades ~ $N(34, 6)$.

The test grade = take-home grade + in-class grade.

Thus, $\mu_{\text{Test grade}} = \mu_{\text{Take-home grade}} + \mu_{\text{In-class grade}} = 40 + 34 = 74$, and

$$\sigma_{\text{Test grade}} = \sqrt{\sigma^2_{\text{Take-home grade}} + \sigma^2_{\text{In-class grade}}} = \sqrt{3^2 + 6^2} = 6.71$$

An easier method of getting the answer is to first note that the mean has to be 74, because $40 + 34 = 74$. This eliminates choices (B) and (C). Next, remember that the variance of a sum is always greater than the variance of each addend (the things that were added). Of (A), (D), and (E), only (D) has a standard deviation higher than that of either the take-home or in-class part.

16. **D** Any observation that falls $1.5(IQR)$ beyond the first and third quartiles is considered an outlier.

17. **A** In this cumulative graph, we need to find $P(\text{Demand} > 12,000)$, because that is the point at which the power company will not be able to meet the demand for electricity. Draw a vertical line at 12,000 until it reaches the curve. From the point at which it crosses the curve, draw a horizontal line to the Y-axis. The line reaches the Y-axis at approximately 97 percent, which means that on 97 percent of days the demand for electricity will be, at most, 12,000. In other words, on about 3 percent of days, the power plant will have more demand for electricity than what they produce. Because none of the other choices are close to 3 percent, you do not need to be accurate with your drawing.

18. **B** The curvature in the residual plot indicates that a line is not an appropriate model to describe the relation between X and Y. If a line is an appropriate model, then the residual plot will show randomly scattered residuals without any pattern.

19. **E** The alternative hypothesis indicates that we need to use a right-tailed test. And because the population standard deviation is unknown, and the population is normally distributed, a t-test is the best option. Sample size 10 gives 9 degrees of freedom, and $\alpha = 0.05$ is used. Therefore, the rejection region is

$$t > t_\alpha(df) = t_{0.05}(9) = 1.833$$

(Hint: Look at Table B, row $df = 9$, column $P = 0.05$.)

20. **A** It is given that the hypothesized value of the proportion is $p_0 = 0.08$. The estimated proportion from a sample of size 300 is

$$\hat{p} = \frac{18}{300} = 0.06$$

Therefore, the test statistic used to test the given hypotheses is

$$z = \frac{\hat{p} - p_0}{\sqrt{\dfrac{p_0(1 - p_0)}{n}}} = \frac{0.06 - 0.08}{\sqrt{\dfrac{0.08(1 - 0.08)}{300}}}$$

21.   **C**   The population standard deviation is unknown and the weights are normally distributed. So we should use a t-test for the mean. The test statistic value is

$$t = \frac{\bar{x} - \mu_0}{s/\sqrt{n}} = \frac{4.3 - 4.0}{0.6/\sqrt{16}} = 2.0$$

Because we are using a right-tailed test, the p-value is the area in the right tail of the t-distribution with 15 degrees of freedom, beyond 2.0.

(Hint: On the TI-83 or TI-84, use the t-test function from the STAT → TESTS menu.)

22.   **D**   Note that $ME = t^* \dfrac{s}{\sqrt{n}}$. The margin of error is inversely proportional to the sample size; in other words, it will be smaller for a larger sample size. So, the confidence interval will be narrower.

23.   **E**   The number of engineers working for the company is so small that the mean salaries were computed using the salaries of all the engineers. Because no samples were taken, whatever difference was observed between the mean salaries is the real difference. There is no probability statement associated with the difference. Therefore, there is no inference.

24.   **B**   It is given that the distribution is skewed with an outlier. Therefore, the distribution cannot be normal, because the normal distribution is symmetric. So, the assumption of normality required for a t-test is not satisfied, and because the sample size is small, the central limit theorem does not apply.

25.   **A**   For a confidence interval with a higher confidence level, the probability of overestimating or underestimating the result is lower. Therefore, there is less area under the sampling distribution beyond the confidence limits. Hence, the confidence interval with a higher confidence level will be wider.

26.   **A**   It is given that P(Successfully selling insurance policy) = 0.20, which means that P(Failing to sell a policy) = 0.80. If we are using one-digit numbers, then there are a total of 10 digits available for selection. If "0, 1" are designated for "selling a policy," then we have P(Selling a policy) = 0.20, and if the remaining eight digits are designated as "failing to sell a policy," then P(Failing to sell a policy) = 0.80 as desired.

27.   **E**   Because the distributions of heights differ for men and women, we cannot compare their heights directly. If you want to, you can compute the z-scores for the height of each one within their respective populations.

$$Z_M = \frac{74 - 70}{4} = 1$$

This means that the man is one standard deviation taller than the mean height of men.

$$Z_W = \frac{70-66}{3} = \frac{4}{3} = 1.33$$

This means that the woman is 1.33 standard deviations taller than the mean height of women. Therefore, the woman should be considered taller within her group. However, no calculation is needed because it should be clear that $\frac{4}{3}$ is larger than $\frac{4}{4}$.

28. **C** X = the amount of rainfall ~ $N(6, 1.6)$.

We need to find amount H such that $P(X < H) = 0.10$.

$H = \mu - Z_{0.10}\sigma = 6 - 1.28(1.6) = 3.95$

(Hint: On the TI-83 or TI-84, use the invNorm function from the DISTR menu.)

29. **C** If we take different samples from the same population, the estimates from the different samples will be different. The difference in percentages may be entirely due to sampling variation.

30. **A** This experiment consists of two treatments, the currently marketed medicine and the experimental medicine. Patients are not matched, and no blocks are formed. Only patients with sickle cell disease are involved in the experiment.

31. **E** Confidence intervals are constructed as Statistic ± Margin of Error. Therefore, the statistic is always right in the center of the confidence interval.

32. **B** One requirement of the binomial distribution is that trials must be independent. The weather in a given week is not independent from day to day—if there's rain on Monday, there's more likely to be rain on Tuesday (more likely than if Monday were sunny).

33. **D** If the probability of the intersection of two events is zero, then those two events cannot both occur. They are disjoint.

34. **D** This is an example of observational study. The reporter collected the data but had no control over the factor (the car's speed).

35. **A** A stratified sample is most appropriate when we have a population divided into subgroups that may have differences of opinions about the issue at hand; by dividing the population into these strata and randomly selecting members from each group, we guarantee that no particular viewpoint is overrepresented or underrepresented in the sample. Choice (B) is incorrect because a cluster sample requires that each group be representative of the population as you choose one entire cluster at random to form your sample. Choices (C), (D), and (E) are incorrect because a simple random sample may overrepresent or underrepresent the viewpoint of one particular office.

36. **C** Blinding in an experiment is achieved by preventing the subjects (or those who could affect the subjects) from knowing which treatment group they are in and by preventing the evaluators from knowing which treatment group the subjects are in. If we have achieved this for both groups, the experiment is double-blind; if we can achieve this for only one group, the experiment is single-blind. In this case, there is no way to keep the subjects from knowing what treatment group they are in, but because the results are evaluated from recorded breathing patterns, the evaluators could be kept from knowing which records belonged to each group.

37. **D** The predicted value of Y for $X = 5$ is $\hat{y} = -2.29 + 1.70(5) = 6.21$.

The residual is $y - \hat{y} = 6 - 6.21 = -0.21$.

38. **B** The slope of the regression line gives the average amount of increase in expected grade for every hour increase in studying. So, if studying is increased by two hours, then the expected grade will increase by $2(10.2) = 20.4$. Note that based on this model the predicted score increase doesn't depend on how many hours the student originally studied, ie. we would expect the same score increase if she had studied for 0 hours and increased her studying to 2, as if she had studied for 1 hour and increased her studying to 3 hours total.

39. **B** The standard deviation of the sampling distribution of the sample proportion is given by $\sqrt{\dfrac{p(1-p)}{n}}$. Therefore, the standard deviation decreases as the sample size increases. In other words, the distribution becomes less spread out as the sample size increases.

40. **D** According to the normal distribution, about 97.5 percent of the data falls within two standard deviations of the mean. $20,500 - 2(3,750) = 13,000$, and $20,500 + 2(3,750) = 28,000$. So $(13,000, 28,000)$ gives an interval two standard deviations from the mean. Therefore, 97.5 percent of data—$0.975(400) = 390$ observations—should fall within the given limits.

Section II—Free-Response

1. (a) The formula for the mean of a probability distribution tells us that the mean parking time is
$$\mu_{hours} = \sum xp(x) = 1(0.15) + 2(0.25) + 3(0.45) + 4(0.15) = 2.6 \text{ hours}$$

(b) For the first hour, the parking fee is $3.00. Each hour after that adds another $2.50; therefore, the probability distribution function for the fee charged for a car is as shown in the table below.

x	$P(X = x)$
3.00	0.15

x	$P(X = x)$
5.50	0.25
8.00	0.45
10.50	0.15

(c) The formula for the mean of a probability distribution tells us that the mean fee is

$$\mu_{fee} = \sum xp(x) = 3.00(0.15) + 5.50(0.25) + 8.00(0.45) + 10.50(0.15) = \$7$$

The formula for the variance of a probability distribution tells us that the variance of the fee is

$$\sigma^2_{fee} = \sum (x - \mu)^2 p(x) = (3 - 7)^2(0.15) + (5.50 - 7)^2(0.25) + (8 - 7)^2(0.45) + (10.5 - 7)^2(0.15) = 5.25$$

Thus the standard deviation is $\sqrt{5.25} = \$2.29$.

(If you are using a TI-83 or TI-84, you can enter the dollar amounts into L_1 and the corresponding probabilities into L_2; then by using 1-Var-Stats L_1, L_2, the mean and standard deviation can be found by checking $\bar{x}$ and σ.)

(d) Eighty percent of the time the cab driver pays $3.00, and the other 20 percent of the time he pays $5.50. Thus his expected cost each time he parks is $0.80(\$3) + 0.20(\$5.50) = \$3.50$. If he parks n times in a month, his expected cost for the month is therefore $3.5n$ dollars. In order for the monthly parking permit to cost less than his expected cost for paying the hourly rate for a month, we would therefore need $100 < 3.5n$ which implies $n > 28.57$. The minimum number of times he would need to use the parking garage is therefore 29 times.

2.   Let D = Sodium deficit and I = Sodium intake.

(a) Prepare a scatterplot, or a residual plot. Figures 1 and 2 are examples of each:

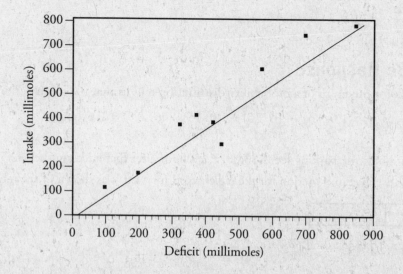

Figure 1: Scatterplot of intake versus deficit

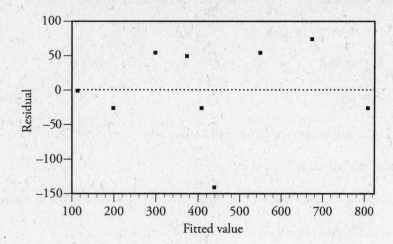

Figure 2: Residual plot for intake as a function of deficit

Using the scatterplot, you could argue that a line appears to be a reasonable model to describe the relation between sodium deficiency and sodium intake.

Using the residual plot, you could argue that the residuals are scattered randomly (they show no patterns or trends), so a line appears to be a reasonable model to describe the relation between sodium deficiency and sodium intake.

(Hint: On the TI-83 or TI-84, use the graph function to make a scatterplot or the regression diagnostics to make a residual plot. Then copy the graph or plot from the calculator screen to the exam paper.)

(b)   From the regression output, estimate the slope of the line of best fit as $b = 0.94211$. This means that for every millimole of deficiency in sodium, the sheep will take in approximately (or on the average) 0.94211 millimoles of sodium.

(c)   The basic summary results provided show that $s_D = 256.4$ and $s_I = 250.0$. The results of the regression analysis show that the estimated slope $b_1 = 0.94211$. Therefore, the correlation coefficient is

$$r = b_1 \frac{s_D}{s_I} = 0.94211 \left(\frac{256.4}{250.0} \right) = 0.966$$

This correlation coefficient shows that there is a strong, positive, linear correlation between the amount of sodium intake and the amount of sodium deficiency among the sheep.

(d) The regression results show that the relation between intake and deficiency is

Intake = 15.55 + 0.94211(deficit)

= 15.55 + 0.94211(800)

= 769.238 millimoles.

A sheep with 800 millimoles deficiency will take in about 769.2 millimoles of sodium.

3. The university officials are interested in testing

H_0: The graduating students major in A&S, Eng, B&M, and Comp in a ratio of 5:6:6:8.

H_a: The ratio differs from that given in the null hypothesis.

The major preference for incoming freshmen is in the ratio

A&S : Eng : B&M : CompSci

5:6:6:8

In other words,

P(A new freshman applies for A&S major) = 5/(5 + 6 + 6 + 8) = 5/25 = 0.20

P(A new freshman applies for Eng major) = 6/(5 + 6 + 6 + 8) = 6/25 = 0.24

P(A new freshman applies for B&M major) = 6/(5 + 6 + 6 + 8) = 6/25 = 0.24

P(A new freshman applies for Comp major) = 8/(5 + 6 + 6 + 8) = 8/25 = 0.32

A total of 200 students were sampled. If the null hypothesis were true, then the officials would expect approximately 200(0.20) = 40 students to graduate with a degree in A&S. The numbers of students expected to graduate in each of the above majors if the null hypothesis were true are as follows:

	Major			
Expected Counts	A&S	Eng	B&M	Comp
	40	48	48	64

A random sample of students is taken and all the expected counts are larger than five. So the chi-square test for goodness of fit is appropriate.

	Major			
	A&S	Eng	B&M	Comp
Expected Counts (E_i)	40	48	48	64
Observed Counts (O_i)	60	30	60	50

Degrees of freedom = df = (4 − 1) = 3. Let's use a 5 percent level of significance.

The rejection rule is "reject the null hypothesis if p-value < 0.05"(or if using the rejection region approach, "reject the null hypothesis if $TS > \chi^2_{0.05}(3) = 7.81$").

$$TS = \sum \frac{(O_i - E_i)^2}{E_i}$$

$$= \frac{(60 - 40)^2}{40} + \frac{(30 - 48)^2}{48} + \frac{(60 - 48)^2}{48} + \frac{(50 - 64)^2}{64}$$

$$= 22.81$$

p-value = $P(\chi^2 > 22.81)$ = 0.000044 with 3 degrees of freedom.

Because the p-value of 0.000044 is smaller than any reasonable level of significance (or if using the rejection region approach, because TS = 22.81 > 7.82, or because the TS falls in the rejection region), we should reject the null hypothesis and accept the alternative hypothesis. At a 5 percent level of significance, we can conclude that the distribution of majors among the graduating students is different from that of the incoming students.

4.   Approximately four out of five students whom the professor interviews are not able to participate in the program. This means,

P(Student is not able to participate) = 4/5 = 0.80
P(Student is able to participate) = 1/5 = 0.20

(a)   To simulate the situation, consider 10 one-digit random numbers 0, 1, 2, 3, 4, 5, 6, 7, 8, 9.

Designate them as follows:

- Assign "0, 1" to "Student is able to participate."
- Assign "2, 3,..., 9" to "Student is not able to participate."

Start at the beginning of the table and read random numbers consecutively, one number for each student contacted. Numbers 0 or 1 mean that the student contacted is able to participate in the program, whereas numbers 2 through 9 mean the student contacted is not able to participate in the program. Continue until three students who are able to participate in the program are found.

(b)   Suppose we start the first simulation at the beginning of the table.

2 5 2 [1][1] | 7 5 [0] 4 9 | 7 0 6 7 8 | 2 4 6 4 6 | 9 6 3 2 9 | 6 3 5 4 7 | 3 7 2 5 5

Our first simulation results in interviewing eight students before finding three students who are able to participate in the program.

Suppose we start the second simulation at the beginning of the second line.

9 7 [0] 7 7 | 8 2 3 8 4 | 3 3 [0] 7 8 | 5 9 5 7 4 | 3 4 9 [1] 6 | 0 9 4 2 2 | 8 5 7 0 0

Our second simulation results in interviewing 24 students before identifying three students who are willing to participate in the program.

Note that the answer to this question depends on how the simulation is designed as well as where in the table one starts the simulation.

(c)   From the chart, we can see nine simulations that resulted in interviewing more than 20 students before three students were found.

P(Interviewing more than 20 students) = $\dfrac{9}{100}$ = 0.09.

There is a 9 percent chance that the professor will have to interview more than 20 students before he can recruit three.

5. **(a)** This is an observational study, not an experiment. Therefore, causal conclusions are not appropriate from this data. In an observational study, there is no control for other variables that might be affecting the results. For instance, the results could be explained by the fact that those who exercised also changed their diet, and that combination may have contributed to the reduced cholesterol, not the exercise regimen alone. Another alternative could be that the patients in the two groups have systematic differences in age, sex, race, or genetic factors that contributed to their cholesterol changes. In all, this leads to the famous saying "correlation does not imply causation."

(b) Recruit a group of patients. Randomly assign the selected patients to two groups. Instruct patients to Group 1 to do specifically assigned exercises regularly. Monitor their exercise activities closely. Instruct patients in Group 2 not to do regular exercises. After one year, measure the cholesterol levels of both groups and compare. To avoid confounding factors and strengthen this experiment, make sure that none of the patients are on a cholesterol reducing medicine or diet. Further, you could have participants matched based on age, sex, race, and genetic factors that contribute to high cholesterol.

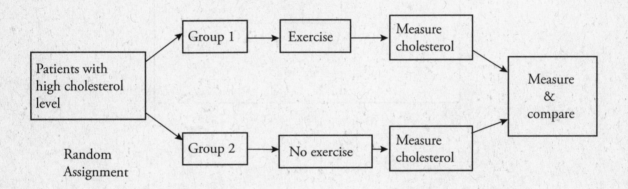

Figure 3: Schematic diagram showing the design of this experiment

6.　　　First, organize the information as follows.

	Sunshine Estates	Pinewoods Estates
Q_1	111.000	112.000
Q_3	116.000	133.000
$IQR = Q_3 - Q_1$	5.000	21.000
Length of Whiskers = (1.5) IQR	7.500	31.500
$Q_1 - (1.5)\ IQR$	103.500	80.500
$Q_3 + (1.5)\ IQR$	123.500	164.500

(a) Then use this information to create the following boxplots.

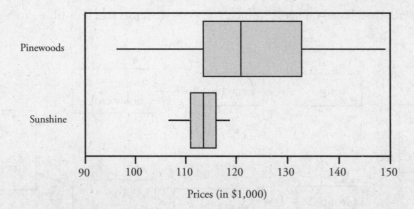

Prices (in $1,000)

The prices of houses in Pinewoods Estates vary a lot compared to the prices of houses in Sunshine Estates. The median price of houses in Sunshine Estates is lower than the median price of houses in Pinewoods Estates. The distribution of prices seems to be fairly symmetric in both the neighborhoods.

(b) Let μ_S = the mean selling price of houses in Sunshine Estates

and μ_P = the mean selling price of houses in Pinewoods Estates

$(\mu_S - \mu_P)$ = the difference in mean selling prices of houses in Sunshine and Pinewoods estates

It is given that the selling prices are normally distributed. The population variances are unknown, but the boxplots indicate that the population variances are more likely to be unequal. So use an unequal standard deviations t-interval to estimate $(\mu_S - \mu_P)$.

$$df = \frac{\left(\dfrac{s_S^2}{n_S} + \dfrac{s_P^2}{n_P}\right)^2}{\dfrac{\left(s_S^2/n_S\right)^2}{n_S - 1} + \dfrac{\left(s_P^2/n_P\right)^2}{n_P - 1}} = \frac{\left(\dfrac{10.8636}{14} + \dfrac{201.101}{15}\right)^2}{\dfrac{\left(10.8636/14\right)^2}{14 - 1} + \dfrac{\left(201.101/15\right)^2}{15 - 1}} = 15.611$$

(smaller sample size) − 1 = 14 − 1 = 13, so use 13 degrees of freedom.

$t_{0.025}(13) = 2.160$

$$95\% ME = t_{\alpha/2}\left(df\right)\sqrt{\frac{s_S^2}{n_S} + \frac{s_P^2}{n_P}} = 2.160\sqrt{\frac{3.296^2}{14} + \frac{14.181^2}{15}} = 8.17155$$

(Hint: On the TI-83 or TI-84, you can get df using the 2-sampTint function on the STATS-Tests menu.)

Therefore, the 95 percent confidence interval for $(\mu_S - \mu_P)$ is: (−19.1475, −2.8045).

We are 95 percent confident that the true difference in mean prices of houses in Sunshine Estates and Pinewoods Estates is between $2,804.50 and $19,147.50, with houses in Pinewoods Estates on the average being more expensive.

(Hint: On the TI-83 or TI-84, use the 2-SampTInt function from the STAT → TESTS menu.)

(c) The prices in Sunshine Estates are approximately normally distributed, with a mean price of $113,357 and a standard deviation of $3,296. Pam and Dave can afford to spend $120,000.

P(Pam and Dave can afford to buy a house in Sunshine Estates)

$$= P(X < 120) = P\left(t < \frac{120 - 113.357}{3.296}\right) = t(Z < 2.015) = 0.9780$$

About 97.8 percent of the houses in Sunshine Estates are within Pam and Dave's budget.

(Hint: On the TI-83 or TI-84, use the normalcdf function from the DISTR menu.)

(d) The prices in Pinewoods Estates are approximately normally distributed, with a mean price of $124,333 and a standard deviation of $14,181. Pam and Dave can afford to spend $120,000.

P(Pam and Dave can afford to buy a house in Pinewoods Estates)

$$= P(X < 120) = P\left(Z < \frac{120 - 124.333}{14.181}\right) = P(Z < -0.3055) = 0.3800$$

About 38 percent of the houses in Pinewood Estates are within Pam and Dave's budget.

From the answer to (c) we know that about 97.8 percent of houses in Sunshine Estates are within Pam and Dave's budget. Comparing these two, we can say that Pam and Dave are much more likely to find a house within their budget in Sunshine Estates.

(Hint: On the TI-83 or TI-84, use the normalcdf function from the DISTR menu.)

(e) This can be argued using several different methods. Some are listed below.

- The boxplots reveal no outliers and the distributions seem symmetric. Median prices are almost the same as mean prices and the median, the first quartile is close to the third quartile. Therefore, the prices are most likely fairly normally distributed.

- Suppose we computed z-scores for the minimum and the maximum prices in both subdivisions. Then we would get:

	Sunshine Estates	Pinewoods Estates
Minimum	$z\text{–score} = \dfrac{107 - 113.357}{3.296} = -1.93$	$z\text{–score} = \dfrac{97 - 124.333}{14.181} = -1.93$
Maximum	$z\text{–score} = \dfrac{119 - 113.357}{3.296} = 1.71$	$z\text{–score} = \dfrac{149 - 124.333}{14.181} = 1.74$

Note that in both neighborhoods, the highest and the lowest prices are less than two standard deviations away from the mean. In a normal distribution, almost all observations fall within three standard deviations from the mean. This could indicate that the prices may not be normally distributed.

- We can still use the z-scores and argue that only about 5 percent of the observations are expected to be beyond two standard deviations from the mean. Because we have only 14 and 15 observations, it is possible to get no z-scores in the intervals $(-3, -2)$ and $(2, 3)$ in such a small data set when sampling from a normal population. The boxplots reveal no outliers and the distributions seem symmetrical. The median prices are almost the same as the mean prices. So the prices should be fairly normally distributed.

Appendix
Formulas and
Tables

I. Descriptive Statistics

$$\bar{x} = \frac{\sum x_i}{n}$$

$$s_x = \sqrt{\frac{1}{n-1}\sum(x_i - \bar{x})^2}$$

$$s_p = \sqrt{\frac{(n_1 - 1)s_1^2 + (n_2 - 1)s_2^2}{(n_1 - 1) + (n_2 - 1)}}$$

$$\hat{y} = b_0 + b_1 x$$

$$b_1 = \frac{\sum(x_i - \bar{x})(y_i - \bar{y})}{\sum(x_i - \bar{x})^2}$$

$$b_0 = \bar{y} - b_1 \bar{x}$$

$$r = \frac{1}{n-1}\sum\left(\frac{x_i - \bar{x}}{s_x}\right)\left(\frac{y_i - \bar{y}}{s_y}\right)$$

$$b_1 = r\frac{s_y}{s_x}$$

$$s_{b_1} = \frac{\sqrt{\dfrac{\sum(y_i - \hat{y}_i)^2}{n-2}}}{\sqrt{\sum(x_i - \bar{x})^2}}$$

II. Probability

$$P(A \cup B) = P(A) + P(B) - P(A \cap B)$$

$$P(A|B) = \frac{P(A \cap B)}{P(B)}$$

$$E(X) = \mu_x = \sum x_i p_i$$

$$Var(X) = \sigma_x^2 = \sum (x_i - \mu_x)^2 p_i$$

If X has a binomial distribution with parameters n and p, then:

$$P(X = k) = \binom{n}{k} p^k (1-p)^{n-k}$$

$$\mu_x = np$$

$$\sigma_x = \sqrt{np(1-p)}$$

$$\mu_{\hat{p}} = p$$

$$\sigma_{\hat{p}} = \sqrt{\frac{p(1-p)}{n}}$$

If $\bar{x}$ is the mean of a random sample of size n from an infinite population with mean μ and standard deviation σ, then:

$$\mu_{\bar{x}} = \mu$$

$$\sigma_{\bar{x}} = \frac{\sigma}{\sqrt{n}}$$

III. Inferential Statistics

Standardized test statistic: $\dfrac{\text{statistic} \; - \; \text{parameter}}{\text{standard deviation of statistic}}$

Confidence interval: statistic $\pm$ (critical value) $\cdot$ (standard deviation of statistic)

Single-Sample

Statistic	Standard Deviation of Statistic
Sample Mean	$\dfrac{\sigma}{\sqrt{n}}$
Sample Proportion	$\sqrt{\dfrac{p(1-p)}{n}}$

Two-Sample

Statistic	Standard Deviation of Statistic
Difference of sample means	$\sqrt{\dfrac{\sigma_1^2}{n_1} + \dfrac{\sigma_2^2}{n_2}}$ Special case when $\sigma_1 = \sigma_2$ $\sigma\sqrt{\dfrac{1}{n_1} + \dfrac{1}{n_2}}$
Difference of sample proportions	$\sqrt{\dfrac{p_1(1-p_1)}{n_1} + \dfrac{p_2(1-p_2)}{n_2}}$ Special case when $p_1 = p_2$ $\sqrt{p(1-p)}\;\sqrt{\dfrac{1}{n_1} + \dfrac{1}{n_2}}$

$$\text{Chi-square test statistic} = \sum \frac{(\text{observed} \; - \; \text{expected})^2}{\text{expected}}$$

Table entry for z is the probability lying below z.

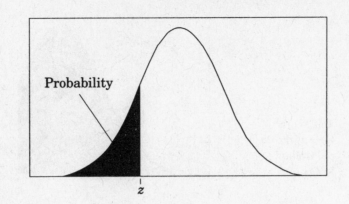

Probability

Table A   Standard normal probabilities

z	.00	.01	.02	.03	.04	.05	.06	.07	.08	.09
−3.4	.0003	.0003	.0003	.0003	.0003	.0003	.0003	.0003	.0003	.0002
−3.3	.0005	.0005	.0005	.0004	.0004	.0004	.0004	.0004	.0004	.0003
−3.2	.0007	.0007	.0006	.0006	.0006	.0006	.0006	.0005	.0005	.0005
−3.1	.0010	.0009	.0009	.0009	.0008	.0008	.0008	.0008	.0007	.0007
−3.0	.0013	.0013	.0013	.0012	.0012	.0011	.0011	.0011	.0010	.0010
−2.9	.0019	.0018	.0018	.0017	.0016	.0016	.0015	.0015	.0014	.0014
−2.8	.0026	.0025	.0024	.0023	.0023	.0022	.0021	.0021	.0020	.0019
−2.7	.0035	.0034	.0033	.0032	.0031	.0030	.0029	.0028	.0027	.0026
−2.6	.0047	.0045	.0044	.0043	.0041	.0040	.0039	.0038	.0037	.0036
−2.5	.0062	.0060	.0059	.0057	.0055	.0054	.0052	.0051	.0049	.0048
−2.4	.0082	.0080	.0078	.0075	.0073	.0071	.0069	.0068	.0066	.0064
−2.3	.0107	.0104	.0102	.0099	.0096	.0094	.0091	.0089	.0087	.0084
−2.2	.0139	.0136	.0132	.0129	.0125	.0122	.0119	.0116	.0113	.0110
−2.1	.0179	.0174	.0170	.0166	.0162	.0158	.0154	.0150	.0146	.0143
−2.0	.0228	.0222	.0217	.0212	.0207	.0202	.0197	.0192	.0188	.0183
−1.9	.0287	.0281	.0274	.0268	.0262	.0256	.0250	.0244	.0239	.0233
−1.8	.0359	.0351	.0344	.0336	.0329	.0322	.0314	.0307	.0301	.0294
−1.7	.0446	.0436	.0427	.0418	.0409	.0401	.0392	.0384	.0375	.0367
−1.6	.0548	.0537	.0526	.0516	.0505	.0495	.0485	.0475	.0465	.0455
−1.5	.0668	.0655	.0643	.0630	.0618	.0606	.0594	.0582	.0571	.0559
−1.4	.0808	.0793	.0778	.0764	.0749	.0735	.0721	.0708	.0694	.0681
−1.3	.0968	.0951	.0934	.0918	.0901	.0885	.0869	.0853	.0838	.0823
−1.2	.1151	.1131	.1112	.1093	.1075	.1056	.1038	.1020	.1003	.0985
−1.1	.1357	.1335	.1314	.1292	.1271	.1251	.1230	.1210	.1190	.1170
−1.0	.1587	.1562	.1539	.1515	.1492	.1469	.1446	.1423	.1401	.1379
−0.9	.1841	.1814	.1788	.1762	.1736	.1711	.1685	.1660	.1635	.1611
−0.8	.2119	.2090	.2061	.2033	.2005	.1977	.1949	.1922	.1894	.1867
−0.7	.2420	.2389	.2358	.2327	.2296	.2266	.2236	.2206	.2177	.2148
−0.6	.2743	.2709	.2676	.2643	.2611	.2578	.2546	.2514	.2483	.2451
−0.5	.3085	.3050	.3015	.2981	.2946	.2912	.2877	.2843	.2810	.2776
−0.4	.3446	.3409	.3372	.3336	.3300	.3264	.3228	.3192	.3156	.3121
−0.3	.3821	.3783	.3745	.3707	.3669	.3632	.3594	.3557	.3520	.3483
−0.2	.4207	.4168	.4129	.4090	.4052	.4013	.3974	.3936	.3897	.3859
−0.1	.4602	.4562	.4522	.4483	.4443	.4404	.4364	.4325	.4286	.4247
−0.0	.5000	.4960	.4920	.4880	.4840	.4801	.4761	.4721	.4681	.4641

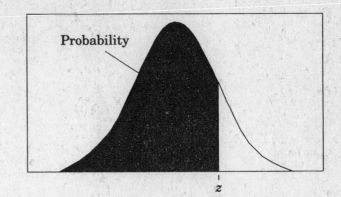

Table entry for z is the probability lying below z.

Probability

Table A (Continued)

z	.00	.01	.02	.03	.04	.05	.06	.07	.08	.09
0.0	.5000	.5040	.5080	.5120	.5160	.5199	.5239	.5279	.5319	.5359
0.1	.5398	.5438	.5478	.5517	.5557	.5596	.5636	.5675	.5714	.5753
0.2	.5793	.5832	.5871	.5910	.5948	.5987	.6026	.6064	.6103	.6141
0.3	.6179	.6217	.6255	.6293	.6331	.6368	.6406	.6443	.6480	.6517
0.4	.6554	.6591	.6628	.6664	.6700	.6736	.6772	.6808	.6844	.6879
0.5	.6915	.6950	.6985	.7019	.7054	.7088	.7123	.7157	.7190	.7224
0.6	.7257	.7291	.7324	.7357	.7389	.7422	.7454	.7486	.7517	.7549
0.7	.7580	.7611	.7642	.7673	.7704	.7734	.7764	.7794	.7823	.7852
0.8	.7881	.7910	.7939	.7967	.7995	.8023	.8051	.8078	.8106	.8133
0.9	.8159	.8186	.8212	.8238	.8264	.8289	.8315	.8340	.8365	.8389
1.0	.8413	.8438	.8461	.8485	.8508	.8531	.8554	.8577	.8599	.8621
1.1	.8643	.8665	.8686	.8708	.8729	.8749	.8770	.8790	.8810	.8830
1.2	.8849	.8869	.8888	.8907	.8925	.8944	.8962	.8980	.8997	.9015
1.3	.9032	.9049	.9066	.9082	.9099	.9115	.9131	.9147	.9162	.9177
1.4	.9192	.9207	.9222	.9236	.9251	.9265	.9279	.9292	.9306	.9319
1.5	.9332	.9345	.9357	.9370	.9382	.9394	.9406	.9418	.9429	.9441
1.6	.9452	.9463	.9474	.9484	.9495	.9505	.9515	.9525	.9535	.9545
1.7	.9554	.9564	.9573	.9582	.9591	.9599	.9608	.9616	.9625	.9633
1.8	.9641	.9649	.9656	.9664	.9671	.9678	.9686	.9693	.9699	.9706
1.9	.9713	.9719	.9726	.9732	.9738	.9744	.9750	.9756	.9761	.9767
2.0	.9772	.9778	.9783	.9788	.9793	.9798	.9803	.9808	.9812	.9817
2.1	.9821	.9826	.9830	.9834	.9838	.9842	.9846	.9850	.9854	.9857
2.2	.9861	.9864	.9868	.9871	.9875	.9878	.9881	.9884	.9887	.9890
2.3	.9893	.9896	.9898	.9901	.9904	.9906	.9909	.9911	.9913	.9916
2.4	.9918	.9920	.9922	.9925	.9927	.9929	.9931	.9932	.9934	.9936
2.5	.9938	.9940	.9941	.9943	.9945	.9946	.9948	.9949	.9951	.9952
2.6	.9953	.9955	.9956	.9957	.9959	.9960	.9961	.9962	.9963	.9964
2.7	.9965	.9966	.9967	.9968	.9969	.9970	.9971	.9972	.9973	.9974
2.8	.9974	.9975	.9976	.9977	.9977	.9978	.9979	.9979	.9980	.9981
2.9	.9981	.9982	.9982	.9983	.9984	.9984	.9985	.9985	.9986	.9986
3.0	.9987	.9987	.9987	.9988	.9988	.9989	.9989	.9989	.9990	.9990
3.1	.9990	.9991	.9991	.9991	.9992	.9992	.9992	.9992	.9993	.9993
3.2	.9993	.9993	.9994	.9994	.9994	.9994	.9994	.9995	.9995	.9995
3.3	.9995	.9995	.9995	.9996	.9996	.9996	.9996	.9996	.9996	.9997
3.4	.9997	.9997	.9997	.9997	.9997	.9997	.9997	.9997	.9997	.9998

Table entry for p and C is the point t^* with probability p lying above it and probability C lying between $-t^*$ and t^*.

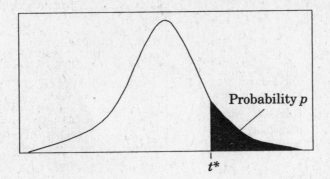

Probability p

t^*

Table B

t-distribution critical values

df	.25	.20	.15	.10	.05	.025	.02	.01	.005	.0025	.001	.0005
1	1.000	1.376	1.963	3.078	6.314	12.71	15.89	31.82	63.66	127.3	318.3	636.6
2	.816	1.061	1.386	1.886	2.920	4.303	4.849	6.965	9.925	14.09	22.33	31.60
3	.765	.978	1.250	1.638	2.353	3.182	3.482	4.541	5.841	7.453	10.21	12.92
4	.741	.941	1.190	1.533	2.132	2.776	2.999	3.747	4.604	5.598	7.173	8.610
5	.727	.920	1.156	1.476	2.015	2.571	2.757	3.365	4.032	4.773	5.893	6.869
6	.718	.906	1.134	1.440	1.943	2.447	2.612	3.143	3.707	4.317	5.208	5.959
7	.711	.896	1.119	1.415	1.895	2.365	2.517	2.998	3.499	4.029	4.785	5.408
8	.706	.889	1.108	1.397	1.860	2.306	2.449	2.896	3.355	3.833	4.501	5.041
9	.703	.883	1.100	1.383	1.833	2.262	2.398	2.821	3.250	3.690	4.297	4.781
10	.700	.879	1.093	1.372	1.812	2.228	2.359	2.764	3.169	3.581	4.144	4.587
11	.697	.876	1.088	1.363	1.796	2.201	2.328	2.718	3.106	3.497	4.025	4.437
12	.695	.873	1.083	1.356	1.782	2.179	2.303	2.681	3.055	3.428	3.930	4.318
13	.694	.870	1.079	1.350	1.771	2.160	2.282	2.650	3.012	3.372	3.852	4.221
14	.692	.868	1.076	1.345	1.761	2.145	2.264	2.624	2.977	3.326	3.787	4.140
15	.691	.866	1.074	1.341	1.753	2.131	2.249	2.602	2.947	3.286	3.733	4.073
16	.690	.865	1.071	1.337	1.746	2.120	2.235	2.583	2.921	3.252	3.686	4.015
17	.689	.863	1.069	1.333	1.740	2.110	2.224	2.567	2.898	3.222	3.646	3.965
18	.688	.862	1.067	1.330	1.734	2.101	2.214	2.552	2.878	3.197	3.611	3.922
19	.688	.861	1.066	1.328	1.729	2.093	2.205	2.539	2.861	3.174	3.579	3.883
20	.687	.860	1.064	1.325	1.725	2.086	2.197	2.528	2.845	3.153	3.552	3.850
21	.686	.859	1.063	1.323	1.721	2.080	2.189	2.518	2.831	3.135	3.527	3.819
22	.686	.858	1.061	1.321	1.717	2.074	2.183	2.508	2.819	3.119	3.505	3.792
23	.685	.858	1.060	1.319	1.714	2.069	2.177	2.500	2.807	3.104	3.485	3.768
24	.685	.857	1.059	1.318	1.711	2.064	2.172	2.492	2.797	3.091	3.467	3.745
25	.684	.856	1.058	1.316	1.708	2.060	2.167	2.485	2.787	3.078	3.450	3.725
26	.684	.856	1.058	1.315	1.706	2.056	2.162	2.479	2.779	3.067	3.435	3.707
27	.684	.855	1.057	1.314	1.703	2.052	2.158	2.473	2.771	3.057	3.421	3.690
28	.683	.855	1.056	1.313	1.701	2.048	2.154	2.467	2.763	3.047	3.408	3.674
29	.683	.854	1.055	1.311	1.699	2.045	2.150	2.462	2.756	3.038	3.396	3.659
30	.683	.854	1.055	1.310	1.697	2.042	2.147	2.457	2.750	3.030	3.385	3.646
40	.681	.851	1.050	1.303	1.684	2.021	2.123	2.423	2.704	2.971	3.307	3.551
50	.679	.849	1.047	1.299	1.676	2.009	2.109	2.403	2.678	2.937	3.261	3.496
60	.679	.848	1.045	1.296	1.671	2.000	2.099	2.390	2.660	2.915	3.232	3.460
80	.678	.846	1.043	1.292	1.664	1.990	2.088	2.374	2.639	2.887	3.195	3.416
100	.677	.845	1.042	1.290	1.660	1.984	2.081	2.364	2.626	2.871	3.174	3.390
1000	.675	.842	1.037	1.282	1.646	1.962	2.056	2.330	2.581	2.813	3.098	3.300
	.674	.841	1.036	1.282	1.645	1.960	2.054	2.326	2.576	2.807	3.091	3.291
	50%	60%	70%	80%	90%	95%	96%	98%	99%	99.5%	99.8%	99.9%

Confidence level C

Table entry for π is the point (χ^2) with probability π lying above it.

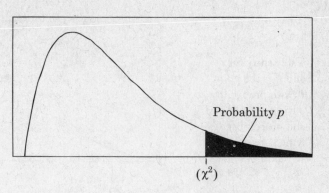

Probability p

(χ^2)

Table C χ^2 critical values

df					Tail probability	π					
	.25	.20	.15	.10	.05	.025	.02	.01	.005	.0025	.001
1	1.32	1.64	2.07	2.71	3.84	5.02	5.41	6.63	7.88	9.14	10.83
2	2.77	3.22	3.79	4.61	5.99	7.38	7.82	9.21	10.60	11.98	13.82
3	4.11	4.64	5.32	6.25	7.81	9.35	9.84	11.34	12.84	14.32	16.27
4	5.39	5.99	6.74	7.78	9.49	11.14	11.67	13.28	14.86	16.42	18.47
5	6.63	7.29	8.12	9.24	11.07	12.83	13.39	15.09	16.75	18.39	20.51
6	7.84	8.56	9.45	10.64	12.59	14.45	15.03	16.81	18.55	20.25	22.46
7	9.04	9.80	10.75	12.02	14.07	16.01	16.62	18.48	20.28	22.04	24.32
8	10.22	11.03	12.03	13.36	15.51	17.53	18.17	20.09	21.95	23.77	26.12
9	11.39	12.24	13.29	14.68	16.92	19.02	19.68	21.67	23.59	25.46	27.88
10	12.55	13.44	14.53	15.99	18.31	20.48	21.16	23.21	25.19	27.11	29.59
11	13.70	14.63	15.77	17.28	19.68	21.92	22.62	24.72	26.76	28.73	31.26
12	14.85	15.81	16.99	18.55	21.03	23.34	24.05	26.22	28.30	30.32	32.91
13	15.98	16.98	18.20	19.81	22.36	24.74	25.47	27.69	29.82	31.88	34.53
14	17.12	18.15	19.41	21.06	23.68	26.12	26.87	29.14	31.32	33.43	36.12
15	18.25	19.31	20.60	22.31	25.00	27.49	28.26	30.58	32.80	34.95	37.70
16	19.37	20.47	21.79	23.54	26.30	28.85	29.63	32.00	34.27	36.46	39.25
17	20.49	21.61	22.98	24.77	27.59	30.19	31.00	33.41	35.72	37.95	40.79
18	21.60	22.76	24.16	25.99	28.87	31.53	32.35	34.81	37.16	39.42	42.31
19	22.72	23.90	25.33	27.20	30.14	32.85	33.69	36.19	38.58	40.88	43.82
20	23.83	25.04	26.50	28.41	31.41	34.17	35.02	37.57	40.00	42.34	45.31
21	24.93	26.17	27.66	29.62	32.67	35.48	36.34	38.93	41.40	43.78	46.80
22	26.04	27.30	28.82	30.81	33.92	36.78	37.66	40.29	42.80	45.20	48.27
23	27.14	28.43	29.98	32.01	35.17	38.08	38.97	41.64	44.18	46.62	49.73
24	28.24	29.55	31.13	33.20	36.42	39.36	40.27	42.98	45.56	48.03	51.18
25	29.34	30.68	32.28	34.38	37.65	40.65	41.57	44.31	46.93	49.44	52.62
26	30.43	31.79	33.43	35.56	38.89	41.92	42.86	45.64	48.29	50.83	54.05
27	31.53	32.91	34.57	36.74	40.11	43.19	44.14	46.96	49.64	52.22	55.48
28	32.62	34.03	35.71	37.92	41.34	44.46	45.42	48.28	50.99	53.59	56.89
29	33.71	35.14	36.85	39.09	42.56	45.72	46.69	49.59	52.34	54.97	58.30
30	34.80	36.25	37.99	40.26	43.77	46.98	47.96	50.89	53.67	56.33	59.70
40	45.62	47.27	49.24	51.81	55.76	59.34	60.44	63.69	66.77	69.70	73.40
50	56.33	58.16	60.35	63.17	67.50	71.42	72.61	76.15	79.49	82.66	86.66
60	66.98	68.97	71.34	74.40	79.08	83.30	84.58	88.38	91.95	95.34	99.61
80	88.13	90.41	93.11	96.58	101.9	106.6	108.1	112.3	116.3	120.1	124.8
100	109.1	111.7	114.7	118.5	124.3	129.6	131.1	135.8	140.2	144.3	149.4

ABOUT THE AUTHOR

Madhuri S. Mulekar received her Ph.D. in Statistics from Oklahoma State University in 1988. She is currently a professor of statistics at the University of South Alabama. She has been involved with AP Statistics since 1997 as both a reader and a table leader. She has given several lectures and workshops on teaching AP Statistics. She also wrote several refereed publications on such topics as statistical education, selection and ranking procedures, estimation and inferential procedures for overlap coefficients, and medical applications. Dr. Mulekar has received grants from the National Science Foundation and the Alabama Center for Estuarine Studies (Environmental Protection Agency).

The Princeton Review

1. YOUR NAME: _____

(Print)   Last   First   M.I.

SIGNATURE: _____   **DATE:** ___ / ___ / ___

HOME ADDRESS: _____

(Print)   Number and Street

_____

City   State   Zip Code

PHONE NO. : _____

(Print)

IMPORTANT: Please fill in these boxes exactly as shown on the back cover of your test book.

2. TEST FORM

_____

6. DATE OF BIRTH

Month	Day	Year
○ JAN		
○ FEB		
○ MAR	⓪ ⓪	⓪ ⓪
○ APR	① ①	① ①
○ MAY	② ②	② ②
○ JUN	③ ③	③ ③
○ JUL		④ ④
○ AUG		⑤ ⑤
○ SEP		⑥ ⑥
○ OCT		⑦ ⑦
○ NOV		⑧ ⑧
○ DEC		⑨ ⑨

3. TEST CODE   **4. REGISTRATION NUMBER**

(bubble grid 0–9 with letters A–G in second column)

7. SEX
- ○ MALE
- ○ FEMALE

The Princeton Review
© 2005 The Princeton Review, Inc.
FORM NO. 00001-PR

5. YOUR NAME

First 4 letters of last name				FIRST INIT	MID INIT
Ⓐ	Ⓐ	Ⓐ	Ⓐ	Ⓐ	Ⓐ
Ⓑ	Ⓑ	Ⓑ	Ⓑ	Ⓑ	Ⓑ
Ⓒ	Ⓒ	Ⓒ	Ⓒ	Ⓒ	Ⓒ
Ⓓ	Ⓓ	Ⓓ	Ⓓ	Ⓓ	Ⓓ
Ⓔ	Ⓔ	Ⓔ	Ⓔ	Ⓔ	Ⓔ
Ⓕ	Ⓕ	Ⓕ	Ⓕ	Ⓕ	Ⓕ
Ⓖ	Ⓖ	Ⓖ	Ⓖ	Ⓖ	Ⓖ
Ⓗ	Ⓗ	Ⓗ	Ⓗ	Ⓗ	Ⓗ
Ⓘ	Ⓘ	Ⓘ	Ⓘ	Ⓘ	Ⓘ
Ⓙ	Ⓙ	Ⓙ	Ⓙ	Ⓙ	Ⓙ
Ⓚ	Ⓚ	Ⓚ	Ⓚ	Ⓚ	Ⓚ
Ⓛ	Ⓛ	Ⓛ	Ⓛ	Ⓛ	Ⓛ
Ⓜ	Ⓜ	Ⓜ	Ⓜ	Ⓜ	Ⓜ
Ⓝ	Ⓝ	Ⓝ	Ⓝ	Ⓝ	Ⓝ
Ⓞ	Ⓞ	Ⓞ	Ⓞ	Ⓞ	Ⓞ
Ⓟ	Ⓟ	Ⓟ	Ⓟ	Ⓟ	Ⓟ
Ⓠ	Ⓠ	Ⓠ	Ⓠ	Ⓠ	Ⓠ
Ⓡ	Ⓡ	Ⓡ	Ⓡ	Ⓡ	Ⓡ
Ⓢ	Ⓢ	Ⓢ	Ⓢ	Ⓢ	Ⓢ
Ⓣ	Ⓣ	Ⓣ	Ⓣ	Ⓣ	Ⓣ
Ⓤ	Ⓤ	Ⓤ	Ⓤ	Ⓤ	Ⓤ
Ⓥ	Ⓥ	Ⓥ	Ⓥ	Ⓥ	Ⓥ
Ⓦ	Ⓦ	Ⓦ	Ⓦ	Ⓦ	Ⓦ
Ⓧ	Ⓧ	Ⓧ	Ⓧ	Ⓧ	Ⓧ
Ⓨ	Ⓨ	Ⓨ	Ⓨ	Ⓨ	Ⓨ
Ⓩ	Ⓩ	Ⓩ	Ⓩ	Ⓩ	Ⓩ

Section 1
Start with number 1 for each new section.
If a section has fewer questions than answer spaces, leave the extra answer spaces blank.

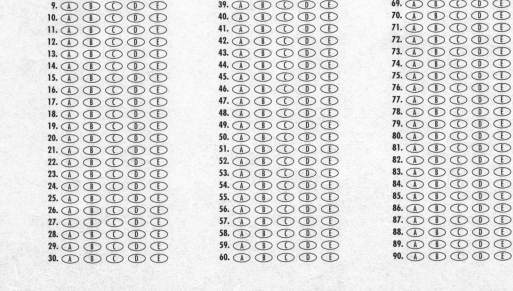

Answer grid questions 1–90, each with bubbles Ⓐ Ⓑ Ⓒ Ⓓ Ⓔ:

1. Ⓐ Ⓑ Ⓒ Ⓓ Ⓔ   31. Ⓐ Ⓑ Ⓒ Ⓓ Ⓔ   61. Ⓐ Ⓑ Ⓒ Ⓓ Ⓔ
2. Ⓐ Ⓑ Ⓒ Ⓓ Ⓔ   32. Ⓐ Ⓑ Ⓒ Ⓓ Ⓔ   62. Ⓐ Ⓑ Ⓒ Ⓓ Ⓔ
3. Ⓐ Ⓑ Ⓒ Ⓓ Ⓔ   33. Ⓐ Ⓑ Ⓒ Ⓓ Ⓔ   63. Ⓐ Ⓑ Ⓒ Ⓓ Ⓔ
4. Ⓐ Ⓑ Ⓒ Ⓓ Ⓔ   34. Ⓐ Ⓑ Ⓒ Ⓓ Ⓔ   64. Ⓐ Ⓑ Ⓒ Ⓓ Ⓔ
5. Ⓐ Ⓑ Ⓒ Ⓓ Ⓔ   35. Ⓐ Ⓑ Ⓒ Ⓓ Ⓔ   65. Ⓐ Ⓑ Ⓒ Ⓓ Ⓔ
6. Ⓐ Ⓑ Ⓒ Ⓓ Ⓔ   36. Ⓐ Ⓑ Ⓒ Ⓓ Ⓔ   66. Ⓐ Ⓑ Ⓒ Ⓓ Ⓔ
7. Ⓐ Ⓑ Ⓒ Ⓓ Ⓔ   37. Ⓐ Ⓑ Ⓒ Ⓓ Ⓔ   67. Ⓐ Ⓑ Ⓒ Ⓓ Ⓔ
8. Ⓐ Ⓑ Ⓒ Ⓓ Ⓔ   38. Ⓐ Ⓑ Ⓒ Ⓓ Ⓔ   68. Ⓐ Ⓑ Ⓒ Ⓓ Ⓔ
9. Ⓐ Ⓑ Ⓒ Ⓓ Ⓔ   39. Ⓐ Ⓑ Ⓒ Ⓓ Ⓔ   69. Ⓐ Ⓑ Ⓒ Ⓓ Ⓔ
10. Ⓐ Ⓑ Ⓒ Ⓓ Ⓔ   40. Ⓐ Ⓑ Ⓒ Ⓓ Ⓔ   70. Ⓐ Ⓑ Ⓒ Ⓓ Ⓔ
11. Ⓐ Ⓑ Ⓒ Ⓓ Ⓔ   41. Ⓐ Ⓑ Ⓒ Ⓓ Ⓔ   71. Ⓐ Ⓑ Ⓒ Ⓓ Ⓔ
12. Ⓐ Ⓑ Ⓒ Ⓓ Ⓔ   42. Ⓐ Ⓑ Ⓒ Ⓓ Ⓔ   72. Ⓐ Ⓑ Ⓒ Ⓓ Ⓔ
13. Ⓐ Ⓑ Ⓒ Ⓓ Ⓔ   43. Ⓐ Ⓑ Ⓒ Ⓓ Ⓔ   73. Ⓐ Ⓑ Ⓒ Ⓓ Ⓔ
14. Ⓐ Ⓑ Ⓒ Ⓓ Ⓔ   44. Ⓐ Ⓑ Ⓒ Ⓓ Ⓔ   74. Ⓐ Ⓑ Ⓒ Ⓓ Ⓔ
15. Ⓐ Ⓑ Ⓒ Ⓓ Ⓔ   45. Ⓐ Ⓑ Ⓒ Ⓓ Ⓔ   75. Ⓐ Ⓑ Ⓒ Ⓓ Ⓔ
16. Ⓐ Ⓑ Ⓒ Ⓓ Ⓔ   46. Ⓐ Ⓑ Ⓒ Ⓓ Ⓔ   76. Ⓐ Ⓑ Ⓒ Ⓓ Ⓔ
17. Ⓐ Ⓑ Ⓒ Ⓓ Ⓔ   47. Ⓐ Ⓑ Ⓒ Ⓓ Ⓔ   77. Ⓐ Ⓑ Ⓒ Ⓓ Ⓔ
18. Ⓐ Ⓑ Ⓒ Ⓓ Ⓔ   48. Ⓐ Ⓑ Ⓒ Ⓓ Ⓔ   78. Ⓐ Ⓑ Ⓒ Ⓓ Ⓔ
19. Ⓐ Ⓑ Ⓒ Ⓓ Ⓔ   49. Ⓐ Ⓑ Ⓒ Ⓓ Ⓔ   79. Ⓐ Ⓑ Ⓒ Ⓓ Ⓔ
20. Ⓐ Ⓑ Ⓒ Ⓓ Ⓔ   50. Ⓐ Ⓑ Ⓒ Ⓓ Ⓔ   80. Ⓐ Ⓑ Ⓒ Ⓓ Ⓔ
21. Ⓐ Ⓑ Ⓒ Ⓓ Ⓔ   51. Ⓐ Ⓑ Ⓒ Ⓓ Ⓔ   81. Ⓐ Ⓑ Ⓒ Ⓓ Ⓔ
22. Ⓐ Ⓑ Ⓒ Ⓓ Ⓔ   52. Ⓐ Ⓑ Ⓒ Ⓓ Ⓔ   82. Ⓐ Ⓑ Ⓒ Ⓓ Ⓔ
23. Ⓐ Ⓑ Ⓒ Ⓓ Ⓔ   53. Ⓐ Ⓑ Ⓒ Ⓓ Ⓔ   83. Ⓐ Ⓑ Ⓒ Ⓓ Ⓔ
24. Ⓐ Ⓑ Ⓒ Ⓓ Ⓔ   54. Ⓐ Ⓑ Ⓒ Ⓓ Ⓔ   84. Ⓐ Ⓑ Ⓒ Ⓓ Ⓔ
25. Ⓐ Ⓑ Ⓒ Ⓓ Ⓔ   55. Ⓐ Ⓑ Ⓒ Ⓓ Ⓔ   85. Ⓐ Ⓑ Ⓒ Ⓓ Ⓔ
26. Ⓐ Ⓑ Ⓒ Ⓓ Ⓔ   56. Ⓐ Ⓑ Ⓒ Ⓓ Ⓔ   86. Ⓐ Ⓑ Ⓒ Ⓓ Ⓔ
27. Ⓐ Ⓑ Ⓒ Ⓓ Ⓔ   57. Ⓐ Ⓑ Ⓒ Ⓓ Ⓔ   87. Ⓐ Ⓑ Ⓒ Ⓓ Ⓔ
28. Ⓐ Ⓑ Ⓒ Ⓓ Ⓔ   58. Ⓐ Ⓑ Ⓒ Ⓓ Ⓔ   88. Ⓐ Ⓑ Ⓒ Ⓓ Ⓔ
29. Ⓐ Ⓑ Ⓒ Ⓓ Ⓔ   59. Ⓐ Ⓑ Ⓒ Ⓓ Ⓔ   89. Ⓐ Ⓑ Ⓒ Ⓓ Ⓔ
30. Ⓐ Ⓑ Ⓒ Ⓓ Ⓔ   60. Ⓐ Ⓑ Ⓒ Ⓓ Ⓔ   90. Ⓐ Ⓑ Ⓒ Ⓓ Ⓔ

1. YOUR NAME:
(Print)   Last   First   M.I.

SIGNATURE: _____ DATE: ___ / ___ / ___

HOME ADDRESS: _____
(Print)   Number and Street

_____
City   State   Zip Code

PHONE NO. : _____
(Print)

5. YOUR NAME

First 4 letters of last name | | | | FIRST INIT | MID INIT

(Bubble columns A–Z for first 4 letters of last name, plus First Init and Mid Init)

IMPORTANT: Please fill in these boxes exactly as shown on the back cover of your test book.

2. TEST FORM

3. TEST CODE

4. REGISTRATION NUMBER

(Bubble grids with digits 0–9 and letters A–G for test code)

6. DATE OF BIRTH

Month	Day	Year
JAN		
FEB		
MAR	0	0 0 0
APR	1	1 1 1
MAY	2	2 2 2
JUN	3	3 3 3
JUL		4 4 4
AUG		5 5 5
SEP		6 6 6
OCT		7 7 7
NOV		8 8 8
DEC		9 9 9

7. SEX
- MALE
- FEMALE

The Princeton Review
© 2005 The Princeton Review, Inc.
FORM NO. 00001-PR

Section 1

Start with number 1 for each new section.
If a section has fewer questions than answer spaces, leave the extra answer spaces blank.

1. Ⓐ Ⓑ Ⓒ Ⓓ Ⓔ   31. Ⓐ Ⓑ Ⓒ Ⓓ Ⓔ   61. Ⓐ Ⓑ Ⓒ Ⓓ Ⓔ
2. Ⓐ Ⓑ Ⓒ Ⓓ Ⓔ   32. Ⓐ Ⓑ Ⓒ Ⓓ Ⓔ   62. Ⓐ Ⓑ Ⓒ Ⓓ Ⓔ
3. Ⓐ Ⓑ Ⓒ Ⓓ Ⓔ   33. Ⓐ Ⓑ Ⓒ Ⓓ Ⓔ   63. Ⓐ Ⓑ Ⓒ Ⓓ Ⓔ
4. Ⓐ Ⓑ Ⓒ Ⓓ Ⓔ   34. Ⓐ Ⓑ Ⓒ Ⓓ Ⓔ   64. Ⓐ Ⓑ Ⓒ Ⓓ Ⓔ
5. Ⓐ Ⓑ Ⓒ Ⓓ Ⓔ   35. Ⓐ Ⓑ Ⓒ Ⓓ Ⓔ   65. Ⓐ Ⓑ Ⓒ Ⓓ Ⓔ
6. Ⓐ Ⓑ Ⓒ Ⓓ Ⓔ   36. Ⓐ Ⓑ Ⓒ Ⓓ Ⓔ   66. Ⓐ Ⓑ Ⓒ Ⓓ Ⓔ
7. Ⓐ Ⓑ Ⓒ Ⓓ Ⓔ   37. Ⓐ Ⓑ Ⓒ Ⓓ Ⓔ   67. Ⓐ Ⓑ Ⓒ Ⓓ Ⓔ
8. Ⓐ Ⓑ Ⓒ Ⓓ Ⓔ   38. Ⓐ Ⓑ Ⓒ Ⓓ Ⓔ   68. Ⓐ Ⓑ Ⓒ Ⓓ Ⓔ
9. Ⓐ Ⓑ Ⓒ Ⓓ Ⓔ   39. Ⓐ Ⓑ Ⓒ Ⓓ Ⓔ   69. Ⓐ Ⓑ Ⓒ Ⓓ Ⓔ
10. Ⓐ Ⓑ Ⓒ Ⓓ Ⓔ   40. Ⓐ Ⓑ Ⓒ Ⓓ Ⓔ   70. Ⓐ Ⓑ Ⓒ Ⓓ Ⓔ
11. Ⓐ Ⓑ Ⓒ Ⓓ Ⓔ   41. Ⓐ Ⓑ Ⓒ Ⓓ Ⓔ   71. Ⓐ Ⓑ Ⓒ Ⓓ Ⓔ
12. Ⓐ Ⓑ Ⓒ Ⓓ Ⓔ   42. Ⓐ Ⓑ Ⓒ Ⓓ Ⓔ   72. Ⓐ Ⓑ Ⓒ Ⓓ Ⓔ
13. Ⓐ Ⓑ Ⓒ Ⓓ Ⓔ   43. Ⓐ Ⓑ Ⓒ Ⓓ Ⓔ   73. Ⓐ Ⓑ Ⓒ Ⓓ Ⓔ
14. Ⓐ Ⓑ Ⓒ Ⓓ Ⓔ   44. Ⓐ Ⓑ Ⓒ Ⓓ Ⓔ   74. Ⓐ Ⓑ Ⓒ Ⓓ Ⓔ
15. Ⓐ Ⓑ Ⓒ Ⓓ Ⓔ   45. Ⓐ Ⓑ Ⓒ Ⓓ Ⓔ   75. Ⓐ Ⓑ Ⓒ Ⓓ Ⓔ
16. Ⓐ Ⓑ Ⓒ Ⓓ Ⓔ   46. Ⓐ Ⓑ Ⓒ Ⓓ Ⓔ   76. Ⓐ Ⓑ Ⓒ Ⓓ Ⓔ
17. Ⓐ Ⓑ Ⓒ Ⓓ Ⓔ   47. Ⓐ Ⓑ Ⓒ Ⓓ Ⓔ   77. Ⓐ Ⓑ Ⓒ Ⓓ Ⓔ
18. Ⓐ Ⓑ Ⓒ Ⓓ Ⓔ   48. Ⓐ Ⓑ Ⓒ Ⓓ Ⓔ   78. Ⓐ Ⓑ Ⓒ Ⓓ Ⓔ
19. Ⓐ Ⓑ Ⓒ Ⓓ Ⓔ   49. Ⓐ Ⓑ Ⓒ Ⓓ Ⓔ   79. Ⓐ Ⓑ Ⓒ Ⓓ Ⓔ
20. Ⓐ Ⓑ Ⓒ Ⓓ Ⓔ   50. Ⓐ Ⓑ Ⓒ Ⓓ Ⓔ   80. Ⓐ Ⓑ Ⓒ Ⓓ Ⓔ
21. Ⓐ Ⓑ Ⓒ Ⓓ Ⓔ   51. Ⓐ Ⓑ Ⓒ Ⓓ Ⓔ   81. Ⓐ Ⓑ Ⓒ Ⓓ Ⓔ
22. Ⓐ Ⓑ Ⓒ Ⓓ Ⓔ   52. Ⓐ Ⓑ Ⓒ Ⓓ Ⓔ   82. Ⓐ Ⓑ Ⓒ Ⓓ Ⓔ
23. Ⓐ Ⓑ Ⓒ Ⓓ Ⓔ   53. Ⓐ Ⓑ Ⓒ Ⓓ Ⓔ   83. Ⓐ Ⓑ Ⓒ Ⓓ Ⓔ
24. Ⓐ Ⓑ Ⓒ Ⓓ Ⓔ   54. Ⓐ Ⓑ Ⓒ Ⓓ Ⓔ   84. Ⓐ Ⓑ Ⓒ Ⓓ Ⓔ
25. Ⓐ Ⓑ Ⓒ Ⓓ Ⓔ   55. Ⓐ Ⓑ Ⓒ Ⓓ Ⓔ   85. Ⓐ Ⓑ Ⓒ Ⓓ Ⓔ
26. Ⓐ Ⓑ Ⓒ Ⓓ Ⓔ   56. Ⓐ Ⓑ Ⓒ Ⓓ Ⓔ   86. Ⓐ Ⓑ Ⓒ Ⓓ Ⓔ
27. Ⓐ Ⓑ Ⓒ Ⓓ Ⓔ   57. Ⓐ Ⓑ Ⓒ Ⓓ Ⓔ   87. Ⓐ Ⓑ Ⓒ Ⓓ Ⓔ
28. Ⓐ Ⓑ Ⓒ Ⓓ Ⓔ   58. Ⓐ Ⓑ Ⓒ Ⓓ Ⓔ   88. Ⓐ Ⓑ Ⓒ Ⓓ Ⓔ
29. Ⓐ Ⓑ Ⓒ Ⓓ Ⓔ   59. Ⓐ Ⓑ Ⓒ Ⓓ Ⓔ   89. Ⓐ Ⓑ Ⓒ Ⓓ Ⓔ
30. Ⓐ Ⓑ Ⓒ Ⓓ Ⓔ   60. Ⓐ Ⓑ Ⓒ Ⓓ Ⓔ   90. Ⓐ Ⓑ Ⓒ Ⓓ Ⓔ

International Offices Listing

China (Beijing)
1501 Building A,
Disanji Creative Zone,
No.66 West Section of North 4th Ring Road Beijing
Tel: +86-10-62684481/2/3
Email: tprkor01@chol.com
Website: www.tprbeijing.com

China (Shanghai)
1010 Kaixuan Road
Building B, 5/F
Changning District, Shanghai, China 200052
Sara Beattie, Owner: Email: sbeattie@sarabeattie.com
Tel: +86-21-5108-2798
Fax: +86-21-6386-1039
Website: www.princetonreviewshanghai.com

Hong Kong
5th Floor, Yardley Commercial Building
1-6 Connaught Road West, Sheung Wan, Hong Kong
(MTR Exit C)
Sara Beattie, Owner: Email: sbeattie@sarabeattie.com
Tel: +852-2507-9380
Fax: +852-2827-4630
Website: www.princetonreviewhk.com

India (Mumbai)
Score Plus Academy
Office No.15, Fifth Floor
Manek Mahal 90
Veer Nariman Road
Next to Hotel Ambassador
Churchgate, Mumbai 400020
Maharashtra, India
Ritu Kalwani: Email: director@score-plus.com
Tel: + 91 22 22846801 / 39 / 41
Website: www.score-plus.com

India (New Delhi)
South Extension
K-16, Upper Ground Floor
South Extension Part–1,
New Delhi-110049
Aradhana Mahna: aradhana@manyagroup.com
Monisha Banerjee: monisha@manyagroup.com
Ruchi Tomar: ruchi.tomar@manyagroup.com
Rishi Josan: Rishi.josan@manyagroup.com
Vishal Goswamy: vishal.goswamy@manyagroup.com
Tel: +91-11-64501603/ 4, +91-11-65028379
Website: www.manyagroup.com

Lebanon
463 Bliss Street
AlFarra Building - 2nd floor
Ras Beirut
Beirut, Lebanon
Hassan Coudsi: Email: hassan.coudsi@review.com
Tel: +961-1-367-688
Website: www.princetonreviewlebanon.com

Korea
945-25 Young Shin Building
25 Daechi-Dong, Kangnam-gu
Seoul, Korea 135-280
Yong-Hoon Lee: Email: TPRKor01@chollian.net
In-Woo Kim: Email: iwkim@tpr.co.kr
Tel: + 82-2-554-7762
Fax: +82-2-453-9466
Website: www.tpr.co.kr

Kuwait
ScorePlus Learning Center
Salmiyah Block 3, Street 2 Building 14
Post Box: 559, Zip 1306, Safat, Kuwait
Email: infokuwait@score-plus.com
Tel: +965-25-75-48-02 / 8
Fax: +965-25-75-46-02
Website: www.scorepluseducation.com

Malaysia
Sara Beattie MDC Sdn Bhd
Suites 18E & 18F
18th Floor
Gurney Tower, Persiaran Gurney
Penang, Malaysia
Email: tprkl.my@sarabeattie.com
Sara Beattie, Owner: Email: sbeattie@sarabeattie.com
Tel: +604-2104 333
Fax: +604-2104 330
Website: www.princetonreviewKL.com

Mexico
TPR México
Guanajuato No. 242 Piso 1 Interior 1
Col. Roma Norte
México D.F., C.P.06700
registro@princetonreviewmexico.com
Tel: +52-55-5255-4495
+52-55-5255-4440
+52-55-5255-4442
Website: www.princetonreviewmexico.com

Qatar
Score Plus
Office No: 1A, Al Kuwari (Damas)
Building near Merweb Hotel, Al Saad
Post Box: 2408, Doha, Qatar
Email: infoqatar@score-plus.com
Tel: +974 44 36 8580, +974 526 5032
Fax: +974 44 13 1995
Website: www.scorepluseducation.com

Taiwan
The Princeton Review Taiwan
2F, 169 Zhong Xiao East Road, Section 4
Taipei, Taiwan 10690
Lisa Bartle (Owner): lbartle@princetonreview.com.tw
Tel: +886-2-2751-1293
Fax: +886-2-2776-3201
Website: www.PrincetonReview.com.tw

Thailand
The Princeton Review Thailand
Sathorn Nakorn Tower, 28th floor
100 North Sathorn Road
Bangkok, Thailand 10500
Thavida Bijayendrayodhin (Chairman)
Email: thavida@princetonreviewthailand.com
Mitsara Bijayendrayodhin (Managing Director)
Email: mitsara@princetonreviewthailand.com
Tel: +662-636-6770
Fax: +662-636-6776
Website: www.princetonreviewthailand.com

Turkey
Yeni Sülün Sokak No. 28
Levent, Istanbul, 34330, Turkey
Nuri Ozgur: nuri@tprturkey.com
Rona Ozgur: rona@tprturkey.com
Iren Ozgur: iren@tprturkey.com
Tel: +90-212-324-4747
Fax: +90-212-324-3347
Website: www.tprturkey.com

UAE
Emirates Score Plus
Office No: 506, Fifth Floor
Sultan Business Center
Near Lamcy Plaza, 21 Oud Metha Road
Post Box: 44098, Dubai
United Arab Emirates
Hukumat Kalwani: skoreplus@gmail.com
Ritu Kalwani: director@score-plus.com
Email: info@score-plus.com
Tel: +971-4-334-0004
Fax: +971-4-334-0222
Website: www.princetonreviewuae.com

Our International Partners

The Princeton Review also runs courses with a variety of
partners in Africa, Asia, Europe, and South America.

Georgia
LEAF American-Georgian Education Center
www.leaf.ge

Mongolia
English Academy of Mongolia
www.nyescm.org

Nigeria
The Know Place
www.knowplace.com.ng

Panama
Academia Interamericana de Panama
http://aip.edu.pa/

Switzerland
Institut Le Rosey
http://www.rosey.ch/

All other inquiries, please email us at
internationalsupport@review.com